LABOUR AND DEVELOPMENT IN TWENTY FIRST CENTURY

Challenges and Perspectives

LABOUR AND DEVELOPMENT IN TWENTY FIRST CENTURY

Challenges and Perspectives

Editor

Prof. G. Saibaba

M.A., Ph.D.

Dean, School of Social Behavioural Sciences,
Coordinator, U.G.C. Special Assistance Programmes
Sri Venkateswara University
Tirupati–517 502

Joint Editors

Dr. G. Erraiah, *M.A., M.Phil., Ph.D.*
Dr. M. Devarajulu, *M.A., Ph.D.*
Dr. M. Chinnaswamy Naidu, *M.A., Ph.D.*

SERIALS PUBLICATIONS
NEW DELHI

First Published–2005

ISBN: 81-86771-71-9

SERIALS PUBLICATIONS

4, B.S.S. Hall, Khyber Pass Market,
Civil Lines, Delhi–110054 (India)
Phone: 23245225
Fax: 91-11-23272135
e-mail: serials@satyam.net.in

Branch Office

4830/24, Prahlad Street, Ansari Road,
Darya Ganj, New Delhi-110002 (India)

Printed at : R.K. Offset Process, Delhi-32

PRINTED IN INDIA

Foreword

I have great pleasure in forwarding the volume entitled "Labour and Development in 21st Century: Challenges and Perspectives". The volume is the outcome of papers presented at the Seminar held in the Department of Economics, S.V. University, Tirupati. The Seminar was organized under the Special Assistance Programme of University Grants Commission.

As all we know that Economic reforms have been introduced in India from July 1991, so that India does not face crisis of the type, which she faced in 1990. The very bass of economic reforms is liberalization, globalization and privatization. This approach was also advocated by International agencies such as IMF and World Bank. A need was felt that World Trade should be more liberal and multilateral in nature. In order to go forward every country was expected to liberalize imports and dismantle controls in the economy. Now this economic philosophy has been not only accepted by a large number of countries in the world but also is being practised. So also India has adopted.

The economic reforms in India have been introduced in certain vital sectors such as labour and real sectors.

The challenges of providing employment in the organized and unorganized sectors, eliminating poverty and achievement of higher economic growth are most complicated in India for their solutions in the current century because of deep-seated social crisis through which India is passing through.

Although India is the most populous country with noteworthy brain power and capital, it bristles with great social diversities as compared to any country or continent in the world with 4000 castes, 6000 social groups, about 400 languages including dialects and a number of religions with wide range of cultures, not to speak of varied levels of social and economic development.

After achieving Independence in 1947, over the last fifty and odd years, its special groups have become quite vocal engendering social struggles and agitation of dimensions. The problems that confront development effort in India are identified as bureaucratic delays and inefficiency, corruption, poor quality of public services and collapsing of judicial system under the weight of a huge backlog cases. In a globalizing environment, no state can afford to be less than efficient. Good governance is a necessary condition for attracting capital and the maintenance of adequate and stable growth. Public leaders have to realize the need to build human capabilities rather than the mere distribution of wealth under the package of reforms. The different papers which were presented in the Seminar have by and large brought out the achievements and shortfalls of reforms. One and all agree that infrastructure, both economic and social, has really become critical and therefore it might lower down the productivity and growth of the Indian economy. In some of the papers by using macro economic indicators, the performance of labour reforms is assessed. Interesting part is that some indicators show the positive performance and others negative. A view was also taken that regional disparities have widened in the period of reforms.

I hope the volume would be of great interest to the general readers, researchers, students and teachers.

Tirupati

Prof. P Murali
Vice-Chancellor
S.V. University
Tirupati

Preface

We have great pleasure in bringing out this volume the research papers originally presented at the two-day national level seminar on "Labour and Development in 21st Century: Challenges and Perspectives" held at the Department of Economics, Sri Venkateswara University, Tirupati, under the Special Assistance Programme of the University Grants Commission.

Forty-one research papers were presented at the Seminar by the participants from different parts of the country. Most of these papers have been revised by the authors themselves.

The University Grants Commission, New Delhi, has been kind enough to us by providing the Special Assistance Programme (SAP) in three phases. We are thankful to the UGC, New Delhi for their generous financial assistance to this seminar.

We would like to thank the contributors to this volume for revising their papers well in time. We are highly thankful to Reserve Bank of India for their generous contribution to organize this seminar. Specially thanks are due to Dr. Y. Venugopal Reddy, I.A.S., governor Reserve Bank of India, for his keen interest in this Seminar. We are thankful to the NABARD for their generous support to publish this book. We would like to thank Serials Publications Pvt. Ltd, New Delhi, for agreeing to publish this volume speedily. We are highly thankful to Prof. P. Murali, Vice-Chancellor, S.V. University for his kind presence and forwarding remarks to this volume.

Colleagues in the Department of Economics have read the text and made useful suggestions. Our thanks are due to all of them. We are thankful to the staff of Library of Special Assistance Programme, Department of Economics and Library of Sri Venkateswara University, Tirupati. Finally, we thank Smt. U. Anitha for typing the manuscript.

Prof. G.Saibaba
Dr. G. Erraiah
Dr. M. Devarajulu
Dr. M.C. Naidu

Editorial Note

"LABOUR AND DEVELOPMENT 21ST CENTURY PROBLEMS AND PERSPECTIVES"

Prof. D.L. Narayana in his keynote address analysed employment and economic development a comparative analysis of China and India. The innovations in science and technology and their utilisation for human development will make the 21st century a century of great knowledge of explosion. According to him knowledge is power, accelerated growth of knowledge will usher much required social change for human progress. Thus knowledge is behind Asia's surge. This paper analysed structural changes in economic development changes in employment of labour, state and market in economic policy, Chinese miracle of economic growth is a reflection on two stabilities viz., political stability and economic stability. China rose to great sight in advancing economic development with the dynamic role of dispose whose perception is that of loyalty. It has a far deeper morale contribution governing Chinese development which is one of the most sweeping historical drama not only of the 20th century and perhaps for all times. In fine Chinese miracle of employment and economic growth is an illustration of the policy of market socialism. Probably, China is destined to make world history for achieving highest economic growth rate in recent times.

The problems that confront developmental effort in India are identified as bureaucratic delays and inefficiency, corruption, poor quality of public services and collapsive judicial systems under the weight of huge backlog of cases. Thus he advocated that in a globalising environment, no state can, efford to be less than efficient. Public leaders come to realise the need to build human capabilities rather than the mere distribution of wealth under the package of reforms.

Prof. Shanmugasunndaram in his article on *"Institutional Theory of Economic Development with special Reference to Employment and Labour—21st Century Approach"*. He says the basic conceptual classification of the term labour and stated that we use a wiser term human resource both in the historical terms of labour and organisation. These are of great importance and the trade unions and human rights forums to persue in defence of human dignity and self respect. He analysed the convergence of employment in modern times. He analysed the relative share of organised and unorganised sectors and advocated for the creation of effective demand in creation of Indian economics. He is very critical about the Budget, Economic Survey and Central Statistical Organisation which feeds the state and ministries with vide range of statistics. He advocated the comprehensive term human resources rather than labour and analysed the institutional theory of labour in economic development.

Prof. Manonmoney in her article *"Economic Reforms and Employment Challenges Ahead"* argued that globalisation is the process by which events, decisions in one part of the world have significant consequences for the other parts of the globe. This economic reform has been a beginning to a series of reforms in the labour sector which has increased the social cost of adjustment. This called for a human approach in the labour sector reforms. Hence employment generation has for reaching consequences which may even threaten the very existence of modern economies and stated that if this objective of generation of employment is ignored in our anxiety for economic reforms would bring about serious consequences in the direction and content of India's economic development

Dr. K.S. Harigopal in his article on *"Post-Reforms Trends in Organised Sector Employment"* stated that 21st century witnessed several changes in the process of economic development and growth due to emergence of globalisation and privatisation. Labour as one of the key variable in the development process assumed significance particularly in the light of declining role of public sector and increasing role of private sector. The analysis in this article was made in terms about public and private sectors and in terms of pre- and post liberalisation periods, to study the impact of economic reforms. The study advocated for a suitable labour policy to generate more employment opportunities in the private sector.

Dr. Sailabala Devi and Prof. P.R. Panchamukhi in their article on *"Impact of Economic Reforms on Rural Women Labour—An Empirical Evidence"* argued that women's involvement in the process of economic development has remained comparatively a neglected area. The introduction of economic reforms seems to be severely effected the participation of female in all the sectors and more so in the agricultural sectors. In this back drop the present study aims at examining the participation of women in the agricultural operations during the process of economic reforms and before reforms. The study is based on a field study covering three districts of Karnataka. The study suggested several measures to avoid victims of any reform or any changed circumstances.

Prof. Uduman Mohiddin and Haroon in their paper *"Enhancing Labour Productivity through Policy Interventions"* attempted to analyse the employment situation, labour productivity, income and period of employment, poverty level and related issues in India. They pointed out that poverty is the most degrading experience of human existence. Hence, central and state governments have been planning and implementing various poverty alleviation programmes, and for them improvement in productivity occures through central and state government policy measures like encouraging intensive and extensive cultivation, implementation of watershed and wasteland development, careful implementation of employment generations, and skill development through training and social measures and suitable credit policy for encouraging the self employment opportunity.

Prof. Saibaba and Dr. K. Vijayalakshmi in their paper on *"Globalisation Economic Reforms and Social Sector Development: Some Emerging Areas in India."* In this article an attempt has been made to analyse the several aspects of social development in pre and post-reform period. Globalisation is a very fast emerging trend on the international scene and experiencing revolutionary changes. As economic growth stress market friendly approach and social development postulates state intervention. They argued for a real need to synthesise the state intervention and market approach for economic development. Around the world there is vide spread unease about the growth of social and economic insecurity and inequality. As such they argue that economic growth is to be pro-social development, pro-jobs and pro-native and pro-people. The eight crisis of global protection are due to new globalised societies. They argued that the glance of the changing intellectual tides and economic policies including the trends of globalization is to be stated that the prime requisite is the social change for human development. It is the pursuit of '*welfare capitalism*' by the market approach along with the social policy of the state. In India since 1991 many significant changes taken place in her economic policy and a large amount of information on theoretical and empirical aspects of economic reforms and the working of economic reforms has brought about a significant stability to the economy. But economic reforms have their drawbacks and brought many changes in our financial position and focused on the need for fiscal discipline in India.

Prof. L.K. Mohan Rao, Narasimha Rao and Ravi Babu in their article *"Mechanization and Labour Absorption in A.P. Agriculture—A Study in the Right Canal Command Area of NSP"* traced historical developments in the mechanization of farm operations in agriculture lead to increase in employment and reduction in under employment. Thus an attempt has been made to examine the impact of mechanization of on human labour employment in Andhra Pradesh. The results of the study reveal that in the production of paddy and cotton mechanization has negative affects on human labour absorption in agriculture in A.P. Thus, the over all effect of mechanization and other farm inputs together according to them, on human labour employment is positive. Hence the agricultural development through mechanization effects are positive and provide employment opportunities.

Mr. Pulinda Rao, Giriyappa and Krishnama Naidu in their article on *"Labour Participation in Leather Goods Industry"* stated the merits and demerits on import and export policies and stated that the current liberal policy signifies restrictions on a few items for export and import. They analysed the global level changes and their impact on the Indian economy having a strong raw-material base and abundant skilled workforce had a definite edge in exploiting the situation. They felt that workers in leather goods manufacturing in Kolkata and Mumbai centres are vulnerable to form self-help groups (SHG) and need for an active non-government organisation to initiate their programme.

Dr. Erraiah in his article on *"Global Integration and Unemployment Among Rural Poor in India"* stated that in India employment elasticity has been decelerated during liberalization period. Further, it attempted to analyse the relation between unemployment and poverty and reasons for decline in poverty in recent years. It is due to improvement in wage rates and coverage of public works programmes in India. Hence, poverty in India has come down irrespective of decline in employment opportunities aseptically in agriculture.

Dr. M.K. Rao and Venugopal in their article on *"Rural Non-Farm Sector in A.P."* pointed out that the structure of work force has undergone a structural change and the share of workers in agriculture declined and the share of workers in industry and service activities have increased their proportion in total work force of the economy. Thus according to them in India the non-farm rural employment has witnessed a steady expansion during the last few decades. They analysed the changes in non-farm sector employment in Andhra Pradesh and shown the regional variation in the different regions. Thus the growth of rural non-farm sector is desirable to alleviate rural poverty and unemployment in India as well as in Andhra Pradesh.

Prof. R.G. Desai and Mrs. Madhumathi in their article on *"Analysis of Industrial Relations in Karnataka State Road Transport Corporation—A Case Study"* emphasised the need for harmonious peaceful and cordial employee—employer relations for the stability, prosperity and growth of any organization. In this paper an attempt has been made to analyse the industrial relations in KSRTC. It is based on secondary data. On the basis of this data they constructed industrial relations index. The industrial relations situation in Karnataka State Road Transport Corporation is rather unsatisfactory except in 1995-96.

Prof. Venkatanarayana in his article on *"Economic Reforms Crisis in Handloom Industry in A.P. A Critical Study"* drawn the attention to the fact that the advent of machine in to industry reduced their artisan industry to size and how power looms and mill sector made their dent in to the rural markets. The economic reforms both at the centre and state level the handloom industry suffered a death blow. Consequently with these economic reforms handloom sector landed in to deeper crisis and resulted in several suicides and became an eye-opener to policy makers.

Prof. Lakshminarasaiah in his article *"Trade and Labour Standards—Using the Wrong Instruments for Right Cause"* examined the issue of the proper labour standards to increase trade and economic growth. The ILO which was created to develop core labour standards and promote workers rights and proper conditions to develop labour standards and economic development.

Mr. Seshadri and Vasudevalu Naidu in their article *"Education for Skills Development and their Utilization in the India Economy"* traced the significant contribution of education for skill formation, besides production and consumption effects. As a result of craze for white collar jobs has been on increase and the member of unemployed and under employed both in rural and urban areas indicate the need for creation of additional employment opportunities in India. Economic reforms must have human face and develop human resources for rapid economic development.

Prof. Raghava Reddy and Dr. Vinodini in their article *"Gender Related Issues of Urban Informal Labour Market"* stressed on the crucial role of urban informal sector in providing jobs for urban poor and rural migrant labour force. According to them gender discrimination and gender gaps in wages and earnings are quite common. These problems are receiving the attention of planners and administrators and reorientation in the development strategies and models are being formulated at national and global level. Thus the authors argued for a labour oriented, equity based welfare—guided state policy is to be harmonized with growth oriented, market driven policies. Hence the need for micro level and macro welfare policies to protect the politically marginalised classes.

Prof. Indrakant and Rajat Kumar in their article on *"Impact of Economic Reforms on Industrial Workers"* collected the secondary data from Annual survey of industries for the 17 year period from 1981 to 1998 and for analytical purpose the time period was divided in to two—pre-reform period 1981 to 1991 and post-reform period 1991-98. They stated that the economic reforms have not had any negative impact on the growth rate of employment for industrial workers and supervisors. Wage rates for both categories have grown in real terms. There are large scale inter-industry differences in all the variables. This study shows that to what the critics of economic reforms had predicted that the Indian industrial worker has not been adversely affected by the reforms. However, they argued for the need to take policy measures to increase employment opportunities in race with the growth of population and labour force in India.

Dr. M.C. Naidu in his article *"Child Labour and Education Policy in India"* emphasised the need for an effective education policy to eradicate child labour in India. He stated that poor parents are sending their children to schools of work clearly shows that motivation and infrastructure are key variables in eradication of child labour rather than poverty. He advocated for the need for local level or village level efforts to eradicate this evil and hence need for coordinated effort on different fronts such as various aspects of child development of which child labour is a part.

Mr. M. Devarajulu and Mr. Prasad in their article on *"Economic Reforms and Organised Sector Employment in India"* pointed out that employment has come down gradually in India after economic reforms been initiated. It is mainly due to adjustment programmes initiated in the economy. As a drive to reduce government expenditure, the disinvestments in public sector units and ban on recruitment in many state departments reduced employment opportunities. They concluded that the employment in organised sector declining because the share of public sector declining. The share of private sector in organised sector has grown at a fast rate as economic reforms in liberalization period. It exercised favourable impact on employment generation in private sector.

Prof. Sambasiva Rao and M.R.S. Babu in their article on *"Women Labour in Agriculture—A Case Study of Bethapudi Village of Guntur District"* amply justifies their argument that 70 per cent of farm work was performed by women and most of labourers in India are women. They examined the wages of women are low and minimum wages are not paid to and women are not paid equal wages for equal work. As such they advocated for better wages, and associations for women, the need to empower women workers and necessary awareness among women regarding their rights and duties through education.

Dr. Santha Kumari in her article on *"Agricultural Labourers in Rural Areas"* stated that agricultural labourers constitute the single most important segment of rural proletariat and over decades their proportion in the total workforce is rapidly growing. She classified agricultural labourers in to three types viz., casual labourers, attached labourers and bonded labourers and most of them live below poverty line due to low income and low wages. All the programmes meant for them are not so successful in reducing the inequalities of income. The economic reforms and new economic policies have further reduced their incomes. As such according to her there is a wide scope to improve their conditions and provision for housing, roads, drinking water, sanitation in rural areas. There is need for critical enquiry of the emerging new labour institutions with an agenda of social unionism.

Prof. V.K. Reddy and Smt. Naga Prasuna in their article examined the *"Male and Female Labour Productivities in Agriculture Across Six Villages in Siadvatham Mandal of Cuddapah District"* for the year 2000-01. The study reveals that marginal value productivity to factor cost ratios of the variables except irrigated areas (x5) in all the farm sizes are less than unity. Further the ratios are negative for female labour (x4). Therefore they argued that efforts should be made to use these resource efficiently by reallocating the timely use of resources with balanced use.

Prof. P.V. Raju and Purnachandra Rao in their article on *"Transition Era and Its Impact on Social Security"* advocated for social protection and social security for two reasons—distinctive Justice and for creation of better conditions of economic growth. Group of Ministers advocated for labour reforms in the process of globalization, which is highly sensitive. The case study of Krishna District milk producers cooperative union limited provided some empirical evidence for economic reforms on labour sector.

The characteristics of the world economy have changed radically over the past few years as a whole a large number of countries have embarked upon dramatic transforms. All most every region of the world has been affected. China and Vietnam as they undertake market reforms, sub Sahara Africa struggle to restore growth, Latin America and middle east responded to debt crisis and oil price shocks, India and South East Asia nations fight against growing population, poverty and unemployment. Most of these transforms involves a shift from a failed development strategy to a new one. Whatever the cause for their collapse of development strategy forced countries to undergo reforms unknown in the history of the world than ever before.

The wide variety of changes and different causes for there changes and starting points of countries forcing unmemorable shocks make it difficult to generalize about their impact on workers and to formulate a suitable policy choices. Yet, the experience of the past decade makes clear that workers suffer more when necessary reforms are delayed or aborted. The key to these changes is to formulate proper government policies, restoring sustainable economic growth and to ease out form transition for workers and preparing labourers to equipping them to successfully adjust to new circumstances. The World Development Report, 1995, focused on the workers in an Integrating world examined the patterns of reforms. The report stated that the Asian agrarian pattern are marked by steady growth in GDP, some institutional reforms, and cover time redeployment of labour. This is the pattern adopted in China, India and Vietnam. In these countries over a billion workers well over a third of the world's workforce, live in the Asian agrarian economies.

The labour market plays an important role in determining the success of adjustment reforms and their impact on living standards. It then focuses on how different initial conditions affect the over all reforms and the role of macro economic policies. At this juncture the pertinent issue is who bears the burden of major changes? Labour is the immediate victim of these changes and capital may gain in the short period. During restructuring and reforms period workers, poorest of the poor in rural areas are the worst effected and may create turmoil in the labour market and uncertainty for these groups. Hence, there is need to equip workers for change which require more resources to develop new skills and job habits so as to take advantage of new opportunities as they arise in fast emerging labour markets. The trade unions. State and managements in developing countries must work hard to develop understanding cooperation and cardinal labour management relations in the context of emergence of new institutions like W.T.O. and other world trading blocks. In this section about 13 papers analysed the various conditions and problems in India and perspectives for 21st century arrived at several expert reports.

Sri. N. Sampath in his article on *"Labour and Development in 21st Century Challenges and Perspectives"* traced the history and role of labour unions in the development of public sector in India specially in the banking sector. He has examined the adverse effects of economic reforms on labour in terms of reduction of jobs, removal of several perks, voluntary retirement schemes and large scale closures and reduction of jobs in public sector. He advocated that there is no way out for them except to fight untidily the concept of globalization.

Prof. R.G. Desai and Dr. Madhumathi examined the *"Vital role of Labour Welfare in Industrial Society and Advocated for the Wider Scope and Content of Labour Welfare"*. They felt that the efficiency of labour increases productivity while cheap food, free medical aid, education, housing etc. increase real income of workers, as such according to them the workers try to avoid the strikes and industrial disputes provided they are given good welfare measures. They analyzed the security measures in the public sector units with a case study of Karnataka state road transport corporation and derived the changing outlook and emerging perspectives.

Prof. K. Narasimhulu and Dr. Snehalatha in their article *"Analysed the various Developments in the theory of human resource development and role of health security for industrial workers"*. They pointed out that the budgetary cuts of Indian state government, poor functioning of government health care delivery system, urban rural disparities, poor safety and occupational hazards in industrial firms undermine the goal of achieving national health policy of *"Health for all by 200 A.D."* The six section of this paper examine the multidimentional nature of social security and health care measures required for ensuring an equitable and efficient system of health security in India.

Dr. Lellavathi in her article *"The Contours of Labour Sector Reforms in India"* called for a human approach to labour sector reforms (LSR) in India. LSR has to create labour market flexibility which is internal with globalization. She analysed the causes for growing opposition by the workers unions, politicization of reforms resulted in creating stumbling blocks. She felt that the need for second generation reforms which hold key for the successful transformation of the economy. As such she called for an integrated as well as human approach for reforms.

Prof. Khurana in his article *"Indian Economic Reforms, Labour Market Mechanisms and the Twenty—first century policy Imperatives"*. Examined the post independent growth experience and privilege of enjoying the benefits of a protected labour market. This paper warns that in the absence of adequate, timely, appropriate safety nets the forces of competition would unlash a reign of uncertainty and the process of ongoing reforms may provide to be counter productive or even backfire culminating into a position in which development if self would become unsustainable. To cope up with such eventualities this paper proposes an alternative focus that would offer better growth prospects together with increased employability of the growing workforce in India in the new millennium.

Prof. K. Sreenivasulu Naidu, Prof. K.M. Naidu and Manjushree stated that *"Economic reforms are expected to benefit the labour both in the organized and unorganized sectors"*. They critically examined the social security measures for the organized sector labour and observed that the amounts allotted are inadequate and the functioning of ESIE scheme is far from satisfactory. Thus they advocated for state intervention is a must in the labour related activities particularly affecting unorganized labour. The proportion of GDP, the share of social sector expenditure has not increased during this reform period. This paper on *"Economic Reforms and Social Security in India"* drive to one significant point that the country like India can ill afford to reduce expenditure on social security measures in the 10th five year plan period. They advocated for grass roots level vigilance, decentralization, participatory approach by people and political power to help the poor workers in the organized and unorganized sectors to over come poverty and deprivation in this century.

Dr. Srinivasulu in his paper on *"Trends in quantum-employment and wage rates of Agricultural Labourers"* found that the total number of agricultural labourers increased significantly in all the states during last 30 years since 1964-65 and the trends in total number of employment days available to make and female labourers increased. He found that the sources of employment changed significantly, particularly, self employment days increase in every state but incremental variations are different. The money wage rates of male agricultural labourers increased in all the states during forty years, despite, some fluctuation in one or two years. The real wages rate for different years, for the same group reveals sudden jumps and downs and only in three states recorded increasing trend. Hence need for proper programmes like employment guarantee programmes, land reforms, and more public investment in agriculture.

Prof. Atchi Reddy and Ms. Senha Nelha in their article on *"Agricultural Labourers in Andhra Pradesh During 1951-2001 and policy perspectives for the 21st century"* pointed out that most of the problems are common to India as a whole through their nature and extent vary from state to state and from region to region depending mainly on the agrarian conditions of the region. In A.P. agricultural labourers constitute about 34 per cent of its main workers in 1991 and the corresponding all India figure was only 26 per cent. The migration of these labourers is mainly from rural to urban areas on the one hand and dry felts to the irrigated tracts on the other. The rates of growth varied over districts in the same decade but exhibited changes over last four decades along with occupational changes. The proportion of agricultural labourers to the total agricultural workers in the state had increased from 18% in 1951 to 50% in 1991 leading to increased volume of unemployment and low wages. As such they advocated for micro level village studies to assertion the changing levels of poverty and deprivation in the rural areas. They call for improvement in training them to improve their skills.

Mr. C.P. Rao, Girappa and Dr. B. Krishnama Naidu in their article *"Problems and Perspectives of Labour in the Indian Leather Industry"* reviewed the various Perspectives and pointed out that in India the main source of labour confines to agricultural sector and non-agricultural sources contribute to some extent. Indian leather industry has witnessed remarkable structural changes and hence remarkable mobilisation of labour force into factory sector of leather industry after 1970s. The level of education is very low for these labourer. Hence, they advocated for proper technical training and skill upgradation which in turn may improve their wages and living conditions. Hence improvement of skills and training for the workers in leather industry are the challenges in the new millennium.

Prof. Sudhakar Rao and Narasimha Rao in their article on *"Child Labour in India—A micro level analysis of Mopidevi Mandal in Krishna district A.P."* stated that child labour occupies an important position in the context of economic development of any country. All most all countries in the world have unanimously resolved to of end exploitative pace of extracting labour from children. They felt that child labour robs the essential qualities of labour and the nations future depends up the healthy growth of children Globally 200 million of the world children under 15 years of age spent most of their working hours at work at the risk of their survival. Finally they advocated several policy measures to combact child labour.

Prof. Savaraiah and Dr. Devarajulu in their article on *"National Child Labour Project: Some Issues"* examined the causes for the growth of child labour in India and the achievements and shot comings of National child labour project. They advocated for the need to adopt the 'Kerala

Model' to eradication of child labour in India. A.P. has surpassed the sanctioned strength and coverage of working children. In Punjab the NCLP has not been implemented.

Mr. Muthuraj in his article of *"Gender and Employment in India: An agenda for the 21st Century"*. Analysed the employment trends in India. Girls lacked education and skills or both and indirectly forced to accept any work either at home or outside. He advocated for a 12 point agenda to tackle the problems of women workers of which entrepreneurial development programmes, vocational courses, need for changes in attitude of men towards women workers, and to develop a gender disaggregated data bases are of vital importance.

Editor
Prof. G. Saibaba

Joint Editors
Dr. G. Erraiah
Dr. M. Devarajulu
Dr. M. Chinnaswamy Naidu

List of Contributors

PART I

Prof. D.L. Narayana, Chairman, Second State Finance Commission, Urdu Hall Lane, Himaytnagar, Hyderabad-29.

Prof. V. Shanmuga Sundaram, Formerly, Professor & Head of the Department of Economics, Madras University, Vice-Chancellor, M.S.N. University, Tirunalvali.

Dr. Manonmoney, Professor, School of Economics Madurai Kamaraj University Madurai-625 021.

Dr. Sai Haragopal, Department of Economics, Osmania University, Hyderabad-500 007.

Dr. Sailabala Debi, Reader, Department of A & A Economics, Utkal University, Bhubaneswar-751 004, Orissa.

Prof. P.R. Panchamukhi, Director, Centre for Multidisciplinary, Development Research, Dharwad, Karnataka.

Dr. KSS Uduman Mohiddin, Professor, Department of Economics, University of Madras, Chennai-600 055, India.

Prof. G. Saibaba, Formerly Dean, SSBS Chairman, BOS, Department of Economics, S.V. University, Tirupati.

Dr. K. Vijayalakshmi, Sree Padmavathi Mahila University College Library, Tirupati-A.P.

Dr. L.K. Mohana Rao, Professor of Economics, Department of Applied Economics, Andhra University, Vishakhapatnam.

Sri. C. Pulinda Rao, Sri. K. Giriappa and Dr. B. Krishnama Naidu, Scientists, Central Leathers Research Institute, Chennai.

Dr. M. Koteswara Rao & P. Venugopal, Associate Professor & Head of the Dept., Department of Economics & Applied Economics, S.V. University, Tirupati.

Dr. G. Erraiah, Asso. Professor, Department of Economics, S.V. University, Tirupati.

PART II

Dr. M. Madhumathi, Professor and Chairman, Department of Economics, Bangalore University, Bangalore.

Dr. R.G. Desai, Lecturer, Department of Economics, Government Arts College, Tumkur.

Prof. K. Venkata Narayana, Professor of Economics, Kakatiya University, Warangal-506 009.

Dr. M. Lakshmi Narasaiah, Professor & Head, Department of Economics, SKU PG Centre, Kurnool-518 002.

Sri Seshadri and Vasudevulu Naidu, Research Scholars, Dept. of Economics, S.V. University, Tirupati.

Prof. G. Raghava Reddy, Director and RA of RDA, Tirupati.

Dr. VMJ. Vinodhini, Director and RA of RDA, Tirupati.

Dr. S. Indrakanth, Professor of Economics, Osmania University, Hyderabad-500 007.

Sri Rajat Kumar, Indian Administrative Services, Joint Secretary, Government of AP.

Dr. M.C. Naidu, Department of Economics, S.V. University, Tirupati.

Dr. M. Devarajulu, Associate Professor, Department of Economics, SVU, Tirupati.

Sri. RSVN, Prasad, Research Scholar, Department of Economics, SVU, Tirupati.

Dr. B. Sambasiva Rao, Associate Professor in Economics, Nagarjuna University, Agarjuna Nagar, Guntur Dist. AP.

Dr. MRS Babu, Sr. Lecturer in Economics, VTJM & IVTR Degree College, Mangalagiri-522 503.

Dr. K. Santha Kumari, Associate Professor of Economics, SVU College, Tirupati.

Prof. V.K. Reddy, Professor of Econometrics, S.V.U. College, Tirupati.

Smt. T. Naga Prasuna, Research Scholar, Department of Econometrics, S.V.U. College, Tirupati.

Prof. S.V. Raju, Department of Commerce & Business Administration, Nagarjuna University, Nagarjuna Nagar-522 510, Guntur.

Dr. P. Purnachandra Rao, Teaching Assistant, N.U.P.G. Centre, Ongole-523 001.

PART III

Prof. P. Murali, Vice-Chancellor, S.V. University, Tirupati.

Dr. N. Sampath, Secretary, All Indian Bank, Employees Association, Chennai.

Prof. R.G. Desai & M. Madhumathi, Res. 23, Arthi Apart, Binny Layout-ii, (Behind Good Will Ganga Apart), Chandra Layout, Bangalore-40. Janana Bharati Campus, Bangalore-560 056.

Dr. D.S. Leelavathi, Reader in Economics, DOS in Economics & Co-operation, Manasagargothri, Mysore-570 006. Karnataka.

Prof. N. Sudhakar Rao, Professor in Economics, Nagarjuna University, Guntur.

Prof. M.R. Khurana, Head of the Department, Punjab University, Chandigarh-160 014 (India).

Prof. K.M. Naidu, UGC Emeritus Fellow, Department of Economics, SVU, Tirupati.

Prof. K.S. Naidu, Professor, Head and Coordinator, Department of Economics, S.V. University, Tirupati, A.P.

Dr. C. Sreenivasulu, Vice Principal & Reader in Economics, Sri Venkateswara College, Suryapet-508 213, Nalgonda Dist., A.P.

Prof. G. Savaraiah, Professor of Economics, S.V. University, Tirupati.

Dr. M. Devarajulu, Associate Professor in Economics, S.V. University, Tirupati.

Dr. C. Muthu Raja, Faculty Member, P.G. Department of Economics, The American College, Madurai-625 002. Tamil Nadu.

Sri K. Giriyappa & C. Pulinda Rao, Central Leather Research Institute, (Council of Scientific & Industrial Research), Adyar, Chennai-600 020, India.

Dr. B. Krishnama Naidu, Head & Deputy Director, Economics Research Division, Chennai-600020, India.

Prof M. Atchi Reddy, Professor of Economics, University of Hyderabad, Hyderabad.

Ms. Sneha Nalla, Research Scholar in Economics, University of Hyderabad, Hyderabad.

Contents

PART II

IMPACT OF ECONOMIC REFORMS ON THE INDIAN LABOUR

Part I

Globalisation, Economic Reforms and Labour

1

Employment and Economic Development Analysis of China and India[1]

Prof. D.L. Narayana

Welfare State

According to Amold Toynbee, World historian, "The twentieth century will be chiefly remembered not as an age of political conflicts or technical innovations, but as an age in which human society dared to think of the welfare of the whole human race as a practical objective"[1] The UNDP's annual reports published since 1990 contain a rich fund of knowledge about economic and social policies to be pursued for achieving the goal of real world welfare state spread over the developed and developing countries.

The innovation in science and technology and their utilization for human development will make the twenty first century of great knowledge exposition. Knowledge is power, accelerated growth of knowledge will usher in much required social change for human progress. "Knowledge is like light, weightless and intangible, it can easily travel the world, enlightening the lives of people everywhere"[2] Knowledge is behind Asia's surge. If so, "knowledge is the key to development-that knowledge is development"[3]. According to Alfred Marshall "Knowledge is our most powerful engine of production".

1. Invited Keynote paper to the U.G.C Seminar

The twentieth century has achieved outstanding accomplishment in the sphere of science and technology. The second part of the century witnessed significant revolutions in three fields: biotechnology, space technology and information technology which are instrumental in knowledge explosion as well as the promotion of global village.

While science and technology provide the tools for advancing physical productivity in varied lines of activity, social institutions, devised by politics, economic sociology, religion and culture determine the quality and quantity of leadership in the country to achieve the possible level of development in the different lines of human activity.

There is a fair degree of correlation between the level of employment and the level of economic development which a country can achieve with effective utilization of manpower. Generally labour intensive techniques as in agriculture and rural areas of developing countries, generate more employment for a given investment as compared to manufacturing industry which is generally more capital intensive. Service sections provide wider scope for both labour intensive and capital intensive and capital intensive techniques as the latest experience reveals.

The two Asiatic countries, china and India are the most populous countries of the world with 1.02 and 1.25 billion of population as per the latest population census. While China has already succeeded in adopting one child norm, India has not been in a position to adopt two child norm. If the current rates of population growth were to continue, by the middle of 21st century, both India and China will have 1901 dimension of world population of 1.5 billion. Other things being equal successful control of population growth will facilitate improvement in the quality of population of a country. Unrestrained population growth will complicate the achievement of welfare state, which postulates accelerated economic growth to meet the challenge of unchecked or less checked population growth. In geographical area, China is three times bigger than India.

Structural Change in Economic Development

History of human civilization reveals that agricultural civilization is about ten thousand years old, as against the modern industrial civilization which is almost three hundred years of age. Organised effort for economic development started after the first World War and it has emerged as a world-wide movement after the Second World war. As the transition from war economy involved some time, peace efforts to build economy on the basis of evolved programme of planning may have commenced from 1950 onwards acquitting about 50 years of experience in the implementation of organized efforts.

Industrial Revolution by virtue of its creative impact on economic growth, industry, agriculture, education, health, population growth, employment structure, international relations, social, political and cultural spheres facilitated radical transformation of social order and generated rich economic history.

The I.L.O. rightly emphasized the importance of facilitating structural change in social systems, "Many societies throughout the World have in the past chosen to resist change and have as a result, stagnation for centuries and even millennia. Modern industrial society, by contrast has accepted and adopted itself to changes that have given people longer lives, better health, more education that vastly more material wealth-and have given these things to a population many times larger than would have been conceivable 200 years age. Spreading widely throughout the world, the spirit of change has generated a revolution of rising expectations-that can be fulfilled only if structural change continues and spreading further".

Structural change is a process of adaptation of an economic system to stimulate economic growth in the course of its evolution. Every dynamic economy experiences the need for adjusting production-and employment undergoes structural change. The more rapid is the growth of an economy, the greater will be the need for assimilation of structural change. Expecting structural change may necessitate organizational effort on the part of state and market to remove the barriers to smooth economic growth.

Simon Kuznets defined structural changes as changes in social and economic institutions or practices emerging in the course of economic growth involving sustained increase in per capita real income and output per worker in spite of increase in population. He identified modern economic growth as a significant orderly and distinctive body of long-term experience. It is a significant process of long-term change in a number of societies affecting most of mankind. It is orderly in so far the nation states develop common characteristics among the various aspects of their economic and social behaviour. It is a distinctive process in so far it differs significantly from the past experience of societies. It constitutes an era of spreading application of science to processes of production and social organization.

The prime structural characteristics of modern economic growth are industrialization, the movement of population from agricultural production to industrial production, urbanization, the process of distribution population between villages and towns a clear shift in employment structure from primary sector to secondary, and tertiary sector, a significant shift in the relative economic position of different groups in terms of employment status, level of per capita income and standard of living and inevitable involvement international aspects of economic growth. In general industrial characteristics and changes as compared to the developing economies, where the problems of structural change and adjustments are far more serious and acute. Economic development of underdeveloped countries, indeed represents and attempt for complete transformation of traditional systems into modern economies depending on the framework of the programme of their development.

Generally structural changes in the industrially advanced countries are of smaller dimension and shorter duration as compared to the developing countries requiring long period for economic transformation.

Structural Change in the Employment of Labour

In the early economic literature immediately after the Second World War, Clark-Fisher hypothesis (Clark 1951, Fisher 1946), later Arthur Lewis in his classic text book "Theory of the Economic Growth", argued in the course of economic development of under developed countries with surplus man-power in their dominant primary sector of agricultural and allied occupations, there will be a substantial shift of labour to the secondary sector of manufacturing industry and later to the tertiary sector of services. This theory of structural change appears to be valid in the traditional pattern of industrialization for some decades. Modern patterns economic growth has experienced by the dynamic South East Asian countries with a greater degree of scientific knowledge utilization, it is found that the tertiary sector would be playing a very significant role in the creation of new jobs.[4]

It may be noted that the impact of policy measures on employment and incomes in the tertiary sector has much less discussed that the effects of public policy on employment in manufacturing. Experience reveals that the tertiary employment which Government can shape is quite considerable on account of direct public sector expenditure, investment infrastructure of transport and construction as well as education and health sectors. As migration of rural people is increasing more rapidly than before, urban planning policies play a crucial role in the expansion of tertiary labour market. Regulatory framework in domestic and foreign trade influence spatial location and capital intensity of jobs created in the sector.[5]

Tertiary sector is heterogeneous sector containing labour which is "pushed" in for want of opportunities for jobs in other sectors, and "pulled" into the sector because of higher incomes.

Another significant feature of the tertiary sector is the significant existence of dualism in the labour market containing so-called informal sector which contrasts with large-scale sub-sectors which coexist together with wide variation in their productivity. A substantial portion of employment created in the tertiary sector of the economy is in the small scale and even one man enterprises which coexist along with large establishments.[6]

Stage and Market in Economic Policy

After the First World War, the Marxian Doctrine of Socialism with proletariat dictatorship inspired U.S.S.R to embark on totalitarian planning, which yielded good success in the early decades of its implementation as analysed by leading lights like Sydney Webb, Beatrice Webb and Mawrice Dobb of U.K.

The Marxian tide promoted the rise of socialism and economic planning after the First World War in U.S.S.R. and the spread of economic planning later, especially after the Second World War to a large number of countries in the world.

The Second World War and its aftermath witness the rise of European democracies and the Chinese Revolution. Several colonial countries achieved independence. Since 1950s, economic planning got spread among the developing and developed countries rapidly. The four decades of democratic planning in the world and seven decades of totalitarian planning in U.S.S.R. revealed their limitations for further dynamic growth by accumulating their own problems that are standing in the way of their reaching their goals and highest economic growth and welfare.

Despite the phenomenal impact of Soviet Economic Development, the totalitarian planning in U.S.S.R. undermined economic freedom and individualism. The Gorbachev Revolution with Perestroika and Glasnost policies initiated changes towards privatization and liberalization coinciding with the emergence of New Economic Policy in the World since 1980s. The New Economic Policy has crystallized into five basic principles of liberalization, privatization, modernization, marketisation and globalization.

Contemporary Russia displays many symptoms of the free market. It has entrepreneurs, stock exchanges and bank; but the Russian businessman is unlike his counterparts elsewhere. Because of the indolence of the state police, he is forced to deploy a private army, because lack of coherent laws, he is forced to bribe officials. The officials like it so much that they are in no hurry to establish a consistent legal system.

Russian entrepreneur is bound to pay a good proportion of his profits to the state treasury and the percentage may rise or fall depending on the goodwill of individual officials. Additional taxes payable to the Mafia rare unavoidable, so the businessman has no alternative but to offer to the official a sweeter for interpreting the law in his favour.

Hence, what Russia is having today is bandit capitalism. It is a unique grafting together of indigenous black market gangsterism, party clientism, ethnic nepotism along with Mafia lines and western joint ventures. The system operates in the twilight world of the hard currency zone, and like all forms of criminal capitalism. It generates large amounts of line quality, growing amounts of political corruption, it is capitalism, red in tooth and claw.

Today, a growing number of Russians have realized that decades of systematic suppression of initiative and enterprise have left a mindset that will take a generation to alter.

Indeed according to the Transparency International, Berlin, study of corruption among 85 countries, Russia was always a top index contender along with Colombia, Bolivia and Nigeria. Its rank is 76th during 1998 out of the 85 countries as for per capita corruption index.

Under the determined leadership of Deng, China switched over to Socialist market policy since 1978 achieving outstanding results as analysed in detail later.

While the World Bank is advocating market friendly approach for economic growth among the different countries of the World, UNDP since 1990s has been emphasizing people's friendly approach for human development and economic growth involving Government intervention in the developing countries in particular. There is a growing realization that ideology driven prescriptions of either of interventionist variety of free may not deliver goods. An appropriate synthesis of State and Market with innovative cooperation and coordination holds the key for world economic development today. The experience of Asian Tigers ranging from Japan to that of South Korea and also China bear testimony to the purpose.

David F. Burton, after evaluation of the challenges of newly industrialized countries as competitors to America asserted that the distinguishing feature of "East Asian economic performance is not the dominance of free enterprise but the higher effective collaboration between the private and public sectors. Shared goals and commitments together with a high degree for professionalism in the service of national economic development have characterized the region's economic strategy. Market forces and Government intervention are not at odds with each other but carefully coordinate for national economic gain".[7]

Competent policy advisers are now inclined to focus on appropriate combination of markets and state intervention. It is now generally recognized that apart from maintaining macro economic stability, governments in developing countries must also strongly intervene in sections like health care, education, development of physical infrastructure such as roads, transportation, power and communications as well anti-poverty programmes and protection of environment. The state has to intervene to minimize government failure and market failure, so that social objectives can be achieved at minimum social cost.

What development requires is good governance and public intervention, which supplement rather than supplant the market mechanism. Hundreds of years ago, Kautilya's Arthasastra postulated; "in the interest of the prosperity of the country the King should be diligent in foreseeing the possibilities of calamities, try to avoid them before they arrive, overcome those which happen, remove all obstructions to economic activity and prevent loss of revenue to the State".

The three hundred years of industrial civilization witnesses the resurgence of market for accelerating economic growth with an intervening phase of totalitarian planning in U.S.S.R. and intensive democratic planning World war. Free market does not mean the withering of the State. Appropriate coexistence of State and market with suitable pursuit of economic activities constitute the enlightened path for high economic development. The State and Market have to adopt innovative cooperation and coordination to generate high economic growth like the dutiful husband and wife to promote the growth of their family. Hence the case is for an appropriate synthesis of State and market for high rate of economic growth for accomplishing welfare State sooner than later for the rapidly growing World population. A crucial requisite for the emergency of the world welfare state is the commitment of the public sector and private sector for advancing the welfare of the people in their decision-making and management of the economy without undermining efficiency.

China's Miracale of Economic Growth

Today, there are nine Asian Tigers Japan, Hongkong, Singapore, Taiwan, South Korea, Indonesia, Malaysia, Thailand and China. While Japan is the classic tiger of Asia known for its rapid growth after Second World War, China's pragmatic policies of achieving one-child-family in population planning, market friendly approach and effective mobilization of capital from foreign countries enabled it to emerge as the most dominant Asian tiger in size since 1970.

In view of their high economic growth rate, the Asian tigers are having high per capita income as compared to that of India. According to the HDR 1999, the per capita income of India in 1977 is only $ 498 as against $ 25,084 of Japan, $ 12, 438 of Hongkong, $ 3,387 of Malaysia, $ 1970 of Thailand and $ 785 of Indonesia. During 1998, the GNP of China is higher by 2.8 times over that of India, per capita income is higher by 2.4 times. The disparity in GNP and per capita income of India and China must have further increased by now with greater advance of China.

The World Bank conducted a state of the East Asia miracle under the leadership of John Page[8]. The study found that the Asian tiger, have the World's fastest growing areas for the past 30 years. The high performing eight nations excluding China grew since 1960 twice as best as East Asia, thrice as fast as South Asia and Latin American Countries. China's southern region has been growing fast, but this is a recent phenomenon since 1978. The World Bank organized a separate study of China. The miraculous growth of Chinese economy is highlighted at the end of this section in view of the special importance for economic policy for development.

The essence of the World Bank study of Asian tigers in that most of East Asia's extra-ordinary growth flowed from a reservoir of physical and human capital they build over the years and allocated to highly productive sectors in much better way than other countries. They also invested in the acquisition of modern technology.

The East Asian experience proved that the acquisition of physical and human capital is the engine and motive force of economic growth. The eight countries spent 7 to 10 per cent of GDP, more than in other countries on education and training. "People in these countries worked harder and saved more than people in other countries" As the state played positive contributive role to economic development in some of those countries, the study found that state intervention is not bad. While the world-wide spread of privatization and the erosion of the role of State in economic policy in developed countries undermined the importance of government intervention in economic policy for development, the extraordinary economic growth rate achieved by Asian tigers has gone a long way to strengthen the case for resurgence of State and market for economic development. East Asia's fastest growth rate is based on several governing factors which are quite significant in visualizing the scope and nature of contemporary economic development although they vary among the different countries in relation to the stage of their development. They are as in the following.

1. Political stability
2. Investment in human capital
3. High rate of saving
4. Attraction of foreign investment
5. Imported technology policies involving state intervention
6. Selective industrial policies involving state intervention
7. Effective implementation and management

8. Improving professionalism
9. Low fiscal deficit and stable macro economic policy
10. Aggressive export development
11. Pursuit of principles of shared growth emphasized and followed by leadership to benefit the middle class and the poor to get the benefit of growth.
12. Educated labour force and its active cooperation
13. The impact of Diaspora in the case of China since 1978 with liberal economic policy.
14. Dominant role of private entrepreneurship
15. Close cooperation between Government and private business on creation of public enterprises with high start-up costs and externalities as components of strategy.
16. Pursuit of middle path without external extreme and drastic policies.
17. Influence of Buddhist and Confucius thought on society contributing to corporate spirit and social efficiency in economic activity.

The China's miraculous economic growth is a reflection on two stabilities-political stability and economic stability. China rose to great height in advancing economic development with the dynamic role of diaspora whose perception is one of loyalty. Loyal and loyalty have a far deeper moral contribution governing Chinese development that is behind China's miracle. China is having one of the most sweeping historical drama not only of the 20th century and perhaps of all time. According to Fredric R. Clairmont "No economy in the world, it would appear, is so favourably poised to meet the competitive challenges of the 21st century as china today"[9]. The Chinese developmental experiment reveals that it revised its original philosophy and vision of creating a new China as an alternative system of classless and stateless communism. Its pragmatic and successful efforts for social and economic development are quite revealing and inspiring about which a detailed note is provided in this section.

China has emerged as a country of rapid economic growth with its vigorous programme of economic reform of 1978. After years of state control of all productive assets, it encouraged the formation of rural enterprises and private businesses, liberalized foreign trade and investment, and released State control of some prices and investment in industrial production and the education of its work force.

As compared to the annual growth rate of 6 per cent a year in pre 1978 China, the post-1978 China witnessed average real growth of more than 9 per cent a year. During the peak years, Chinese economy grew more than 13 per cent. Per capita income nearly quadrupled in the last 15 years, 1985-2000. A few analysts are predicting that the Chinese economy will be larger than that of U.S.A. in about 20 years. Its growth compares favourably, as compared to 7-8 per cent average growth of the Asian Tigers, Hongkong, Korea and Singapore during the last 15 years.

An important lesson of Chinese development experience for Countries with a large segment of population underemployed in agriculture, is inspiring the growth of rural enterprises and not focusing exclusively on the urban industrial sector that has successfully moved million of workers off the farms into factories without creating an urban crisis, as a large proportion of China's explosive industrial growth took place in township village enterprises (TVEs). TVEs grew in strength and in 1995-96 they produced 61% industrial output and facilitated take-off in China. TVEs are collectively owned by the respective township and villages. Their surpluses accrue to the township and village authorities and not to individual capitalists. As they are located on land owned by local authority itself, they need not pay any rent for land.

Capital in China is substantially cheaper than India. China's saving rate is more than 40 per cent as compared to India's 23 percent.

As compared to price advantage of land and capital, the most outstanding feature of China's competitiveness is the dynamic advantage of higher labour productive of labour efficiency. Indeed China's recent productivity performance is quite remarkable. While the productivity of Asian Tigers hovered around 2 per cent, China's rate of about 4 per cent puts it simply in a class by itself.

Moreover China's open door policy has spurred foreign investment into the country apart from the Diaspora. The foreign investment has added power to economic transformation as it facilitated the building of factories, creation of jobs and linking China to international market. It helped the important transfers of technology with greater advantage for a dozen open coastal areas where foreign investors enjoy tax advantages. Further, economic liberalization boosted exports, which rose to 19 per cent a year during 1981-94. Strong export growth, in turn, appears to have fuelled productivity growth in domestic industries.

"China's strong productivity, growth, spurred by the market-oriented reforms, is the leading cause of China's unprecedented economic performance."

The absence of land market, production for export, educated labour force and greater identification of labourers in a large number of enterprises, i.e. TVEs with result of their labour are some of the factors accounting for China's higher productivity and its competitiveness in the World market". Thus, Chinese economy has become a market socialist economy. It may be noted that China achieved a GDP growth rate of 13.3 per cent during 1991-92 to 1995-96 as against 5.3 per cent of India.

In fine, China's miracle of employment and economic growth is an illustration of the policy of market socialism, which constituted a successful experiment in effective implementation of the collaborative effort of State and market.

It may be further noted that the annual growth rate of 6 per cent in pre 1978 China, post 1978 China witnessed average real growth of more than 9 per cent a year. During the peak years Chinese economy grew more than 13 per cent. Per capita income has nearly quadrupled in the last 15 years, 1985-2000. A few analysts are predicting that the Chinese economy will be large than that of USA in about 20 years. Probably, China is destined to make world history for achieving highest economic growth rate.

Although East-Asian countries experienced foreign currency account deposit problems since 1997 on account of "inadequate foreign exchange reserves in relation to short term external liabilities, China, like Japan, Taiwan and Singapore in spite of some financial turbulence, maintained surplus in their current account. Consequently they did not experience any recession and unemployment as in the case of Latin American countries. (Mr. Rakshit: "The East Asian Currency Crisis", 2000).

The following Table reveals the comparative superiority of China over India as regards some important economic indicators.

It is obvious from the Table China possesses outstanding superiority in the availability of capital, electricity generation and utilization and agricultural productivity of important crops like paddy, maize, groundnut and cotton.

Performance of the Indian Economy, Employment and Social Crisis

Indian is considered to be the fifth largest economy in the World in purchasing power next to the economics of U.S.A., China, Japan and Germany. In terms of growth rate as noted already, it compares less favourably with most of the South East Asian Countries which maintained a

Table 1. Some Economic Indicators of Contrast between India and China

S. No.	Description	India	China	Remarks
1.	Saving Rate	23% of GDP	45% of GDP	Approximately double that of India
2.	Annual F.D. Flow	$ 2.16 billion	$ 40 billion	About 19 times over India
3.	Power Generating capacity	90,000 MW	1.6 lakh MW	About 3 times over that of India
	(a) Transmission and Distribution loss in Power	1.8 per cent	6.8 per cent	Cost of loss of power in India is 3.5 times over that of China
	(b) Power cost per twice 100 kwh	47.83	44.3	India is nearly that of China
	(c) Per capita consumption	350 Kwh	1000 Kwh	About 3 times over that of India.
4.	Agricultural Productivity per hectare in KG			
	Paddy	2,915	6,331	About 2½ times over that of India
	Maize	1,594	4,481	About 2½ times over that of India
	Groundnut	998	2,574	About 3 times higher that of India
	Cotton	311	943	About 3 times over that of India
	Wheat	Lower in China by 54 per cent over that of India		
	Sugarcane	Lower in China by 10 per cent over that of India		

sustained growth rate of 6 to 7 per cent over a long period of time not to speak of China with highest growth rate.

India is a developing country with a moderate rate of economic growth. It's annual average growth rate from 1950 to 1980 was only 3.5 per cent which was characterized as Hindu growth rate as it was too low. It's average growth rate from 1981-82 to 1998-99 is 5.6 per cent with a range of variation from 10.6 per cent during 1988-89 to 0.8 per cent during 1991-92. It's growth rate from 1994-95 to 1996-97 was above 7 per cent. Since 1999 to 2000, its' growth rate is slightly above 5 per cent. Thus, the growth rate of Indian economy experienced market fluctuations.

The ration of debt of GNP in 1999 was 21.3, the only other developing country with a more favourable ration is China. India's fiscal deficit is among the highest out of 74 major countries with a population more than 10 million. Further more, public savings in the nineties in India, which reached peak of 2.0 per cent GDP in 1995-96 turned negative, 1.2 per cent GDP by 1999-2000[12].

India has achieved an appreciable decline in its poverty. The all India poverty ration fell to 27.09 per cent in rural areas, 23.52 per cent in urban areas and 26.10 per cent at the all-India level in 1999-2000 from 53.1 per cent, 45.2 per cent in 51.3 per cent recorded during 1977-78. Life expectations moved up from 50.4 years in 1980-81 to above 61 years in 1998. There has been an improvement in life expectations at first for males from 50.1 years to 60.4 years for females from 50 years to 61.8 years. The over all literacy has increased from 43.7 per cent in 1980-81 to 63.1 per cent in 1998-99. Moreover for the first time in four decades the population growth has decelerated to below 2 per cent according to 2001 census. Mortality rate declined from 12.5 per cent per 1000 in 1980-81 to 8.0 per 1000 in 1998-99. Nevertheless, India still accounts for a very large concentration of poverty and illiteracy[13].

Although the annual growth rate of India's population came down to below 2 per cent the work force population seeking employment above the age of 20 years increased to 2.5 per cent since 2001. Accordingly, one of the most daunting challenges facing India is to provide employment not only for the additions of the labour force but also reduce the backlog accumulated unemployment in the past. The secular downward pressure in employment postulates rapidly, increasing economic growth rate. Moreover, economic growth and employment opportunities may not be sufficient to improve the living conditions of the poor. It is therefore, necessary also to shift the focus of employment strategies towards creating conditions whereby employment opportunities lead to significant betterment in living and working conditions of the people. It is alarming to note that the average annual growth rate of over all employment in the organized and unorganized sectors declined continuously from 2.75 per cent in the period 1997-78 to 1.77 per cent in 1987-88 but increased to 2.37 per cent in the period 1987-94[14].

With reform policies of disinvestments in public sector and the pursuit of V.R.S. to reduce the surplus manpower in public sector, employment in the public sector has been declining. The following Table reveals the annual growth rates of employment in the organized public and private sector during 1991 to 1998.

It is obvious from the Table that the private sector contributed predominantly to the increase in organized sector employment in the post-reform period except in the year 1993. The employment in the public sector declined in 1998, where as organized public sector employment grew by 1.72 per cent. The rate of growth of employment, however, in public and private sectors during 1998 were lower as compared to the preceding year.

Apart from the increasing trend of unemployment in the un-organized sector of India, the number of candidates with educational qualifications and industrial skills registered with Employment Exchanges in India has gone up beyond four crores in the year 1998, touching the figure of 40,224,000.

Table 2. Growth Rate of Employment in Organised Sector (per cent)

Year	*Public Sector*	*Private Sector*	*Total Organised*
1991	1.52	1.24	1.44
1992	0.80	2.21	1.21
1993	0.60	0.06	0.44
1994	0.62	1.01	0.73
1995	0.11	1.63	0.55
1996	0.19	5.62	1.51
1997	0.67	2.04	1.09
1998	-0.09	1.72	0.46

Source: "Economic Survey 1999-2000", p. 168 (Govt. of India).

Although population explosion has registered a marginal fall in its growth, unemployment explosion in the organized and unorganized sectors is most conspicuous. Presently India's greatest challenges in advancing of employment opportunities during the 21st century for the increased ration of work force aspiring jobs.

The challenges of providing employment in the organized and unorganized sectors, eliminating poverty and achievement of higher economic growth are most complicated in India for their solution in the current century because of deep-seated social crisis through which India is passing.

Although India is a most populous country with note-worthy brainpower capital, it bristles with greatest social diversities as compared to any country or continent in the world with 4000 castes, 6000 social groups, about 4000 languages including dialects and a number of religions with wide ranging cultures, not to speak of varied levels of social and economic development. Although India is a country of great spiritual wealth, Hinduism is the most autonomous and horizontal religion unlike Islam Buddhism or Christianity that is conductive for better corporate spirit as vertical religions.

After achieving Independence in 1947, over the last fifty and odd years, its social groups have become quite vocal engendering social struggles and agitation of dimensions. Indeed India today has about 600 political parties threatening national political stability. The visible social consequences worthy of note are the emergence of materialism as a religion and transformation of rampart politics into a profession.

According to Transparency International of Berlin, India is one of top ten countries of highest incidences of parallel economy. While economic growth is moderate, with a serious incidence of social struggle, India is experiencing a metamorphosis of transforming its social trends into evil that has engendered a deep social crisis on ethical values upsetting political stability, administrative efficiency, effective management of the country not to speak of decades old cross border terrorism. Percolation of less ethical values in different walks of life will influence adversely the achievement of welfare state not to speak of socialist pattern of society.

The problems that confront development effort in India are identified as bureaucratic delays and inefficiency, corruption, poor quality of public services and collapsing of judicial system under the weight of a huge backlog of cases. In a globalising environment, no state can afford to be less than efficient. Good governance is a necessary condition for attracting capital and the maintenance of adequate and stable growth. Public leaders have to realize the need to build human capabilities rather than the mere distribution of wealth under the package of reforms.

"A society that periodically indulges in events of barbarism, whose intensity seems to increase with time, cannot possibility hope to build an economy on organized lines."[15] India experienced abnormal communal violence in 1947, Delhi in 1984, Mumbai in 1992-93 and Gujarat in 2002. All of them witnesses a serious break down of civil society resulting in murders on a large scale. The wide prevalence of social conflict undermined economic prospects leading the economy in high unemployment. Rapid economic growth provides a greater stake for citizens in a peaceful civil society and facilitates dissolution of communal tensions.

In fine, while employment generation proved to be a growth engine in china which altered its original institutional arrangements of State Policy for achieving a historical record of social and economic development. India in spite of its brainpower is experiencing a deep-seated social crisis of conflicting interests without the required corporate support to work for nation development.

References

1. D.L. Narayana: *Employment and Economic Growth in India"* (ILO. 50th Anniversary Lectures", Madurai University, 1970 p. 21.
2. The World Bank: *"World Development Report", "Knowledge for Development"*, 1998-99, Oxford University Press, p. 3.
3. *Ibid*, p. 19.
4. Dipak Mazundar: *"Labour Market and Employment in Economic Growth of East and South-East Asia-Some Key Issues"*, "The Indian Journal of Labour Economics", Vol. 43, No. 3, July-September, 2000, p. 422.
5. *Ibid*, p. 422.
6. *Ibid*, p. 422.
7. "Challenge of Nies: *"America's New Competitor" "Economic Impact"*, 1989, p. 31.
8. *"The Hindu"*, Madras, September 27, 1993, p. 5.
9. Fredric F. Clairmount, *"The Awakened Prometheus", Economic and Political Weekly"*, April, 1993, p. 748.

10. Zulieu Hu and Moshim S. Khan: "*Why is China Growing so Fast*", p. 9, Reprint, June-2000, I.M.F.
11. "Economic and Political Weekly", February 17-23, 2001, Vol. XXXVI, No. 7, p. 524.
12. Y.V. Reddy: "*Revising Confidence in the Indian Economy*". "The Indian Economic Journal", Vol. No.1.p. 11.
13. *Ibid*, p. 12.
14. Government of India: Economic Survey 1999-2000, p. 168.
15. C. Mohan Reddy: "*The Hindu*" 16.3.2002, p. 10.
16. Prem Shankerdha "*The Silent Crisis of Unemployment*", The Hindu, 22-8-2001, p. 19.

2

Institutional Theory of Economic Development

With Special Reference to Employment and Labour: Twenty First Century Approach

Prof. V. Shanmugasundaram

The Hangover of Marshall and Allied British Economic Thought:

Sometime in the evolution of economic theory, the classificatory approach gave birth to the four fold factors Land, Labour, Capital and Organisation, and related distribution of income as rent, wages, interest and profits. Compared with recent advances in economic sciences, this is obsolete, misleading, irrelevant and if persisted in by pedagogues is tantamount to corrupting the minds of the scholars committed to their care. Marshall in the high tide of British empire, in whose domains the sun was ever shining, in the east or west possessions. It is classification of convenience when economies were less developed and arbitrary divisions would satisfy the gullible. Not many economists believed in these distinctions.

The Basic Conceptual Classification

The term labour, should not have been accepted by Marx. He was a victim of standard English school of Adam Smith, Ricardo, Mill and Cairnes. (Ref:1. Philop H. Wicksteed:

The Common Sense of Political Economy and Selected Papers and Reviews of Economic Theory) (With Introduction by Lionel Robbins) London, 1933, p. 725) Finally, since we know that land and capital are remunerated on one identical principle, in conformity with their marginal efficiency, we see that the attempt to distinguish accurately between them is as unnecessary as it is hopeless. (Source: Philip H. Wicksteed: The Common Sense of Political Economy and Selected Papers and Reviews of Economic Theory (With Introduction by Lionel Robbins London, 1933, p. 574). It is on this hopeless, distinction between labour and organization, and equally outworn differences between wages and profits, we can seek reduction of the profession of economists and their younger siblings. I venture to demolish as much as I can, these classificatory monstrosity in Indian economics. And in the temple city of Tirupathi, this amounts to worship at the shrine of economics, with faith in nothing but the veracity of contemporary turn of human affairs. I am deeply conscious that my search is for a term other than that in wide use among economists, and many professional associations who for want of a better term stick to "labour". What they mean is the exertion of a person who is not learned enough and rich enough to set up his own firm and get what the income tax authorities will hail as profits. It is time we use a wiser term Human Resource to cover both the historical terms labour and organization. This may be a matter of degree, but surely one of improvement which recognizes the inalienable use of mental faculties, always with mere physical exertion, like that of other vertebrate animals, the cattle or horses. The matter is important and it is for the trade union and human right forums to pursue further, in defence of human dignity and self respect.

And the Emergence of Employment as a Concept

The iconoclastic writings of the mathematician turned art critique, journalist, businessman and also economist John Maynard Keynes, wrote and published a book based on his lectures of 1934 on 'The General Theory of Employment. Earlier he authored a book on Indian Currency and Finance (1913), A Treatise on Probability (1921) A Treatise on Money (2 Vols. 1930) Essays in Biography (1933). One should delve deep into these outpourings to know how he launched the book 'The General Theory" (Source: The General Theory of Employment, Interest and Meony, published in London, 1936). This carried a preface to the English edition dated 13 Dec. 1935, and it was reprinted 17 times without any change, and remains as such to this day. This German edition has a preface on 7 Sept. 1936, the Japanese edition on 4 Dec. 1936 and the French Edition on 20 Feb. 1939. He was a product of economic climate of Great Depression, during which he penned his widely read pieces though they were carefully ignored by British economic policy makers. It was Samuelson, Galbraith and other younger group of Economists, in the Roosevelt Era who saw the prospects of healing the ravages of the Great Depression who widened the market for what is now known as Keynesian Economics. The question to be posed and answered is how is it that the term employment so widely used in current economic literature, was hidden in other words and phrases like wages and labour, profits and organization. Labour was for a long term the output of inferior human beings, who are to use an old saying "rowers of water and hewers of wood", a little more work-horses, and cattle whose subsistence is taken care of by food, and shelter, and a little protective covering. To extent it did not care for it. The attitude of economists and political activists towards human beings was that bulk of them constituted means for the ends of others, the means by a vast bulk of men and women as toilers, and few as beneficiaries of their toil. The palaces the former built, in hovels the rest lived. (Source: I Vedagiri Shanmugasundaram: The General Theory of Change from Poverty of Plenty, Surat, 1979, Poem). For too long a time, humanity has used economists as apologists for the order of the day and the upholders of distributive injustice. And currently, those of us in the profession of economics are in many of its avatars, as theoreticians for agriculture, industry, and services another simplistic sector. And the subject has widened so much in the 20th century as to accommodate the countless specialities, by prefiixing economics to whatever is marketable as a subject in luxurious combination with it, like economics of ethics, economics of sports and games, economics of health, economics of environment, and of course, the subject of our concern today is Economics of Labour. (Source: conversations with Dr. B. Natarajan: First Economic Adviser to the Govt. of Madras Presidency; First Development Commissioner, Andhra Pradesh: "Economics will shamelessly associate with everything. See also his writings: Economics is Not All") In our extensive conquests comparable to those of the Prince of Macedona in the past, Alexander the Great we have vast territories to claim, but the governance of it is dubious, and often ephemeral. With this rider, we may start our sojourn.

The Employment Situation in India: The Demand Side

There are two sides to employment. One the demand side and the other supply side. The uniqueness of Indian employment environment is the ground to base our employment theory. Whatever Keynes and those of his school may offer. It is good to recognize that in Indian cultural milieu the demand for employment, by which we mean marketable use of time and human exertion is not as much as it is in many west European and North American countries. This is due to what Professor Peter Bauer cited as Reserve Price Theory. (Source Peter Tomas Bauer; Economics of Under-Developed Countries, Visbet, London, Cambridge handbook Series, 1950s several editions.) In a joint family, if one member can get food and shelter, and a little to spend clothing and other services, it is not likely that the person concerned will go for work, unless the income from such exertion is substantially more than what he gets in return for his membership of the joint family. This is not to deny that the person concerned does render some services in return for his reserve price based real income. This is only to confirm that he is not an active person so far as demand for wage employment is concerned, unless the income is many times over the reserve price. This, is in one set of persons, in joint family, extended family etc. (ii) In another are women who due to social, cultural and allied social reasons do not enter employment in unorganized sectors, where employment-related security concerns do not meet the household to which she belongs, which household intern being responsible for her marriage, with attendant costs of dowry, marriage ceremonies, etc. She would rather remain unemployed, if regid social criteria of employment could not be met, and be an eligible bride, instead of taking any employment, which do not mesh with their concerns. (iii) The same reasons would prevent any young person, man or women from taking up work in far off places, which may give them culture or social shock. (iv) And from any other reason, if young persons in search of high-income safe Government-secure job, are waiting this period could well be considered non-demand period of employment. (v) In organized private employment especially in firms whose growth is based on restrictive practices like licenses, quotas, permits etc., with easy profit, pressures by those in authority, or other influential persons would count for recruitment. Some candidates would wait for this manna to fall from heaven, and would be outside the employment market (vi) In all cases where there is no transparency as regards vacancies terms of employment, period of service, job description etc., there is imperfect employment market: (vii) In the fast changing economic environment of the 21st century, continuous upgrading of the skills is required; if one is not ready for it, and if one wants to rest on prior skills, the eligibility criterion would preclude the person from employment market.

The Creation of Effective Demand in Indian Economics

Education is the Key to unlock this rigidity in employment demand. And this is happening. Education among women in all communities, the increasing age of marriage, the preference of employed women in both arranged and other forms of marriage, the strength of women's movements which assert security concerns, have removed many of the erstwhile unique features of the rigidity in the employment market, cited above in (i) to (vii) Nevertheless, the mismatch of skills required and the demand thereof remain. The push factor is that, the means of livelihood are becoming expensive and under the stress of price rise, the joint family is breaking up. Employment opportunities in far off places, bring about geographic factors to have full play. And the Keynesian remedy, is to crate money and encourage public works schemes, even such projects like digging ditches and filling them. We notice hereunder a few schemes under the current exercises of the Government of India.

The Relative Share of Organized and Unorganized Sectors

It is a matter of great concern for the current generation of Indian, is not that the growth if employment in the organized sectors is meagre. When we consider the growth of population, the increase in the size of the labour force, and the percentage of growth in employment, the obvious inference is that employment is shrinking. Recognizing the back log and additions to labour force, (Source; ibid, p. 238. para. 10.7) the report adds: "Economic reforms in the areas of abolishing quantitative restrictions (QRs). Reducing tariffs, reforming labour laws and abolishing SSI reservations have aimed at fostering labour- intensive production in India." The economic fact is that measures would increase employment potential in the countries with which we trade. And surely SSI would have less employment, and more employment. This is what we call tongue in the cheek argument. Facts are followed by wishes, which are not consistent. The reasons for this are not far to seek, *There is no consistent and persistent full employment policy in India.* In most of the industrial countries, the level of unemployment forms the basis of electoral manifestos. Not so in India. And agricultural under-employment apart, there is something more hazardous. The Agricultural Price Commissions instead of fixing a floor price which covers the cost of production plus income for the farmer, is biased to support the fiscal consideration of supply of subsidized food to the urban lobby. As a consequence, there double disadvantage to the agricultural population, mostly small holders under historical socialist land reforms regime. Let some figures speak for themselves.

Sectors	*1983*	*1999-2000*	*Growth rate 1994/00*
Total Population	718 Millions	1004 Millions	1.93
Total Labour Force	308	406	1.03
Total Employment	302	397	0.98
Organized Sector	24	28	0.53
Private Sector	16	19	-0.03
Private Sector	7	9	1.87

Source: Economic Survey, op. cit. p. 240.

The inference to the extent these figures are realistic, is that relative to labour force the employment generation is inadequate and in recent years negative. A person should have either full employment or social security to care of this educational, health and nutritional needs. This happens in all the developed countries, and because of this happens the countries are developed.

An Institutional Critique of the Annual Economic Survey of India

We may approach the issues form Institutional angle and notice some of the logical inconsistencies in official documents not excluding the current Economic Survey (Source: The Economic Survey, 2001-2002, Ministry of Finance, Economic Division, Government of India. 2002, pp. 268+Statements 1214). Next only to the documents of the

Reserve Bank of India, this publication is a mine of information, thought, being a product of officials mainly for official use, and defence of government policy and practice, it is insulated from academic and other intellectual influences. The title commits the logical fallacy of mistaking the part for the whole. There is economics in it starting with public finance, money & banking, capital markets, prices and food management, external sector, industrial policy, agriculture, infrastructure, and social sectors. All these serve the purpose of the Finance Minister in presenting his budget, this document being a curtain raiser. These selective topics could bear a more modest title, Background to the Budget, or to deserve the title Economic Survey, in macro and micro foundations and analyses thereof the economy in the year preceding the budget. The Central Statistical Organization feeds this Ministry with wide range of statistics. A critical study of the definitions, the aggregates, limitations of surveys on which the data are compeled, etc., should be part of the document. And the demographic data provides the human resources available, the means of education, health and nutritional characteristics essential to reach the ends of good health and citizenry could form the first part. The growth apart the distributive content of the growth process should find a mention. It is the duty of the non-governmental bodies to express value judgements and give critiques of the official documentation. The govt. cannot criticize itself; surely it can give data on which the rest of the World can base their judgements. And the Economics profession has a right to seek wide circulation of the Economic Survey, at affordable price. Out of the 14,000 copies of this year Survey, bulk of it will be at the official desks, leaving a meagre stock for academies, and other opinion makers. I would consider 300% increase in its print order, and wider distribution network. An alternative Economic Survey has been in the making for some years past, and this is a welcome commencement. (Source: this document is produced by a body which is guided by Professor Kalyan Kabra of the Indian Institute of Public Administration, besides others, who form informal economic pressure groups.) More resources, human and material, are essential for this document to be an effective challenge; it is for the parliamentarians and academics to plan for this institutional counter force. The Brookings Institutional in the USA produces similar documents, and many foundations fund critical studies of official documents. Firstly, these documents should be available widely, not only on Website, but also in hard copies, and secondly, public economic opinion should be based on informed debate on economic policy alternatives.

Areas for Research in Human Resource and Human Needs Research. Human being constitute the ends more than means: Legal, Social, Ethical & Political:

It is important to use the comprehensive term Human Resources (HR) rather than labour. Granted this we may list major research concerns in this area. (Source: Vedagiri Shanmugasundaram: Methodology of Research in Social Sciences, Madras, 1962, 1974, pp. 59-75.) The hypotheses we may set are many, and among them are (i) the voters are educated enough to demand that full employment be condition on which the electors decide on their political masters; (ii) there are economic experts who form public opinion in favour of full employment with sufficient home work on the means, techniques time span etc., to realize this goal; (iii) given the time span for the structural adjustment for this goal, means of social security should be in position; (iv) countries without full employment or social security, are under-developed; (v) Employment which provides for skill up gradation has high productivity for the economy and happy work force; (vi) to ensure economic welfare, a country should benefit without another country put to loss, to ensure Pareto welfare criterion. (vii) Trade unions or workers organizations should grow into humanitarian forces for production and consumption of healthy, educational, environmental products and towards this, cooperative organizations have high credibility.

References

1. J.B. Rebitzer: Radical Political Economy and the Economics of Labour Markets (Jrl. Econ. Literature, Sept.. 1993.) (ii) Paul Ekins (Edr.) The Living Economy (A New Economics in the Marketing) London, 1996. (iii) Denis Barnes and Eileen Reid: Governments and Trade Unions, (Policy Studies Institute. London, 1980) (v) Yasodha Shanmugasundaram: Women Employment in India (IASR, Chennai, 1993) (vi) S.P. Verma (Editor): Spl. Number: Indian Judicial System (IIPA, New Delhi, 1999, Vol. XI. V, No. 3 (vii) V.N. Balasubramanian: Conversations with Indian Economists (London, 2001) (viii) K.G.J.C. Knowles: Strikes-A Study in Industrial Conflicts (London, 1954) (ix) K. Appanraj & V.R. Chandran: NJJA NENGAN S.CC. Anthony Pillai (Chennai, 1995) (x) Keith Griffin: Institutional Reform and Economic Development in the Chinese Countryside (London, 1984) (xi) Fred Hirsch & John H Goldthorpe: The Political Economy of Inflation (London, 1978) (xii) David Gowland: International Economics (New Jersey, 1983) (xviii) IBIDI: The Brandt Commission Papers: International Development Issues (Geneva, 1981).

3

Economic Reforms and Employment Challenges Ahead

Dr. N. Manonmoney

Economic Reforms has led to a series of reforms in the labour sectors which has increased the social cost of adjustment. This has called for a human approach in the labour section reforms. Creation of employment opportunities is an important objective in the process of economic planning and development over a period of time. In the regime of economic reforms, many questions have been raised about the positive impact of reforms on employment. In a developing country like India where the magnitude of the problems of unemployment and underemployment is very serious. An examination of employment scenario in terms of rate of growth of employment over the rate of growth of labour force, sectoral trends in employment generation, and policies pursued by the Government would help to evaluate the employment implication of economic reforms.

In this paper an attempt has been made to analyse the salient features of Economic Reforms and its implication on the job market, the state of private sector and public sector in India.

The following are the two main issues to be discussed in this paper.

1. Why globalisation has led to unemployment in DCs and LDCs?
2. What is the impact of globalisation on the job market in India?

Globalisation and Unemployment

Record of economic development is full of challenges. In the past fifty years there have been many success stories; cases of failure, and of disappointed expectations. One solved problem may open new issues. Aspirations, environment, gola's policies and instruments go on changing. The emphasis on development theory shifted from national income to human development, reduction of poverty, unemployment and inequalities. At present the emphasis is not only on sustainable development but on interdependent development. That is, the emphasis has shifted to market-driven forces but alone with state playing the role of facilitator and providing safety nets for those who are put to disadvantageous position; thereby preventing the market failures. Thus globalisation is the process by which events, decision and activities in one part of the world have significant consequences for other parts of the globe. Globalisation has led to the need of firms to compete internationally, and international competition has reinforced globalisation. Cost reduction, greater efficiency and higher incomes have achieved at the cost of uncertainty, unemployment and inequality. Globalisation has reduced the ability of many governments both to maintain full employment and to take care of the victims of the competitive struggle. Persistent high unemployment in many countries in the world has been a leading policy issues due to globalisation and the new technologies of information and communication.

Jobless Growth in Advanced Countries

Productivity growth means growth of output of goods without more unpleasant work and employment is a basic need today both in DCs and LDCs. The concern in the DCs has become jobless growth. Many types of monotonous, dirty, hard or dangerous work are a burden. There is a need to increase the output growth to absorb all those seeking work of the reduced work load can be spread evenly; with corresponding equally distributed rises in income. But in last decade, output grew insufficiently fast to generate employment for the whole workforce and the work is unevenly distributed which has resulted in private affluence and private squalor. Thus the causes of unemployment in the DCs are global competition, lack of skill in an age of advancing technology, slow growth and imports from low-wage countries.

Jobless Growth Socialist Countries

China has been enjoying high growth rates but unemployment particularly urban unemployment is a major problem. The result of globalisation has been the need to cut unit labour costs. Before globalisation there was the system of unemployment insurance and guaranteed employment. When China began to be integrated into the global economy it had to reduce the labour costs in order to become competitive and attract direct foreign investment. In 1986, a new regulation was passed that employment in government enterprises had to be based on fixed-term contracts, and these enterprises were given the power to dismiss workers. The decline in employment in these enterprises was 15.5 per cent during 1991 to 1994. In Russia, the official figures on unemployment are low due to non-registration of many of those thrown out of employment. In Bulgaria, the Czech Republic, Poland, Romania and Russia real wages fell between 18 and 40 per cent in the first phase of transition to market development.

Jobless Non-Growth in LDCs

In many developing countries, the main reason for unemployment is the need to close down inefficient, overmanned public sector undertakings and to relocate labour to more efficient work and produce goods in demand. The main causes for unemployment in LDCs are:

- Absence of factors like capital, markets, management, infrastructure, etc.
- Absence of institution like labour, exchanges, training scheme and system of wide-spread land ownership.
- Inhibition and aspiration in attitudes to work.
- Barriers to work due to low levels of living, such as poor nutrition, health and education.
- Low level of LDCs exported goods in DCs due to slow growth, technical progress and trade barriers.
- Policies of many LDCs often over-price labour, under-price capital and over-value exchange rates which prevent efficient labour utilization.

According to available statistics, there are 15 million surplus workers in China accounting for 12.5 per cent of China's work force. The European Union Countries are experiencing unemployment of 20 million which is about 11 per cent of the work force. The current unemployment rates in the European Union Countries vary from 12 per cent in France, 24 per cent in Spain, 11 per cent in Germany. Japan and Britain are also facing rising unemployment. In October 1997, the unemployment ration in Japan reached a record high of 3.5 per cent. In Britain unemployment is rising due to privatization, with increased globalisation and liberalization, there is threat to unskilled labour. The ILO Years book 'Labour Statistics' reveals that unskilled work-force employment opportunities are scarce and they are becoming 'endangered species' on the labour scene in many countries as occupational patterns shift towards jobs calling for an increased skill level.

With 22 million people out of work across Europe and numbers rising every three months, business and political leaders are bluntly telling workers that jobs for life are a theory of the past. The model of job for life will be reserved for just a few people. Low wage competition is becoming ever more of a force. German economy with record unemployment of 10.5 per cent has contracted a flood of job alliances where union has been forced to agree to relax working practices and swallow low pay deals to halt lay off.

Thus free trade, capital export, reduced number of workers, as well as of wage for economy and rapid technological development in the regime of globalisation thus thwart volume of employment, wage rate of the workers and their share in the gross domestic product of DCs to a large extent. Globalisation is clearly the strategic design for the self-expansion and more rapid concentration of monopoly capitals through higher rate of profit, It is expected that much worse would be the condition of workers not only in DCs but also in LDCs in the times to come. Of the world's 2.5 billion workers, 1.4 billion live in countries struggling with transitions from state sector, high degree of trade protection or central planning. In many developing countries these changes have caused an acceleration in the destruction of a far greater number of jobs with the creation of a fewer ones. The result has been that unemployment rises and employment shifts into information activities of precarious condition. According to World Bank, "The change can be wrenching". Economic reforms can create opportunities for some workers but have un-renching effects on others and that employment and wages often decline particularly to those workers who move from old to "new" jobs.

Impact of Economic Reforms on the Employment in India

Economic liberalization was introduced in India in 1991 and it would be of interest to know about the process of employment growth in the post-liberalisation period. The reform process resulted in an acceleration of GDP growth, but it was not accompanied by a corresponding increase in employment. Public sector employment has declined as the public sector began to withdraw from several areas. Even in the private sector, employment would not grow at a much faster rate and industrial units are getting rid of redundant labour. As per NSS data, the growth rate of employment in the economy was of the order of 2.0 per cent annum during 1983-93 and it has declined to less than one per cent during 1993-94 to 1999-2000. It has shown that the process of economic reforms is that of "jobless growth".

In India, the reform process has gained momentum only during 1993-94 even though reform was introduced in 1991(1991-92 was a depressed year). In India NSS data show the following:

- The growth rate of employment declined from 2.04 per cent per annum during 1983-1993 and 0.93 per annum during 1993-94 to 1999-2000. It implies that the growth rate in employment is less than the growth rate in labour price and has resulted in increase in unemployment.
- In agricultural sector, the growth rate of unemployment was 1.51 per cent during 1983-1993 and it became negative(-0.34 per cent) during 1993-94 to 1999-2000.
- In the manufacturing sector, employment growth rate was 2.14 per cent during 1983-1993 but declined marginally to 2.05 per cent during 1993-94 to 1999-2000.
- In Trade Transport, storage and communication and financial services, employment growth rate increased sharply during 1993-94 and 1999-2000.
- Community, social and personal services witnessed a sharp deceleration in growth rate during 1993-94 to 1999-2000.

In India, 20 lakh total employment in the 265 central public undertakings excludes temporary labour employed by the undertakings. On a broader assessment, it appears that one-half to two-thirds of labour in surplus which implies that nearly 10-12 lakh workers out of 20 lakh are to be retrenched. The unemployment problem in our country seems to have been swept under the carpet without realizing that such a method can blast the economic system sooner or later. Mass unemployment in the Indian economy will lead to more terrorism, increasing anti-social elements and communal violence.

Pragmatism in Indian Economic Reform cannot bypass the major objectives of generating fuller employment for the increasing work force and also for high wage employment for those who are in the low wage group. If this objective is ignored in our anxiety for economic reforms; unemployment would cause tremendous labour unrest and it would bring about serious consequences in the direction and content of India's economic development.

References

1. K.R. Gupta (ed.): *Liberation and globalisation of Indian economy.* Altantic Publishers and Distributors, New Delhi, 1997.
2. Ruddar Dutt, *Economic Liberalisation and its Implications for Employment in India.* Indian Economic Association of 84th Annual Conference Volume, 2001.
3. Adrian Wood & Michele Calandrino, When Other Giant Awakens: Trade & Human Resources in India. *Economic and Political Weekly,* December 30, 2000.
4. Paul Streeten, globalisation; International Integration and Disintegration, *Political Economy Journal of India,* Vol. 9, No. 2.
5. Nanjundappa, Economic Reforms and Employment Policy: Restructuring of Public Sector Enterprises. Presidential Address, National conference on Globalisation Dimensions & Impact, J.S.S. College, Mysore, March 2001.
6. R.S. Bawa, Challenges and Opportunities of globalisation: Implication for India. Presidential Address, 84th Annual Conference of Indian Economic Association, December 2001.

7. N. Manonmany, Challenges of Globalisation of Employment Opportunities in India. Paper presented in the Seminar on *Elusive Labour Policy in India,* Organized by Department of Labour Studies, Madurai Kamaraj University, April, 2001.

4

Globalisation Economic Reforms and Social Sector Development

Some Emerging Areas in India

Prof. G. Saibaba, Dr. K. Vijayalakshmi,

It is mere truism that a large proportion of population in most regions of the world does not enjoy any special protection or covered a very few partially. This is the case for the vast majority of population in developing economies and even in some of the richest industrialized countries. There are many gaps in social protection. Precise measurement of the problem is not easy. In practice, it bristles with many practical problems. A further complication is that social protection coverage often varies from one branch of social protection to another. To cite a real example a country may have health care coverage almost hundred per cent of population, Britain mostly. But it may reimburse on average only about 50 per cent of the cost of the hospital care, leaving individual families to bear a large part of the risk. Furthermore, health care coverage may be relatively wide, but the quality of the health care provided woefully inadequate. Thus it may be quite misleading to compare social protection coverage in different countries on the basis of single measure. In this paper an attempt has been made to analyse the several aspects of social development in the pre and post-reform period. The first section of the paper examines the frame work for sector development and focus on the need for Decent work as a major goal of economic development at global and consequently, with national economies. Second section of the paper examines economic reforms and social sector development in India. The final section of the paper analyses the emerging trends and the urgent areas of social development in India and conclusion.

SECTION-I

Globalisation is a very fast emerging trend on the international scene. Shrinking space, shrinking time and eclipse of boarders are linking peoples in the developed and developing countries, with more intensely and more rapidly than ever before in the history of world. Global economy is experiencing revolutionary changes. The new economic policy since 1980's has been rapidly advancing the market friendly approach to economic growth. With several set backs and disappearance of stateless communism in Soviet union and China, the market based development by the centrally planned economies and many developing countries, international market are being opened for facilitation of easy flow of goods, capital and ideas around the world. As economic growth stress as market-friendly approach, social development postulates state intervention. Social development approach has been advocating human rights and place people at the centre of all development programmes in developing and developed countries. It is a real need for synthesis of the state intervention and market approach for economic development. Further, capitalism that gives appropriate consideration, the actual persuit of the guiding principles of social development can be treated as welfare capitalism as it is conductive to social and national welfare. Globalisation opens up new opportunities to the world economy, especially the developed countries, but it also bristles with several deleterious consequences to the developing countries in the absence of effective international cooperation, equitable partnership of developed and developing countries for formulating policies and their implementation requiring effective governance. Human Development Report 1999 has drawn attention of this and pointed out, 'over the past 20 years increasing privatization of research and development, ever-growing liberalization of markets and tightening of intellectual property rights have set of a race to lay a claim to knowledge, and this has changed technologies path. The risk is that poor people and poor countries interests are being left on the sidelines.'

Globalisation is creating new threats to human security both in rich and poor countries, such as financial volatility and economic insecurity as on East Asia in 1997-99. Job and income insecurity as the pressure of global competition have led countries are exposed in the course of spread of 'Welfare Capitalism'. National and global governance have to be reinvented with social and human development and equity at the core of control effectively the risk to which people and countries are exposed to the emerging trends of globalisation. The Human Development Report 1999, proposed the key institutions of global governance needed for 21st century. The stronger and more coherent United Nations has to prove a forum for global leadership with equity and human and social concern. The statement 1 provides a glance of the changing intellectual tides and economic policies including the trends of globalisation. A prime requisite is the social development stress on human development is the pursuit of welfare capitalism by the market approach along with social policy of the state and human rights.

Globalisation of Economic Growth and Human Security

Around the World, there is wide spread unease about the growth of social and economic insecurity and inequality. Whatever the system, people look to systems of social retention to overcome the worst effects, whether the system is the

Statement 1

Economic Tides and Public Policies

1.	Economic Tide	Adam Smith Tide; 1776-1889	Marxian Tide 1985	Hayek Tide Since 1980s
2.	State Action	Laisses-faire	Economic planning totalitarian and democratic patterns	Decline of State in planning, liberalization and Privatization
3.	Market Action	Free Market	Fall of Free Market	Resurgence of Market
4.	Economic Growth Response	Autonomous Economic growth with the spread of industrial revolution	Acceleration of Economic Growth by economic planning	Achievement of extra-ordinary growth by the Asian Tigers.
5.	Economic System	Capitalism with industrialism; in U.K. European Countries and USA	Socialist eco-economies of USSR & China and mixed economies of developed and developing countries	Emergence of Prosperous capitalism
6.	Reaction	Fabianism and Collectivism	Increasing economic inefficiencies and liabilities of public sectors	Trend for free enterprise, downfall of dictatorship in USSR

(Cont...)

Statement 1 (Contd...)

7.	Remarks	Growth of Colonialism	Achievement of Freedom by colonial countries after Second World War	Market domination for economic growth
8.	Economic Tide	The Asian Tigers Tide Since 1950	The Human Development Tide Since 1990	Globalisation Trend Tide
9.	State Action	Resurgence of State	Crucial Role of State for peoples' welfare	Positive Role of State
10.	Market Action	Resurgence of Market	Welfare Capitalism	Promotion of Competitive Markets
11.	Economic Growth Response	Higher Rate of Economic Growth	Peoples' Welfare with economic growth	Sustained economic growth in the World
12	Economic System	Evolution of Welfare State	Goal of Welfare State	International Institutional Set-up to strengthen policies and action for human welfare
13.	Reaction	Better Climate for Economic Growth	Radical Changes for improving peoples' welfare	Emergence of new threats to human security in rich and poor countries
14.	Remarks	The Asian Tigers experienced economic crisis due to the exodus of foreign capital	Human Development at the centre of global debate for action	Globalization should avoid the imposition of capitalist order on the world.

informal net work of family relationships or a complex web of state policies. They look to institutions to enhance the security of themselves and their families and communities. Globalization requires the pace of economic growth has to be higher than earlier and demands several reforms on various fronts and sectors. The recent decades show clearly that there is no automatic link between growth and social development. Even when links are established which may gradually erode unless fortified by skilful, time bound and regular policy management.

The search for security in such a milieu lies in development but not in arms. Thus sustainable economic growth is pro-social development, pro-jobs, pro-native and people. So the purpose of growth should be to enrich people lives. But for too often it does not. It is about this economic protection of the social embedding the economy in society through structures of systems of regulation, protection and distribution that limit social and economic insecurity, reduce inequalities and provide patterns of opportunity. Recently Prof. Guy studying, ILO attempted to put the development policy in the context of recent-economic political changes globalization argued and presented a stage where they induced eight crises in social protection, which can only be resolved by a profound but eminently feasible change in direction.

The eight crises of social protection are due to new globalised socio-economic stratification. Thus it is no exaggeration to describe the emerging tensions and dilemmas in social policy as crises. They are:

1. Linguist Crisis;
2. A Fiscal Crisis;
3. A Legitimation Crisis;
4. A Oral Crises;
5. A Social Dumping Crisis;

6. A Governance Crisis;
7. A Work Crisis; and
8. A Social Justice Crisis.

In view of space limitation the details of these aspects of emerging crises are not presented (GUY standing 2002)

SECTION II

In India a vigorous thrust for social protection and justice is an integral part of our development strategy. Poverty alleviation and rising the standard of living have been the central aim of economic planning in India. The general contention was that economic growth would automatically take care of social justice and protection. This phenomena was to work through the process of trickle down effect. Unfortunately, it was realised that growth has failed to trickle down in order to fulfil the objectives of social protection, so special targeted programmes were framed in India. Further, it is realised that a strategy based on growth or on equity and poverty alleviation could not be made effective in isolation. Now a greater concern with the distribution of income emerged in the reforms period. It appears that development was seen as going beyond economic growth and bringing changes in the structure of the economy. Hence, equitable distribution of economic growth becomes an independent goal. The concept of equity was translated into provision to every one of basic needs. Further, more the concept of basic has been widened and the objective of growth been set as human development.

In general the need for social sector's development along with economic infrastructure has been highlighted in post sixties and the need for human development has been stressed by T.W. Schultze in his famous presidential address to the American Economic Association. It has brought into a sharp focus of the crucial role played by social sector development in economic growth and development. Generally speaking social sector refers to human resource development on all the activities which contribute to human capital formation. Traditionally per capita income was regarded as the best indicator to judge the level of economic growth in any economy. But this has been questioned by many in recent years. It is the human development aspect which has assumed prime importance. Further more UNDP has taken greater care for the past ten years in computing and publishing the human development index which is designed to reflect the well being and welfare of the people in a better way. In fact one of the primary reasons why economic growth has not had an impact on the lives of ordinary people is the current state of India's backwardness in human development.

In 1991 India witnessed many significant changes in her economic policy when we adopted the economic reform measure in the wake of acute balance of payments crisis and mounting fiscal deficit. There is a large body of literature on the theoretical and empirical aspects of economic reforms in developing countries including India. There are several studies and some found that economic reforms have positive effects in terms of opening of economies of developing countries (Sachs, Bhargavati and Srinivasan expected good performance of economic reforms in India). They advocated structural adjustment programme. The first generation reforms initiated in 1991 were crisis-driven. The crisis in balance of payments and mounting fiscal deficits both at the central and state level prompted the congress led government under the leadership of P.V. Narasimha Rao to initiate economic reforms. Finance minister Mr. Yashwant Sinha in his budget speech 2000-2001 stated very clearly that NDA government intends to carry forward the process of implementation of the second generation reforms in which he stated that growth is just an end in itself. It is the critical vehicle for increasing employment and raising the living of our people, especially of the poorest. In his speech he laid stress on the need for sustained and broad-based growth, combined with programmes for accelerating rural development, boosting knowledge-based industries and enhancing the quality of human resources. Since economic reforms were born out of an economic crisis, the prevailing thinking among economists and policy makers has a keen desire to go in for a programme of structural adjustment which should help to strong then the process of stabilization by pulling the economy out of the crisis of balance of payments and fiscal deficits. Nearly a decade of working of the reforms has brought about a significant stabilization of our economy.

It was found that importance of social sector has been much recognised in India in our five-year plans. Social welfare programmes were introduced from time to time, besides, focusing on education, primary health and other basic facilities. Infact there is nothing in the new economic policy which restricts the governments from giving more importance to social sector and to the needs of the vulnerable sections of the society. In this context, let us analyse the trend of public expenditure of the state governments on social sector over a period of time. Data given in Table 1 reveals the percentage of expenditure as states in India to total expenditure during pre-reform and post-reform period. It is evident from Table 1 that the non-plan expenditure during the reform period has increased to 81-85 per cent as compare to 78.86 per cent during pre reform period. Expenditure both in plan and non-plan expenditure on social services has fallen during reform period as compared to pre-reform period. Infact there has been a slight decline of plan expenditure by 0.47 per cent in the reform period, where as the non-plan expenditure has also witnessed a decrease of 2.90 per cent. Therefore, these trends of plan expenditure in relation to the total expenditure have not registered a robust increase during the reform-period; on the other hand they have actually shown a relatively declining trend. Recent economic policy contains an important fiscal component to bring down the size of fiscal deficit. In fact

Table 1: Percentage of Expenditure of States in India on Social Sector to Total Budgeted Expenditure. (Revenue Account) Pre-Reform and During Reform Period.

Items		*Pre-Reform Period*			*During Reform Period*		
		Plan	*Non-Plan*	*Total*	*Plan*	*Non-Plan*	*Total*
1.	Total Revenue Expenditure	21.14	78.86	100.00	18.85	81.85	100.00
2.	Development Expenditure	20.75	47.95	68.70	17.70	43.87	61.57
3.	Social Services	9.15	30.18	39.32	8.68	27.28	35.95
	(a) Education, Sports, arts & Culture	2.12	18.95	21.08	2.32	17.38	19.70
	(b) Medical & Public health	2.16	4.58	6.73	1.77	3.98	5.74
	(c) Water Supply and Sanitation	1.70	0.84	2.53	1.28	0.90	2.18
	(d) Housing	0.17	0.37	0.54	0.23	0.26	0.49
	(e) Urban development	0.36	0.45	0.81	0.58	0.38	0.96
	(f) Welfare of SC, ST, OBC	1.29	1.24	2.53	1.22	3.76	4.98
	(g) Labour	0.17	0.53	0.70	0.14	0.41	0.55
	(h) Social Security	0.66	1.35	2.01	0.62	1.14	1.77
	(i) Nutrition	0.46	0.29	0.75	0.36	0.61	0.97

Source: P. R. Panchmukhi: 'Social Impact of Economic Reform in India- A critical Appraisal' E.P.W., March 4, 2000.

the need for such reforms at state level is more important now than ever before. However, economic reforms have transitional cost which fare to be borne more by poorer sections, so we need a special correction mechanism to plug the loopholes of the new economic policy. Further more, there is no conflict between social sector reforms and economic reforms because a country can not achieve higher level of human development without having high rate of economic growth. Thus there is no trade off between the two as both are complementary to each other. Normally the economic sector gets the priority over the social sector's spending. Hence if any cut has to be made to reduce the fiscal deficit, it is always the social sector which has to bear the brunt of deficit reduction.

The 9th Five Year Plan mentions that while the government was over active in industry, which was under active in many areas, especially relating to social development. This was reflected in a very slow pace of improvement in critical social indicators. The development strategy of the 9th plan has therefore indicated the following objectives relating to social development sector as;

1. Ensuring food and nutritional security for all, particularly the vulnerable sections of the society;
2. Providing basic minimum services of safe drinking water, primary health care facility, universal primary education, shelter and connectivity to all in a time-bound manner;
3. The empowerment of women and society disadvantaged groups such as SCs and STs and other backward classes and minorities as agents of socio-economic change and development. Therefore the 9th plan underlies the need for state intervention in three broad areas to take care of the imperfections of the market force. These forces are: 1. Quality of life of people 2. Generation of productive employment and 3. To bring regional

balance. The chief ministers of the states focused on seven services such as safe drinking water, primary health facilities, universal primary education, nutrition to school and pre-school children, shelter for the poor, road connectivity for all villages and public distribution system with a focus on the poor.

A critical examination of the data on some of these variables has been made in this section. The goal of universalisation of elementary education has not yet been achieved. Still, half of the Indian adult population continues to be illiterate and a two-third of women are illiterates.

Data in Table 2 reveals the achievements on enrolment of students during 1970-71 to 1996-97. It is very interesting to note that the primary enrolment reached an all time record of 101 per cent in 1990-91 declined to 89 per cent in 1996-97. The girls enrolment 76.2 per cent in 1996-97 as against 85.6 per cent in 1990-91. Similarly middle level

Table 2. Enrolment of Students

	1996-97	*1990-91*	*1980-81*	*1970-71*
Primary (Mn.)	110.4 (89.0)	97.4 (101.0)	73.8 (80.5)	57.0 (76.4)
Of which Girls	47.9 (76.2)	40.4 (85.6)	28.5 (64.1)	21.3 (59.1)
Middle (Mn.)	41.1 (54.9)	34.0 (60.1)	20.7 (41.9)	13.3 (34.2)
Of which girls	16.4 (44.3)	12.5 (46.1)	6.3 (28.6)	3.9 (20.8)
High/Higher Secondary (Mn.)	27.0	19.1	11.0	7.6

\+ Figures in brackets show percentages of gross enrolment in classes I-V (6-11 Years) and VI-VII (11-14 Years) to total population.

Source: Statistical Outline of India, 1998-99 Tata Services Ltd., Department of Economics and Statistics.

enrolment of boys has also declined by 5.25 per cent (from 60.1 per cent to 54.9 percent). Girls enrolment also registered a decline of 1.8 per cent (46.1-44.3) during the same period.

Another important indicator of human resource development is the provision for safe drinking water. Infact the existence of safe drinking water or even drinking water in rural areas is one of the most important indicators of social development. In India about one half of all villagers do not have any source of protected drinking water. Data in Table 3 shows the population covered with drinking water and sanitary facilities. Government is committed to provide safe drinking water to every village in the country within five years (Economic Survey 1999-2000). However, it seems a very difficult task because various reports that have come up showing that the water in the country has been declining at alarming rate every year. Similarly from the data given in Table 3 it is clear that most of the facilities are concentrated only in the urban areas, and the rural people are not still benefited by these facilities. Drinking water schemes in rural areas are formulated and implemented by the states under Basic Minimum Services (BMS programme) with the over all objective of improving the quality of life in rural areas.

Housing is the another basic human requirement that needs to be met on priority basis. The national housing policy of 1994 recognized the importance of both rural and urban housing in the over all development of the poor people. The national building organization has estimated urban housing shortage at 7.57 millions in 1997 and expected that the absolute shortage will decline to 6.64 millions in 2001. It is mainly due to tax incentives given for housing construction. But the estimation of the Habit 11 has shown that this shortage in shelter will increase upto 9.49 millions by the year 2001. Hence the National Housing Policy 1994 has to be reformulated to meet this heavy demand for shelter in the coming five years.

Table 3. Households Having Drinking Water, Electricity and Toilet Facilities (percentage)

		*1991**	*1981**
1.	Household with safe drinking water	62.72	37.91
	Rural	55.92	26.34
	Urban	81.59	74.13
2.	Household with Electricity	42.98	25.74
	Rural	31.1	14.29
	Urban	75.93	61.6
3.	Household with Toilet facility	23.55	n.a.
	Rural	8.84	n.a.
	Urban	63.58	57.44

* Excluding Jummu & Kashmir in 1991 and Assam in 1981.

Source: Statistical Outline of India, 1998-99 Tata Services Ltd., Department of Economics and Statistics.

Health

Treatment of sickness and containment of disease is basically the realm of the medical and epidemiological science. Yet, social scientists have a role to play in tracking morbidity and health pattern and in explaining health seeking behaviour in order to devise appropriate policies and programmes to protect and maintain health. The existing health system in the rural areas are in a state of chaos too. The health facilities for the people living in the rural areas are in the worst condition. The high mortality rate, in the rural areas, has been due to lack of knowledge and information about many diseases and the adverse distances of the health centres. The health centres that are established in rural areas are operating without infrastructural facility and also medical or para medical staff. Table 4 clearly depicts the scenario which is prevailing in the country.

Although, due to some measures, which were adopted in the Fourth Five year plan, the vital statistics are now

Table 4. Rural Primary Healthcare Infrastructure

Category of Centres	*Requirement for 1991*	*Functioning as on 30.06.1996*	*Gap*
Sub Centers	13,4108	13,2730	1,378
Primary Health Centers	22,349	21,854	495
Community Health Centers	5,587	2,424	3,163

Source: Ninth Five Year Plan (Draft) 1997-2002. Planning Commission GOI, p. 189.

IEA Conference (83rd) Volume of the Millennium 2000.

showing good results, data in Table 5 provides information on vital statistics since 1951 to 1991. It is necessary to keep its momentum, enhanced outlay on health and family welfare should continue. Further proper care has to be taken to provide medical facilities in rural areas. Therefore it is necessary that the officials should maintain their vigilance on the medical facilities that are provided in the rural areas to achieve better results. The expenditures that have been made in the different plans are very much meagre especially in the context of larger problems related to the health and nutrition. After the Fourth Five year plan, there is a decline in the expenses that were made on the health and it has

Table 5. Vital Statistics Related to Health

Parameter	*1951*	*1981*	*1991*	*Current levels*
Birth rate (per 1000 population)	39.9	33.9	29.5	26.4
Total Fertility Rate	6.0	4.5	3.6	3.3
Infant Mortality Rate (per 1000 live birth)	146	110	80	72
Child Mortality Rate (0-4) year per thousand children	57.3	39.1	26.5	23.9
Couple protection Rate (%)	10.4	22.8	44.1	44.0

Source: Economic Survey, 1999-2000, p. 173.

gone down upto 1.56 per cent of the total plan outlay in the year 1990-91 and marginally increased by 0.19 per cent in the year 1997. Likewise the expenditure on family welfare has also gone down upto 1.26 per cent of the total plan outlay in the Sixth Five year plan. Here also the plan outlay has marginally increased by 0.24 per cent only. It is not ironical to notice that the government is expressing a seriousness of the problem of population disaster on one hand and measures to control them and downsizing the expenditure to combat it on the other hand.

SECTION III

Some Emerging Trends and Areas of Action

Old age. Since a break-through in fertility and mortality is expected, the proportion of the elderly in India is likely to increase in the coming years. The old age population (60+) has increased from about 19.8 million in 1951 to 56.7 million in 1990-91 and its share in the total population has risen from 5.5 to 6.8 per cent during the same period. According to the population projections prepared for the 9th plan, the number of those aged 60 and above will rise from 54.5 million in 1991 to 70.6 million in 2001 and to 13 million by 2016. As such there is an urgent need to take proper action and planning for the welfare of the elderly as suggested by World Assembly on Ageing. Hence social security for the elderly of more appropriately social insurance against poverty (income security) and ill health (health security) has to be tackled by the government at the earliest. That is why social insurance provision needs government intervention. Data given, Table 6 shows the changing and increasing aged-population in India since 1901-2001.

Child labour. It may be *naïve* fact that poverty is one of the main determinants of the supply of child labour. The Indian constitution is sensitive to the rights of children. According to article 24 of the constitution of India, no child

Table 6. Age Structure of Population in India: 1901-2001

Census Years	*Males*			*Females*		
	0-14	*150-59*	*60+*	*0-14*	*15-59*	*60+*
1901	39.2	56.2	4.6	38.0	56.5	5.5
1911	38.8	56.4	4.8	38.1	56.4	5.5
1921	39.4	55.6	5.0	39.0	55.6	5.5
1931	40.0	56.1	3.9	40.0	55.8	4.2
1941	38.1	57.1	4.9	38.4	56.7	4.9
1951	37.1	57.4	5.5	37.9	56.3	5.8
1961	40.9	53.6	5.5	41.2	53.0	5.8
1971	42.0	52.3	5.7	42.2	51.8	6.0
1981	39.8	54.1	6.1	39.6	53.8	6.6
1991	37.7	55.6	6.7	37.8	55.5	6.7
2001*	34.0	59.0	7.0	34.5	58.4	7.1
2011*	28.4	63.5	8.1	28.5	63.2	8.3
2020**	25.1	64.0	10.9			

Note: * Figures based on Technical Group Projection on Population (1996)

** UN projections or combined male & female population, see Bhat (1992, p. 44)

Source: Decennial Population Censuses.

below the age of 14 years shall be employed to work in any factory or mine or engaged in any other hazardous employment. Further, according to article 45 of the constitution, the state is direct to provide pre and compulsory education for all children until they complete the age of 14. The government strategy since the early 1980s has been guided by the view that *'Child labour is a necessary evil'* and a product of poverty, social discrimination and economic exploitation, etc. Thus the National policy on education calls for a large and a systematic programmes of non-formal education as an alternative for the large number of children who don't attend schools. The establishment of compulsory education for children appears to be a necessary condition for the reduction and abolition of child labour. It may be noticed that non coercive means can be used for promoting compulsory education. The girl child will be particularly benefited from the establishment of compulsory education.

Informal Sector Employment

Now-a-days, they appears to be wider realisation in the organised labour movement that lack of protection in the informal economy is bad not only for those directly concerned but also for workers in general. There are two main reasons for this, more and more workers are at risk themselves of having to work in the informal economy, because of the informalisation of their jobs or unemployment and lack of social protection in the formal economy. The problem of low coverage under social protecting is of course not new, especially in countries where large member of people work in subsistence agriculture. However, in recent years, prospects of resolving or atleast mitigating it have taken a dramatic turn for the work, as an increasing proportion of urban labour force has had to resort to working in the informal economy. In various countries of Asia and Latin America almost all new jobs being created in the informal economy. Informal economy workers have little or nor security of employment. They have no income security and their earning tend to be very low and to fluctuate more than those of other workers. A brief period of incapacity can leave the worker and her or his family without enough income to live on. The sickness of a family member can result in costs which destroy the delicate balance of the house-hold budget. Women face additional disadvantages owing to discrimination related to their reproductive role or upon marriage. Therefore, it is now widely recognised that there is a pressing need to find effective ways to extend social protection in the structured adjustment programme. Thus there is need for economic reforms with human face.

Employment Creation and Security

In the context of globalisation and implementation of economic reforms in India requires higher purchasing power for attaining food security, the youth and the poor have to be provided employment. In case of workers in the organised sector there are some social security measures off course be inadequate, but for the workers in the unorganised sector who have nor regular jobs or assured income to meet their primary needs employment creation is the basic need. The trends in employment in recent years are not encouraging and demand a proper employment-oriented reforms to meet the challenges of trends on this front underline the need for employment creation and for some job security. The summary of the recent trends are:

1. Growth rate of employment during the period 1972-73 to 87-88 showed declaration. It increased during 1988-94 but the rate of growth was still lower than that of 1970s. The growth of employment over the past two and half decades has, on average, been lower than the rate of growth in the labour force. The elasticity of employment has also indicated the similar trend.
2. There has been a slow change in the structure of work force and there are some indicators of unfavourable distribution of work force and hence undesirable consequences on the economy.
3. The proportion of self-employment indicates a steady decline over the years. The corresponding increase has been mostly observed for casual laboureres.
4. The search of the organised and unorganised sectors in employment has remained constant at 10 and 20 per cent respectively, but the proportion of the unorganised has significantly increased in manufacturing what some stated this as

'informalization of formal sector' transport and construction sectors and

5. The unemployment rates for the period 1973-88 showed the open unemployment increase while daily status rate declined, there was no sign of increase in open unemployment as well as CDS unemployment rate at the level of All India expects male under daily status. The crucial aspect of unemployment has been increasing. Therefore, there is immediate need to shift to high 'labour intensive pattern of economic growth' for creation of employment and thereby job security. As such there is immediate need for 'employment orientation built' in the growth strategy itself. To protect the poor from the onslaught of globalisation, and market forces, state or public intervention is necessary to ensure adequate opportunities and also enable the labour force to access these opportunities.

Women and Development

The process of economic development should reflect the provision for empowerment of women, reduction of feminization of poverty, gender blindness of macro-economic policies, all forms of violence against women, and provision for removal of barries encountered by women in accessing legal entitlements. Thus the process of empowerment has to be accelerated by all methods within a time period. All these issues are very complicated and certainly not easy to overcome. It may require to empower women by ensuring them a share in decision making at the local level. Further, it demands a fine combination of state intervention, public pressure and community support. Provisions must be made for women to participate in all the developmental programmes and ensure that development will empower women in all the spheres of economic activity without discrimination.

Financial of Social Development and Security Programmes

A reforms and Finance on Social Sector

The provision for social development which includes security programmes for the poor depends considerably on the efficient functioning of delivery systems of the government reflects the quantum and quality of services rendered therein. The provision of social security in this wider connotation of the term, promotes human development, which in turn contributes to economic growth. Table-7 high lights the problem with respect to the responsibility for implementation of various schemes introduced during five year plans with a plethora of schemes and programmes for poverty alleviation, health and nutrition, education specially primary and secondary levels, and social security and welfare sectors. As such given the notorious lack of inter-department, inter-ministerial coordinating, it is not surprising that the provisions of social security in India are piece meal and haphazard. A close scrutiny of public expenditure on social sector during post-reform period in the central and states budgets and the total of all states expenditure during the post-reform period, reveals some interesting facts. Given concludes that in the final outcome, what is of concern is that the GDP ratio of total outlays at both levels taken together declined in the first four years of adjustment. Further, he pointed out, 'given the magnitude of poverty and deprivation in India, their absolute levels are less than 7 per cent of GDP is also grossly inadequate for rural development and the entire gamut of social services.

Seetha Prabhu and Iyer V analysed the level and patterns of financing social security and summarized the main features that emerge from the perusal of the data presented in Table 8 and 9. They are:

1. Total expenditure on social security as the level of 15 major states constituted only 2.63 per cent

Table 7. Distribution of Social Security Programmes Across Departments and Ministries: Union Government, 1998

S. No.	*Social Security Programme*	*Sub-Department / Department*	*Ministry*
		Income Security; Assets and Employment	
1.	Jawahar Rojgar Yojana	Rural Employment/Dept. of Rural Employment & Poverty Alleviation	Ministry of Rural Areas and Employment
	(a) Indira Awas Yojana	Housing/Dept. of Rural Employment and Poverty Alleviation	-do-
	(b) Million Wells Scheme	Other Rural Development Programme/ Dept. of Rural Development	-do-
2.	Integrated Rural Development Programme	Special Programmes for Rural Development/Dept. of rural Employment and Poverty Alleviation	-do-
3.	Employment Assurance Scheme	Rural Employment/Dept. of Rural Employment and Poverty Alleviation	-do-
4.	Training of Rural Youth for Self-employment	Special Programmes for Rural Development/Dept. of Rural Employment and Poverty Alleviation	-do-
5.	Development of Women & Children in Rural Areas	Other Rural Development Programmes/Dept. of Rural Employment and Poverty Alleviation	-do-

(Cont...)

6.	Mahila Samrudhi Yojana	Women's Welfare/Dept. of Women and Child Health	Ministry of Human Resource Development
	(a) Support to training & Employment Programme	Women's Welfare/Dept. of Women and Child Health	-do-
7.	Nehru Rojgar Yojana	Urban Development/Dept. of Urban Development	Ministry of Urban Affairs & Employment
8.	Prime Ministers' Integrated Urban Poverty Eradication Programme for Small Towns	Urban Development/Urban Employment and Poverty Alleviation	-do-
9.	Swarna Jayanti Rojgar Yojana	Urban Development/Urban Employment and Poverty Alleviation	-do-
10.	Prime Minister's Rojgar Yojana	Khadi and Village Industries/Dept. of Small Scale Industries and Agro and Rural Industries	Ministry of Industry
		Health and Nutrition	
1.	Disease Control Programmes like TB, Leprosy, AIDS, etc.	Public Health/Department of Health	Ministry of Health and Family Welfare
2.	Reproduction and Child Health Programme-Maternal and Child Health	Family Welfare Services/Department of Health and Family Welfare	-do-

(Cont...)

3.	Integrated Child Development Services	Social Security & Welfare-Child Welfare/Department of Women and Child Health	Ministry of Human Resource Development
		Social Security and Welfare	
1.	Hut Insurance Scheme for the Poor Through the GIC etc.	Social Security and Welfare/ Department of Economic Affairs	Ministry of Finance
2.	Pensions and Other Retirement Benefits	Pensions Department of Economic Affairs	-do-
3.	Social Security and Welfare-Deposit Linked Insurance Schemes	Pensions/Department of Economic Affairs	-do-
4.	Labour and Employment Coal mines Labour Welfare	Ministry of Coal	Ministry of Coal
5.	National Transfer from Labour Welfare Funds-Beedi Workers; Mica Mines Labourers; Iron Ore Mines; Manganese Ore Mines Chrome; Limestone and Dolomite Mines Labour; and Cine Workers Welfare Fund	Labour and Employment-Labour/Ministry of Labour	Ministry of Labour
6.	Employees Pension Scheme; Family pension- cum-Life Insurance Scheme & Deposit Link Insurance Scheme	Social Security for Labour/ Ministry for Labour	-do-

Source: Complied from Government of India, *Expenditure Budge—1998-99*, Vol. 2 (June, 1998) (incorporating Notes on Demand for Grants).

Table 8. State-wise Share of Government Expenditure on Social Security in NSDP: 1991-95

(per cent)

Sl. No.	States	Level I					Level II			Level I+II	Level III	Level I+II+III
		Ele. Edn.	Rl. & Ph.	F.W.	Nutrition	Total	Assets	Emplt.	Total	Promo-tional	Protec tive	Total
1.	AP	1.19	0.15	0.18	0.04	1.56	0.29	0.29	0.58	2.14	0.19	2.33
2.	ASM	2.92	0.22	0.20	0.04	3.38	0.23	0.07	0.30	3.68	0.20	3.88
3.	BIH	2.16	0.18	0.23	0.03	2.60	0.22	0.81	1.04	3.64	0.51	4.15
4.	GUJ	1.60	0.14	0.13	0.25	2.13	0.18	0.21	0.39	2.52	0.10	2.62
5.	HAR	0.99	0.11	0.11	0.08	1.29	0.07	0.10	0.17	1.46	0.63	2.09
6.	KAR	1.59	0.04	0.17	0.16	1.95	0.22	0.21	0.43	2.39	0.44	2.83
7.	KER	2.37	0.16	0.21	0.04	2.77	0.12	0.27	0.39	3.16	0.39	3.55
8.	MAH	0.73	0.10	0.09	0.04	0.95	0.04	0.29	0.33	1.28	0.15	1.44
9.	MP	1.81	0.18	0.17	0.06	2.22	0.12	0.49	0.61	2.83	0.21	3.04
10.	ORS	1.53	0.16	0.24	0.12	2.05	0.15	0.55	0.70	2.75	0.48	3.24
11.	PUN	0.72	0.16	0.10	0.00	0.98	0.02	0.07	0.09	1.07	0.26	1.33
12.	RAJ	2.09	0.24	0.24	0.08	2.65	0.28	0.33	0.62	3.27	0.14	3.41
13.	TN	1.71	0.12	0.19	0.62	2.64	0.11	0.31	0.42	3.06	0.38	3.45
14.	UP	1.67	0.22	0.25	0.02	2.16	0.22	0.43	0.65	2.82	0.23	3.04
15.	WB	1.16	0.14	0.13	0.02	1.45	0.10	0.31	0.41	1.86	0.21	2.07
16.	MEAN	1.46	0.15	0.17	0.11	1.89	0.15	0.33	0.48	2.37	0.26	2.63
17.	CENTRE.	0.02	0.00	0.01	0.00	0.03	0.02	0.04	0.07	0.10	0.05	0.15

Source: Computed from NIPFP Data Bank and Reserve Bank of India (1998), *Report of Currency and Finance 1997-98*, Vol. II. Statistical Statements, p. 6.

Table 9. State-wise Share of Government Expenditure on Social Security in Total Revenue Expenditure: 1991-95

(per cent)

Sl. No.	*States*	*Level I*					*Level II*			*Level I+II*	*Level III*	*Level I+II+III*
		Ele. Edn.	*Rl. & Ph.*	*F.W.*	*Nutrition*	*Total*	*Assets*	*Emplt.*	*Total*	*Promo-tional*	*Protec tive*	*Total*
1.	AP	7.84	0.97	1.20	0.25	10.26	1.91	1.94	3.84	14.11	1.26	15.36
2.	ASM	15.47	1.18	1.05	0.23	17.93	1.21	0.37	1.58	19.51	1.08	20.59
3.	BIH	11.48	0.98	1.20	0.15	13.81	1.18	4.32	5.50	19.31	2.73	22.04
4.	GUJ	10.55	0.95	0.86	1.68	14.04	1.19	1.35	2.54	16.58	0.64	17.22
5.	HAR	6.98	0.76	0.75	0.55	9.05	0.51	0.70	1.22	10.26	4.46	14.73
6.	KAR	9.88	0.25	1.03	0.98	12.14	1.36	1.32	2.69	14.82	2.75	17.57
7.	KER	12.57	0.84	1.09	0.20	14.71	0.64	1.43	2.07	16.77	2.05	18.82
8.	MAH	5.99	0.80	0.73	0.30	7.81	0.36	2.40	2.75	10.57	1.25	11.82
9.	MP	10.56	1.08	0.99	0.33	12.96	0.71	2.85	3.56	16.52	1.25	17.77
10.	ORS	8.04	0.85	1.26	0.63	10.77	0.79	2.88	3.67	14.44	2.54	16.98
11.	PUN	5.20	1.18	0.70	0.02	7.10	0.13	0.49	0.63	7.73	1.90	9.63
12.	RAJ	11.20	1.26	1.30	0.44	14.21	1.52	1.79	3.32	17.52	0.76	18.28
13.	TN	9.05	0.64	1.03	3.26	13.99	0.60	1.63	2.23	16.22	2.03	18.25
14.	UP	9.75	1.28	1.48	0.11	12.62	1.29	2.53	3.82	16.44	1.33	17.77
15.	WB	8.71	1.06	1.02	0.12	10.90	0.78	2.33	3.11	14.01	1.55	15.57
16.	MEAN	9.23	0.94	1.06	0.67	11.91	0.97	2.08	3.05	14.96	1.67	16.63
17.	CENTRE	0.10	0.03	0.07	0.01	0.21	0.13	0.28	0.40	0.62	0.30	0.91

Source: Computed from NIPFP Data Bank.

of GDP and 16.63 per cent of total revenue expenditure. However, considerable variations found across states.

2. Overall social security expenditures with the emphasis on various components differed across states. There Southern states Kerala, Karnataka and Tamil Nadu have given greater importance for elementary education, rural and public health, family welfare and nutrition.

3. When the shares considered interms of promotions and protective measures, it was found that promotional measures accounted for a share of 70 per cent (Haryana) to 96 per cent in Gujarat. Across states data given in Table-10 with the 15 states average being 90 per cent on promotional measures. Protective measures, which immediate relief to the destitute, were paid less attention, with relative share in total security expenditure exceeding 30 per cent in only Haryana, and.

4. The centres allocations to social security constituted only 0.15 per cent of gross domestic product and less than 1 per cent of total revenue expenditure (see Table 9, Sl. NO. 17 centre). It is evident from the data given in Table 9 that 44 per cent of centre's expenditure was spent on asset and employment programmes (level II measures), 32 per cent on social assistance programmes (level II) and 23 per cent on level 1 measures. Within level 1 elementary education constituted a major share followed by family welfare and rural public health in the order of preference.

The empirical analysis indicated that overall, the level of expenditure by the centre and states on social sector seems exceedingly peltry in relation to the magnitude of deprivation in the country especially during post-reforms period (1990-2002) and till to date.

Table 10. State-wise Share of Government Expenditure on Components of Social Security in Total Social Security Expenditure: 1991-95

(per cent)

Sl. No.	*States*	*Level I*					*Level II*			*Level I+II*	*Level III*
		Ele. Edn.	*Rl. & Ph.*	*F.W.*	*Nutrition*	*Total*	*Assets*	*Emplt.*	*Total*	*Promo-tional*	*Protec tive*
1.	AP	51.06	6.29	7.80	1.63	66.79	12.42	12.61	25.03	91.81	8.19
2.	ASM	75.11	5.74	5.10	1.14	87.09	5.87	1.79	7.67	94.75	5.25
3.	BIH	52.09	4.44	5.43	0.70	62.65	5.37	19.58	24.95	87.60	12.40
4.	GUJ	61.28	5.53	4.97	9.75	81.53	6.91	7.86	14.76	96.29	3.71
5.	HAR	47.42	5.13	5.12	3.77	61.44	3.48	4.77	8.25	69.69	30.31
6.	KAR	56.23	1.42	5.85	5.58	69.08	7.76	7.54	15.29	84.37	15.63
7.	KER	66.78	4.47	5.82	1.08	78.14	3.39	7.58	10.97	89.12	10.88
8.	MAH	50.67	6.74	6.15	2.54	66.10	3.03	20.27	23.30	89.40	10.60
9.	MP	59.43	6.06	5.55	1.88	72.92	4.02	16.03	20.05	92.97	7.03
10.	ORS	47.31	4.99	7.43	3.70	63.43	4.66	16.95	21.61	85.04	14.96
11.	PUN	54.02	12.23	7.32	0.16	73.73	1.36	5.14	6.49	80.22	19.78
12.	RAJ	61.28	6.89	7.11	2.42	77.71	8.34	9.79	18.13	95.84	4.16
13.	TN	49.60	3.53	5.62	17.88	76.63	3.30	8.94	12.24	88.87	11.13
14.	UP	54.87	7.22	8.30	0.63	71.03	7.26	14.23	21.49	92.52	7.48
15.	WB	55.99	6.78	6.53	0.77	70.06	4.98	14.98	19.96	90.02	9.98
16.	MEAN	55.52	5.66	6.40	4.05	71.63	5.81	12.51	18.32	89.24	10.06
17.	CENTRE	11.44	3.14	7.46	1.26	23.30	14.07	30.17	44.24	67.54	32.46

Source: Social Security Expenditure from NIPFP Data Bank.

Some other Issues

There are some other issues which need urgent action. They are gender discrimination employment of the poor, and people participation in promoting voluntary coverage and supporting voluntary schemes such as proven programmes of training for administrators etc. The different options for extending social protection have been assessed individually and most of these social protection systems are to be mixed and linkages between different components be designed.

Conclusion

In India basic services and needs such as education, health, shelter, safe drinking water and transport and communications have received the attention of the planners. In the 9th plan a special action plan envisages expansion and improvement of social infrastructure and focused on providing integrated preventive, promotive, creative and rehabilitative services in primary, secondary and tertiary health care institutions with appropriate linkages. Similarly the 9th plan treats education as the most crucial investment in human development. Eradication of illiteracy is a top priority in the national agenda for the governance. In the process of heavier economic reforms, there are many distortions in the socio-sector domain. The going economic reforms process should be reappraised and revitalized to give the entire national development effort a more human face. Finally, the goal of social protection is not mere survival but, social inclusion and preservative of human dignity. The economically globaling world with all its opportunities as well as problems, calls for similarly globalised understanding of the priority of the Decent work as development objective (Rogers, 2000). Further, it demands the need for proper economic, political and social arrangements under economic reforms to meet the challenge of globalization.

Further, an important constraint which aggregates the dismal situation is the fiscal crunch being forced by the state governments since the mind-1980's the situation, further, deteriorated in the 90's with the initiation of financial sector reforms. Thus the question of development of social sector is inextribly linked with fiscal reforms. Thus it is needless to all, reforms are also required for improving the pattern of expenditure within education and health sectors. These measures should be aimed at making the delivery systems for social sector, function more efficiently as they play a leading role in translation increased allocations to better social sector development for the poor. Finally, according to Sen and Dreze (1995) economic reforms would lead to greater economic opportunities for the population. However in the context of free marketisation, there is a substantial section of society which does not have the resource power to enter into market operations. If these people have to survive the state and those who are already in the market have the responsibility to provide provision for social sector development and more so for the unorganized workers and other groups who are out of the market. Regional differences in human development seem to be increasing after liberalization. Public action in terms of public investment in physical and social infrastructure is required in order to reduce regional disparities.

References

1. Rogers, "Decent Work as Development Objective", Lecture delivered at annual conference of ISLE, Jabalpur, December, 2000.
2. Rangarajan.C (2000), "Social Development and Economic Growth in Perspectives on Indian Economy A collection of Essays", New Delhi.
3. Arun Glosh (20000, "Whither the Tickle Down Effect of Growth", Business Line, March, 21.
4. Nayyar Deepak (1990), "Social Sector and Development: Experiences and Challenges" in the D.K. Dos (ed) Social Sector and Development. Deep and Deep, Publication, New Delhi.
5. Panchamukhi, P. R. (2000) "Social Impact of Economic Reforms in India, A critical Approach", EPW, Vol. XXXC No. 10.

6. Amartya Sen, "Work and Rights" Special Issues; Social Policy and Social Protection, ILO Review, Vol. 139, No. 2, 2000/2, Geneva.

7. Roger. Beattie, "Social Protection for All: But How?" ILO, Review, Vol. 139, No. 2, 2000/2.

8. UNDP, "Human Development Report, 1999, Oxford University Press, p. 22.

9. Guy Standing, "Globalization: The Eight Crises of Social Protection", V.V. Giri Memorial Lecture, December 19, 2001, ISEC, Bangalore.

5

Post-Reform Trends in Organised Sector-Employment

Dr. K. Sai Haragopal

Introduction

India embarked on reform process in tune with the changing scenario in the world economy. The 21st century witnessed several changes in the process of economic development and growth due to the emergence of globalization and privatization. Labour, as one of the key variables in the development process assumed greater significance particularly in the light of declining role of public sector and increasing role of private sector. It has been reported that public sector started to get rid of redundant labour and employment generation in the public sector became thin. Organised private sector has been looked upon to lead in income generation in the economy through generating more employment opportunities. Reform process was expected to result in higher growth rate with significant expansion of employment in the organized sector. Hence an attempt is made in this paper to examine the trends in the growth of employment in the organized sector. The analysis was dealt in terms of public and private sectors. Both public and private sectors were further divided into several sectors for an indepth analysis. The analysis was also carried out in terms of pre and post liberalization periods to study the impact of economic reforms.

Objectives

The basic objectives of the study are:

1. To examine the trends in employment in the organized sector
2. To examine the trends in public and private sectors
3. To examine the trends in different sectors of the industry for public and private sectors.

Data Base and Indicators

Relevant data for the study was collected from various economic surveys published by the Government of India. Organised sector data on employment was collected for Public and Private sectors. Public and private sectors were further divided into 9 sub sectors namely, (1) Agriculture and Hunting, (2) Mining & Quarrying, (3) Manufacturing, (4) Electricity, Gas, and Water, (5) Construction, (6) Wholesale and Retail Trade, (7) Transport Storage & Communications, (8) Finance, Insurance and Real Estate, (9) Community, Social and Personal Services. The period of study was 20 years beginning from the year 1980-81. The entire period was further divided into two sub periods namely pre-reform period and post-reform period.

The Author wish is to acknowledge the help received from Professor S. Indrakant, Department of Economics, Osmania University for his help in preparation of this paper.

The pre-reform period was covered 12 years from 1980-81 to 1991-92 and the post-reform period was covered 8 years from 1992-93 to 1999-2000. Basic analysis was carried out in terms of 9 sectors for two sub-periods namely pre-reform period and post-reform period. To analyse trends in the growth of employment we have employed the following important indicators.

1. Sectoral proportions.
2. Ratio of public sector to private sector.

3. Incremental Values.
4. Simple Growth Rates.
5. Linear Growth Rates.

Results of the Study

Sectoral Proportions

Public Sector. Table 1 presents sectoral proportions of employment in the public sector in the pre-reform period. The Table reveals that roughly fifty per cent of the total employment in the public sector is in *Community, Social and Personal services sector.* Next is Transport Storage and Communications with around 17 per cent employment and Manufacturing sector with around 10 per cent employment. The remaining 25 to 26 per cent of the employment is distributed among the other 6 sectors. In the manufacturing sector the proportions have shown an increase during 1983-84 to 1988-89.

When we look at the Table 2 we final that the post-reform trends in the compositional changes of sectoral allocations, Community, Social and Personal services sector continue to provide higher volume of employment. However, there is a decline in the volume of employment in the sectors, Transport Storage and Communications and Manufacturing during the post reform period.

Private sector. Sectoral proportions of employment in the private sector present altogether different picture. Table 3 presents data pertaining to different sectors in terms of proportions of employment during the pre-reform period. Roughly 90 per cent of the employment is in three sectors namely Manufacturing, Community Social & Personal services and Agriculture & Hunting. The remaining 10 per cent or so is distributed among other 6 sectors. The manufacturing sector itself corners around 60 per cent employment followed by Community Social and Personal services with 18 to 19 per cent and then Agriculture and

Table 1. Employment in the Public Sector Sectoral Proportions in Percentage Pre Reform Period

Year	Agriculture Hunting etc.	Mining and Quarrying	Manufa-cturing	Electricity Gas and Water	Constr uction	Wholesale and retail trade	Transport storage and communi-cation	Finance Insurance and real estate	Community social & personal services	Total
1980-81	2.99	5.28	9.70	4.41	7.03	0.76	17.50	4.83	47.50	100.00
1981-82	2.87	5.22	9.98	4.38	6.97	0.71	17.44	5.11	47.33	100.00
1982-83	2.89	5.37	9.93	4.38	6.81	0.72	17.17	5.30	47.43	100.00
1983-84	2.90	5.50	10.18	4.35	6.64	0.74	16.98	5.42	47.31	100.00
1984-85	2.88	5.64	10.20	4.40	6.64	0.76	16.76	5.69	47.04	100.00
1985-86	2.97	5.46	10.26	4.44	6.68	0.74	16.56	5.82	47.05	100.00
1986-87	3.09	5.23	10.33	4.38	6.57	0.74	16.48	5.86	47.32	100.00
1987-88	3.02	5.22	10.19	4.63	6.63	0.76	16.44	5.98	47.13	100.00
1988-89	3.01	5.18	10.10	4.71	6.21	0.81	16.12	6.09	47.76	100.00
1989-90	2.93	5.15	9.97	4.78	6.04	0.80	16.11	6.15	48.07	100.00
1990-91	2.92	5.24	9.72	4.75	6.03	0.79	15.88	6.27	48.42	100.00
1991-92	2.98	5.14	9.69	4.77	5.99	0.82	15.95	6.32	48.34	100.00

Table 2. Employment in the Public Sector and Sectoral Proportions in Percentage Post-Reform Period

Year	*Agriculture Hunting etc.*	*Mining and Quarrying*	*Manufac turing*	*Electricity Gas and Water*	*Constr uction*	*Wholesale and retail trade*	*Transport storage and communi-cation*	*Finance Insurance and real estate*	*Community social & personal services*	*Total*
1992-93	2.91	5.16	9.58	4.82	5.97	0.77	15.81	6.48	48.52	100.00
1993-94	2.80	5.22	9.17	4.82	6.00	0.83	15.86	6.55	48.74	100.00
1994-95	2.77	5.22	9.02	4.80	5.98	0.83	15.96	6.59	48.82	100.00
1995-96	2.78	5.11	8.95	4.87	5.97	0.83	15.91	6.59	49.00	100.00
1996-97	2.73	5.00	8.49	4.89	5.80	0.84	15.81	6.62	49.83	100.00
1997-98	2.73	4.83	8.32	4.91	5.71	0.84	15.88	6.63	50.14	100.00
1998-99	3.17	4.77	8.08	4.95	5.70	0.84	15.88	6.67	50.45	100.00
1999-00	3.18	4.78	7.93	4.90	5.65	0.84	15.93	6.71	50.59	100.00

Table 3. Employment in the Private Sector and Sectoral Proportions in Percentage Pre-Reform Period

Year	*Agriculture Hunting etc.*	*Mining and Quarrying*	*Manufac turing*	*Electricity Gas and Water*	*Constr uction*	*Wholesale and retail trade*	*Transport storage and communi-cation*	*Finance Insurance and real estate*	*Community social & personal services*	*Total*
1980-81	11.60	1.76	61.46	0.47	0.97	3.75	0.81	2.65	16.52	100.00
1981-82	11.28	1.71	61.76	0.48	0.94	3.67	0.80	2.70	16.68	100.00
1982-83	11.22	1.59	61.65	0.49	0.90	3.64	0.78	2.74	16.99	100.00
1983-84	11.15	1.54	60.89	0.53	0.90	3.76	0.78	2.91	17.55	100.00
1984-85	11.04	1.55	60.49	0.53	0.96	3.79	0.74	3.00	17.91	100.00
1985-86	11.15	1.51	60.32	0.54	0.94	3.76	0.73	3.00	18.06	100.00
1986-87	11.52	1.24	59.89	0.54	0.79	3.76	0.71	3.11	18.45	100.00
1987-88	11.42	1.26	59.46	0.55	0.68	3.83	0.69	3.22	18.90	100.00
1988-89	11.65	1.29	58.81	0.52	0.93	3.84	0.68	3.14	19.17	100.00
1989-90	11.55	1.31	58.78	0.53	0.90	3.84	0.69	3.15	19.26	100.00
1990-91	11.61	1.30	58.37	0.52	0.95	3.91	0.69	3.31	19.34	100.00
1991-92	11.62	1.36	58.20	0.51	0.99	3.77	0.69	3.39	19.46	100.00

Hunting with 11 per cent. The manufacturing sector that is providing almost 61 per cent employment in the private sector reduced its share in total employment from the year 1984-85 onwards. However the sector Community Social and Personal services has been increasing its share continuously in total employment of the private sector.

Sectoral proportions of employment in the post-reform period in private sector are presented in Table 4. The Table shows even though the Manufacturing sector provides higher volume of employment, its share in total employment has come down. Post-reform period saw less than 60 per cent share in Manufacturing sector except in the year 1996-97 when its share was around 60 per cent. The sector Community Social and Personal services maintained around 19 per cent share with slight variations. The sector Agriculture and Hunting share has declined from around 11 per cent from 1992-93 to 10 per cent after 1995-96.

The analysis in terms of shares of total employment in different sectors for the public and private sectors shows, firstly, only three sectors in public and private sectors contribute larger volume of employment i.e. 75 per cent in the public sector and 90 per cent in the private sector. The remaining 25 per cent in public sector and 10 per cent in private sector are shared by the remaining 6 sectors. Secondly, while the sector of Community Social and Personal services contributes more share (i.e. around 50 per cent) to total employment in the public sector, the Manufacturing sector in private dominates with around 60 per cent. Thirdly post reform period saw a declining share in the Manufacturing sector in both public and private sectors.

Sectoral Ratios of Public Sector to Private Sector

Table 5 presents sectoral ratios of public sector to private sector during the pre reform period. The ratio indicates that if the ratios are lesser then the employment is more in the private sector. A glance through the Table reveals that at

Table 4. Employment in the Private Sector and Sectoral Proportions in percentage Post-Reform Period

Year	Agriculture Hunting etc.	Mining and Quarrying	Manufac turing	Electricity Gas and Water	Constr uction	Wholesale and retail trade	Transport storage and communi-cation	Finance Insurance and real estate	Community social & personal services	Total
1992-93	11.67	1.22	57.89	0.48	0.93	3.83	0.70	3.53	19.74	100.00
1993-94	11.13	1.27	58.39	0.50	0.64	3.81	0.71	3.56	19.99	100.00
1994-95	11.09	1.28	58.39	0.50	0.66	3.82	0.72	3.64	19.89	100.00
1995-96	10.80	1.26	59.32	0.49	0.62	3.72	0.70	3.59	19.48	100.00
1996-97	10.50	1.06	60.32	0.47	0.62	3.65	0.73	3.71	18.93	100.00
1997-98	10.33	1.04	59.82	0.48	0.85	3.67	0.74	3.90	19.17	100.00
1998-99	10.01	1.00	59.53	0.47	0.82	3.71	0.79	4.12	19.54	100.00
1999-00	10.46	0.94	58.82	0.47	0.66	3.82	0.81	4.14	19.93	100.00

Table 5. Sectoral Ratios of Public Sector to Private Sector Pre-Reform Period: 1980-81 to 1991-92

Year	*Agriculture Hunting etc.*	*Mining and Quarrying*	*Manufac turing*	*Electricity Gas and Water*	*Const-uction*	*Wholesale and retail trade*	*Transport storage and communi-cation*	*Finance Insurance and real estate*	*Community social & personal services*	*Total*
1980-81	0.54	6.29	0.33	19.51	15.13	0.42	45.15	3.82	6.02	2.09
1981-82	0.54	6.45	0.34	19.39	15.66	0.41	46.35	4.00	5.99	2.11
1982-83	0.56	7.37	0.35	19.49	16.47	0.43	47.90	4.21	6.08	2.18
1983-84	0.60	8.20	0.38	18.79	16.97	0.45	50.25	4.27	6.19	2.30
1984-85	0.62	8.62	0.40	19.49	16.37	0.47	53.59	4.49	6.21	2.36
1985-86	0.64	8.70	0.41	19.63	17.12	0.47	54.24	4.66	6.25	2.40
1986-87	0.66	10.35	0.42	19.73	20.43	0.48	57.12	4.61	6.28	2.45
1987-88	0.66	10.28	0.42	20.71	24.28	0.49	59.04	4.60	6.18	2.48
1988-89	0.64	9.96	0.43	22.28	16.61	0.52	58.31	4.80	6.17	2.48
1989-90	0.63	9.76	0.42	22.43	16.68	0.52	58.13	4.83	6.18	2.47
1990-91	0.62	9.99	0.41	22.63	15.74	0.50	57.09	4.70	6.21	2.48
1991-92	0.63	9.22	0.41	22.90	14.76	0.53	56.74	4.56	6.08	2.45

aggregate level, the ratio has increased from 2.09 to 2.45 indicating an increase in employment in the public sector. At the disaggregate level also in all sectors the ratios are on the rise. In the case of Mining and Quarrying the ratios are increased substantially when compared to other sectors. In the case of construction sector the ratios are fluctuating.

Table 6 presents the ratios of public sector to private sector in different sectors during the post reform period. The Table reveals that the ratios in the post reform period has a declining and fluctuating trend. At aggregate level the ratios have fallen from 2.46 to 2.23. At disaggregate level also the ratios are falling. This indicates the private sector is not able to generate more employment opportunities as anticipated by the reformists.

The ratios of public sector to private sector indicates that the post-reform period have not been able make much dent on employment generation through private sector.

Incremental Values

Incremental values are nothing but the difference between the current year employment and to the preceding year employment. In fact, these values show the additional employment generated in the succeeding years.

Public Sector. Table 7 presents incremental values of employment during the pre-reform period in the public sector. The Table shows that there is not much increase in the employment. No consistent trend is seen in the employment generation. In fact the values are declining.

Table 8 presents incremental values of employment during post-reform period. The post reform period show a drastic reduction in the employment generation in the public sector. Perhaps it is in tune with the privatization process. The same trend can be seen in almost all sectors. In fact there are negative values recorded at aggregate level and in almost in all sectors.

Table 6. Sectoral Ratios of Public Sector to Private Sector Post-Reform Period: 1992-93 to 1999-00

Year	*Agriculture Hunting etc.*	*Mining and Quarrying*	*Manufac turing*	*Electricity Gas and Water*	*Constr uction*	*Wholesale and retail trade*	*Transport storage and communi-cation*	*Finance Insurance and real estate*	*Community social & personal services*	*Total*
1992-93	0.61	10.39	0.41	24.50	15.81	0.49	55.55	4.52	6.05	2.46
1993-94	0.62	10.05	0.39	23.45	22.88	0.53	55.07	4.51	5.98	2.45
1994-95	0.60	9.86	0.37	23.38	21.96	0.53	53.55	4.38	5.93	2.42
1995-96	0.59	9.28	0.34	22.52	21.87	0.51	51.53	4.18	5.74	2.28
1996-97	0.58	10.63	0.32	23.32	21.00	0.52	49.08	4.02	5.93	2.25
1997-98	0.59	10.30	0.31	22.71	14.99	0.51	47.45	3.78	5.81	2.22
1998-99	0.71	10.64	0.30	23.46	15.59	0.50	44.70	3.62	5.76	2.23
1999-00	0.68	11.41	0.30	23.07	19.16	0.49	43.96	3.62	5.67	2.23

Table 7. Employment in the Public Sector Incremental Values-Pre-Reform Period

Year	*Agriculture Hunting etc.*	*Mining and Quarrying*	*Manufac turing*	*Electricity Gas and Water*	*Constr uction*	*Wholesale and retail trade*	*Transport storage and communi-cation*	*Finance Insurance and real estate*	*Community social & personal services*	*Total*
1980-81										
1981-82	-0.06	0.14	0.90	0.15	0.23	-0.04	0.72	0.67	1.92	4.62
1982-83	0.19	0.52	0.42	0.23	0.08	0.05	0.45	0.57	2.59	5.11
1983-84	0.13	0.43	0.83	0.12	0.00	0.06	0.38	0.42	1.75	4.12
1984-85	0.09	0.47	0.44	0.27	0.26	0.07	0.30	0.69	1.42	4.01
1985-86	0.28	-0.08	0.54	0.25	0.35	0.00	0.35	0.47	1.98	4.14
1986-87	0.31	-0.24	0.47	0.04	0.04	0.03	0.41	0.26	2.08	3.40
1987-88	-0.03	0.14	0.05	0.60	0.29	0.05	0.41	0.39	1.06	2.96
1988-89	0.01	0.00	-0.04	0.20	-0.68	0.11	-0.37	0.28	1.76	1.27
1989-90	-0.06	0.10	0.07	0.28	-0.12	0.00	0.49	0.31	2.08	3.15
1990-91	0.07	0.33	-0.18	0.08	0.15	0.00	0.03	0.40	2.08	2.96
1991-92	0.17	-0.12	0.09	0.11	0.02	0.07	0.38	0.20	0.60	1.52

Table 8. Employment in the Public Sector Incremental Values—Post-Reform Period

Year	*Agriculture Hunting etc.*	*Mining and Quarrying*	*Manufac turing*	*Electricity Gas and Water*	*Constr uction*	*Wholesale and retail trade*	*Transport storage and communi-cation*	*Finance Insurance and real estate*	*Community social & personal services*	*Total*
1992-93	-0.11	0.10	-0.10	0.15	0.03	-0.09	-0.09	0.38	0.90	1.16
1993-94	-0.17	0.18	-0.67	0.07	0.13	0.13	0.29	0.21	1.01	1.19
1994-95	-0.06	0.01	-0.28	-0.03	-0.03	0.01	0.22	0.10	0.26	0.21
1995-96	0.01	-0.23	-0.18	0.11	-0.05	0.00	-0.14	-0.03	0.16	-0.37
1996-97	-0.07	-0.15	-0.77	0.10	-0.25	0.02	0.00	0.14	2.27	1.30
1997-98	-0.03	-0.41	-0.45	-0.02	-0.25	0.00	-0.08	-0.06	-0.10	-1.41
1998-99	0.85	-0.11	-0.47	0.08	-0.02	-0.01	0.00	0.07	0.57	-0.03
1999-00	-0.01	-0.02	-0.38	-0.16	-0.15	0.00	-0.07	0.01	-0.23	-1.01

Private Sector. Table 9 presents incremental values of employment during the pre-reform period. The private sector employment in the pre-reform period is marked by low, negative and fluctuating incremental values. This indicates not much employment is being generated in the private sector during the pre-reform period.

Table 10 presents incremental values of employment during the post reform period. The post reform period records low, fluctuating and even negative employment in the private sector. Only in the year 1995-96 there was a higher incremental value showing some positive impact of liberalization. Otherwise the values clearly indicate contrary to the expectations of privatization.

The analysis in terms of incremental value of employment generation in the public and private sectors during the pre and post reform periods clearly show the reform process has not been able to generate more employment opportunities in the economy particularly in the private sector.

Simple Growth Rates

To analyze the trend in the growth rates, we have computed simple growth rates or in other words, percentage change over previous year. Simple growth rates were calculated for the public and private sectors during the pre and post-reform periods. Simple growth rates were computed using the formula $[\{(Y_t)-(Y_t-1)\}/(Y_t-1)]*100$ Where Y_t is the current year value and Y_t-1 is the previous year value. This simple growth rate indicates the year-to-year performance of a studied variable.

Public Sector. Table 11 presents simple growth rate or percentage change over preceding year of employment during the pre-reform period. It appears on year-to-year basis the employment has grown to somewhat consistently upto 1985-86 and later declined in its growth. An analysis

Table 9. Employment in the Private Sector Incremental Values—Pre-Reform Period

Year	Agriculture Hunting etc.	Mining and Quarrying	Manufacturing	Electricity Gas and Water	Construction	Wholesale and retail trade	Transport storage and communication	Finance Insurance and real estate	Community social & personal services	Total
1981-82	-0.07	-0.01	1.16	0.01	-0.01	0.00	0.00	0.08	0.37	1.52
1982-83	-0.04	-0.09	-0.05	0.01	-0.03	-0.02	-0.01	0.03	0.24	0.05
1983-84	-0.28	-0.07	-1.83	0.02	-0.02	0.01	-0.02	0.07	0.06	-2.06
1984-85	-0.12	0.00	-0.52	0.00	0.04	0.01	-0.03	0.05	0.20	-0.37
1985-86	0.15	-0.02	0.27	0.01	-0.01	0.00	0.00	0.02	0.23	0.65
1986-87	0.26	-0.20	-0.38	0.00	-0.11	0.00	-0.02	0.08	0.27	-0.10
1987-88	-0.04	0.02	-0.15	0.01	-0.08	0.06	-0.01	0.09	0.38	0.28
1988-89	0.24	0.03	-0.12	-0.02	0.19	0.03	0.00	-0.04	0.32	0.61
1989-90	0.08	0.03	0.74	0.01	-0.01	0.05	0.01	0.05	0.31	1.29
1990-91	0.15	0.01	0.24	0.00	0.05	0.09	0.01	0.15	0.25	0.95
1991-92	0.21	0.07	0.85	0.00	0.05	-0.04	0.01	0.12	0.42	1.69

Table 10. Employment in the Private Sector Incremental Values—Post-Reform Period

Year	*Agriculture Hunting etc.*	*Mining and Quarrying*	*Manufac turing*	*Electricity Gas and Water*	*Constr uction*	*Wholesale and retail trade*	*Transport storage and communi-cation*	*Finance Insurance and real estate*	*Community social & personal services*	*Total*
1992-93	0.04	-0.11	-0.21	-0.02	-0.05	0.05	0.01	0.11	0.23	0.05
1993-94	-0.33	0.05	0.85	0.02	-0.22	0.01	0.01	0.05	0.35	0.79
1994-95	0.11	0.02	0.76	0.00	0.02	0.06	0.02	0.11	0.18	1.29
1995-96	0.25	0.04	3.43	0.02	0.00	0.09	0.02	0.13	0.55	4.53
1996-97	-0.07	-0.15	1.90	-0.01	0.01	0.00	0.03	0.16	-0.14	1.74
1997-98	-0.08	-0.01	-0.06	0.01	0.20	0.04	0.02	0.19	0.33	0.62
1998-99	-0.33	-0.04	-0.55	-0.01	-0.03	0.02	0.04	0.17	0.23	-0.50
1999-00	0.33	-0.06	-0.93	0.00	-0.14	0.07	0.01	0.00	0.23	-0.53

Table 11. Employment in the Public Sector Percentage Change Over Previous Year-Pre-Reform Period

Year	*Agriculture Hunting etc.*	*Mining and Quarrying*	*Manufac turing*	*Electricity Gas and Water*	*Constr uction*	*Wholesale and retail trade*	*Transport storage and communi-cation*	*Finance Insurance and real estate*	*Community social & personal services*	*Total*
1981-82	-1.30	1.71	5.99	2.20	2.11	-3.42	2.66	8.96	2.61	2.98
1982-83	4.16	6.25	2.64	3.30	0.72	4.42	1.62	6.99	3.43	3.20
1983-84	2.73	4.86	5.08	1.66	0.00	5.08	1.34	4.82	2.24	2.50
1984-85	1.84	5.07	2.56	3.68	2.32	5.65	1.05	7.55	1.78	2.38
1985-86	5.62	-0.82	3.07	3.29	3.05	0.00	1.21	4.78	2.44	2.40
1986-87	5.89	-2.48	2.59	0.51	0.34	2.29	1.40	2.52	2.50	1.92
1987-88	-0.54	1.49	0.27	7.60	2.45	3.73	1.38	3.69	1.24	1.64
1988-89	0.18	0.00	-0.21	2.36	-5.60	7.91	-1.23	2.56	2.04	0.69
1989-90	-1.08	1.05	0.38	3.22	-1.05	0.00	1.65	2.76	2.36	1.71
1990-91	1.28	3.42	-0.96	0.89	1.32	0.00	0.10	3.47	2.31	1.58
1991-92	3.06	-1.20	0.49	1.22	0.17	4.67	1.26	1.68	0.65	0.80

of the sectoral trend also shows fluctuating, declining and negative growth in almost all the sectors during the pre-reform period in the public sector. Only three sectors namely (1) Electricity, Gas and Water (2) Finance Insurance and Real estate and (3) Community Social and Personal services have not recorded any negative growth.

Table 12 presents employment growth in simple terms during the post reform period. The post-reform scenario show a drastic change in the employment growth in the public sector. There appears to be virtually no growth at all. At aggregate level it has not grown even at one per cent. At disaggregate level many sectors recorded negative growth.

The trends in the growth of employment in the public sector during the post-reform period clearly show the anticipated declining role of the public sector and the economy in the aftermath of economic reforms.

Private Sector. Table 13 presents the growth of employment during the pre-reform period. The trends in the employment in the private sector in the pre-reform period are not much to the satisfaction. The trend in growth rates depicts fluctuating negative and declining values. Same trends are seen in almost all sectors with more number of negative growth rates. This shows that private sector was not performing well in terms of employment generation during the pre-reform period.

Table 14 shows the growth of employment during the post-reform period. It appears there is a slight improvement in the growth of employment during the post reform period in the private sector. At aggregate level up to 1997-98 the growth rates were positive. Subsequently the growth rates were negative. At the disaggregate level in different sectors there are less number of negative growth rates when compared to the pre reform period. However negative growth

Table 12. Employment in the Public Sector Percentage Change Over Previous Year-Post-Reform Period

Year	*Agriculture Hunting etc.*	*Mining and Quarrying*	*Manufac turing*	*Electricity Gas and Water*	*Constr uction*	*Wholesale and retail trade*	*Transport storage and communi-cation*	*Finance Insurance and real estate*	*Community social & personal services*	*Total*
1992-93	-1.92	1.01	-0.54	1.64	0.26	-5.73	-0.29	3.13	0.97	0.60
1993-94	-3.02	1.81	-3.62	0.75	1.13	8.78	0.95	1.68	1.08	0.62
1994-95	-1.10	0.10	-1.57	-0.32	-0.26	0.62	0.71	0.79	0.27	0.11
1995-96	0.19	-2.26	-1.03	1.18	-0.43	0.00	-0.45	-0.23	0.17	-0.19
1996-97	-1.30	-1.51	-4.43	1.06	-2.16	1.23	0.00	1.09	2.38	0.67
1997-98	-0.56	-4.19	-2.71	-0.21	-2.20	0.00	-0.26	-0.46	-0.10	-0.72
1998-99	16.04	-1.17	-2.91	0.84	-0.18	-0.61	0.00	0.54	0.59	-0.02
1999-00	-0.16	-0.22	-2.42	-1.66	-1.36	0.00	-0.23	0.08	-0.23	-0.52

Table 13. Employment in the Private Sector Percentage Change Over Previous Year-Pre-Reform Period

Year	Agriculture Hunting etc.	Mining and Quarrying	Manufac-turing	Electricity Gas and Water	Constr uction	Wholesale and retail trade	Transport storage and communi-cation	Finance Insurance and real estate	Community social & personal services	Total
1981-82	-0.82	-0.77	2.55	2.86	-1.39	0.00	0.00	4.08	3.03	2.06
1982-83	-0.47	-6.98	-0.11	2.78	-4.23	-0.72	-1.67	1.47	1.91	0.07
1983-84	-3.31	-5.83	-3.93	5.41	-2.94	0.36	-3.39	3.38	0.47	-2.73
1984-85	-1.47	0.00	-1.16	0.00	6.06	0.36	-5.26	2.34	1.55	-0.50
1985-86	1.86	-1.77	0.61	2.56	-1.43	0.00	0.00	0.91	1.76	0.89
1986-87	3.16	-18.02	-0.85	0.00	-15.94	0.00	-3.70	3.62	2.03	-0.14
1987-88	-0.47	2.20	-0.34	2.50	-13.79	2.17	-1.92	3.93	2.80	0.38
1988-89	2.84	3.23	-0.27	-4.88	38.00	1.06	0.00	-1.68	2.29	0.83
1989-90	0.92	3.13	1.69	2.56	-1.45	1.75	1.96	2.14	2.17	1.73
1990-91	1.71	1.01	0.54	0.00	7.35	3.09	1.92	6.28	1.71	1.25
1991-92	2.36	7.00	1.90	0.00	6.85	-1.33	1.89	4.72	2.83	2.20

Table 14. Employment in the Private Sector Percentage Change Over Previous Year-Post-Reform Period

Year	Agriculture Hunting etc.	Mining and Quarrying	Manufac turing	Electricity Gas and Water	Constr uction	Wholesale and retail trade	Transport storage and communi-cation	Finance Insurance and real estate	Community social & personal services	Total
1992-93	0.44	10.28	-0.46	-5.00	-6.41	1.69	1.85	4.14	1.51	0.06
1993-94	-3.60	5.21	1.87	5.26	30.14	0.33	1.82	1.81	2.26	1.01
1994-95	1.25	1.98	1.64	0.00	3.92	1.99	3.57	3.90	1.14	1.63
1995-96	2.80	3.88	7.29	5.00	0.00	2.92	3.45	4.44	3.43	5.62
1996-97	-0.76	14.02	3.76	-2.38	1.89	0.00	5.00	5.23	-0.84	2.04
1997-98	-0.88	-1.09	-0.11	2.44	37.04	1.26	3.17	5.90	2.01	0.71
1998-99	-3.65	-4.40	-1.05	-2.38	-4.05	0.62	6.15	4.99	1.37	-0.57
1999-00	3.79	-6.90	-1.80	0.00	19.72	2.17	1.45	0.00	1.35	-0.61

rates are indicative of not so good performance of the private sector in the post reform period even though it was expected to take a lead role in employment generation.

The analysis in terms of simple growth rates clearly indicates that the performance of public sector in terms of employment generation has declined drastically in the post-reform period in accordance with the reform process. However the private sector could not take a lead role in employment generation in the post-reform period as anticipated.

Results of Regression Analysis

We have also analysed sectoral growth of employment in public and private sectors for the two sub periods with the help of regression analysis. Regression technique is used to compute linear growth rates for the selected sectors. We have selected three sectors from each group i.e. public and private sectors for analyzing employment trends in terms of linear growth rates. As mentioned earlier, three sectors in public sector namely, (1) Community Social and Personal Services, (2) Transport Storage and Communications and (3) Manufacturing sectors have cornered roughly 75 per cent of employment. Likewise in private sector also three sectors namely, (1) Manufacturing, (2) Community Social and Personal Services and (3) Agriculture and Hunting have covered about 90 per cent of employment. We have fitted linear equations for these selected sectors against time. We have employed the formula Y= a+bt where Y (employment) is the dependant variable, 'a' is the intercept and 'b' is coefficient. Growth rate (linear) is calculated as coefficient over mean of dependent variable multiplied by 100. The results are presented in Tables 15,16,17, and 18.

Sectoral analysis of public sector for the two sub periods is presented in Table 15 & 16. A glance through the Tables reveals that linear growth rates of employment in all the selected sectors in the post-reform period have decelerated in the public sector. 'T' ratios are significant in all the three sectors in the pre reform period. The value of R^2 attributes the variation in employment reasonably to the time factor in all the three sectors in the pre-reform period.

Table 15. Regression Results of the Selected Variables in the Public Sector

Pre-Reform Period: 1980-81 to 1991-92

Function	*Estimated Equation*	*'t' value*	*LGR*	*R^2*
CSP = f (t)	Y = 72.331 + 1.7747t	47.97	2.11	0.99
TSC = f (t)	Y = 27.309+0.2947t	12.09	1.00	0.93
Mf=f (t)	Y =15.609+0.3159t	6.33	1.78	0.80

Table 16. Regression Results of the Selected Variables in the Public Sector

Post-Reform Period: 1992-93 to 1999-00

Function	*Estimated Equation*	*'t' value*	*LGR*	*R^2*
CSP f(t)	Y = 93.34+0.6266t	6.95	0.65	0.89
TSC = f (t)	Y = 30.795+0.0104t	0.43	0.03	0.03
MF = f(t)	Y = 18.924 – 0.4538t	-21.37	-2.68	0.98

The regression results of the selected variables of private sector are presented in Table 17 & 18. The results of the three sectors show, the manufacturing sector in the post-reform period has shown a positive growth when compared to pre-reform period. However the growth rate of the other two sectors has decelerated in the post-reform period. The coefficients of the equation also show that except for the manufacturing sector for the other two sectors they have fallen in the post-reform period. With regard to manufacturing sector, the value of R^2 attributes the variation in employment to time factor only in the post-reform period. In the case of Community Social and Personal Services, 98 per cent of variation in the pre-reform period and 96 per cent of variation in the post-reform period are attributed to the time factor. However this is not the case with Agriculture and Hunting sector.

Table 17. Regression Results of the Selected Variables in Private Sector

Pre-Reform Period: 1980-81 to 1991-92

Function	*Estimated Equation*	*'t' value*	*LGR*	R^2
Mf=f(t)	Y=47.674-0.1170t	-1.55	-0.26	0.20
CSP =f(t)	Y=11.894+0.2663t	24.57	1.95	0.98
AH =f(t)	Y=8.186+0.0538t	2.64	0.63	0.41

Table 18. Regression Results of the Selected Variables in Private Sector

Post-Reform Period: 1922-93 to 1999-00

Function	*Estimated Equation*	*'t' value*	*LGR*	R^2
Mf=f(t)	Y=45.139+0.9870t	3.91	1.99	0.72
CSP=f(t)	Y=15.356+0.2373t	12.06	1.44	0.96
AH=f(t)	Y=9.068-0.0144t	-0.52	-0.15	0.04

The regression analysis of the selected sectors for both public and private shows that employment growth has declined in the post-reform period for the public sector. However, the performance of private sector in terms of generating more employment opportunities has not been successful.

Summery of Results

1. The analysis in terms of shares of total employment in different sectors for the public and

private sectors points out that only three sectors in public and private sectors contribute larger volume of employment. Post-reform period saw a declining share in the manufacturing sector in both public and private sectors.

2. The ratios of public sector to private sector indicate the post-reform period has not been able to make much dent on employment generation through private sector.
3. The analysis in terms of incremental value of employment generation in the public and private sectors during the pre- and post- reform periods clearly shows the reform process has not been able to generate more employment opportunities in the economy particularly in the private sector.
4. The analysis in terms of simple growth rates clearly indicates that the performance of public sector in terms of employment generation has declined drastically in the post-reform period in accordance with the reform process. However, the private sector could not take a lead role in employment generation in the post-reform period as anticipated.
5. The linear growth rates in selected sectors of public sector undertakings have declined during the post-reform period. In case of private sector except in manufacturing sector in other two sectors the rate growth rate has fallen.

Conclusions

The 1991 crisis of unsustainable fiscal deficits, collapse of international credit worthiness has resulted in economic reforms wherein privatization was given a lead role to sustain economic development. The controls hitherto practised were given a slip to give a free hand to the private sector in order to increase the income levels of the community through generating more employment opportunities. However it appears, after a decade of economic reforms the economy has not reached anywhere. The study of trends in organized sector employment amply demonstrates that private sector has not lived up to its expectations. Lack of employment opportunities will result in lesser incomes in the economy. This will further affect the consumer demand of a product resulting in reduced production. Hence, it is time a suitable labour policy to generate more employment opportunities in the private sector has to be evolved.

References

1. Economic Surveys, Government of India.
2. Statement on Industrial Policy, July 1991, Government of India.
3. India's Economic Reforms—Montek S. Ahwalia—Future of Economic Reform in India' edited by Robert Cassen and Vijay Joshi.
4. Economic Liberalisation and Its Implications for Employment in India—Ruddar Dutt—Indian Economic Association Conference, Volume 2001.

APPENDIX TABLES

Employment in the Public Sector—Lakh Persons Pre-Reform Period

Year	*Agriculture Hunting etc.*	*Mining and Quarrying*	*Manufac turing*	*Electricity Gas and Water*	*Constr uction*	*Wholesale and retail trade*	*Transport storage and communi-cation*	*Finance Insurance and real estate*	*Community social & personal services*	*Total*
1980-81	4.63	8.18	15.02	6.83	10.89	1.17	27.09	7.48	73.55	154.84
1981-82	4.57	8.32	15.92	6.98	11.12	1.13	27.81	8.15	75.47	159.46
1982-83	4.76	8.84	16.34	7.21	11.20	1.18	28.26	8.72	78.06	164.57
1983-84	4.89	9.27	17.17	7.33	11.20	1.24	28.64	9.14	79.81	168.69
1984-85	4.98	9.74	17.61	7.60	11.46	1.31	28.94	9.83	81.23	172.70
1985-86	5.26	9.66	18.15	7.85	11.81	1.31	29.29	10.30	83.21	176.84
1986-87	5.57	9.42	18.62	7.89	11.85	1.34	29.70	10.56	85.29	180.24
1987-88	5.54	9.56	18.67	8.49	12.14	1.39	30.11	10.95	86.35	183.20
1988-89	5.55	9.56	18.63	8.69	11.46	1.50	29.74	11.23	88.11	184.47
1989-90	5.49	9.66	18.70	8.97	11.34	1.50	30.23	11.54	90.19	187.62
1990-91	5.56	9.99	18.52	9.05	11.49	1.50	30.26	11.94	92.27	190.58
1991-92	5.73	9.87	18.61	9.16	11.51	1.57	30.64	12.14	92.87	192.10

Source: Economic Survey, Government of India.

Employment in the Public Sector—Lakh Persons

Post-Reform Period

Year	*Agriculture Hunting etc.*	*Mining and Quarrying*	*Manufac turing*	*Electricity Gas and Water*	*Constr uction*	*Wholesale and retail trade*	*Transport storage and communi-cation*	*Finance Insurance and real estate*	*Community social & personal services*	*Total*
1992-93	5.62	9.97	18.51	9.31	11.54	1.48	30.55	12.52	93.77	193.26
1993-94	5.45	10.15	17.84	9.38	11.67	1.61	30.84	12.73	94.78	194.45
1994-95	5.39	10.16	17.56	9.35	11.64	1.62	31.06	12.83	95.04	194.66
1995-96	5.40	9.93	17.38	9.46	11.59	1.62	30.92	12.80	95.20	194.29
1996-97	5.33	9.78	16.61	9.56	11.34	1.64	30.92	12.94	97.47	195.59
1997-98	5.30	9.37	16.16	9.54	11.09	1.64	30.84	12.88	97.37	194.18
1998-99	6.15	9.26	15.69	9.62	11.07	1.63	30.84	12.95	97.94	194.15
1999-00	6.14	9.24	15.31	9.46	10.92	1.63	30.77	12.96	97.71	193.14

Source: Economic Survey, Government of India.

Employment in the Private Sector—Lakh Persons. Pre-Reform Period.

Year	*Agriculture Hunting etc.*	*Mining and Quarrying*	*Manufac turing*	*Electricity Gas and Water*	*Constr uction*	*Wholesale and retail trade*	*Transport storage and communi-cation*	*Finance Insurance and real estate*	*Community social & personal services*	*Total*
1980-81	8.58	1.30	45.45	0.35	0.72	2.77	0.60	1.96	12.22	73.95
1981-82	8.51	1.29	46.61	0.36	0.71	2.77	0.60	2.04	12.59	75.47
1982-83	8.47	1.20	46.56	0.37	0.68	2.75	0.59	2.07	12.83	75.52
1983-84	8.19	1.13	44.73	0.39	0.66	2.76	0.57	2.14	12.89	73.46
1984-85	8.07	1.13	44.21	0.39	0.70	2.77	0.54	2.19	13.09	73.09
1985-86	8.22	1.11	44.48	0.40	0.69	2.77	0.54	2.21	13.32	73.74
1986-87	8.48	0.91	44.10	0.40	0.58	2.77	0.52	2.29	13.59	73.64
1987-88	8.44	0.93	43.95	0.41	0.50	2.83	0.51	2.38	13.97	73.92
1988-89	8.68	0.96	43.83	0.39	0.69	2.86	0.51	2.34	14.29	74.53
1989-90	8.76	0.99	44.57	0.40	0.68	2.91	0.52	2.39	14.60	75.82
1990-91	8.91	1.00	44.81	0.40	0.73	3.00	0.53	2.54	14.85	76.77
1991-92	9.12	1.07	45.66	0.40	0.78	2.96	0.54	2.66	15.27	78.46

Source: Economic Survey, Government of India.

Employment in the Private Sector—Lakh Persons

Post-Reform Period

Year	Agriculture Hunting etc.	Mining and Quarrying	Manufac turing	Electricity Gas and Water	Constr uction	Wholesale and retail trade	Transport storage and communi-cation	Finance Insurance and real estate	Community social & personal services	Total
1992-93	9.16	0.96	45.45	0.38	0.73	3.01	0.55	2.77	15.50	78.51
1993-94	8.83	1.01	46.30	0.40	0.51	3.02	0.56	2.82	15.85	79.3
1994-95	8.94	1.03	47.06	0.40	0.53	3.08	0.58	2.93	16.03	80.59
1995-96	9.19	1.07	50.49	0.42	0.53	3.17	0.60	3.06	16.58	85.12
1996-97	9.12	0.92	52.39	0.41	0.54	3.17	0.63	3.22	16.44	86.86
1997-98	9.04	0.91	52.33	0.42	0.74	3.21	0.65	3.41	16.77	87.48
1998-99	8.71	0.87	51.78	0.41	0.71	3.23	0.69	3.58	17.00	86.98
1999-00	9.04	0.81	50.85	0.41	0.57	3.30	0.70	3.58	17.23	86.45

Source: Economic Survey, Government of India.

6

Impact of Economic Reforms on Rural Women Labour-An Empirical Evidence

Dr. Sailabala Debi, Prof. P.R. Panchamukhi

Introduction

Women play a crucial role in all societies. However, their low socio-economic status in an historical perspective is largely based on the myth that they are inferior agents of production. Much of the labour contributed by them specially in the domestic chores and outside, though highly productive, is not recognized in its proper perspective. Their work is equally essential for the smooth functioning of the economy, whether it is at the community, firm/farm or at the household level.

In India, women constitute nearly 50 per cent of the total population and they play a significant role both as housewives and also as workers, but hardly any attention has been paid to assess their contribution to the economy. Women's involvement in the process of economic development in the country has remained comparatively a neglected area. Thus, women's economic role in a static framework as well as dynamic setting remains unrecognized.

The UN report prepared at the time of women's decade rightly conducted that when women and girls constituted, half of the world's population, did two thirds of the worlds work hours, yet received only one tenth of the worlds property.

The World Women Conference at Nairobi in 1985 asserted that if the domestic work of women is paid and if it is estimated in terms of GNP, it would account for half of the National income. The consensus view of this conference was for economic independence of women.

There is a general notion that productivity of women is always less than that of their male counterparts. In view of this notion there exists a wage differential between male and female particularly in the unorganised or informal sector of our economy. But the contributions made by women to these sectors (here we consider agricultural sector) are very significant. They contribute about three-fourth of the labour required for agricultural operations. Their involvement in agricultural operations is, besides their domestic obligations. Most of the contributions made by women to this sector also go unaccounted for as they are not directly paid for the same.

The Economic reform measures were in operation in almost all the sectors of our economy since June 1991. It has emphasized the role of the market economy. *The dominance of market process generally undervalues everything which is not directly calculable in those terms.* Household work and the works in the unorganized sectors of our economy are the prime examples, in which particularly women play a significant role. The market dominance of the economy makes the labour market more competitive. Access to a job depends not only on education and skill formation but also the sheer availability of such jobs in a diversified and growing economy. An economy, which is emphasizing cheap, and unorganized labour as the main attraction for export oriented production or multinational investment, is hardly likely to generate many such jobs.

In a predominantly agrarian economy like India, a sustainable increase in agricultural production cannot be achieved by unsustainable resource use. Peasant farming system in which women are an integral part, combine elements of traditional farming system with new technologies. The natural resource base, which is closely linked to the livelihood and well being of the rural households, seems to be fast getting weakened during the recent years. As a result of economic reform, the control over these resources is getting shifted from local to national and international agencies. The agricultural sector (subsistence economy as a whole) can no longer be operate resource-intensive technology. Hence this sector is coming under increasing pressure from the market-led forces. The type of technology, the market system would use, is likely to affect adversely the women-participation in this sector.

In this background, the following issues deserve a special attention in the context of different regions of the Indian economy.

1. What are the areas in agricultural operations where women are mostly engaged in?
2. Has the technological change as a result of economic reform adversely affected the employment of women labour?

The present study makes an attempt to address the aforesaid issues in three different regions of varying levels of development in the state of Karnataka. The districts covered under the study are Dharwad (medium developed district), Mangalore/Dakshina Kannada (developed district) and Gulbarga (less developed district).

Studies Done

Even though researchers have not paid adequate attention to these issues, several studies on women's contribution to activities at the domestic front as well as outside home have come up in favour of women's contributions to the hosuehold income. Some of the important studies are presented here.

Acharya and Bennett (1963), Reddy (1981), Jain and Chand, (1982), Ashok Mitra (1981:52), Sisodia (1985), Marothia and Sharma (1985), Dhongade et al (1985), Guleria and Agnihotri (1985), Dutta and Sharma (1985), Mungial et al (1985), Suryawanshi and Kapase (1985), Joshi and Alshi (1985), Bhati and Singh (1987), Unni (1992), Agrawal (1994), Ghosh (1994), Hirway and Roy (1999), Subrahmanyam (1999), Rajkishor et al (1999), Despande (1994), Bhatt (1992), Ranadev (1994) and many others focused on various aspects of women labour and different dimensions of the economic reforms and its impact on women labour in general at the macro level. *But micro level studies are yet to be undertaken to examine the real impact of reforms on the most important sector of our economy i.e. agricultural sector and the women labour therein.*

Since a decade has elapsed after the reform is initiated (1991, June), it is now high time to examine its impact in different sectors of the economy. *The present study attempts to examine the (i) impact of reform on the employment of women in the agricultural sector.*

Objectives of the Study

The specific objectives of the study are stated below:

1. To identity the works done by women in agricultural operations as well as on the domestic chores in rural area;
2. To examine the implications of economic reforms on the employment pattern of women in various agricultural operations.

Hypothesis

1. The reform process is likely to affect adversely the female participation in the agricultural sector (due to technological change).

Coverage of the Study

The study is conducted for the *State of Karnataka,* a medium developed state covering three districts in it. *The logic of including three districts is* (i) Inter district analysis could be made to get a clear idea about the role of women in agricultural operations and their contribution in the context of differential development status; (ii) There is an implicit hypothesis that the participation of women is inversely related to the economic status of the family. In order to test this hypothesis in the wider context i.e. at the district and at the state level, we have included the three categories of districts.

Data Base and Sampling Design

The study concentrated on primary data collected through field survey. All the required information was collected through a well-structured questionnaire designed for the purpose.

The sample selected for the study was based on *multi-stage stratified random sampling method.* The first stage of sampling was the state i.e. Karnataka, the second stage of sampling procedure was the districts from the state. i.e. one developed (Mangalore), one medium developed (Dharwad) and one less developed (Gulbarga), thus comes to 3 districts. The third stage was blocks from each of the districts i.e. three blocks (3 blocks). In the fourth stage we selected two villages from each block. The villages again be divided as irrigated and un-irrigated i.e. two villages from each block which come to six villages in the state. A list of all households of the selected villages was prepared as per the size of the holding of their farms i.e. marginal, small and large which were the strata for drawing the sample. Depending on the size of the total population (household here) and keeping in view, the cost and time constraint, the desired sample was drawn. We selected randomly 300 households from each village (100 households from each farm size i.e. marginal, small and large farmers). Thus a total of 1800 households was selected for the final household survey. The details of sampling breakup are given in Table 1 and 2.

Analytical Framework

The official statistics provided for the participation rate of women do not consider all the works performed by women at home, and outside home as most of these works are invisible and hence unpaid. In this study we took into consideration all the activities done by women at home and outside the home. Taking into consideration all the works done by women, we estimated their hours of work before the economic reforms and after the economic reforms. Here we have considered the working age group of 15-59 years as taken by Census and other official statistics.

Organisation of the Paper

The paper is divided into *four sections.* The *second section* provides all the relevant information relating to the participation of females according to the socio-economic status of the households. The impact of economic reforms on the females is discussed in the third section. The *last section* summarizes the main findings along with the concluding observations.

Participation of Females

The participation of females in the present study is estimated in different activities like agriculture, animal husbandry, domestic activities, gathering and other types of activities like manufacturing etc. But the emphasis is laid here on agriculture (both traditional and HYV paddy in different farm sizes (marginal, small and large farmers).

Table 1. Sampling Design

Districts	*Blocks*	*Type of village*	*Name of village*	*No. of schedule*			
				Marginal	*Small*	*Large*	*Total*
Dakishna Karnataka	Belatangadi	Irrigated	Ujare	100	100	100	300
(Developed)	(Developed)	Non irrigated	Laila	100	100	100	300
Dharwad	Navalgund	Irrigated	Morab & Tirlapur	100	100	100	300
(Med. Developed)	(Med. Developed)	Non irrigated	Annigeri	100	100	100	300
Gulbarga	Afzalpur	Irrigated	Gabbur B	100	100	100	300
(Less Developed)	(Less Developed)-	Non irrigated	Deval Ganagapur	100	100	100	300
Grand Total				600	600	600	1800

Table 2. Labour Rose Pattern in Different Types of Work (Land Holding Size)

	Before SAP								
	Marginal			*Small*			*Large*		
Agriculture	*Female*	*Male*	*Total*	*Female*	*Male*	*Total*	*Female*	*Male*	*Total*
Dharwad									
Land Prep.	16.05	26.46	21.97	24.44	28.20	26.28	29.70	28.46	29.05
Sowing	39.62	12.54	24.20	49.78	8.48	29.58	41.65	4.51	22.15
Inter Cultiv	16.74	38.14	28.93	8.72	35.13	21.63	12.02	42.57	28.06
Harvesting	27.59	22.86	24.90	17.06	28.19	22.50	16.63	24.45	20.74
Total	100.00	100.00	100.00	100.00	100.00	100.00	100.00	100.00	100.00
	After SAP								
Land Pre.	14.42	19.31	17.10	25.17	18.39	22.42	27.55	20.96	24.54
Sowing	44.32	13.11	27.20	52.24	9.43	34.87	44.15	6.67	27.02
Inter Cultiv	11.63	44.11	29.45	4.14	42.41	19.66	9.82	48.26	27.39
Harvesting	29.63	23.47	26.25	18.45	29.77	23.04	18.48	24.11	21.05
Total	**100.00**	**100.00**	**100.00**	**100.00**	**100.00**	**100.00**	**100.00**	**100.00**	**100.00**

(Cont...)

Agriculture	*Marginal*			*Small*			*Large*		
	Female	*Male*	*Total*	*Female*	*Male*	*Total*	*Female*	*Male*	*Total*
				Before SAP					
Mangalore									
Land Prep.	11.05	32.27	21.24	23.47	46.73	34.51	40.53	39.43	40.02
Sowing	37.21	3.43	20.99	38.00	2.46	21.13	8.02	2.07	5.28
Inter Cultiv.	4.97	27.69	15.89	4.55	18.84	11.33	4.05	20.01	11.40
Harvesting	46.77	36.61	41.88	33.98	31.97	33.03	47.40	38.50	43.30
Total	100.00	100.00	100.00	100.00	100.00	100.00	100.00	100.00	100.00
				After SAP					
Land Prep	9.10	24.75	16.49	17.90	28.34	22.97	34.16	34.37	34.26
Sowing	39.66	4.76	23.18	32.43	3.30	18.29	12.68	2.64	7.69
Inter Cultiv.	3.73	32.42	17.28	4.41	23.35	13.60	4.77	22.51	13.59
Harvesting	47.51	38.07	43.05	45.26	45.01	45.14	48.38	40.48	44.46
Total	**100.00**	**100.00**	**100.00**	**100.00**	**100.00**	**100.00**	**100.00**	**100.00**	**100.00**

(Cont...)

	Before SAP								
	Marginal			*Small*			*Large*		
Agriculture	*Female*	*Male*	*Total*	*Female*	*Male*	*Total*	*Female*	*Male*	*Total*
Gulbarga									
Land Prep.	4.96	21.78	14.09	1.79	19.81	10.99	0.90	28.85	13.73
Sowing	37.58	9.63	22.41	45.65	9.65	27.28	47.69	9.38	30.10
Inter Cultiv.	15.45	40.02	28.79	10.79	36.52	23.92	13.66	33.14	22.60
Harvesting	42.01	28.57	34.71	41.76	34.01	37.81	37.75	28.63	33.57
Total	100.00	100.00	100.00	100.00	100.00	100.00	100.00	100.00	100.00
	After SAP								
Land Prep	5.18	18.23	11.75	1.65	14.31	7.95	0.73	20.89	9.75
Sowing	36.76	9.30	22.93	44.14	10.13	27.22	48.91	9.35	31.22
Inter Cultiv.	21.85	42.29	32.15	16.75	41.36	28.99	14.01	39.40	25.36
Harvesting	36.21	30.19	33.18	37.46	34.20	35.84	36.36	30.35	33.67
Total	**100.00**	**100.00**	**100.00**	**100.00**	**100.00**	**100.00**	**100.00**	**100.00**	**100.00**

In our study the works done by women in a household are divided as; agriculture, animal husbandry, domestic, manufacturing, gathering, and food processing. The activities in agriculture included in our study are; ploughing, land preparation, levelling, trimming, weeding etc., sowing, transplanting, manuring, carrying manures to the field, spreading the manure, spraying pesticides, irrigation, threshing, winnowing, harvesting, packing, storing, drying the crops etc. Under animal husbandry we included the activities like, herding, feeding, collection of fodder, breeding, milking, cleaning the shed, extraction of ghee etc. The domestic works included cooking, serving, cleaning utensils, washing clothes, fetching water, caring children and old persons, teaching children etc. The works under gathering are; forest materials collection (honey, edible oil fruits, and mushrooms), fuel collection, etc. The manufacturing works included weaving, rope making, pottery, sewing etc. The works of food processing included the works like husking grains, dying, winnowing roasting, grinding oil processing, food preservation etc...

Across the districts, it was found that the participation of females varies with the development status of the districts. In other words, the higher the development status of a district, the higher is the participation of females (Table 3).

Table 3. Work Participation by Gender in Three Districts

Districts	*Traditional Crop*		*HYV Crop*	
	Male	*Female*	*Male*	*Female*
Dharwad	47.99	55.17	44.83	52.01
Mangalore	46.47	58.19	41.81	53.53
Gulbarga	45.88	54.12	48.54	51.46

It is found that the female work participation rate is much higher than that of their male counterparts in case of traditional paddy cultivation and it declined substantially in HYV paddy. It is also found that there is a constant decline in female labour when it has shifted from traditional to HYV paddy cultivation. Across the districts, similar pattern was found. The decline in female labour was not only due to the adoption of HYV crops but mostly due to the reason that most of the operations which were traditionally done by women are now done by machines. The consequence was the displacement of female labour. The above chart supports the explanations already provided.

In this context, we may raise the questions, viz; *what actually affects the participation of female labour in agricultural activities? Is it due to the mechanization of agriculture as a result of economic reforms? Or has their participation been under estimated?* These are some of the issues we discuss in the following section.

Impact of Economic Reforms on Work-participation by Gender for Different Activities

We estimated different activities done by women in a day. A female member does different activities starting from the kitchen to the agricultural field. The activity status of females for all the districts is summarized in Table 4.

While estimating the time allocation pattern of females and males in the periods before and after reforms, it was found that female's work participation declined after reforms. The working hours per day by females were about 12 hours as against eight hours for male and this was reduced after reforms. This supports the hypothesis that *'reform affects employment of women adversely'*. While the time allocation to different agricultural operations before and after reforms was examined, it was found that there was a substantial decline (about 67 per cent) in working hours by women after reforms while this was about 36 per cent for male. This implies that economic reforms have affected severely

Table 4. Labour Use Pattern in Different Type of Agricultural Works (hours/day)

Types of work	*Before reforms*		*After reforms*	
	Female	*Male*	*Female*	*Male*
Land Preparation	0.08	3.95	0.01	2.11
Sowing	2.12	0.12	2.08	0.02
Inter cultivation	0.71	1.87	0.03	1.51
Harvesting	2.01	1.01	0.83	1.46
Total	**4.92**	**6.95**	**2.95**	**5.10**

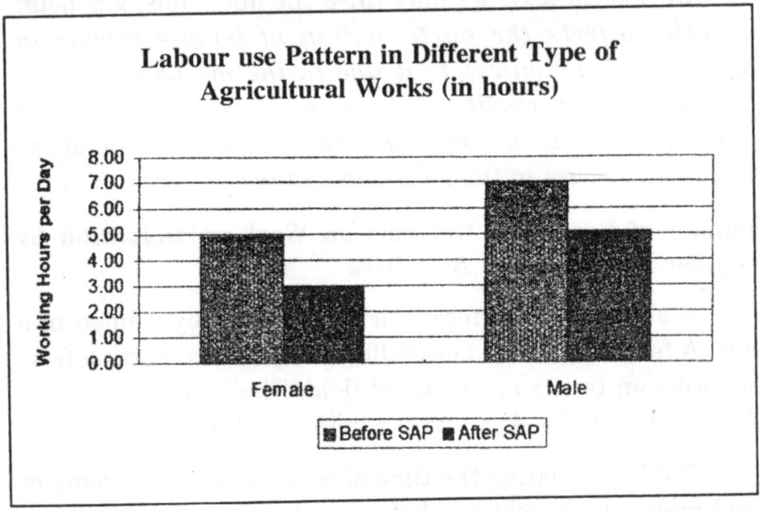

the employment of women. The time allocated by women is examined before economic reforms and after reforms. It is found that except marginal farmer households, female spend less time in all the activities after the reforms. Again in the large farming households, the females devote more time in domestic activities after the reforms have been introduced. During the day women spend more time in cooking, tending animals, gathering forest materials, fuels and in agriculture. Further more they also take care of children, old and sick persons at home which normally men do not do.

The jobs traditionally done by women in the region were harvesting, threshing, showing and weeding, winnowing and other miscellaneous works accounted for more than 50 per cent of the agricultural activities in 1990-91 (Before reforms) and it declined to about 25 per cent in 1999-2000 (after reforms). The animal-based tasks are done by females. They spend about 14% of their time in a day for cake making, ghee preparation, milking, removing cow dung, feeding animals etc. done by women. They spent 49 per cent of the total time for domestic activities and this time increases with increase in farm size. Women spend more time in domestic activities when size holding becomes larger and larger. Within the agricultural operations, it is found that women mostly perform the activities like sowing, harvesting and the works like land preparation and other activities like irrigation, spraying pesticides, manuring, etc. are mostly done by man. It is observed that after the reforms, the women's activities of agricultural operations in harvesting have reduced substantially because of mechanization in certain operations. The working hours of females before reforms were 4.92 hours per day and declined to 2.95 hours per day after reforms showing about 67 per cent decline in their time. The time allocated by men also has declined after reforms. But this decline is about 36 per cent. *It indicates that reform process has severely affected our rural women's employment in the field of agricultural activities.* This supports our hypothesis that 'Reform has adversely affected female employment'.

Conclusion, Policy Implication and Suggestions

Female participation in general is much higher than participation of their male counterparts. The introduction of HYV paddy affects women's participation significantly. Their participations is reduced when there is a shift from traditional to HYV paddy. Not only this, but their participation also declined after the initiation of reform process. In agricultural operations, their working hours declined significantly after the reforms largely due to technological change.

In spite of substantial contribution of our women to the economy, our official statisticians do not accurately measure the works performed by women and also women in unorganised sector are not reported as workers. Hence, their contributions are not included in GDP. This is largely due to the problem of identifying and defining the work of women with a proper perspective. Hence, the concept of their work needs to be classified and defined properly in economic terms adopting strict economic methodology. The methodology for estimation of their time allocation needs to be properly understood by the policy makers and planners.

It is a fact that efforts are made by the Government to reduce gender inequality, to estimate their work properly, but it is not yet done in a proper manner with seriousness. The constraints of the large labour force are not properly understood to be included in the policy and are still continuing.

Occupational diversification among rural women is till lacking. The bulk of our rural women are still working in the primary sector. It is also observed that within the primary sector, they concentrate on the agricultural sector. This is mainly because of the reason that they work in this sector as unpaid family workers. Further more, when the male workers change their occupation form primary to other sector, the female workers have no other option but to look after the family activities. Hence, due to low occupational diversification of women workers in rural areas, they are mostly unpaid or under paid.

The reform process aimed at replacing the unskilled/ incompetent and uneducated labourer by skilled/highly educated and competent labourers. The traditional and outdated technology is replaced by modern and sophisticated technology. In this background, whatever income generating or employment programmes are undertaken, it should give priority to such technology, which are adaptable to women. Most of the activities done by females (grain processing, weaving, oil processing, and many such activities) are now done by machines. *Introduction of new technology should try to involve women directly and make sure that female labour is not displaced in the process of technological change. Above all the access to ownership of resources by women like land and credit should be given high priority.*

Obviously, agriculture is seasonal in nature and in the slack period more male surplus labour is available than female surplus labour throughout the year, because women are already over employed in their domestic activities and other activities and have little or extra time. Keeping this in view, employment policies should emphasize increase in the efficiency and productivity of time spent by women rather than just providing employment through some rural development/public works programmes. Hence, the schemes designed for women, should be designed with a lot of flexibility to allow our women folk to adjust themselves to the current situation. It should be situation-specific and target-oriented, so that they should not be just victims to any reform or any changed circumstances.

References

1. Agarwal, Bina (1984) "Rural Women and HYV Rice Technology", *Economic and Political Weekly,* Vol. XIX, Issue, March, P-A-39.
2. Acharya, M. and Bennett, L (1983) "Women and the Subsistence Sector: Economic Participation and Household Decision-making in Nepal", World Bank Staff Working Paper, No. 526, World Bank, Washington, D.C. USA.
3. Afshar, H and C, Dennis (eds.) (1992) "Women and Adjustment Policies in the Third World", Mac Millan, London.

4. Bhati, J.P. and Singh, D.V. (1987) "Women's Contribution to Agricultural Economy in Hill Regions of North West India", Economic and Political Weekly, Volume-XXII, issue-17, April 30, p-ws-7.
5. Baud, I and Smyth, I (Eds.) (1996) "Searching for Security: Women's Responses to Economic Transformations", London and New York, Routledge.
6. Despande, S. and L.K. Despande (1992) "New Economic Policy and Female Employment", EPW. Oct, 10.
7. Dhongade, M.P. *et al* (1985) "Participation of Women Labour in Agriculture in Maharastra", *Indian Journal of Agricultural Economics,* Vol. XL, No. 3, July-Sept, pp. 235-239.
8. Dutta, L.N. and Sharma, N (1985) "Contribution of Female Labour in Agriculture: A Case Study of Ranchi District of Bihar", *IJAE,* Vol. XL, No. 3.
9. Ghosh, Jayati (1994) "Gender Concerns in Macro Economic Policy", *Economic and Political Weekly,* April, 30.
10. Guleria, A.S. and Agnihotri, B. (1985) "Contribution of Female Workers in the Farm Sector", *Indian Journal of Agricultural Economics,* Vol. XL, No. 3. July-Sept. p. 271.
11. Hirway, I and Roy, A (1999) "Women in Rural Economy: The Case of India", *Indian Journal of Agricultural Economics,* Vol. 54, No. 3, July-Sept, pp. 251-271.
12. Jain, Devaki, and Chand Malini (1982) "Report on a Time Allocation Study, its Methodological Implications" (New Delhi, Institute of Social Studies).
13. Joshi, C.K. and Alshi, M.R. (1985) "Impact of HYV on Employment Potential of Female Labour—A Study in Akola District (Maharashtra)", *Indian Journal of Agricultural Economics,* Vol. XL, No. 3. July-Sept. pp. 230-234.
14. Joy, R. Ranadev (1994) Gender Implications of Adjustment Policy Programme in India, Significance of the Households, EPW, Vol. XXIX, No. 18, April 30, pp. ws-12-18.
15. Kumud, S. (1994) Gender, Environment and Structural Adjustment, *Economic and Political Weekly,* Vol. XXIX, No. 18, pp. ws-5-ws 11.
16. Marothia, D.K. and Sharma, S.K. (1985), "Female Labour Participation in Rice Farming System of Chhatisgarh Region",

Indian Journal of Agricultural Economics, Vol. XL, No. 3, July-Sept. pp. 235-239.

17. Mungial, S. *et al.* (1985), "Womens Econom'c Contribution in Farm Household in Haryana", IJAE, Vol. XL, No. 3.

18. Mitra, Ashok (1979) "The Status of Women: Literacy and Employment", (New Delhi, Allied).

19. "Participation of Women in Socio-Economic Development: Indicators as Tools of Development Planning: The Case of India", in Women and Development, (Paris, UNESCO). 1981.

20. Raj Kishore *et al.* (1999) "Role of Rural Women in Decision Making Process in Agriculture in District Sitapur (Uttar Pradesh)", *Indian Journal of Agricultural Economics,* Vol. 54, No. 3, July-Sept, pp. 282-286.

21. Reddy, K.N. (1981) "Appropriate Technology for Rural Development" in the Proceedings of National Workshop on "Appropriate Technology for Health Care", New Delhi, Indian Council of Medical Research (April 23-26, 1981).

22. Sisodia, J.S. (1985) "Role of Farm Women in Agriculture: A Study of Chambal Area of MP", *Indian Journal of Agricultural Economics,* Vol. XL, No. 3, July-Sept, pp. 223-230.

23. Subramanyam, S. (1999) "Female Labour Absorption in Andhra Pradesh Agriculture", Indian Journal of Agricultural Economics, Vol. 54, No. 3, July-Sept, pp. 272-281.

24. Suryawanshi, S.P. and Kapase (1985) "Impact of Ghod Irrigation Project on Employment of Female Agricultural Labour", Indian Agricultural Economics, Vol. XL, No. 3, July-Sept. pp. 240-244.

25. Unni, Jeemol, (1992) Women's Participation in Indian Agriculture, Oxford & IBH Publishing Co., Pvt. Ltd., New Delhi.

7

Enhancing Labour Productivity Through Policy Interventions

Dr. K.S.S. Uduman Mohideen, R.K. Haroon

The proportion of population engaged in productive work, the nature of employment and remuneration received by the working population are important determinants of human development. Lack of adequate opportunity for gainful employment results in lowering of income level, which pushes people to a condition of poverty. Thus there is a close relationship between employment and income and employment and poverty. Economic development is invariably associated with change in income (GDP) and Employment. A characteristic feature of the developing economy is a declining trend in the share of primary sector in GDP. In the process of diversification of the economy, one would expect a shift in the share of workers from primary to secondary and tertiary sectors. The problem of poverty is directly related to the existence of unemployment and under-employment, and low productive employment. Therefore, the redistribution of income and consumption in favour of the poor basically meant expanding employment opportunities to the growing labour force. There are very few methods of distributing income as effective as offering employment. The prevalence of poverty in rural areas is widespread, mainly due to the low productivity of workers in agricultural sector and seasonal nature of employment. In order to get a proper understanding of the interplay of force, an attempt is made in this paper to analyse the employment situation, labour productivity, income, period of employment, poverty level and related issues in India.

Employment Situation in India

An important objective of development planning in India is to increase employment opportunities not only to clear the backlog of the unemployment but also to add to the new additions to the labour force. The increasing diversification of the economy together with acceleration in economic growth has resulted in structural changes in the nature of the job market. The various rounds of survey conducted by the NSSO reveal that the average annual growth rate of overall employment was 2.73 per cent per annum in the period from 1972-73 to 1977-78 but declined to 1.54 per cent per annum during 1983 to 1987-88. However, the growth rate of employment increased to 2.43 per cent per annum over 1987-88 to 1993-94. As per the 55th round (1999-2000) of the Survey on Employment conducted by the NSSO, overall, employment grew by about 1 per cent per annum during 1993-94—1999-2000. Employment in absolute numbers has risen from 303 million in 1983 to 374 million in 1994 (2.04%) and to 397 million in 2000(0.98%), as given in Table 1.

The sector-wise growth of employment as shown in Table 2 indicates that the employment growth rate decelerated from 1983-1994 to 1994-2000, and it was primarily due to slower growth in agricultural sector employment, with the absolute number of persons employed in agricultural sector showing a decline for the first time. Employment in sectors like trade, construction, and financial services, transport, storage, and communication has grown faster than the annual national average. This reflects the structural changes in product markets in the post-reforms period.

Table 1. Rate of Growth of Population, Labour Force and Employment

Period	*Rate of growth of population (% per annum)*	*Rate of growth of labour force (UPSS)* (% per annum)*	*Rate of growth of employment UPSS (% per annum)*
1972-73 to 1997-98	2.27	2.94	2.73
1977-78 to 1983	2.19	2.04	2.17
1983 to 1987-88	2.14	1.74	1.54
1987-88 to 1993-94	2.10	2.29	2.43
1993-94 to 1999-2000	1.93	1.03	0.98

UPSS— Usual principal and subsidiary status.

Source: Economic Survey 2001-02, GOI.

Table 2. Growth of Employment by Sectors (UPSS) in Per cent

Industry	*Annual growth rate*	
	1983-94	*1994-2000*
Agriculture	1.51	-0.34
Mining and quarrying	4.16	-2.85
Manufacturing	2.14	2.05
Electricity, gas and water	4.50	-0.88
Construction	5.32	7.09
Trade	3.57	5.04
Transport, storage and Communication	3.24	6.04
Financial Service	7.18	6.20
Community Social and Personal Services	2.90	0.55
Total	**2.04**	**0.98**

Source: Planning Commission, Government of India.

Labour Productivity

Productivity of Labour is measured by Gross Value Added (GVA) can be arrived by dividing Gross Domestic Products (GDP) by total number of workers. In the analysis the GDP at Constant price (1993-94 New Series) and Workers on Usual Principal Subsidiary Status are taken for GVA measurement. The just released quick estimates of GDP for 1999-2000 make it possible to assess the changes between 1993-94 and 1999-2000 in gross value added per (usual status) worker at constant 1993-94 prices by broad industry division. The estimates of the number of workers, gross value added (GVA) at 1993-94 prices and of GVA per worker as a measure of productivity per worker for 1983, 1993-94 and 1999-2000, by industry division-wise details are presented in Annexure I.

Taking the economy as a whole, the GVA per worker has grown, in real terms, from Rs. 15581 in 1983 to Rs. 29017 in 1999-2000 i.e. at a compound annual rate of over 5.30% per annum during 1993-2000 and 3.73% per annum during 1983-2000. In agriculture and allied sector, which still employs 60 per cent of the workforce, has grown at a little over 2.94 per cent per annum during 1993-2000 and 1.95 per cent during 1983-2000. GVA in agriculture in real terms has increased from Rs. 8606/- in 1983 to Rs. 12222/ in 1999-2000 at constant prices. Apart from agriculture, three largest employing sectors are trade, hotel and restaurant, (5.20 crores) manufacturing (4.8 crores) and Community and social service (3.32 crores). In these three sectors, average labour productivity measured by GVA per worker has grown at an annual rate of 2.43,4.11 and 4.24 per cent respectively. Among all, the construction sector which employing 1.76 crores of workers, however, the GVA per worker has virtually stagnated and even growth rate is on negative trend. In two other infrastructure sectors (Electricity, Gas, and Water) and Finance, Insurance and Business service, labour productivity has grown at, respectively, 4.78 and 2.14 per cent per annum.

Overall, with the sole exception of the construction sector, labour productivity has grown in the long run (1983-2000), in real terms close to over 3.73 per cent per annum in all the sectors of the economy. In the economy as a whole and in two of the three largest employing sectors outside agriculture, (manufacturing and community and social service) real gross value added per worker has grown at over 6 per cent per annum over the six years from 1993-94 to 1999-2000.

Labour Productivity in Tamil Nadu

The NSDP for Tamil Nadu stood at Rs. 57482 crores in 1993-94. The share of primary, secondary and tertiary sectors in NSDP was 26.6 per cent, 29.9 per cent and 43.5 per cent, respectively. The aggregate employment in the State for the year 1993-94 stood at 285.60 lakhs. The share of primary, secondary and tertiary sectors in the aggregate employment was 54.1 per cent, 21.8 per cent and 24.1 per cent, respectively. The dissimilar distribution of income and employment had naturally led to high inequitous average output per worker among the sectors. More than half of the working population (primary sector) in the State had contributed only a little over one fourth to the NSDP. Tertiary sector employed less than one fourth of the working population but its contribution to the NSDP was 43.5 per cent. The secondary sector, which accounts for about 22 per cent of the total employment, contributed nearly 30 per cent to the NSDP.

The average output generated per worker during 1993-94 stood at Rs. 20119/-. The per worker contribution in the agricultural and allied sector has been less than half (Rs. 9024/-) of the average per worker contribution at the aggregate level. On the other hand, the average output per worker in the manufacturing sector (Rs. 29885) was higher by 49 per cent and that of tertiary sector (except community and social works) (Rs. 50590) by more than cent per cent and community and social work service (Rs. 17396) less by 14%.

The average output generated per worker during 1999-2000 stood at Rs. 29977/-. The per worker contribution in the agricultural and allied sector has been one third (Rs. 10368/-) of the average per worker contribution at the aggregate level. On the other hand, the average output per worker in the manufacturing sector (Rs. 39533) was higher by 32 per cent and that of construction sector (Rs. 38753/) by 29 per cent. The estimates of the number of workers, gross value added (GVA) at 1993-94 prices and of GVA per worker as a measures of productivity per worker for 1993-94 and 1999-2000, by industry division details for Tamil Nadu are presented in Annexure II.

Wage Income, Person Day Worked, and Relationship

Table 3 below presents, the average person-days of wage employment in agriculture and non-agricultural work. For rural India the overall duration of agricultural wage employment is 137 days per annum but it is substantially lower in Tamilnadu slightly below Kerala. The average for AP, and Karnataka was 183 and 146 respectively. The average rural agricultural employment is highest in North East region, followed by AP. Agricultural employment opportunities are relatively higher in AP and Karnataka in South India.

The average non-agricultural employment for rural India is 152 days per annum. The non agricultural employment days are high as 206 days in North East region followed by Tamilnadu (188). The overall average daily wage rate for agricultural and non agricultural work constituted Rs. 21 and 28 respectively. The daily agricultural wage rate was high in Harayana (Rs. 42), Kerala (Rs. 41), lower in Karnataka (Rs. 17/Rs. 23) and was highest in Kerala (Rs. 41/Rs. 40).

The average annual income per wage worker from agricultural and non-agricultural work for rural India work out to Rs. 2848 and Rs. 4313 respectively.

Table 3. Agricultural and Non-Agricultural Wage Employment and Wage Per Adult wage Earners (Aged 15+) in South India During 90's

Item	*AP*	*Karnataka*	*Kerala*	*Tamilnadu*	*All India*
Avg.annual wage income per household (Rs.)					
Agriculture	9900	5892	9461	7745	6341
Non agriculture	9287	8489	11335	14796	7844
Avg. annual wage income per earner (Rs)					
Agriculture	4208	2530	5295	2725	2848
Non agriculture	4221	4049	5828	5898	4313
Total	**4405**	**2923**	**6397**	**4059**	**3768**
Avg. person days					
Agriculture	183	146	130	119	137
Non agriculture	169	174	146	188	152
Total	188.3	156.2	148.7	151.2	159.8
Avg. Wage per day (Rs.)					
Agriculture	23	17	41	23	21
Non agriculture	25	23	40	31	28
Total	**23**	**19**	**43**	**27**	**24**

Source: India Human Development Report 2000.

This estimate is computed by multiplying actual number of wage-employment-days and actual wages received by all those who worked for wages during the previous year. The total worker income from agricultural wage was highest in Kerala (Rs. 5295) per annum, followed by AP with Rs. 4208 and TN with Rs. 2725. The non-agricultural income per wage worker is Rs. 4313 for rural India and is highest in Tamilnadu (Rs. 5898) in Southern states followed by Kerala (Rs. 5828) and lower in Karnataka (Rs. 4049) and AP (Rs. 4221).

Suggestions for Enhancing the Labour Productivity

Financial capital alone is not enough and human capital is an essential element. While capital and labour are often complementary inputs, these complementarities are best implemented in the presence of human capital. A manifestation of this can be seen in the growth of labour productivity in economics. The increase in labour productivity is therefore an important ingredient in the current emphasis on growth through globalization.

A simple measure of labour productivity is output per worker. This can be increased in three different ways:

1. Labour can become more skilled over times, embodying greater amount of human capital.
2. New capacity can come up using better techniques that increase the quality of output produced from the same amount of input, including labour.
3. New techniques that substitute capital for labour, can also increase output per worker.

While the first two are usually good for labour, the third may increase unemployment or at the very least, reduce the growth of employment.

The enhancement of productivity may be improved through

- Wage regulation/improvement-Minimum wage implementation.
- Productivity improvement in production process-Employment Generation.
- Income generation through export promotion.
- Diversification.

Better Implementation of Minimum Wages in Agriculture

Agricultural workers have been getting very low wages except in Punjab and Kerala. Measures should be taken to raise the wages of farm workers. Unless this is done, it is impossible to raise the economic condition of the agricultural workers. Minimum wage legislation alone is not sufficient but steps should be taken to enforce it. In 1999, the

Tamilnadu government revised the minimum wages for agricultural labourers whose number is nearly 20 lakh. Based on Kolappan Committee Report, the Government hiked the wage for ploughing with bullocks from Rs. 55 to Rs. 100 per day. For those without bullocks and all others engaged in harvesting and post-harvesting operations, the wages have been raised from Rs. 32 to Rs. 54. If an operation involves both men and women, the wages should equal, the government stated. When the work is performed on hourly basis, the agricultural labourers are to be paid Rs. 9 per hour. However, the actual wages, prevailing in the state are more or less equal to the wages fixed by the state, making the law redundant. *Peasant Union for agricultural workers* wherever trade unions are organised for agricultural workers, their wages are protected and their exploitation by powerful landlords and moneylenders can be eliminated. Hence, great emphasis should be placed on the formation of unions in unorganized sectors and the Government should help actively the formation of such unions.

Intensive and Extensive Agriculture

Owing to large scale under employment and disguised unemployment in the agricultural sector, there is need to divert the existing agricultural labourers to more productive segments in the agricultural sector itself. The agricultural labourers do not have full time employment because of the seasonal nature. Both intensive cultivation and extension of irrigation are much needed to increase agricultural work. Besides, there will be increase in productivity of labourers, which will also increase the wages of workers.

For improvement in employment generation and to improve productivity, more areas need to be brought under cultivation, for which there is great scope by developing Wasteland available in the country.

Similarly Saline and Alkaline land should be treated properly and put into use.

As the productivity of dry land is very low, there is need for proper utilisation of technology and also through proper planning crop-rotation, multiple-cropping, and inter-cropping; the cropping intensity may be improved, which will increase the crop and output, land productivity, farm income and above all, the labour productivity.

Crop Planning

Promotion of diversified growth is an important strategy for raising the growth rate and expanding of employment opportunities in the economy. Requirement of labour for the crops depends on factors like variety, technology followed, duration of crops, method and mode of irrigation, use of implements and machinery. Use of high yielding variety to local variety will achieve more production and more income, apart from higher employment generation[1] as could be seen from the following Table-4.

Table 4. Labour Requirement Per ha.(man days)

Crop	*Variety*	
	HYV	Local
Paddy	160	147
Cumbu	181	100

Therefore, High yielding Variety needs to be encouraged so as to improve the productivity of labour and production.

The results of the study conducted by Centre for Agricultural and Rural Development Studies reveal that Well-irrigation is providing more employment and tank irrigation is providing less employment as could be seen from Table 5.

Non-availability of water in time and quantity restricted the tank-irrigated farmers to cultivate more number of crops and intensified use of inputs. Labour intensive and highly commercial crops such as Banana, Turmeric and Sugarcane were cultivated in Canal and Well-irrigated farms where

Table 5. Source-wise Employment Generation

Source	*Days of employment (mandays)*
Canal	240.48
Tank	118.12
Well	339.40
Dry farming	253.03
Overall	240.91

there is assured water supply. In dry farming areas groundnut, cotton, cumbu and fodder cholam are important crops. Demand for labour occurred in this area during sowing and harvesting of crops since agricultural operations would commence at the same time on receipt of the rains. Average mandays per ha for various crops are given below in the Table 6.

Table 6. Average Mandays Per ha for Various Crops

Mandays generated	*Crops*
50-100	Vegetable, Tamarind, Chillies, Fodder crops
100-150	Green gram, Coriander (122), Jasmine (115), Cashew (117)
150-200	Paddy (156), Cholam (155), Cumbu (177), Ragi (189), other cereal crops
200-250	Groundnut (201)
Above 250	Cotton (370)

Labour Intensive Programmes

A variety of labour intensive activities such as land reclamation, soil conservation, land leveling, minor irrigation, watershed planning, horticulture, sericulture, village and farm forestry on degraded and wasteland will not only create immediate employment but will also contribute towards the development of backward regions, protection of the environment and promotion of employment in the subsequent phase. This could be seen from Table 7.

Table 7. Estimated Mandays Generated Per Lakhs of Expenditure

Works	*Labour cost to total cost*	*Monday generated per lakhs of expenditure*
Contour punding	100	3125
Checkdam, percolation ponds and land leveling	60	1875
Modernisation of tank	35	673
Maintenance and repair of tank	40	769
Maintenance and repair of Canal	30	372
Raising of plantation, agro forestry	90	2813

Rural Industries

There is great scope for setting up of village and rural industries which will use the raw materials readily available in the villages, and provide employment for the rural population. Development of Handicarfts, Khadhi and Village Industries offers a potential source for employment generation along with good scope for exports and increase in income and the productivity of labourers, Organising Rural Industry Enterprises as China has done. China has already provided a billion of new jobs in the non-farm sector and they have effective plan to encourage the non-farm sector. India has to learn the Chinese way of imparting dynamics and economics of small-scale rural units.

Export Growth-Labour Productivity

In WTO regime, with the removal of restriction in export of large number of agricultural products, there is substantial scope for export of agricultural products particularly processing of agricultural products of horticulture and sericulture offer good export potential for employment generation.

Skill Development

Many organizations are forced to become cost effective and competitive through various measures including down sizing. This results in loss of employment and reduction in employment opportunity. This calls for separate institutions and training centres, which retain surplus labour to be accommodated in new jobs calling for new skills. In order to improve the productivity to match international standards, an awareness programme should be initiated to educate all employees.

Self employment Programmes can play very important role in the generation of employment for labour.

Privatisation has the benefits of improved efficiency of the industry (by eliminating bureaucratic/political controls), eliminating Monopolies in key sectors like power generation, telecommunications etc. These generate more employment. The ongoing economic reforms exposing Indian industry to international competitions have underlined the need for promoting a certain degree of flexibility in deployment of labour.

Government Interventions

Government legislations, such as Minimum Wage Act, social security legislation and social institutions (see Annexure III) have been in existence in India to protect labour. They have been improving wage and the socio-economic position of the poor and the under privileged sections in the labour markets. (Kannan, Kumar 1998). The Centre and State Governments, over the years developed a wide spectrum of employment programmes. (See the annexures IV and V).

Comprehensive Law

There is a need to enact a comprehensive law which would include provisions regarding social security, labour welfare, health, safety and rehabilitation of the landless agricultural labourers exclusively. In fact, in Annual Report of the Ministry of Labour, GOI, for the year 1999-2000 pointed out that the existing Acts and welfare schemes have not adequately protected the interest of agricultural workers. The Ministry has envisaged alternative strategies such as creating 'Welfare Fund' by enacting yet another 'comprehensive' legislation for agricultural workers. However, not approved or placed in Parliament.

Poverty Alleviation Programmes and Employment

As poverty is the most degrading experience of human existence, Central and State Government have been planning and implementing various poverty-alleviation-programmes which are actually programmes for employment-generation and strengthening the productive capacity of population. These programmes have been launched to create more productive job-opportunities through development of agriculture, irrigation, village and cottage industries and small-scale industries. A number of specially designed poverty alleviation programmes are in operation in rural and urban areas to encourage self and wage employment. (see Annexure III) The performance of the major anti-poverty and employment generating programmes are given below:

Table 8. Physical Performance of Special Employment and Poverty Alleviation Programmes

Programme	*1998-99*	*1999-00*	*2000-01*	*2001-02*
A programmes in Rural Area				
1. JGSY (Manday of Employment Generated)	375.21	268.3	268.83	97.7
2. EAS (Manday of empl. generated)	416.53	278.6	217.49	93.07
3. TRYSEM-Youth trained	0.17			0.32
4. DWCRA-Groups formed	0.05			
5. IAY house constructed	0.83	0.93	1.17	0.40
6. MWS-Well constructed	0.09			
PMRY-Micro enterprise	0.19	0.14	0.04	
-Employment generated	0.29	0.33	0.61	
SJSRY- UWEP mandays generated	6.60	10.14	15.87	3.36

Source: Economic survey-1999-2000 and 2000-01.

Conclusion

- To sum up, in term of labour productivity, except for the construction sector, the GVA per worker has grown significantly in all the sectors with a 5% compound growth rate per annum during 1993-94 to 1999-2000 in the economy as whole.
- The average days of work available to a wage earner are 137 in agriculture and 152 in non-agriculture employment. Employment opportunities in agriculture are high in Andhra Pradesh, and Karnataka and in non-agricultural wage employment in Tamilnadu (with reference to South India).
- Average wage received by wage earner is the highest in Kerala may be due to the great unionism and lowest in Karnataka in South India.
- Both Centre and State Government may intervene in employment opportunity and improve the productivity through their policy measures like, implementation of Labour laws and Acts, through encouraging intensive and extensive cultivation, implementation of programme like Wasteland development, careful implementation of employment generation and poverty alleviation programmes, skill development through training and social measures and suitable credit policy for encouraging the self employment opportunity.

Annexure I

Workers, Gross Domestic Product at 1993-94 Prices, and Labour Productivity-by Industry Division Wise Details-in India

(^*Workers in crores) (GDP increases)*

Industrial Classification	1983			1993-94		
	GDP	*workers*	*GVA*	*GDP*	*workers*	*GVA*
Agriculrural and allied sect	182498	20.72	8806.5	241967	242.46	9979.667
Mining and Quarring	11010	0.18	62556.8	20092	0.27	74414.81
Manufacturing	70306	3.40	20660.0	125493	4.25	29527.76
Electricity, gas and water	8470	0.09	99647.1	18984	1.35	14062.22
Construction	25216	0.68	37191.7	40593	1.17	34754.28
Trade, hotel, restaurant Transport, storage Communication	86013	2.66	32323.6	150500	· 3.51	42865.28
Financing, Insurance etc.,	34391	0.17	202300.0	90084	0.35	255920.5
Community and social service	53838	2.38	22621.0	93632	3.51	266.53
Total	**471742**	**30.276**	**15581.4**	**781345**	**38.66**	**20210.68**

(Cont...)

						(GDP-Rs. in crores)
	1999-2000			Growth rates		
Industrial Classification	*GDP*	*workers*	*GVA*	*1983-93*	*1993-2000*	*1983-2000*
Agriculrural and allied sect	290334	23.756	12221.5	1.26	2.94	1.95
Mining and Quarring	26446	0.227	116502.2	1.75	6.61	3.73
Manufacturing	196763	4.801	40983.75	3.64	4.79	4.11
Electricity, gas and water	28225	0.128	220507.8	-17.78	48.17	4.78
Construction	58728	1.762	33330.31	-0.68	-0.60	-0.64
Trade, hotel, restaurant	252832	5.201	48612.19	2.86	1.81	2.43
Transport, storage Communication						
Financing, Insurance etc.,	146546	0.505	290190.1	2.38	1.81	2.14
Community and social Service	152117	3.32	45818.37	1.65	8.05	4.24
Total	**1151991**	**39.7**	**29017.41**	**2.64**	**5.30**	**3.73**

Annexure II

Workers, Gross Domestic Product at 1993-94 Prices, and Labour Productivity-by Industry Division Wise Details-in Tamil Nadu

		(^Workers in lakhs)			(GDP-Rs. in lakhs)			
			1993-94			*1999-2000*		*Growth rate*
Sl. No.	*Industrial Classification*	*GDP*	*workers*	*GVA*	*GDP*	*workers*	*GVA*	*1993-2000*
1.	Agricultural and allied sector	1384293	153.4	9024.07	1497203	144.4	10368.44	2.00
2.	Mining and Quarring	42173	1	42173.00	41555	1.4	29682.14	-4.89
3.	Manufacturing	1509239	50.5	29885.92	2095224	53	39532.53	4.08
4.	Electricity, gas and water	129467	1.1	117697.27	260241	1	260241	12.00
5.	construction	299387	10.8	27721.02	561923	14.5	38753.31	4.90
6.	Trade, hotel, restaurant							
7.	Transport, storage							
8.	Communication							
9.	Financing, Insurance etc.,	1806066	35.7	50590.08	3156662	46.7	67594.48	4.23
10.	Community and social Service	577576	33.2	17396.87	1074405	28.8	37305.73	11.51
	Total	**5748201**	**285.7**	**20119.71**	**8687213**	**289.8**	**29976.58**	**5.86**

Annexure III

Employment Generation and Poverty Alleviation Programme

Jawahar Gram Samridhi Yojana (JGSY): JGSY was introduced in April 1999 by restructuring the Jawahar Rozgar Yojana and is being implemented as Centrally Sponsored Scheme on a cost sharing ratio of 75:25 between centre and states. The programme is implemented by Gram Panchayat and works which result in creating of durable productive community assets are taken up. The secondary objective, however is generation of wage-employment for the rural unemployed poor.

Swarnjayanti Gram Swarozgar Yojana (SGSY): was launched with effect from April 1, 1999, as a result of amalgamating certain erstwhile programme viz: Integrated Rural Development Programme, Development of Women and Children in Rural Areas (DWCRA), Training of Rural Youth for Self Employment (TRYSEM), Million Well Scheme (MWS) and other, into a Single-Self Employment Programme. It aims at promoting micro enterprises and helping the rural poor into Self-Help Groups (SHG). This scheme covers all aspects of self-employment like organization of the rural poor into SHG and their capacity of building, training, planning of activity clusters, infrastructure development, financial assistance through bank credit and subsidy and marketing support.

Employment Assurance Scheme (EAS): was started on oct 2, 1993 for implementation in 1778 identified Backward Panchayat Samitis of 257 districts situated in drought prone areas, desert areas, tribal areas and hill areas in which the revampled PDS was in operation. It was subsequently expanded by 1997-98 to all the 5448 rural Panchayat Samitis of the country. It was restructured in 1999-2000 to make it a single way of employment programme and implemented as a CSS on a cost sharing ratio of 75:25.

Sampoorna Grameen Rozgar Yojna (SGRY): Launched w.e.f. September 2001, the scheme aims at providing wage employment in the rural areas as also, food security, along with ratio of 75:25 between the Centre and States. The ongoing EAS and JGSY would subsequently be fully integrated within the scheme with effect from April, 2002.

Pradhan Mantri Gramodaya Yojana (PMGY): was introduced in 2000-01 with the objective of focusing on village level development in five critical areas i.e. health, primary education, drinking water, housing and rural roads with the overall objective of improving the quality of life of the people in the rural areas.

Swarna Jayanthi Shahri Rozgar Yojna (SJSRY): The Urban Self Employment Programme and the Urban Wage Employment are two special schemes of the SJSRY initiated in Dec. 97, which replaced various programmes operated earlier for rural poverty alleviation.

Food for Work Programme: This programme was initially launched w.e.f. February 2001, for five months and was further extended. The programme aims at augmenting food security through employment in the drought-affected rural areas in 8 States ie., Gujarat, Chattisgarh, Himachal Pradesh, Madhya Pradesh, Maharashtra, Orissa, Rajasthan and Uttranchal. The Centre makes available the appropriate quantity of food grains at free of cost of each of above State. Wages by the State Government can be paid partly in kind and partly in cash. The workers are paid the balance of wages in cash, such that the they are assured of the notified Minimum Wages.

Krishi Shramik Samajik Suradsha Yojana: The scheme was launched in July 2001 for giving social security benefit to agricultural labourers on hire in the age group of 18-60 years.

Annexure IV

Task Force on Employment Opportunities

The Planning Commission under the Chairmanship of Shri M.S. Ahluwalia set up a Task force on Employment opportunities. M.S. Ahluwalia, Member, Planning Commission to examine the existing employment and unemployment situation in the country and to suggest strategies of employment generation for achieving the target of providing employment opportunities to 100 million people over the next 10 years. A summary of strategy for employment generation recommended by the Task force is given below:

- Accelerating the rate of growth of GDP with a particular emphasis on sectors likely to ensure the spread of income to the low-income segment of the labour force.
- Pursuing appropriate sectoral policies in individual sectors which are particularly important for employment generation. These sector level policies must be broadly consistent with the overall objective of accelerating GDP growth.
- Implementing focused special programme for creating additional employment and enhancing income generation from existing activities aimed at helping vulnerable groups that may not be sufficiently benefited by the more general growth promoting policies.
- Pursuing suitable policies for education and skill development, which would upgrade the quality of the labour force and make it capable of supporting a growth process which generates high quality jobs.
- Ensuring that the policy and legal environment governing the labour market encourage labour absorption, especially in the organized sector.

Second National Labour Commission

The Government is presently examining the issue of rigidities in labour legislation, promotion of industrial investment in labour intensive activities and measures for safeguarding the interests of workers. The Government has also set up the *Second National Labour Commission in Dec. 1998,* to suggest rationalization of existing labour laws in the organized sector and also to suggest an umbrella legislation for ensuring a minimum level of protection to the workers in the unorganized sector.

Kollappan Committee (for Agricultural Labourers) TN.

Government of Tamil Nadu constituted a Committee under the chairmanship of Thiru. Kollappan, IAS during 1997 to analyse the nature and extent of socio-economic problem confronted by the agricultural labourers in Tamilnadu and to suggest the ways and means of improving their levels of living, at least above the poverty line. The Committee submitted its report during 1998.

According to the report, in TN, a male agricultural labourers gets on an average 150 days of work in a year, and a female gets about 100 days in a year. It ranged from a minimum of 90 days to a maximum of 120 days for women and 120 days to a maximum of 150 days for men.

Minimum wages for agricultural labourers need to be set as follows by the committee for the year 1998-99 and revised every five years.

Men labourers (6 hours)-Rs. 54/- Women labourers (5 hours)-Rs. 45/-

Annexure V

Welfare Schemes

- Group Insurance Scheme for Landless Agricultural Labour operated by Insurance Division, Ministry of Finance.
- Group Life Insurance Scheme for IRDP beneficiaries operated by Department of Rural Development.
- Insurance-cum-Retirement Benefit Special Scheme for the workers in the unorganised sector of Tamil Nadu Government.
- Scheme for Financial Assistance to Landless Women Agricultural Labourers during Pregnancy operated by Gujarat Government.
- Personal Accident Insurance Social Security Scheme for Poor Families.
- Hut Insurance Scheme.
- Kerala Agricultural Workers' Pension Scheme.
- Andhra Pradesh Landless Agricultural Workers' Pension Scheme.
- Old Age Pension (Destitute Agricultural Labourers) Scheme of Tamilnadu.
- Old Age Pension Schemes of other States / Union Territories.

Acts

- Minimum Wages Act, 1948.
- Plantation Labour Act, 1951.
- The Payment of Wages Act, 1936.
- The Employees State Insurance Act, 1948.
- The Maternity Benefit Act, 1961.
- The Payment of Gratuity Act, 1972.

- The Personal Induries (Compensation) Act, 1963.
- The Employees' Provident Fund & Miscellaneous Provisions Act, 1952 and
- TN payment of subsistence allowance Act 1981.

Above Acts are applicable to agricultural workers.

Besides these, certain provision in other Acts, viz., (i) Contract Labour Act, 1970 (ii) Equal Remuneration Act, 1976; (iii) Inter State Migrant Workmen (Regulation of Employment and Conditions of Service) Act, 1979 and (iv) Child Labour (Prohibition and Regulation) Act, 1986 give protection to the agricultural workers.

References

1. Institute of Applied Manpower Research, New Delhi, "Employment Generation through decentralized development of Agriculture—A case study of Ramanathapuram district of Tamil Nadu" (1990)
2. Economic Survey 2000-01.
3. Economic Survey 2001-02.
4. National Council for Economic Research, "India Human Development Report"
5. Government of India, "Ninth Five Year Plan" (1997).
6. Indian Labour Year Book 1975 and 1976.
7. Reserve Bank of India Yearly Hand Book-1999-2000.
8. Muragesan. R. "Problem of Agricultural Labourers" (1999).
9. Mahendra Dev - "Labour productivity in Indian Agriculture" EPW, Vol. XXIII, Sep. 24, 1998.
10. Radhakrishnan, R. "Agricultural Growth, Employment and Poverty-A Policy Perspectives" EPW, Jan, 19, 2002.
11. Sundram K. "Employment and Unemployment Situation in the 90's", EPW, Jan 17, 2001.
12. Sundram K. "Employment and Poverty in the 90's" EPW Aug 11, 2001.

8

Mechanisation and Labour Absorption in Andhra Pradesh Agriculture—A Study in the Right Canal Command Area of NSP

Prof. L.K. Mohana Rao, Dr. P. Narasimha Rao, Dr. K. Ravi Babu

Since the dawn of the industrial revolution mechanization has become an irreversible process, sub-suming developed and developing economies with a spurt in technological innovations during the last forty years, there has been a phenomenal acceleration of mechanization in the less developed countries. In the current era of progressive economic globalization and transnationalisation of capital, production systems and markets are often compelled to respond to a single global logic of exchange. This process, geared to unlimited competition, puts a premium on consideration of efficiency even in the operations of remote farms, which were once islands of subsistence-agriculture for small and marginal farmers, or pockets of random neglect of the absentee land lord. In developing economies like India, where unemployment or under employment is a serious problem, divergent views are expressed with regard to the mechanization of farm operations in agriculture. One set of writers (Ashok Mitra and others) who are somewhat ideologically inclined, express the view that the mechanization has deleterious effects, as it is perceived to result in reduction of employment. The other set of studies are empirically oriented and based on fieldwork. Among them, the findings of Bose and Clark, Billings and Singh, Grewal and Kalon, Suzuki, Sison, etc., suggest that mechanization leads to reduction in employment. On the other hand, the findings of Raj Krishna, Rao, Wolf, Chopra, Jhol, etc., are categorical that mechanization does not result in reduction in employment. Keeping this in view, an attempt has been made in this study to examine that impact of mechanization on human labour employment in Andhra Pradesh where mechanization particularly use of combined harvester in agriculture is going at rapid rate.

Objective

The objective of the study is to examine the impact of mechanization of human labour absorption in agriculture in Andhra Pradesh.

Methodology

The data for this study is drawn from a Research Project Equity in Irrigation-A study in the Right Canal Command Area of Nagarjuna Sagar Project' sponsored by UGC, New Delhi. The sample comprises 230 farm households and the distribution of sample holdings among different categories are presented in Table 1. Decomposition analysis is carried out to capture the changes in human labour employment caused by different factors. The analysis is carried out at the aggregate level (all crops put together) and at the disaggregate level (for two predominant crops paddy and

Table 1. Distribution of Selected Holdings

Category of Farm	*Mechanized*	*Non-Mechanized*	*Total*
Marginal	32 (31.07)	50 (39.37)	82 (35.65)
Small	33 (32.04)	38 (29.92)	71 (30.87)
Medium	25 (24.27)	24 (18.90)	49 (21.30)
Large	13 (12.62)	15 (11.87)	28 (12.17)
Total	**103 (100.00**	**127 (100.00**	**230 (100.00**

cotton). The final equation adopted to decompose the changes in human labour employment into different components is

$1_n [X_{M1} / X_{N1}] = \{1_n (A_M / A_N) + [(A_2 / B_2) 1_n X_{N2} + (A_3 - B_3) 1_n X_{N3} + (A_4 - B_4) 1_n X_{N4} + (A_5 - B_5) 1_n X_{n5}]$

In the above, the suffix 'N' denotes for mechanized and non-mechanised farm respectively.

$A_2 1_n (X_{M2} / X_{N2}) + A_3 1_n (X_{M3} / X_{N3}) + A_4 1_n (X_{M4} / X_{N4}) A_5 1_n (X_{M5} / X_{N5})$

X_1: Human labour employment per acre of cropped area

X_2: Size of the land in acres

X_3: Value of fertilizers and manures per acre

X_4: Value of pesticides per acre

X_5: value of capital services per acre

A_M and A_N are the intercept terms

A_2, A_3, A_4 and A_5 are the elasticity coefficients associated with employment with respect to land, fertilizers, pesticides and capital services respectively on mechanized farms.

B_2, B_3, B_4 and B_5 are the elasticity coefficients associated with employment with respect to land, fertilizers, pesticides and capital services respectively on non-mechanized farms.

In the equation used for decomposition analysis, the bracketed expression on the left-hand side is the natural logarithm of ratio of per acre, labour used on mechanized and non-mechanized farms and reflects the approximate total percentage change in per acre labour employment due to mechanization. The first two bracketed expressions on the right hand side of the equation measures the changes in employment per acre due to change in the intercept term and employment elasticities. The second bracketed expression calculates the sum of changes in the employment elasticities weighted by the logarithm of farm size; value of fertilizers, pesticides and capital services used per acre used non-mechanized conditions. Therefore, the first two bracketed expressions together give the percentage change in the human labour-demand exclusively due to mechanization or represent the net impact of mechanization on human labour-demand. The child-bracketed expression is the sum of the logarithm of the ratio of the farm size and of the ratios of fertilizers pesticides and capital services under mechanized and non-mechanized conditions. This measures the percentage change in human labour demand due to change in farm size, and changes in the use of fertilizers, pesticides and capital services, given the employment elasticity of these inputs on mechanized farms.

Results

The estimated results of the decomposition exercise are presented in Table 2 for all crops, paddy and cotton. The results reveal that there is close association between the observed change and the estimated change in the employment in all the crop situations. This may imply that the decomposition equation specified for this purpose is robust.

All Crops

As all the crops put together, the labour use per acre on mechanized farms is found to be higher by 2.56 per cent as compared to non-mechanized farms. The decomposition analysis suggests a decline of 13.41 per cent (Table 2.1) in the use of human labour employment with the adoption of mechanization. The difference in the farm size between mechanized and non-mechanized farms has resulted in a decline in human labour employment by 1.76 per cent, given the elasticity of employment with respect to farm size of non-mechanized farms. On the otherhand, given the elasticity of employment with respect to fertilizers, pesticides and capital services of non-mechanized farms, the difference in the level of use of these inputs has resulted

Table 2.1. Decomposition Anlysis Results of Total Difference in Human Labour

Employment - All Crops

Item	*Percentage attributable*			
	All Crops	*Marginal*	*Small*	*Marginal and large*
Total observed difference	2.56	2.54	5.60	0.50
1. Mechanization	-13.41	-14.00	-4.67	-11.51
2. Changes in Inputs	15.62	16.34	10.30	11.89
(a) Land	-1.76	2.71	-0.05	-4.55
(b) Fertilizer	8.18	14.91	8.58	8.34
(c) Pesticides	8.18	1.98	2.70	5.22
(d) Capital Services	1.32	-3.26	-0.93	2.88
Total Estimated Change due to all sources	2.51	2.34	5.63	0.38

in an increase in the human labour employment by 17.68 per cent. This may imply that the positive effects of fertilizers, pesticides and capital services inputs outweigh the negative effects of mechanisation on employment. A similar pattern with variations in the relative impact of different factors on employment is discernable among different size groups of farms. The total estimated increase in human labour employment with the adoption of mechanization on marginal, small and large farm categories worked out to 2.34 per cent, 5.63 per cent and 0.38 per cent respectively. This may mean that the overall effect of mechanization on human labour employment is positive and higher on small and marginal farms as compared to large farms.

Paddy

With regard to paddy crop, the labour use per acre on non-mechanized farms is higher by 1.57 per cent than mechanized farms. However, different pattern is found among different size groups (Table 2.2) The average labour use

Table 2.2. Decomposition Analysis Results of Total Difference in Human Labour

Employment—Paddy

Item	*Percentage attributable*			
	All Crops	*Marginal*	*Small*	*Marginal and large*
Total Observed difference	-1.57	2.54	8.82	-6.18
1. Mechanisation	-13.29	-14.00	-6.76	-13.75
2. Changes in Inputs	11.79	16.34	15.61	7.98
(a) Land	-2.70	2.71	-6.47	-10.04
(b) Fertilizer	10.02	14.91	17.11	8.78
(c) Pesticides	4.42	1.98	2.38	5.33
(d) Capital Services	0.05	-3.26	2.59	3.91
Total Estimated Change due to all sources	-1.50	2.34	8.85	-5.77

per acre on marginal and small farms of mechanized category is higher by 2.54 per cent and 8.82 per cent respectively as compared to the corresponding size groups of non-mechanized category. On the otherhand, on medium and large farms, the per acre labour use on non-mechanized category is higher by 6.18 per cent than mechanized category.

The results of the decomposition analysis reveal that mechanization alone has reduced labour employment by 13.29 per cent given the input use levels of non-mechanized farms. The farm size differential between mechanized and non-mechanised farms has resulted in a decline in human labour by 2.70 per cent given the elasticity of human labour with respect to land on mechanized farms. On the other hand, given the elasticities associated with fertilizers and pesticides on mechanized farms these inputs together have increased human labour employment by 14.44 per cent. The capital services inputs have also increased the human labour employment on mechanized farms marginally.

A similar pattern, with few exceptions, is observed among different size groups with respect to the change in employment caused by mechanization and changes in the use of other inputs. Here also the difference between observed and estimated change in employment is found to be marginal.

Cotton

Unlike in paddy, cotton under mechanized conditions has absorbed 7.34 per cent higher human labour per acre compared to the human labour employment under non-mechanized conditions (Table 2.3). The estimated results of the decomposition analysis indicate that mechanization in cotton cultivation has declined the human labour employment by 15.01 per cent given the input use level of non-mechanized farms. The differences in the use of other inputs, viz., land, fertilizers and pesticides has resulted in an increase in the human labour employment on mechanized holdings by 1.28 per cent, 10.42 per cent and 10.10 per cent respectively. The total estimated increase in labour

Table 2.3. Decomposition Analysis Results of Total Difference in Human Labour

Employment—Cotton

Item	*Percentage attrinutable*			
	All Crops	*Marginal*	*Small*	*Marginal and large*
Total Observed difference	7.34	13.08	20.45	2.62
1. Mechanization	-15.01	6.59	-7.70	-3.50
2. Changes in Inputs	21.76	6.48	26.71	5.91
(a) Land	1.28	-3.63	-0.83	-5.62
(b) Fertilizer	10.42	1.41	15.08	6.14
(c) Pesticides	10.10	7.29	10.90	5.63
(d) Capital Services	-0.04	1.41	1.56	-0.24
Total Estimated Change due to all sources	6.75	13.07	19.01	2.41

employment per acre in cotton production from all sources is 6.75 per cent. The same pattern prevails among different size groups of farms also.

Conclusions

From the above discussion, it can be inferred that in the overall crop production as well as in the production of paddy and cotton, mechanization has negative effects on human labour employment in a direct manner. However, in all the crop situations, the impact of other inputs, specifically fertilizers and pesticides, on labour employment is positive. This may mean that mechanization by way of promoting intensive cultivation may lead to the intensive use of farm inputs and thereby enhancing human labour employment. Consequent to this, the overall effect of mechanization and other farm inputs put together on human labour employment is positive.

References

1. Abercrobie, K.C (1973), "Agricultural Mechanization and Employment in Latin America," Mechanization and Employment in Agriculture: Case Studies from Four Countries, International Labour Office, Geneva.
2. Anderson, et. al (Ed), (1982), Science, Politics and Agricultural Revolution in Asia, Westview Press, Colarado.
3. Bergman, Theodor (1978), Mechanization of Indian Farming, Popular Prakashan, Bombay.
4. Bhattacharya, N and Saini, G.R. (1970), "Mechanization and Rural Employment with Some Implications for Rural Income Distribution," Economic and Political Weekly, Vol. 5, No. 26.
5. Billings, M.H. and Singh, A. (1970), "Mechanization and the Wheat Revolution Effects of Female Labour in Punjab," Economic and Political Weekly, Vol. 5, No. 52.
6. Bose S.R. and Clark, E.H. (1969), "Some Basic Considerations on Agricultural Mechanisation in West Pakistan," The Pakistan Development Review, Vol. 9, No. 3.

7. Clayton, E.S. (1974), "Farm Mechanisation and Employment in Developing Countries," International Labour Review, Vol. 110, No. 1.

8. Grewal, S.S. and Kahlon, A.S. (1972), "Impact of Farm Mechanisation on Farm Employment in Punjab, Indian Journal of Agricultural Economics, Vol. 27, No. 4.

9. Johl, S.S. (1970), Mechanisation, Labour Use and Productivity in Indian Agriculture, Economics and Sociology Occasional Paper No. 23, Ohio State University, Columbus, Ohio.

10. Johnsoton, Bruce, F and John Cowine (1969), "The Seed Fertilizer Revolution and Labour Force Absorption, " American Economics Review, Vol. 59, No. 4.

11. NCAER (1973) Impact of Mechanisation in Agriculture on Employment, National Council of Applied Economic Research, New Delhi.

12. Stewart, Frances (1972), "Choice of Techniques in Developing Countries," Journal of Development Studies, Vol. 9, No. 1.

13. Suzuki, F(1983), Farm Mechanisation in Asia, Asian Publishing Organisation, Tokyo.

9

Labour Participation in Leather Goods Industry

Giriyappa Kollannavar, C. Pulinda Rao
Dr. B. Krishnama Naidu

Introduction

Indian leather industry with historical background is poised for modernization with technological inputs. It has grown from cottage to factory sector. In the light of significant policy shift in 1991 towards globalization of Indian economy, except duty drawback, the other export incentives for leather products were withdrawn. However, restrictions on the export of finished leathers products with 5% export duty along with ISI norms was introduced and withdrawn later. Liberal imports of raw materials, machinery, chemicals and anxiliaries have been the major highlights of the new policy. The essence of the current liberal policy signifies restriction of a few items for export and import.

Large raw material reserves, access to low cost labour and encouraging support from the government, are the contributing factors for the factory sector of the product industry towards making rapid strides in the production and export of leather products. The Government's industrial and trade policies, institutional support, coupled with aggressive entrepreneurship and the growing demand for exports are the other factors attributing to its growth. Apart from tanners setting up of product units, leading companies like Tata, Wipro, Ponds India, Hindustan Lever, etc. have also set up product units with 100% export orientation. Some of them entered into technical and marketing tie-ups with reputed overseas companies. Setting up of such modern product units opened new avenues to technologists, machine operators, skilled and unskilled workers.

At the global level, increasing labour costs and strict enforcement of pollution control measures in the developed countries have led to a shift of leather industry to developing countries of Asia and South America, due to comparative cost advantage. India, having a strong raw material base and abundant skilled work force, has a definite edge in exploiting the situation.

Despite these developments, the Indian leather product industry attained special feature and presents a complex structure with respect to investment capabilities. The scale of production, quality of the products and adherence to the delivery schedule are the problems faced. However, these problems are temporary in nature. The products made out of the leather are footwear, leather garments and leather goods such as handbags, belts, wallets, travel bags, gloves, sports goods of leather, harness, and saddlers. Of all these items, it is the footwear that consumes about 60% of the total leather produced. The manufacture and export of leather products are systematically promoted as their value addition works out to the extent of four to five times over raw material. While leather was grouped among the thrust sectors, the footwear and leather products are the extreme focus areas. Nearly 25 lakh people are involved in various activities of leather industry. One third of them are in traditional vocations like flaying, collection of hides and skins, and footwear fabrication. Women employment in leather products industry is sizable.

Trends in Export of Leather and Allied Products

India's export of leather and leather products phenomenally increased during the last two decades. The data presented in Table 1 reveals that export of value added products has increased over the years. During 1970-80, the semi finished leathers, in 80's the finished leathers and in 90's the value added products were dominated in the export structure of leather and allied products. Presently the export of this sector claims one among the top 7 commodity exports of the country.

Of the total export value of Rs. 8886 crores during 2000-01 leather products segment claimed major share of 80% and rest is finished leather. Among the products again, the export of leather goods and sports goods of leather is the major item valued at Rs. 2318 crores (33%). Hence it is clear, that the development of leather products industry particularly the leather goods is in tune with the promotional policy of the Government which is contemplating to export only value added leather products.

Major Importing Countries of Leather Goods

USA, Germany, France, Netherlands, Spain are the major importing countries for India's leather goods. These five countries together imported 70% of the total leather goods exported from India. Major items of leather goods exported are ladies hand bags, wallets, purses, hand gloves, leather art wares and saddletrees.

Objectives of the Paper

The main aim of this paper is to analyse the employment pattern and problems of labour in leather goods manufacture. The "Nationwide Survey on Leather Product Units in India" carried out by the Central Leather Research Institute in 1997 found that most of the leather goods manufacturing units are in Kolkata and Mumbai. They follow different pattern of employment and recruitment. The survey has

Table 1. India's Exports of Leather & Leather Products (1975 to 2000-2001)

(Figures in Rs. Crores)

Year	*Semi finished lea.*	*Finished Lea*	*Lea footwear*	*Footwear components*	*Lea goods*	*Lea garments*	*Sports goods of leather*	*Total*
1975-76	144	55	19	1	8	1	-	232
1976-77	150	105	26	6	13	3	6	309
1977-78	122	108	19	15	15	6	7	292
1978-79	111	192	23	18	24	8	11	387
1979-80	113	321	30	37	35	8	9	553
1980-81	51	227	34	45	39	5	10	411
1981-82	54	226	30	77	42	7	8	444
1982-83	46	210	29	87	46	10	6	434
1983-84	52	235	31	122	52	12	7	511
1984-85	65	361	45	175	73	22	7	748
1985-86	68	334	41	224	79	28	5	779
1986-87	59	408	69	229	102	69	7	943
1987-88	56	538	123	295	149	120	8	1289
1988-89	30	650	140	381	188	182	9	1580

(Cont...)

Year	*Semi finished lea.*	*Finished Lea*	*Lea footwear*	*Footwear components*	*Lea goods*	*Lea garments*	*Sports goods of leather*	*Total*
1989-90	16	729	199	439	288	361	7	2039
1990-91	13	799	303	573	372	557	8	2625
1991-92	11	717	425	700	551	761	8	3173
1992-93	-	808	555	605	740	1044	9	3758
1993-94	-	753	803	659	761	1009	13	3998
1994-95	-	1201	1000	652	1006	1224	30	5113
1995-96	-	1241	1103	814	1335	1387	48	5928
1996-97	-	1068	1170	786	1194	1511	72	5801
1997-98	-	1097	981	888	1593	1603	82	6244
1998-99	-	1130	1327	1001	1938	1614	77	7087
1999-2000	-	1061	1595	918	1864	1509	49	6996
2000-2001	-	1757	1658	1037	2262	2116	56	8886

Note: @Included in Leather Goods.

Source Exports: "Monthly Statistics of the Foreign Trade of India - Volume I Exports & Re Exports March Issues of 1976 to 2001. Published by D.G.C.I.S. Calcutta - 700 001.

Compiled by: Economics Research Division, CLRI., Chennai - 600 020.

intensively covered these clusters. These two clusters account for 65% of leather goods exported from India.

Structure of Leather Goods Industry

According to the Nation wide Survey on Leather Products units in India, there are 391 leather goods manufacturing units operating in different scales of production in the country. The merchant exporters/dealers and job work units are excluded from this, as they are not directly involved in manufacturing. The units registered with state industry department are taken for the study. Major highlights of the survey are, most of the leather goods manufacturing units in India are owned by sole proprietor or on partnership basis. The owners or partners control the entire manufacturing activity. Major centres for production of leather goods are Kolkata, Mumbai, Kanpur, Chennai, Bangalore, Indore, and Pondicherry. Availability of finished leather and the accessories that go into the production, and existence of skilled labour are the prime factors for the location of the industry in these clusters. Based on this intensive survey, this paper is prepared with an objective to analyse the nature of labour involvement, migration of labours, and problems faced by them in the leather goods manufacturing units.

Production of Leather Goods

All major centres put together produce around Rs. 3500 crores worth of leather goods in India. Out of this Rs. 2318 crores worth of leather goods items accounting for 66% were exported during 2000-2001. Ladies handbags, wallets, purses, jewellery boxes, hand gloves harness items are considered as sustainable products in the leather products segment for export purpose. Leather waist belts constitute major share in the domestic consumption of leather goods.

Employment Pattern

Manufacture of leather goods is considered as labour intensive and has the high potential value addition to the products. The production pattern is more amenable to small scale operations in view of the intrinsic nature of the industry. The leather goods products are fashion oriented and subjected to frequent changes in designs/styles and hence need to be organized at a limited scale so as to adopt quickly to modifications. The employment pattern of workers engaged in the leather goods units of the major centers is shown in Table 2.

Total employment in the leather goods industry is estimated at 30000 persons. Kolkata and Mumbai centres have the more number of leather goods production units in small and tiny sectors. Both centres together account for 75 per cent of the total employment. However majority of the units in these centres are in unorganized sector. Hence the employment pattern in these centres are different from the organized sector of leather goods production units in Chennai and Bangalore. It is interesting to note that in the decentralized sector only 10 per cent of the total workforce are qualified skilled workers and rest are unskilled. These unskilled workers join as apprentice workers and gradually upgrade to skilled over the years. Such scenario is going to be changed in the WTO regime. Under the social security cover to labourers, minimum wages, labour welfare and working conditions are going to play an active role in manufacture and export of leather goods.

Women Labourers

Around 46% of the total workers are women in leather goods industries. However, in case of south, the proportion of women employment is more than 60% and majority of them are young unmarried girls in the age group of 16-30 years. On the other hand women employment, excluding the decentralized sector in Kolkata and Mumbai centres is restricted to 21% and 5% respectively.

Scenerio of Kolkata and Mumbai

The small scale factory sector in south employs the workers on monthly salary basis and offer some social

Table 2. Pattern of Employment in Leather Goods Units

Category	*Calcutta*	*Chennai*	*Mumbai*	*Kanpur*	*Bangalore*	*Pondicheery*	*Others*	*Total*
Managers	371	140	22	52	11	9	48	653(3.9)
Supervisors	421	435	43	85	30	45	117	1176(6.9)
Cutters	106	557	110	87	66	69	280	1275(7.5)
Stitchers	358	1194	229	196	147	132	1102	3358(19.8)
Supporting Staff	136	896	100	149	42	28	53	1404(8.3)
Administrative Staff	160	224	75	134	37	40	69	739(4.4)
Workers	533	4332	1129	486	448	913	468	8309(49.1)
Total	**2085*** **(12.3)**	**7778** **(46.0)**	**1708** **(10.1)**	**1189** **(7.0)**	**781** **(4.6)**	**1236** **(7.3)**	**2137** **(12.6)**	**16914**** **(100)**
Males	1982 (95)	2930 (38)	1355 (70)	1049 (88)	284 (36)	514 (42)	990 (46)	9104 (54)
Females	103 (5)	4848 (62)	353 (21)	140 (12)	497 (64)	722 (58)	1147 (54)	7810 (46)

Note: Figures in brackets are given in percentage.

*: Including those engaged in the decentralized household sector in Kolkata, total employment is around 12,000 persons.

**: Including those engaged in the decentralized household sector in Kolkata, total employment is around 30,000 persons.

benefits. In contrast to this, majority of leather goods units in Kolkata, Mumbai, and Kanpur employ workers on piece rate basis. In the later case workers who undertake the manufacture of leather goods are not directly controlled by the owner, but sub contracting system of employment pattern is practised. Owner of the leather goods unit procure all the raw material, accessories and with few skilled labourers produce components for leather goods. The ready made components are distributed to the middlemen to get assembled into finished products. The quality and timely delivery of the products are entrusted to middlemen and payment is made on piece rate basis of the finished products. The piece rates vary depending upon the design and style of the product. The contact and contract of the owner is up to middleman and there is no liability for him to control and manage the other workers.

Role of Middle Man (Tekidar)

Real link between owner and workers is middleman (Tekidar) who is responsible for hiring and distributing the work to individual workers. The contractor distributes the leather components which he receives from the factory owner and gets back finished products from the labourers after assembling. Paying wages to workers is sole responsibility of the Tekidar. The workers are at the mercy of middleman to get the work regularly. Sometimes, the wages are deducted for the rejected goods. Although the labour is involved in the production of export quality leather goods, by virtue of their participation in the decentralized sector they are subjected to underpayment, and irregularity of work. This situation clearly demonstrates the exploitation of the middlemen in organizing the labour.

Out of Labour Act Perview

Most of the leather goods manufacturing units do not follow the minimum wage Act as they are not directly dealt with the labourers. The workers who depend on the mercy of the Tekidar are not able to demand more wages. Infact the Tekidar has complete control over workers as majority of them are in the habit of taking advance from him. In other words the bonded labour type of situation is prevailed in these centers of the industry.

Poor Living Conditions

Migrants from Bihar are in more number in the leather goods manufacturing industry of Kolkata. Whereas migrated labourers from Maharastra, Rajasthan, Madhya Pradesh are involved in leather goods manufacture activities of Dharavi area of Mumbai. These migrated workers (single person) living in rented and congested small huts attend to the leather goods assembling work. It was found during the survey that on an average each worker is earning Rs. 2100 per month (2000-01). Out of this Rs. 1000 is sent to his family in the native place to meet the monthly expenditure. With the rest of the amount he has to meet the expenditure of rent for hut, and food. Considering the meare amount earned by these workers that too in a metro city many of them work overtime risking their health. It is a common feature that majority of the workers are suffering from multiple health problems even at productive age. Unhygienic environment, loneliness, uncertainty of regular work lead create depression among these workers, and there were instances that few have become anti social elements due to meager earnings.

Conclusions

Minimum wage Act, Labour welfare Act, and many more labour protective measures, announced by Govt. are not followed in the unorganized leather goods manufacturing units. Though the products are fetching premium price in the export market, the skilled-labour ers behind such products are not justifiably remunerated.

On the other hand workers who have been working for the last 10-15 years are not able to come out of this profession as they tied their hands with the Tekidar by taking advance payment. There is no labour union among them nor any trade union is intervened. Illiteracy, ignorance, backwardness, under employment are part of their living conditions.

However, there is going to be a sea change in the employment pattern in the light of WTO regulations. The labour welfare and working conditions are part of the new regulation. In the changing scenario, leather goods industry being labour intensive may play a vital role in creation of employment to the unemployed youth. Continuous demand exists for leather products in the international market. Although the managerial and supervisory skills are available, there is an urgent need for training the floor level workers. Improvement in labour wage cannot change the present scenario of the exploitation. Formation of Self Help Groups among these workers may be the best solution. Under SHG workers with 15-20 member groups could take the work from employer and distribute among themselves to sustain their earnings. Success of SHG's of various products is highlighted and encouraged by Central and State Govts. (Kurukshetra September 1999) Under these circumstances workers in leather goods manufacture, particularly in Kolkata and Mumbai centres are vulnerable to form the SHG's among them and an active Non Government Organizations (NGO) should initiate this programme.

References

1. Nationwide Survey on Leather Product Units in India, Central Leather Research Institute, Chennai 1997.
2. Shakuntala Narasimhan, Empowering Rural Women: An Overview of Part State Initiatives, Kurukshtra, September 1999, Vol. 47 No. 12.
3. Statistical Bulletin on Eexports and Imports of Leather and Allied Products 2000-01, Central Leather Research Institute, Chennai.

10

Rural Non-Farm Sector in Andhra Pradesh

Dr. M. Koteshwara Rao, Mr. P. Venu Gopal

In India like other developing countries, labour absorption in agriculture and in urban and service sectors have not been enough to absorb the growing labour force. Consequently, problems of poverty and unemployment and underemployment and out-migration have persisted in both rural and urban areas. Under these conditions the diversification of rural economy appears to be an important element of development strategy. Being a long-term strategy, the non-farm avenues of employment and earnings are inevitable for rural households. Generally speaking, non-farm activities can include all those activities which are undertaken outside agriculture. In the sensem, rural non-agriculture activity is essentially a residual category. The empirical evidence shows that labour absorption of agriculture has been falling in many years due to the faster and manifold growth of population.

Table 1 shows structural changes in workforce in India. It can be observed from this Table that, it is no longer true that three-fourths of the workforce depends on agriculture. About 76 per cent of total workforce was there in agriculture in 1961. But it has gone down to about 60 per cent by 1999-2000. Industry and service activities have increased their proportion in total workforce of the economy.

Table 1. Structural Change in Workforce in India

Sector	*1961*	*1999-2000*
Agriculture Forestry & Fishing	75.9	59.9
Live Stock	2	4.1
Agricultural Services	0	0.9
Logging Forestry and Fishing	0.5	0.5
Mining and Quarrying	0.5	0.6
Electricity Etc	0.1	0.3
Construction	1.5	4.4
Trade and Transport etc	6	13.1
Services	6.4	9.6
Total	**100**	**100**

Like other developing countries in the World, the share of national income originating from the primary sector has been declining steadily while respective shares of secondary and tertiary sectors have been increasing steadily ever since the beginning of the planning era in India. This trend is prevalent in Table 2. In 1950-51 the ratio of the three sectors was 56:15:29, it has got transformed to 31:24:45 by 1998-99.

Table 2. Sectprial Composition of G.D.P. (%)

Year	*Agriculture & Allied*	*Industry*	*Service*	*Total*
1950-51	54.6	14.6	29.0	100
60-61	46.7	19.8	33.5	100
70-71	46.0	21.0	33.0	100
80-81	39.7	24.3	36.0	100
90-91	33.7	26.7	39.6	100
94-95	33.3	25.7	41.0	100
98-99	31.2	23.6	45.2	100

Source: Statistical survey, 1999-2000, Tata Ltd.

On the other hand, the industrial sector (organized) is also not offering much scope in absorption of growing labour force, as the production process in this sector is becoming more and more capital intensive. Therefore, non-farm sector, particularly, in rural areas is positioned as a potential sector for absorption of rural labour in more productive manner. Infact, there has been a variable boom in rural non-farm employment, not only in India, but also in other developing countries of Asia and Africa. Rural non-farm sector comprises a number of activities other than agriculture. These are manufacturing trade and commerce, transport, construction and service. Thus, the non-farm activities are regarded as logical extension from crop production in the process of diversification of the rural economy by giving support to local livelihood and to prevent the migration of workers from rural areas to urban areas. So we can state that the major future thrust in job creation should depend on the non-farm sector in order to utilize the local resources and to provide maximum employment opportunities in rural areas.

Rural Non-Farm Employment in India

To analyse the nature, character, growth and determinants of non-farm rural employment in India several attempts have been made over time. For instance, the studies by Krishnamurthy (1984), Vaidyanathan (1986), Badant and Rakesh (1989), Kashyap and Desai (1990), Singh (1990, 1991) Basant and Parthasarathy (1991), Rayappa (1986), Unni (1991), Basu and Kashyap (1992) and Papola (1993) are some of the notable studies in this area of research.

In India the non-farm rural employment has witnessed a steady expansion during the last few decades. The work-force in rural areas is gradually moving out of agriculture. This process of structural change would lead to the emergence of problems of farm-non-farm relations especially from the point of employment for the rural household. Table 3 explains

Table 3. Sexwise Distribution of RNF Workers

State	*1987-88*		*1993-94*		*1999-2000*	
	Male	*Female*	*Male*	*Female*	*Male*	*Female*
Andhra Pradesh	25.9	17.9	24.4	16.3	25.6	15.7
Assam	23.5	17.7	21.8	16.8	35.3	20.6
Bihar	20	9.8	18	8.1	21	14.3
Gujarat	31.4	24.2	28.9	9.4	28.6	8.0
Haryana	29.1	7.5	39.1	6.8	40.4	7.9
Himachal Pradesh	31.3	3.6	34.2	4.5	46.2	4.9
Jammu-Kashmir	36.9	6.1	38.7	4.6	32.1	6.5
Karnataka	20.4	14.5	21.2	15.4	21.5	12.2
Kerala	45.8	34.3	46.8	37.0	57.2	40.2
Madhya Pradesh	14.7	8.9	12.8	6.1	15.8	8.4
Maharashtra	24.2	8.6	24.7	8.8	26.2	6.1
Orissa	25.1	22.0	21.3	15.0	33.0	19.6
Punjab	31.2	8.4	31.8	7.3	36.3	9.4
Rajasthan	34.7	16.7	30.4	7.3	32.7	8.1
Tamil Nadu	34.8	22.9	36.0	21.5	31.8	24.1
Uttar Pradesh	21.1	8.7	23.7	10	28.2	12.5
West Bengal	27.8	29.2	35.3	41	33.6	45.9
All India	25.5	15.3	26	13.8	28.6	14.6

Source: Computed from Different Quinquennial Reports & on Employment and Unemployment of NSSO, GOI.

the proportion of the sex-wise distribution of rural non-farm employees in different states of Indian Union. It can be observed from the Table that in the states like Andhra Pradesh, Tamil Nadu, Haryana, Jammu & Kashmir etc., the share of male employment in rural non-farm has been increasing continuously and is almost equal to national average. It is certainly surprising that the West Bengal and Tamilnadu, there has been a tremendous fall in the ratios of the male workforce absorbed in non-farm activities from 35.3 per cent and 36.0 per cent in 1993-94 to 33.6

per cent respectively in 1999-2000 accompanied by rise in share of non-farm activities in female workers while in all other states even at all India level there has been a substantial increase in the same between these two periods.

State-wise growth rates of workforce in India are shown in Table 4. It can be observed from the Table that between 1987-88 and 1993-94, the states like Haryana, Himachal Pradesh, Jammu & Kashmir, Karnataka, Kerala, Maharashtra, Punjab, Tamilnadu, Uttar Pradesh and West

Table 4. Sex-Wise Growth Rates of RNFE in India

	Male		*Female*	
	1987-88 to 93-94	*1993-94 to 99-2000*	*1987-88 to 93-94*	*1993-94 to 1999-2000*
Andhra Pradesh	-1.5	1.2	-1.6	-0.6
Assam	-1.7	13.5	-0.9	3.8
Bihar	-2	3	-1.7	6.2
Gujarat	-2.5	-0.3	-14.8	-1.4
Haryana	10	1.3	-0.7	1.1
Himachal Pradesh	2.9	12	0.9	-3.2
Jammu-Kashmir	1.8	-6.6	-1.5	2.1
Karnataka	0.8	0.3	0.9	-3.2
Kerala	1	10.4	2.7	3.2
Madhra Pradesh	-1.9	3	-2.8	2.3
Maharashtra	0.5	1.5	0.2	-2.7
Orissa	3.8	11.7	-0.7	4.6
Punjab	0.6	4.5	-0.9	2.1
Rajasthan	-4.3	2.3	-9.4	0.8
Tamil Nadu	1.2	-4.2	-1.4	2.6
Uttar Pradesh	2.6	4.5	1.3	2.5
West Bengal	7.5	1.7	11.8	4.9
All India	0.5	2.6	-1.5	0.8

Computed from Table - 3.

Table 5. Trends of RNFE in India and Andhra Pradesh

Industry Group	*India*			*Andhra Pradesh*			*% Age change*	
	1971	*1981*	*1991*	*1971*	*1981*	*1991*	*INDIA 1971-91*	*A.P. 1971-91*
Mining & Quarrying	2.67	2.7	2.64	2.33	1.73	3.88	72.66	146.8
Manufacturing V	36.26	39.13	43.29	39.4	43.22	45.13	55.7	35.73
Manufacturing Va	21.16	18.5	12.2	27.4	26.64	18.82	0.98	1.67
Manufacturing Vb	15.11	20.63	20.04	12.2	16.59	17.49	132.31	112.24
Construction	4.88	6.19	5.88	5.87	4.91	4.53	110.93	14.35
Trade and Commerce	16.1	16.75	18.51	17.3	18.56	19.4	101.46	65.99
Transport, Storage	5.38	6.63	6.97	4.18	5.27	5.98	126.91	111.84
Other Services	34.69	28.6	33.78	30.73	26.31	29.91	70.6	44.1
Total	**100**	**100**	**100**	**100**	**100**	**100**		

Source: Computed from 1971, 1981, 1991 Census Reports.

Bengal have shown growth rate in male workforce. Regarding females, in the same period, the states like Himachal Pradesh, Karnataka, Kerala, Maharashtra, Uttar Pradesh and West Bengal have shown growth rates and for all India level, it is increased in case of males and decreased in case of females. The states like Andhra Pradesh, Assam, Bihar, Madhya Pradesh, Orissa and Rajasthan have in growth list between 1993-94 and 1999-2000 and Jammu & Kashmir and Tamilnadu have included in the list. Rajasthan had shown tremendous growth rate. It reached 0.8 (+) from (-) 9.4. Karnataka and Maharashtra have shown negative. Andhra Pradesh and Gujarat remain in negative performance between 1993-1994 and 1999-2000.

Rural Non-Farm Employment in Andhra Pradesh

Development of Agriculture is likely to result in positive impact on rural non-farm activity. It generates employment through the development of agro-based industries and growth of the tertiary sector. In this connection, the composition of rural non-farm employment in India and Andhra Pradesh of employment in the activities like Manufacturing, Transport, Construction and Trade and Commerce at India level, whereas in Andhra Pradesh, Mining and Quarrying, Manufacturing and Transport etc. have shown growth per cent in RNFE.

Table 6 explains the trends of rural non-farm employment in Andhra Pradesh, industry-wise and sex-wise. It shows that there are significant differences, if one takes into account the rise or decline in the composition of workforce in various components of rural non-farm employment during 1971-91. Such differences are notable in respect of mining and quarrying. The Table depicts that most of the male and female are concentrated in manufacturing and other services. The share of female in construction and transport is decreased during 1961-91 in Andhra Pradesh.

Table 6. Sex-Wise Distribution of RNF Workforce in A.P

Industry	*1971*		*1981*		*1991*	
	Male	*Female*	*Male*	*Female*	*Male*	*Female*
Mining & Quarrying	2.26	2.59	1.81	1.48	4.03	3.45
Manufacturing	39.03	41.68	40.36	52.45	31.55	50.56
Construction	6.1	5.01	5.64	2.55	5.35	2.08
Trade and Others	17.82	15.42	19.51	15.5	20.97	14.69
Transport, Storage etc	5.1	0.8	6.8	0.32	7.85	0.37
Other Services	29.7	34.5	25.88	27.7	30.26	28.86
Total	**100**	**100**	**100**	**100**	**100**	**100**

Source: Computed from 1971, 1981, 1991 Census Reports.

The Table 7 depicts the share of RNFE in rural employment and changes during 1971-91 in various districts of Andhra Pradesh. It can be observed from the Table that Telangana region showed higher shares in the years in comparison, followed by Coastal Andhra and Rayalaseema. In Coastal Andhra, the shares of RNFE remained almost constant in all the three periods while in the other two regions they declined in 1981 compared to 1971 but attained 1971 levels by 1991. Among the districts Nizamabad topped all others with relatively higher shares in RNFE during the three points of time followed by Karimnagar, East Godavari in Coastal Andhara and Cuddapah in Rayalaseema region maintained higher levels compared to other districts in their respective regions. The share of RNFE has steeply declined in Prakasam of Coastal Andhra, Cuddapah of Rayalaseema and Warnagal of Telangana.

Conclusion

The major conclusions of the study are as follows. Firstly, the analysis reveals that there has been a continuous process of diversification of rural workforce from farm to non-farm

Table 7. District-Wise Profile of RNFE in A.P.

District Region				*Change*		
	1971	*1981*	*1991*	*1971-81*	*1981-91*	*1971-91*
S+V+VI	15.68	17.43	17.2	1.75	-0.23	1.52
East Godavari	20.36	20.44	20.62	0.08	0.18	0.26
West Godavari	16.87	17.64	19.45	0.77	1.81	2.58
Krishna	17.72	16.88	16.26	-0.84	-0.62	-1.46
Guntur	17.15	15.04	14.42	-2.11	-0.62	-2.73
Prakasam	19.61	16.25	13.94	-3.36	-2.31	-5.67
Nellore	16.65	16.12	17.13	-0.53	1.01	0.48
Coastal Andhra	17.44	17.04	17.04	-0.22	-0.18	-0.4
Chittoor	13.19	13.97	15.78	0.78	1.81	2.59
Cuddapah	18.1	17.95	16.58	-0.15	-1.37	-1.53
Anantapur	12.78	12.1	13.22	-0.68	1.12	0.44
Kurnool	14.19	12.78	13.81	-1.41	1.03	-0.38
Rayalaseema	14.28	13.94	14.7	-0.34	0.76	0.42
Mahabubnagar	14.37	13.76	12.75	-0.61	-1.01	-1.62
Hyd+RR	20.37	22.51	18.73	2.14	-3.78	-1.64
Medak	14.72	15.4	16.36	0.68	0.96	1.64
Nizambad	23.85	23.67	26.53	-0.18	2.86	2.68
Adilabad	16.71	16.37	20.5	-0.34	4.13	3.79
Karimnagar	23.77	20.74	23.83	-3.03	3.09	0.06
Warangal	18.39	16.25	15.59	-2.14	-0.66	-2.8
Khammam	16.23	15.22	14.33	-1.01	-0.89	-1.9
Nalgonda	19.23	16.65	19	-2.58	2.35	-0.23
Telanga	18.61	17.62	18.39	-0.99	0.77	-0.22

Source: Computed from 1971, 1981, 1991 Census Reports.

activities i.e., industrial and service activities. So that the share of agricultural employment in total workforce has been decreasing from the last few decades. Andhra Pradesh in terms of composition of Rural Non-Farm Employment. manufacturing and trade and commerce accounted for higher share of rural workforce. However, there are differences in the sex-wise composition at national and state levels. For instance, other services accounted for the highest share of rural non-farm employment for males at the all India level. In Andhra Pradesh, the manufacturing accounted for highest share of females. To sum up, males had a clear edge over females both at the national and state levels. However, thus, the growth of Rural Non-Farm Sector is desirable to alleviate rural poverty and unemployment in India as well as in Andhra Pradesh.

11

Global Integration and Unemployment Among the Rural Poor in India

Dr. G. Erraiah

Introduction

Global integration refers to economic organization having some laws of behaviour that widens the frontier of economic activities across the political boundaries of nation states and help the process of increasing economic integration and growing economic interdependence among countries in the World economy. This intensified integration of global economy increased the pace of privatisation and liberalisation and the domineering role of WTO in World affairs.

India is a founder member of WTO. It has abundant man power but scarce in capital. In view of this, it has followed labour intensive approach to generate more employment opportunities. This approach is reversed in the wake of liberalisation from 1991 in the name of economies to scale, global integration and market friendly approach. This technology-upgradation with more capital, leads to decrease in employment opportunities in the economy. The Task Force on Employment opportunities appointed by Planning Commission also admitted that employment elasticity has been decelerating during liberalisation.

The positive co-relation between unemployment and poverty is well established in India. But World Development Report 2000-2001[1] stated that global integration helped member countries to reduce poverty including India and China irrespective of decreasing employment opportunities. National Sample Survey 1999-2000 also confirms it. But its earlier thin sample studies stated that rural poverty has not declined in India. (Gaurav Datt, 1999).

In this paradoxical situation, an attempt is made in this paper to know the relationship between poverty and unemployment, nature of unemployment among the poor and also factors contributed in decelerating poverty in India.

Poverty Alleviation in India is an Age Old Ambition

In the 18th Century, Dadabai Naoroji a distinguished Indian Economist felt that India is rich in economic resources and culture but Indians are poor because of foreign rule. He propounded Resource Drain Theory to explain this paradox on which independence movement is originated. After independence, India opted planned approach to speed-up economic development based on macro level approach until IVth Five Year Plan. It opined that fruits of development should percolate among all sections and regions of the economy and help in reducing poverty.

But the research study 'Poverty in India' (1971) conducted by V.M. Dandekar and N. Rath based on NSS data, through disclosing the fact that trickle down theory did not work out properly to reduce poverty influenced in changing the future strategy of our planning. From V Plan onwards, planned approach has gradually changed towards target group approach to help the poor directly so as to alleviate poverty effectively. Planning Commission has paid attention to estimate poverty periodically so as to know the nature and dimensions of the poverty and various committees are appointed to analyse the causes of poverty from time to time[2].

Dimensions of Poverty in India

There has been a steep rise in poverty inspite of planned development since 1951. However in 1970s, poverty began to decline and the same has been established in different individual and government studies.

Since 1973-74 onwards Planning Commission has been estimating poverty for every five years based on National Sample Survey data. The analysis reveals that poverty has been decreasing gradually from 54.9 per cent in 1973-74 to 26.1 per cent by 1999-2000 as shown in Table 1.

Table 1. Poverty Estimates in India

(in Millions)

Year	*Number of Total Poor*	*Rural Poor*	*Urban Poor*	*Percentage of Rural Poor to Total*
1973-74	321 (54.9)	261 (56.4)	60 (49.0)	81.3
1977-78	329 (51.3)	264 (53.1)	65 (45.2)	80.2
1983-84	323 (44.5)	252 (45.7)	71 (40.8)	78.0
1987-88	307 (38.9)	232 (39.1)	75 (38.)	75.5
1993-94	320 (36.0)	244 (37.3)	76 (32.4)	76.2
1999-2000	260 (26.1)	193 (27.1)	67 (23.6)	74.2

Source: Economic Survey 2001-2002 p. 238 (Computed).

Note: Figures in Brackets Refer Poverty Ratios to Respective Population.

Table 1 denotes that poverty in India is basically rural in nature. As per Dandekar and Rath, urban poverty is nothing but over flow of rural poverty. (Dandekar V.M. and Rath N.p. 25). Rural poverty accounts for 81 per cent of total poor in 1973-74 and has come down slightly to 74 per cent by 1999-2000.

Poverty projections for the 21st Century

Indian Planning Commission (1998) worked out the poverty projections upto 2011-12 based on the annual growth rate (6.5 percent) experienced between 1993-94 and 1996-97 with the hope that economic growth is likely to have considerably larger impact on poverty reduction than before (Ninth Plan 1997-2002, p. 30-31).

Table 2. Poverty Ratio Projections (India)

Region	*1996-97*	*2001-02*	*2006-07*	*2011-12*
Rural	30.55	18.61	9.64	4.31
Urban	25.58	16.46	9.28	4.49
Total	**29.18**	**17.98**	**9.53**	**4.37**

Source: Planning Commission (1998), Ninth Five Year Plan (1997-98), Vol. 1, p. 35.

Table 2 presents poverty projections for a period of 15 years from 1996-97 onwards. The Planning Commission optimistically estimated the rural poverty has come down to 18 per cent by 2001-2002 and to 4 per cent by 2011-12.

But in early 1990's, there are apprehensions about liberalisation process that it would lead to increase in poverty because of more use of technology in production process in the name of global integration. Surprisingly, NSS study 1999-2000 brought forth the fact that rural poverty in India has declined from 37 per cent in 1993-94 to 26 per cent by 1999-2000. However this decrease is said to be much lower than 18.6 per cent target set by IX Five Year Plan (IX Plan, p.35).

Relation Between Poverty and Unemployment

Poverty and unemployment are said to be the two sides of the same coin because incidence of unemployment is more among the poor due to lack of income generating assets like land, seasonal fluctuations especially in agriculture. The following Table depicts the co-existence of poverty and unemployment.

Table 3. Incidence of Unemployment in India (1971)

Household Monthly income (in Rupees)	*Percentage of unemployed to total work force*
100 and less	45.4
101-200	29.5
201-500	17.9
500 and above	7.2
Total	**100**

Source: Report of the Committee on Unemployment, May (1973).

Table 3 reveals that three- fourths of unemployed belong to households with an income level less than Rs. 200 per month. All these families can broadly be classified as living below the poverty line. Obviously, unemployment is widely spread in poor families and as income level improves, the proportion of the unemployed to the total number declines because upper sections are able to manage jobs for the members of their families due to good education and training and higher social status. This tendency emphasises the need for provision of work to the poor so as to allow them to come out of the poverty trap. For better appreciation of this tendency, awareness about the nature of unemployment among the poor is required.

Nature of Unemployment among Poor Households

In India underemployment generates more concern than open unemployment. Dantwala Committee on unemployment also stated that in an economy like India, there is little open or outright unemployment but there would be considerable seasonal unemployment or underemployment. In India, to estimate unemployment mainly two criteria are used i.e. (1) Usual Principle and Subsidiary Status (UPSS), that measures open-unemployment throughout the year and (2) Current Daily Status (CDS) which takes into account not only open-unemployment but also underemployment. The following Table explains the varied nature of unemployment in relation to the level of monthly expenditure.

Table 4. Unemployment Rates by Household Monthly Per Capita Expenditure (MPCE) 1999-2000

(as per cent of labor force)

MPCE	*Rural*		*MPCE*	*Urban*	
Rs.	*UPSS*	*CDS*	*Rs.*	*UPSS*	*CDS*
0-225	1.06	11.31	0–300	2.91	9.61
225-255	1.02	9.62	300–350	5.21	9.67
255-300	0.98	7.46	350–425	4.08	8.20
300-340	0.98	7.46	425–500	5.43	9.20
340-380	1.20	6.56	500–575	5.81	9.20
380-420	1.43	6.18	575–665	8.12	8.63
775-950	2.44	5.57	1500–1925	3.49	4.67
950 and above	2.54	5.25	1925 and above	2.99	4.10
All	1.43	7.21	All	4.63	7.65

Source: NSSO Survey 55th Round (1999-2000).

Quoted by Ruddar Datt, Indian Economic Association Conference Vol.-2001, p. 469.

A close perusal of data in Table 4 reveals that both in rural and urban areas the lower consumption groups show much lower rate of unemployment on the basis of UPSS criteria but this pattern gets reversed on the basis of CDS criterion. But as the expenditure levels improve, there is increase in unemployment rate of UPSS criterion, fall on the basis of CDS criterion. In other words, the difference between UPSS and CDS rates indicates a decline with an increase of MPCE of the class. This highlights the stark reality, that the poor cannot afford to remain unemployed since their waiting power is very weak and take up any work low paid or high paid, full time or part time, continuous or intermittent to make both ends meet (Ruddar Datt p. 469).

Sharp Decline in Employment Generation During Post Liberalisation Era

There is a sea change in the post-liberalisation era in employment generation as a consequence of shedding down of the load of redundant workers in public sector and technological upgradation in private sector including agriculture. The Task Force on Employment Opportunities admitting deceleration in employment-growth mentions: "This sharp deceleration in the growth of employment naturally has been the focus of much attention and comment, raising fears that economic growth in 1990's has been of a jobless

Table 5. Growth of Employment by Sectors

Industry	*Employed Workers (in million)*			*Annual growth rate*	
	1983-84	*1993-94*	*1999-2000*	*1993-94*	*1994-2000*
A. Primary	208.99 (69.0)	245.16 (65.5)	239.83 (60.4)	1.60	-0.34
Agriculture	207.23 (68.4)	242.46 (64.8)	237.56 (59.8)	1.51	-0.34
B. Secondary	41.66 (13.8)	55.53 (14.8)	66.91 (16.8)	2.90	3.14
(a) Manufacturing	34.03	42.50	48.01	2.14	2.05
(b) Construction	6.78	11.68	17.62	5.32	7.09
C. Tertiary	52.11 (17.2)	73.76 (19.7)	90.26 (22.7)	3.5	2.42
(a) Trade	19.22 (6.3)	27.78 (7.4)	37.32 (9.4)	3.57	5.04
(b) Transport storage & communications	7.39 (2.4)	10.33 (2.87)	14.69 (3.7)	3.24	6.04
(c) Community, Social and personal services	1.70 (7.9)	3.52 (8.6)	33.20 (8.4)	2.90	0.55
Total Employment	**302.76 (100.0)**	**374.5 (100.0)**	**397.00 (100.00)**	**2.04**	**0.98**

Note: Figures in Parenthesis Give the Percentage of the Sector in the Total Employees During the Respective Years.

Source: Compiled and computed from the Data Provided by the Planning Commission (2001), Report of Task Force on Employment Opportunities. Table 3.2 Quoted in Ruddar Datt, Op. Cit. p. 464.

one variably" (Govt. of India 2001 p. 26). This implies that the growth rate in employment is less than growth rate in labour force and this has resulted in an increase in the unemployment rate.

As shown in Table 5 there is deceleration of growth rate of employment during the post liberalisation period. In agriculture, the growth rate of employment observed during 1983 to 1993-94 was 1.51 per cent but during the period of liberalisation, the growth rate of employment became negative (-0.34 percent). In absolute terms workers employed, decreased from 245 million to 240 million.

In the secondary sector, the combined effect of manufacturing and construction resulted in a modest improvement in the growth rate from 2.9 per cent in the pre-liberalisation decade to 3.14 per cent in the post-liberalisation period.

However in tertiary sector (service) there is a deceleration in growth rate of employment to 2.24 per cent in the post liberalisation period as against 3.53 per cent in pre-liberalisation period. It is mainly as the consequence of sharp decline in employment growth in the community, social and personal services to 0.55 per cent in post liberalisation period as against 2.90 per cent in the pre-liberalisation period.

Reasons for Decreasing Poverty

The Rural poor are mostly agricultural labourers, small and marginal farmers and artisans. Wage income is the main source for their livelihood. But in post-liberalisation period employment opportunities have come down especially in agriculture irrespective of increase in labour force. However, incidence of poverty has surprisingly slid down because of the following two reasons.

(a) Increase in wage earnings of the casual labour.

(b) Effective coverage of poor people through poverty alleviation programmes.

Increase in Wage Earnings of Casual Labor

Amount of income earned by labour, depends on wage rate and number of working days. Since the information about number of working days is not published by NSSO available data about wage rates shows an increase in post-liberalization period.

Table 6. Growth of Average Daily Wage Earnings in 1993-94 prices in Rural India

Category	Male		Female	
	1987-88 to 1993-94	*1993-94 to 1999-2000*	*1987-88 to 1993-94*	*1993-94 to 1999-2000*
1. Public works	1.55	3.83	1.90	5.04
2. Casual labour in agriculture	1.36	2. 80	2.34	2.94
3. Casual labour in non-agriculture	1.33	3.70	1.32	5.07
4. Casual labour in all activities	0.77	3.59	1.95	3.19

Source: NSSO Survey for 1987-88, 1993-94 and 1999-2000.

It is noticed from Table 6 that average daily earnings of rural males employed as casual labours indicated a growth rate of 0.77 per cent in the pre-reform period but indicated a sharp increase by 3.59 per cent in the post-reform period. Similarly there was also an improvement in the average daily earnings of rural female casual labour from 1.95 per cent to 3.19 per cent. The average daily earnings of workers employed in public works improved still higher than all other categories of rural labour. These factors indicate an improvement in quality of employment.

Poverty Alleviations Programs

To alleviate poverty two types of measures are required i.e., short term and long term measures. Long term measures include growth inducing investment in agriculture in rural areas. In view of existing labour market and land distribution conditions in rural areas, investment in agriculture does not lead positive results unless land reforms are effectively implemented.

In short run poverty alleviation programmes aimed at directly helping the poor instead of entire population. Helping the poor directly, demands proper identification of the poor for its successful implementation. The rationale for targeting the poor is that the benefits or social returns are higher for the population at lower end of the income distribution than at the upper end. Thus identifying the poor is important for successful implementation of poverty alleviation programmes.

Self Employment Programs Vs. Wage Employment Programs

In terms of targeting success, self targeting schemes like rural public works score over income based targeting. For example, 90 per cent of workers working under the Employment Guarantee Scheme were poor according to some estimates (Dankekar, 1983). A comparison of public works programmes and IRDP (Self-Employment programmes) in Maharashtra (Mahendra Dev S. & Ajit Pande p. 58) shows that participation in public works is highest among the poorest households during the year 1987-88 (See figure 1). But IRDP data reveal that participation is more or less similar across expenditure classes (a horizontal straight line). In other words, participation in IRDP has no relationship with expenditures. These data suggest that public works are much better targeted and that income-based does not ensure better targeting as per 1987-88 data used by Ravallion and Datt. (Mahendra Datt S. and Ajit Pande, p. 58)

But the later study for the year 1993-94 indicates changing tendency. According to the data (1993-94) even in IRDP the percentage of participating households is higher for some of the lower expenditure class as compared to upper expenditure classes as shown in Figure 1. The success in

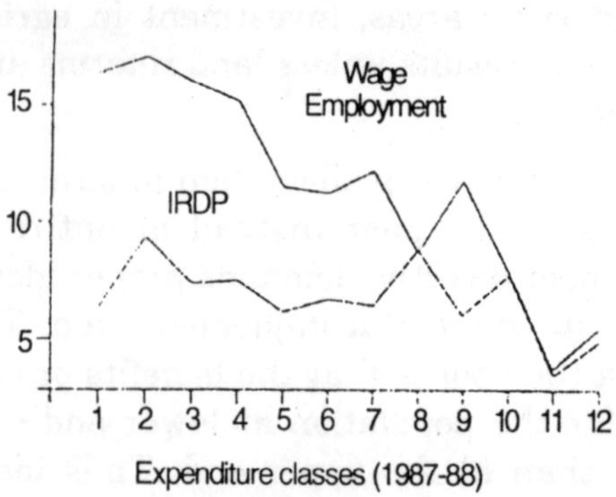

Expenditure classes for 1987-88 are as follows:

1	< Rs65	5	110-25	9	180-215
2	65-80	6	125-40	10	215-80
3	80-95	7	140-60	11	280-325
4	95-110	8	160-80	12	> Rs385

Figure 1: Targeting Success of Wage Employment and IRDP Programmes in Maharastra During 1987-88-1983-84.

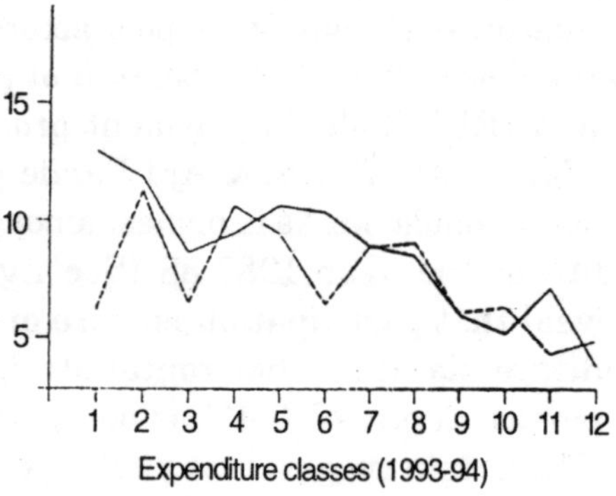

Expenditure classes for 1993-94 are as follows:

1	< Rs120	5	100-210	9	300-55
2	120-40	6	210-35	10	355-445
3	140-60	7	235-65	11	445-560
4	160-90	8	265-300	12	> Rs560

Figure 2: Participation of Households in Wage Employment and Credit (IRDP) Programmes (by expenditure classes) 1987-88, 1993-94. Quoted in S. Mahendra Dev and Ajit Pande, Ibid., p. 58.

targeting is more effective in NGO based community participated programmes rather than government run programmes (Ibid p. 59). Similarly to make government run self-employment programmes more successful targeting group lending is more effective than lending for individuals.

There is another argument that if the country depends more on wage-employment programmes, skills cannot be improved for the poor. Self employment programmes on the other hand can increase the skills of the workers. In future, skill-based workers will get much higher wages and wage-employed people continue to get lower wages particularly in the post-economic-reforms period. In other words if self employment programmes are successful, they are better in terms of income sustainability than public works programmes. However, the Indian experience of IRDP is not satisfactory. (Mahendra Dev S. & Ajit Pande p. 59). Hence there is need to rely on wage-employment-programmes to benefit the poor more effectively and to reduce poverty in short period.

Conclusion

Globalisation is a modern version of the Theory of Comparative Cost Advantage of Ricardo. Its aim is to look upon the world as a "global village." It has four parameters namely - reduction in barriers relating to trade, technology, capital and labour movement among the member countries.

In the process of liberalisation, technology upgradation is the prerequisite for all countries so as to withstand in the global market. In the liberalisation movement economic growth is promoted in many member countries at the cost of bottom sections of the society since employment opportunities to the unskilled labourers are adversely affected. Hence, government no longer act, as facilitator to the globalisation movement but more than that-it has to protect and promote bottom sections of the society.

In India, poverty is rural in nature and incidence of unemployment among the poor is more. In general, the rural labour are engaged as casual labourer due to lack of education and skills. In the process of liberalisation the rural poor are the worst victims when employment opportunities are declining in agriculture. But increasing farm and non-fam wage rates give some relief. Under these circumstances government must act as guardian to the poor through implementing poverty-alleviation-programmes.

The success of these programmes depends on proper identification of the poorest among the poor. These poverty eradication programmes are broadly classified into wage employment and self employment programmes. Between these two, wage employment-programmes score more in targeting of the poor and there is an improvement in targeting of the self-employment-programmes through following group approach, in selection of beneficiaries through NGO's participation. Emprovement of Panchayat system can help in selecting the poorest among the poor better.

In India decrease in poverty during liberalisation period to 26 per cent irrespective of increasing unemployment is mainly due to an improvement in wage rates, an improvement in coverage of poor under poverty alleviation programmes. However, India failed in the reduction of rural poverty upto 18.61 per cent as targeted in IX Plan. Thus there is more need to focus government's attention and support towards the poor than pre-liberlisation period by taking up more and more wage employment and self employment-programmes in addition to effective implementation of Minimum Wage Act in agriculture.

Notes

1. The potential for global integration to reduce poverty is well illustrated by the cases of China, India, Uganda and Vietnam. Though some aspects of data are controversial, the evidence for substantial poverty reduced in India in the 1990's is strong.
2. Danwala Committee on Unemployment Estimates, B. Bhaghavathi Committee (1973) on Unemployment, Task Force on Employment Opportunities (2001).

3. IX Five Year Plan of India, Emphasis on group lending in case of IRDP. See World Bank Report (1998) for information of problems associated with credit programmes.

References

1. Dandekar K. (1983), Employment Guarantee Scheme: An Employment Opportunity for Women, Gokhale Institute of Polities and Economies, Pune.
2. Dandekar V.M. & Rath N. (1971) Poverty in India, The Ford Foundation, New Delhi. Govt. of India (1998) Planning Commission, IX Five Year Plan: 1999-2002.
3. Dandekar V.M. & Rath N. (2001) Report of the Task Force on Employment Opportunities.
4. Gaurav Datt (1999), Has Poverty Declined Since Economic Reforms? Economic and Political Weekly, Dec. 11-17.
5. Mahendra Dev and Ajit Pande (2000), Persisting Poverty and Social Insecurity: A Selective Assessment, India Development Report.
6. Ruddar Datt (2001), Economic Liberalisation and Its Implications for Employment in India, I.E.A., 84th Conference Volume.
7. World Bank (2000) World Development Report: 2000-2001—Attacking Poverty, Oxford University Press, New York.

Part II

Impact of Economic Reforms on the Indian Labour

12

Analysis of Industrial Relations in Karnataka State Road Transport Corporation (KSRTC)–A Case Study

Dr. (Smt.) M. Madhumathi, Prof. R.G. Desai

Introduction

Harmonious relations in every sphere of human activity is a prerequisite for socio-economic progress. Establishing and maintaining smooth and cordial relationship between labour and management is of utmost importance. For every nation to achieve the expected rate of industrial development, among other factors, the most important one is the existence of healthy labour management relations. It is responsible in a large measure for the stability, prosperity and growth of any organisation. Harmonious, peaceful and cordial employee-employer relations contribute much for carrying on the productive activity in a smooth fashion, stepping up the levels of efficiency and profit earning etc. in the organisation and improving the standard of living, welfare, prosperity and happiness of the employees. Thus establishing and maintaining cordial industrial relations is a fundamental pre-requisite not only for the growth, stability and prosperity of the organisation, but also for the welfare of the management and workers in the organisation and the society, nation and world at large.

Objectives

1. To examine the Industrial Relations' in Karnataka State Road transport Corporation.
2. To assess the Impact of strikes in Karnataka State Road Transport Corporation with certain variables.
3. To know the Index of Industrial Relations in Karnataka State Road Transport Corporation.

Material and Method

Material is collected from the official records, and annual administrative reports of the organisation. Simple tabular analysis is followed in this paper. The study covers the time series data over a period of 10 years from 1988-89 to 1997-98. One of the objectives of this paper is to examine the Industrial Relations in Karnataka Road Transport Corporation based on secondary data pertaining to strikes. Accordingly, this paper discusses the number of strikes, growth of strikes, workers' involvement ratio and workers participation rate, causes for strikes and its impact. The index of industrial relations has been constructed in the same way as in Nair (1973). It gives an approximate idea about the Industrial Relations Situation in Karnataka State Road Transport Corporation.

Growth of Strikes in KSRTC

Strike is a weapon in the hands of workers. It is used to fulfil their demands. The growth rate of strikes is shown in the Table 1.

The table shows the annual percentage growth rate of strikes in KSRTC from 1989 to 1998. The number of strikes was highest in 1993. During the year 48 strikes took place and the growth rate was also high to the tune of 300%. It was due to the protest against the implementation of duty rotation of crew in several Depots and supporting the Bharath Bundh on 9.9.1993. Apart from this, KSRTC staff and Workers Federation gave a call for one day strike on 28.7.1993 to implement the Memorandum of Understanding (MoU) signed on 10.5.1993. The growth of strike activity shows ups and downs in the KSRTC during the period under study.

Table 1. Annual Percentage Growth Rate of Strikes in KSRTC from 1989 to 1998

Year		*Number of Strikes*	*Annual Growth rate*
	Phase I		
1989		5	-
1990		18	260
1991		14	-22
	Phase II		
1992		12	-14
1993		48	300
1994		21	-56
	Phase III		
1995		29	38
1996		7	-76
1997		19	171
1998		23	21

Source: Computed from Records of Labour Section, KSRTC.

Workers' Involvement Ratio and Workers Participation Rate

There are two different measures, which help us to understand the size and magnitude of a strike. They are:

(a) Workers' involvement ratio—It is a ratio between the number of workers involved in strikes and the total number of workers. This measure is in no way a perfect one because some workers are likely to strike more than once a year.

(b) Workers' participation rate—it is calculated by dividing the number of workers involved in strikes by the total number of strikes and it gives the average number of strikers per strike.

Table 2. Workers' Involvement (in strikes) Ratio During 1989 to 1998 in KSRTC

Year	*Total Number of workers involved in strikes*	*Total Number of workers employed in KSRTC*	*Workers involvement ratio* $\frac{Col\ 2}{Col\ 3} \times 100$
1988-89	230	50169	0.45
1989-90	257	54315	0.47
1990-91	400	54844	0.72
1991-92	519	55296	0.93
1992-93	41492	56465	73.4
1993-94	15440	58911	26.2
1994-95	49179	57512	85.5
1995-96	152	57806	0.26
1996-97	5919	58603	10.10
1997-98	6706	58807	11.40

Source: Figures in Column (2) have been Compiled from the Labour Section, Central Office, KSRTC Administrative Reports, and Records of Recognised Federations during that period.

Figures relating to the workers' involvement ratio are given in the Table 2. A higher worker involvement ratio indicates greater intensity in the strike activity. The Karnataka State Road Transport Corporation witnessed intense strike activity during 1992-93 to 1994-95 and 1996-97 to 1997-98. On 11.3.1992 KSRTC Staff and Workers Federation (recognised Federation during that time) gave a call for strike to protest against the bifurcation of BTS and privatisation. In this all the workers of several depots had participated. Again on 28.7.1993, the same Federation gave a call to protest against the delay in implementing the Memorandum of Understanding. In this the employees engaged in depots, division, regional workshops and central office had participated. KSRTC Staff and Workers Federation and Karnataka Stage Transport Employees Union together gave a call to support the Bharat Bundh on 9.9.1993. Majority of the workers supported this.

Once again the KSRTC Staff and Workers Federation jointly gave a call to support the Dharni Satyagraha of the Federation Secretary from 9.6.1994. This was supported by the majority of the workers in all the Divisions.

From 1996 onwards the strike activity in KSRTC against took a turn. This was due to the conclusion of referendum on 15/16.7.1996. The workers urged for the referendum to be held quickly. The leaders submitted the new 'Charter of Demands'. Owing to this, strike activity increased during the period.

Table 3. Workers Participation (in Strikes) Rate in KSRTC During 1988-89 to 1997-98

Year	*Total No. of Workers involved in Strike*	*Total No. of Strikes*	*Workers Participation Rate (Col 2 ÷Col 3)*
1988-89	230	5	46
1989-90	257	18	14
1990-91	400	14	28
1991-92	519	12	43
1992-93	41492	48	864
1993-94	15440	21	735
1994-95	49179	29	1695
1995-96	152	7	21
1996-97	5919	19	311
1997-98	6706	23	248

Source: Computed from Records of Labour Section, KSRTC.

The Table shows the workers' participation rate in KSRTC from 1988-89 to 1997-98. They indicate the average number of workers participating in strike. Except in 1994-95, the average size of strike has varied from 14 to 864. This figure was the highest in 1994-95, i.e., 1695 and 14 in 1989-90, it is very less during the period under study.

Causes for Strikes

The major causes which result in the strikes in KSRTC can be grouped under two heads. They are:

1. Internal causes leading to Bad Industrial Relations. and
2. Public Causes—external to KSRTC.

The causes which are responsible for work-stoppage and damage to industrial relations are dismissal of the workers for various reasons, protest against prosecution of a driver and conductors, protest against abuse of Divisional Traffic Officer, Publication of Conductors' misbehaviour, assault on conductor for not sanctioning leave by the higher officials, slapping of the driver, quarrel among fellow workers, action taken by the officers on driver, to pay extra wages for the paid holidays, bonus, allowances, cancellation of schedules, publication in the Vartha Pathra not maintaining vehicles properly, to transfer traffic inspector etc.

The public causes are due to quarrel between police and crew, quarrel between crew and passengers, assault on the crew by the police and public, during various bundhs etc. Anything happens in the society, that directly effects on the transport. During various times, the damage was caused to the buses of KSRTC and started strike due to these reasons many a time.

Impact of Strikes

The number of strikes and man-days lost are increasing on an average. The workers recruited now-a-days in KSRTC are more educated than earlier. They understand their rights and they can fight for them. There are trade unions to support them. Though the number of strikes are few, the impact of strike in terms of man days lost, loss of schedules and loss of KMS is very high. We come to know that these strikes are a great impediment in the development of the KSRTC.

The Average time loss due to strikes is calculated by dividing the total number of man-hours lost with the total number of strikes in that year. Annual average time loss was 3242.01 hours. Similarly Average revenue loss, Average kilo-meter loss and Average schedule loss were calculated.

Annual average revenue loss was Rs. 537611.4. The annual average kilometer loss was 137212.06 kms. and the annual average schedule loss was 26.1.12 schedules.

Index of Industrial Relations

In order to sharpen our results, we have calculated Index of Industrial Relations. This Index is calculated by multiplying with 100 the figure that is obtained by dividing the total man-days worked with the total man-days lost for the given year as compared to the similar figure for the base year. This formula can be presented as follows:

$$\text{Industrial Relations Index} = \frac{\text{Total Man-days worked}}{\text{Total Man-days Lost}} \times 100$$

For example, in 1990-91 the index was

$$= \frac{5003.51}{7960.6} \times 100 = 62.85$$

The Index of Industrial Relations gives us an approximate idea about the industrial relations' situation in the Karnataka State Road Transport Corporation.

When the time-loss gets reduced due to a smaller volume of strike activity, the industrial relations index will be relatively larger and vice-versa. Likewise given the time loss, a possible reduction in man-days worked (on grounds other than strike activity), the index will be smaller. In all circumstances, generally speaking a large index will denote a greater degree of industrial peace as observed by Nair (1973). It may be seen from Table 4, in no year, except 1995-96, the index was larger than that of the base year. In 1995-96 the index was 174.35, this denotes that there was less number of strikes during that year and industrial peace was restored in that particular year. Except that year, the industrial relations in Karnataka State Road Corporation are rather unsatisfactory.

Table 4. Index of Industrial Relations in KSRTC During 1988-89 to 1997-98

Year	*Man-days Worked*	*Man-days Lost*	*Man-days worked÷ Man-days Lost*	*Index of Industrial Relations (Base 1988-89)*
1988-89	1830938	230	7960.60	100.00
1989-90	1982240	257	7712.99	96.88
1990-91	2001406	400	5003.51	62.85
1991-92	2017784	519	3887.83	48.83
1992-93	20194798	41492	486.71	6.11
1993-94	21348115	1540	1382.64	17.36
1994-95	160758	49179	3.26	0.04
1995-96	2109767	152	13880.00	174.35
1996-97	2133089	5919	360.37	4.52
1997-98	2139748	6706	319.07	4.00

Source: Computed from Records of Labour Section, KSRTC.

Major Findings

1. An important finding of the study is that over a period of 10 years, the number of strikes was highest in 1993. During this year as many as 48 strikes took place in the organisation and the growth rate was also high to the tune of 300 per cent. This was due to the protest against the implementation of duty rotation system of crew in several depots. The growth of strike activity shows ups and downs in the Karnataka State Road Transport Corporation during the period under study.
2. Another important finding of the study is that the Karnataka State Road Transport Corporation witnessed another intense strike activity during 1995 and 1998. During this period, there was a protest against Bifurcation of BTS and privatization of Karnataka State Road Transport

Corporation. The workers urged for the referendum to be held quickly, as the referendum was concluded on 15/16 of July 1996.

3. The major causes for strikes in Karnataka State Road Transport Corporation are internal causes leading to bad industrial relations and public causes external to Karnataka State Road Transport Corporation, such as exigencies and misbehaviour of conductors, quarrel between crew and passengers, etc.

4. The impact of strike is measured through average time loss, average revenue loss, average kilometer loss, and average schedule loss of the organisation for a period of 10 years.

5. The index of Industrial Relations is calculated. It gives an approximate idea about the Industrial relations' situation. A large index denotes a greater degree of industrial peace. In no year (except 1995-96), the index was larger than that of the base year. In 1995-96, the index was 174.35, this denotes that there were less number of strikes during that year and industrial peace was restored only in that year. Remaining years, the industrial relations situation in Karnataka State Road Transport Corporation is rather unsatisfactory.

References

1. Administrative Reports of KSRTC from its inception to 1998.
2. Memorandum of Settlement, KSRTC, 1958 to 1989.
3. Memorandum of Understanding KSRTC-1994.
4. Nair. K. Ramachandra (1973), Industrial Relations in Kerala, Sterling, New Delhi.
5. Michael V.P. (1979), Industrial Relations in India and Workers involvement in management, Himalaya Publishing House, Bombay.

13

Economic Reforms: Crisis in Handloom Industry in A.P. A critical note

Prof. K. Venkat Narayana

Introduction

Textile industry is one of the oldest non-agricultural occupations in rural India. Traditionally handloom sector was only popular in each and every village offering employment to a sizable section of population in the ancient village economy. However due to advent of British rule and the introduction of machine into the industry, this artisan industry was reduced to size. Powerloom and mill sectors also made their dent into the market. In recent decades the power loom products also entered into rural and urban market on a large scale replacing the remaining of the traditional handloom industry. Similarly automatic jet machines imported from Japan and other advanced countries also began to dominate the textile industry. As a result artisan communities are thrown out of the traditional industry, reducing them to the status of labourers on casual basis.

Presently, we find handloom sector getting it's base thinning while the powerloom sector occupying significant place in our textile industry. Similarly in recent times the shares of mill sector in total production of cloth also declined from 79 per cent in 1951 to 24 per cent in 1987. Further, the share of Powerlooms in total cloth production was 47.9 per cent in the same year. By the year 1998-99 the share of mill sector in total production has fallen to 5.4 per cent while that of powerlooms increased to 72.2 per cent. Consequently, handloom sector is confined to only silk weaving and quality products of cotton to meet the requirements of upper echelons in the domestic and export markets.

The textile industry was subjected to radical transformation during the 1990's. It included introduction of highly mechanized machines which have replaced the workers to a large extent, exposing the Indian textile market to the world market, withdrawal of state support to the handloom sector consequently growing unemployment among textile workers and leading to casualisation of labour force.

In this paper an attempt is made to focus on the changing role of the state for sustaining the handloom industry in Andhra Pradesh state during 1950-1995. It also presents consequences of sudden withdrawal of state strategic support in the form of marketing, subsidy and other protectionist measures after 1995.

Since ages, the textile industry was confined to household sector. It was the biggest cottage industry in the countryside. It was based on self-employed working members of the household. Wage labour concept was negligible in the industry. Basically it was a family industry. Gradually the concept of master weavers those who organized the production of cloth with investment and hired labour came into existence beginning with second half of nineteenth century. Through the production was carried on with labour intensive techniques, it was a step towards pre-capitalist mode of production. By beginning of the sector, half of 19th century an improved version of machine over the handloom units was also introduced in the country particularly, in and around Bombay and Ahmedabad cities. The process of modernization of textile industry still was continued by introducing capital intensive machines like Jet and automatic looms, still it appraises in the important centres of textile industry in the country.

Andhra Pradesh Scenario

Traditionally three geographical parts of Andhra Pradesh namely Telangana, Rayalaseema and Coastal Andhra regions have been major handloom weaving regions catering to the needs of local people. It also provided employment to sizable rural section of community, particularly weavers. There were about 5.26 lakh handlooms in 1985 and this declined to 2.19 lakh in 2002. Even now this activity provides full time employment to about 3.67 lakh persons and part time employment to more than 85000. During 1980's and 1990's there was a marked decline in loom age in the state accompanied by a fall in the output of cloth. Handloom weaving in the state experienced a sudden and sharp decline. The decline was most sharp in the Telangana region especially in Karimnagar, Nizamabad, Nalgonda, Warangal and Adilabad districts.

The handloom industry in erstwhile Telangana was also flourishing. There was no dearth of market for it's products. Siricilla sarees were national famous. Similarly Cheerala, Mangalagiri, Venkatagiri, Dharmavaram and many other places were known for quality. The industry was providing all varieties of cloth catering to the needs of the rich and poor. But the penetration of mill industry into the rural market began to effect it adversely, as a result the government of A.P. initiated certain supportive measures to sustain the industry and the dependants during 1960-95.

State Government Policy (1950-1994)

Both Centre and State government have supported handloom industry since independence. Keeping in view the significance of the industry, the state government also introduced (1976) certain steps to sustain the industry particularly handloom units. These measures can be classified into three categories (a) organizational measures (b) Modernization measures (c) Protection measures.

Organizational Measures

A great deal of emphasis was placed on formulating and strengthening Weavers Co-operatives, with apex bodies at the State and Central levels. The organizational structure was designed for providing inputs, credit and marketing channels and to protect the weavers community from machine industry and middle men. As part of this, APCO was established in 1976 for supply of inputs like yarn, Credit and marketing of products. This organisational structure was continued till 1995 with the intention to protect the industry.

Marketing Measures

Emphasis was laid to increase productivity through improved looms also. One of the objectives of APCO was supplying required inputs like yarn, cotton to the affiliated silk and wool Primary Co-operatives and purchasing the finished products like sarees, dhoties, furnishings etc. from member societies bridging their marketing gap through the network of sales outlets. Opportunities were provided to upgrade the skills of weavers. There were 401 primary societies in Andhra, 419 in Rayalaseema and 363 in Telangana. All of these 1183 societies are affiliated to APCO, of which about 160 are silk yarn weaving societies and about 50 are wool societies. There were 387 show rooms of APCO through out Andhra Pradesh and in the States of Karnataka, Tamilnadu, Kerala, Orissa, Maharashtra, Utter Pradesh, West Bengal and Delhi as by middle of 1998. The main pride products of APCO are dye silk sarees, Dharmavaram silk sarees, Gadwal, Narayanpet and Venkatagiri sarees besides ikkat furnishing dress material, floor coverings, bedsheets and kalamkari dress material. The total strength of employees in APCO was 1913 by the end of 2000. APCO had been running in profits till the financial year 1994-95.

Protectionist Measures

Both centre and state governments provided marketing and subsidy support to the handloom industry as part of the policy for it's sustainability. This involved a package of schemes to boost up the handloom sales such as reservation of certain varieties of products exclusively for this industry. Similarly subsidized cloth (Janatha cloth) for distribution to the lower income groups was made available by central assistance. Construction of houses and work-sheds for weavers was also included in the package. Provision of subsidies through Marketing Direct Assistance (MDA) schemes funded by the state government, provision of each credit for working capital to the Co-operatives by NABARD, providing Yarn at concessional rates to the industry were some of the measures included in the package of assistance.

The state government has initiated steps to increase the sales by supplying handloom cloth to Government Offices, Social Welfare Hostels, Road Transport Corporation employees and other agencies. It was made compulsory to purchase handloom cloth by all the government offices. The government also promoted production of Janatha cloth for distribution among the weaker section at nominal prices by providing central subsidy. To promote sale of handloom products, the state government also allocated grants in its budget for providing handloom products at discounted rates. Further, the state Government also provided credit facility to it's employees for purchase of handloom products. All these measures were introduced to promote and sustain the handloom industry in view of it's labour intensity. Through it's fiscal policies, the central government was also protective of the handloom industry. As much as 167 per cent excise duty was levied on synthetic yarn till 1994-95 to make mill made cloth dearer compared to handloom products. With the active support of state and central government the APCO, the apex body of handloom industry state level was able to reach a turnover of Rs. 128.41 crores in 1992-93, shows in the Table 1.

Table 1. Turnover of APCO 1992-2001

(Rs. in crores)

Year	*General Cloth Sale*	*Livery Cloth Sale*	*Janatha Cloth Sale*	*Yarn Sale*	*Total*
1992-93	50.29	10.90	36.81	30.41	128.41
1993-94	48.03	16.59	27.58	30.48	122.68
1994-95	59.39	10.84	23.82	31.48	125.53
1995-96	55.07	11.50	13.83	11.64	92.04
1996-97	35.06	9.95	7.57	7.94	60.52
1997-98	42.48	7.98	—	8.41	58.87
1998-99	51.36	10.08	—	8.49	69.93
1999-2k	50.01	6.65	—	9.41	66.07
2000-01	18.80	0.53	—	1.05	20.38

The Crisis in the Industry

With the introduction of economic reforms both at centre and state level the handloom industry suffered a deathblow, Central government had withdrawn incentives hitherto given for producing janatha cloth. Several products exclusively reserved for handloom sector were revoked. The state government also initiated several measures much against the interests of the handloom workers. As part of economic reforms, the centre began to withdraw it's strategic support since 1995-96. It has gradually reduced the excise duty on synthetic yarn from 167 per cent in 1994-95 to 25 per cent in 1996 and totally abolished in the budget for 2002-2003. It also levied excise duty on handloom yarn making the price dearer. This has become a deathblow to the handloom industry. During the last ten years the prices of synthetic yarn has been declining. On the other hand the prices of cotton cloth have increased four times during the same period.

Cotton made cloth has become unaffordable to the poor and lower middle class people. The centre has also withdrawn subsidized handloom Janatha cloth hitherto was distributed to poorer sections at nominal price.

The state government also initiated reform measure in 1995-96 by withdrawing the supportive measures. They are:

1. Refusal of discount sale provision in the state budget;
2. Dispensing with the credit facility to the state employee for purchase of handloom products; and
3. Withdrawal of departmental purchases of handloom products.

Owing to the state withdrawal of purchase of livery and Janatha cloth from APCO, the total sale amount sales which was Rs. 128.41 crores in 1992-93 declined to 20.38 crores in 2000-2001. General cloth sales also declined drastically due to the refusal to reimburse the discount amount by the state government.

Procurement of different varieties of cloth by APCO also declined drastically (Table 2).

Table 2. Procurement of Handloom Products for the Years 1992-2001

(Rs. in crores)

Year	*General*	*Livery*	*Janatha*	*Yarn*	*Total*
1992-93	39.93	31.05	31.41	10.06	112.45
1993-94	50.43	28.68	30.98	15.08	125.17
1994-95	50.25	18.26	30.19	5.11	103.81
1995-96	21.58	6.26	11.97	4.62	44.43
1996-97	28.58	—	6.88	6.56	42.02
1997-98	26.46	—	10.28	5.86	42.60
1998-99	36.40	—	7.21	7.63	51.54
1999-2k	26.18	—	8.17	6.65	41.00
2000-01 (upto Jan' 2001)	4.08	—	0.72	1.56	6.36

All the categories of items for sale have declined as shown the bottom in the year 2000-2001. It is only due to government's deliberate policy initiated in 1995-96 to withdraw the support to the handloom sector.

The stock position of APCO also declined due to the withdrawal of state support.

Table 3. Stock Position as on 31st March

Year	*General Sale Value*	*Janatha*	*Yarn Cost Value*	*Livery*	*Total*
1995-96	36.23	—	—	2.77	39.00
1996-97	56.23	—	—	2.36	50.59
1997-98	51.98	—	1.52	3.97	57.47
1998-1999	58.77	—	0.99	4.22	63.98
1999-2k	51.98	—	0.54	3.87	56.39
2000-01	48.30	—	—	4.36	52.56
(Upto Jan' 2001)					

APCO has been landed in economic crisis. As much as Rs. 52.12 crores of discount amount dues and departmental purchases due are pending the with state government. The state government as part of it's economic reforms has withdrawn it's support base. It has not paid the discount allowance to APCO amounting to Rs. 32.44 crores. Loan amount on account of accumulated and unsold Janatha cloth was Rs. 8.84 crores pending with the government. In addition to this, three loss making units (i) AP state industrial Co-operation Society Ltd., (ii) AP Textile processing Co-operation Society Ltd., (iii) Heat setting plant (Nellore), with total loss of Rs. 11.84 crores were merged with APCO. The APCO was also suffering with high fixed overhead expenditure towards non-commercial staff recruited from time to time and this has become heavy burden to the organisation.

The state government has initiated a deliberate policy of disovning the handloom industry. It has implemented the policy in two-phased manner.

In the first phase the state has withdrawn it's contribution towards discount sale of handloom products. Sale of janatha cloth was also dispensed with. Purchase orders for livery cloth used in government offices were also withdrawn. Government also initiated steps to convert handloom sector into powerloom sector. Government also delayed the payment of outstanding dues to APCO in lieu of earlier discount and purchase of cloth etc.,

The second phase of measures initiated during 1999-2000 in the form of restructuring of APCO, was considered to be deathknell to the handloom sector. Some of the measures are mentioned hereunder:

1. The total strength of staff both commercial and non-Commercial workers in APCO was reduced from 1830 to 805 by Offering VRS.
2. The state government also offered APCO properties such as lands and production units acquired earlier for sale.
3. It was also decided to close down 146 sales units leaving only 200 in various districts and other states. Several divisional offices were also closed down.

It is to be noted that govt of India also appointed Satyam Committee to suggest measures for restructuring handloom sector. To the dismay of handloom workers, this committee also recommended for withdrawal of concessions hitherto enjoyed by the handloom sector. Some of them are:

(a) Yarn mills need not provide yank yarn. It was obligatory to Produce yank yarn used by handloom sector.

(b) Eleven products reserved to handloom sector have to be dispensed with.

(c) Janatha products hitherto supplied by the handloom sector be shifted to powerloom sector or mill sector.

Conclusion

As a result of recent reforms, the handloom sector has landed in deeper crisis. The production has gone down. Lakhs of workers have become jobless and underemployed. The employment days have gone down to 4 or 5 days a month. Similarly their daily wages were brought down to below subsistence level. Recent trends in the labour market, in textile industry provide the evidence of casualisation and informalisation; Whether it is handloom sector, or powerloom sector or mill sector the workers were either self employed or regularly employed. But Post-liberalization scenario suggests that there is neither security of employment nor protection to the workers. Low quality of employment or casualisation of employment is fast replacing the traditional known organised labour market leaving the workers more insecure and vulnerable for exploitation. Handloom workers joined the ranks of labour in powerloom sector could not survive the onslaught of economic reforms and succumbed to suicide deaths. The Siricilla episode is an example.

Emergencies of powerloom sector in the place of handloom sector are supposed to be development oriented, employment creative and ensure social justice. But any change or modernization initiative should not lead to destruction and dislocation of way of life for majority of people who depending upon the system. Otherwise it should ensure the social security. Recent crisis in powerloom sector of Siricilla should become an eye opener to the policy makers.

14

Trade and Labour Standards: Using the Wrong Instruments for the Right Cause

Prof. M. Lakshmi Narasaiah

A moral value is a shared concern of humanity; hence its enforcement should be a cooperative task implemented for the benefit of humankind. Would we qualify recent approaches to the issue of trade and labour standards as non-inquisitory but shared and cooperatives ones? The purpose of this brief is to shed some light on this question.

In fact, nobody, will deny any country the right to raise and fight for uses which are of moral concern for humanity, as they are supposed to benefit humankind. The issue of implementing and enforcing a core of labour standards is one of these.

However, a problem remains: who has the negotiating power to raise and impose them? The key issues is that trade coercive attempts by some become inquisitorial as soon as they are backed by moral concerns which are supposed to be shared by all, while the same "all" lack the negotiating power to be, in turn, coercive if they so wish. In other words, trade related coercion forcedly becomes "inquisition" when moral concerns are introduced into the functioning of an international trading characterized by large imbalances in the negotiating power of the participating countries. Only a few governments have the negotiating leverage and strength to develop what we may qualify as "trade-related inquisitory practices".

The issue of trade and labour standards seems to have arisen when "uniform competition" has been regarded as a threat to employment and economic growth in some industrial countries.

However, without attaining a certain degree of international agreement and coherence as to whether and under what conditions a given competitive advantage is, or is not, related to social or other conditions, and whether or not it may be considered as "unfair". With protectionist views in mind, such an approach may only be interpreted as "unfair competitiveness seekers".

If the motivation behind the introduction and further use of moral argumentation is to seek a justification for the possible use of trade measures as enforcement mechanisms to achieve certain goals. Particularly for harmonization of labour standards, one may wonder why the labour standards issue has not been linked to North-North trade in the current debate on the considerable variation in labour standards among developed countries. The motivation may be that in the post-Uruguay round era, when tariffs have been reduced substantially and "grey area measures" put under stricter control or even banned, we may be facing the possible revival of new forms of protectionism wearing "blue", "green" or "multicolour" masks. On the contrary, if the motivation behind the introduction of such moral labour rights argumentation reflects a real commitment by the international community to enforce labour standards, a door may be opened for embarking, in the future, on a series of international initiative, not necessarily under the trade umbrella.

It should also be stressed that the linkage between trade and labour standards has been seriously misinterpreted. Most analysts remain blind to the two-way character of the link between trade and labour standards. On the one hand, trade liberalization is to promote growth and development by promoting a more efficient allocation of resources and to ease the adoption and implementation of labour standards, as well as to promote job raising labour standards-not keeping them low-should increasingly be seen as the real source of competitiveness and economic growth, among others, increase in the quality of labour. There is a case for considering economic progress and the rise in labour standards as mutually reinforcing.

Turning to the low labour standards debate, much more empirical and analytical evidence is needed to assess the extent to which low labour standards are correlated to lower wages and labour costs. Although raising labour standards may not primarily be intended to maximize efficiency, it is becoming increasingly evident that efficiency and the further potential of the firm may not necessarily be maximized by keeping labour standards low. In this context, it is the development to human capital in LDCs which is a top priority, not because failing to respect labour standards in these economies threatens the welfare of the workers in the industrialized countries but, more simply, because it is the only strategy for enhancing the productivity of labour and ultimately increasing the people's standard of living. Thus, if raising labour standards and ensuring their effective implementation is important for economic progress, developed and developing countries, as well as workers and employers in each region, should adopt a cooperative, not confrontational, approach in order to deal with this urgent and pressing problem. For this very reason, adherence to trade sanctions would be wrong approach. Trade is essential for enhancing workers' productivity because it ensures that a country's resources will be employment in the activities that it is best at. In turn, increased productivity is the key to development, higher labour standards and higher wages. Moreover, the issue of labour standards is of a moral nature: it has an undeniable development dimension which needs to be more clearly perceived but, as discussed, it is certainly not an issue to be dealt with through trade measures.

Labour standards should be dealt with in the WTO. The capacities of the ILO will prove invaluable for renewed multilateral effort to improve working conditions in developing countries. Its tripartite structure has proved to be the best suited to the tasks of conciliation and dialogue.

Improving the standards of living and labour standards for workers or eradicating child labour is what matters it is the right cause for humankind, a cause to fight for, through various approaches and by using all the mechanisms at our disposal in order to ensure its success. Thus, the issue is not one of trade and order standards, but of labour standards and economic development, an issue of human dignity and human rights nature. It is a universal issue, the solutions to which should be found by all nations, taking into account equity considerations. Each country should participate in the process, depending on its level of economic development. It is precisely because economic development, including trade, is positively correlated with the adoption and effective implementation of labour standards that solutions to low labour standards should not necessarily come from negative and coercive approaches. Solutions for universal problems must not only be efficiency-based but also equity-based. Therefore, the case is for cooperation rather than coercion and for applying positive instruments. As in the case of environmental issues, developing countries should be recipients of funds, technical cooperation and other similar forms of support when the implementation of labour standards involves an inequitable cost burden.

The initiative of "grouping" a core of existing conventions into a new global convention on core labour standards of universal value may, in view of its new and distant qualitative nature, generate strong support from the international community for its implementation. The ILO was created to promote workers' right, so the initiative could be launched under its aegis, in direct collaboration with other intergovernmental organizations dealing with social, trade and development issues in an interrelated manner. The support to this or other similar approaches by the international community, and in particular by those developed countries that have recently shown a special and strong interest in the reinforcement and implementation of labour rights in developing countries, will be a clear sign of their degree of sincerity and their willingness to share the social concerns of universal value which seem to be paramount interest to most of their citizens.

15

Education for Skills Development and their Utilisation in the Indian Economy

A. Seshadri & C. Vasudevulu Naidu

Introduction

Education is no longer a privilege, it is considered as a birth right of every citizen in a civilized society. The great progress made by science and technology and the complexities of modern life have necessitated universal education of a reasonable good quality. Education, human skills, innovative knowledge and human resources mobility are real factors in economic growth of nations and the welfare of a citizen.

One of the trends in modern society is the expansion of formal education which is separated from the production process itself. Education may be regarded as an investment as well as consumption. It makes a direct contribution to the standard of living and creates a lasting consumption asset. The consumption effects and the production effects of education may be regarded as complementary to each other from the point of view of the social values which of them form the basis for economic growth, is a wide sense.

Article 26(1) of the Universal Declaration of Human rights (1948) was proclaimed "Every one has the right to education". Education shall be free, as least in the elementary and fundamental stages. Elementary education shall be universal. Technical and professional education shall be made generally available and higher education shall be equally accessible to those who deserve basis of merit.

The human character of educational capital, as distinct from that of real capital, creates a special problem for analysis and polity. By educating youth, we may create people able to provide skills in several fields of science and technology.

Skills Development and Utilisation in the Economy

The most important economic resource in the world consists of the acquired abilities of people, their education, experience, skills and health.

In India nearly 53 per cent are observed to be engaged as production workers. The remaining 47 per cent are engaged in supervision. However, the proportion of production workers among the working proprietors varies very widely from 12 per cent extent in the case of Agro-industries to 63 per cent in the case of agro-equipments.

A large majority of (61%) hired workers are employed as un-skilled workers. Among these unskilled workers the majority are engaged as seasonal workers. In this regard it is of interest to observe that Agro-industries which have the largest percentage of workers as hired workers employ the lowest proportion of skilled workers and the highest proportion of seasonal workers[2].

A large majority of the working proprietors i.e. 85% are literates and 42 per cent of them have minimum of matriculation level of education. Agro-industries are the largest proportion of working properties with minimum level of matriculation education.

Dropout rate is very high. Half of the number of the children enrolled in First standard leave the school before reaching Fifth standard and only one fifth of them reach Tenth standard. Failure rate is also high in the class mainly due to ineffective teaching the contents of the courses are not in relation to the needs and requirements of the people and the quality education is very poor. As such there is a great need for more investment of elementary education.

Education, Various Programmes and Achievements

Eradication of illiteracy is a major task which demands a major initiative by the people, community agencies and state. In poor countries it difficult to meet their social objectives without large scale funding of education as the state involvement in the education of its future citizens is in the increase.

The realisation of illiteracy is the major source of under development in any society. The United Nations Organizations and the developing countries have launched literacy programmes to reach the under privileged.

In recent years higher education has become more responsive to the job market than everbefore. Technocrats are rarely appointed as vice-chancellors of universities and leading experts in agriculture and industry are excluded in boards of studies. Job-oriented degree courses are offered, while non-utility courses are discouraged. This is the real trend in higher education in India. Further, higher education is now offered under self-supporting course.

National Policy on Education

The proposal cannot be applied to occupation specific courses like Engineering, Medicine, Law, Teaching etc. Similarly, the services of specialists with academic qualifications in humanities, social sciences, sciences etc. will be required in various job positions.

The delinking will be applied to services for which, a university degree need not be a necessary qualification. Its implementation will lead to a re-fashioning of job-specific courses and offered greater justice to those candidates who despite being equipped for a given job, are unable to get it because of an unnecessary and too much preference for graduate candidates.

Literacy and Education

While china has adult illiteracy rate of 16.5 per cent, India and Pakistan continue to have huge illiteracy rate of 43.5 per cent and 55 per cent respectively. India made some progress on literacy levels but the proportion of children in primary and secondary school remains very low. India ranks below sub-Saharan Africa's average of 60.5 per cent literacy rate.

Table 1. Trends Literacy and Education

Country	*Adult Literacy % age 15 and above 1999*	*Public expenditure as % of GNP*		*As % of Govt. expenditure*	
	1999	*1985-87*	*1995-97*	*1985-87*	*1987-99*
India	56.5	3.2	3.2	8.5	11.6
China	83.5	2.3	2.3	11.1	12.2
Pakistan	45.0	3.1	2.7	8.8	7.1
Developing Countries	73.1	N.A	N.A	N.A.	N.A.

Note: NA= Not Available.

Source: Human Development Report 2001.

China's state education programme has helped the country's record on adult illiteracy rate that outperforms not only developing countries average but almost some of the high-income country average of 85.5 percent[3].

Education Under the Five Year Plans

There has been phenominal expansion of education under the five year plan. Universalisation of primary education, vocationalisation of society education and equalisation of educational opportunities and improving the content and qualify of higher-education are the goals to be achieved in the shortest possible time[4].

Plans-strategies

1. Combination of formal and non-formal methods, educational technology, Teacher-training,

improvement of physical resources and involvements of the community.

2. Orientation courses to teachers to upgrade their competence.
3. Special education programmes for girls and weaker sections.
4. Effective use of electronic media to promote national integration and cultural heritage.
5. Technology mission to eradication of illiteracy.

Allocation of education in terms of money has multiplied several times but the outlay in terms of percentage to the total volume of investment in the plans has decreased. Planners have not chosen to give education priority in our plans. Therefore, there is an urgent need to increase the educational outlay atleast upto 10 per cent of the total plan out-lay and effective physical management are necessary to create a healthy, democratic, egalitarian and forward looking welfare society.

Education outlays for all the five year plans are given in Table No.2.

Table 2. Education in the Five Year Plan

Five Years Plans	*Total Outlay (in crores)*	*Outlay for education (in crores)*	*Expenditure (Percentage)*
First Plan (1951-56)	2.069	170	7.9
Second Plan (1956-61)	48,100	277	5.8
Third Plan (1961-66)	*7,500	560	6.9
Fourth Plan (1969-74)	15,902	822	5.2
Fifth Plan (1974-78)	38,853	1,284	3.3
Sixth Plan (1980-85)	97,500	2,524	2.6
Seven Plan (1985-90)	1,80,000	6,383	3.5
Eight Plan (1992-97)	4,34,100	21,217	3.5
Ninth Plan (1997-2002)	8,75,000	N.A	N.A

Note: NA = Not Available.

Source: Planning Commission, Eight Five Year Plan, New Delhi.

It is real surprise to note that all the skills created in the economy are not utilized. As such, there is some degree of underutilisation and wastage of skills. The increasing number of unemployed on the live registry of employment is an indication of un-utilization of these educated skills. Further, in some professional courses there is a very high degree of brain drain to the developed countries. Hence, there is a need for national policy on manpower planning for creation, utilization of skills. Proper policy orientation is urgently needed in the context of new economic policies of Liberalisation, Privatisation and Globalisation (GLP). A policy of proper returns to educational investment is the real need of the hour in India.

Achieving the objective and sustaining the anticipated benefits of the educational reforms programmes in a federal set up will pose many problems for the 21st century. As such, every effort must be made to develop proper relationship between centre and state in a federal set up. Therefore, a three-fold strategy may select the most effective strategy of education and training. These past strategies may cover the crucial issues like dropout rates, and low level of learning achievement and prevailing wastages in India's educational system. Such weakness is to be avoided by adopting suitable techniques and improving returns from investment in the development of education. The present capacity of individual states to sustain past investments to be further strengthened. Further, efforts will be needed to support the required new schemes and subjects[5].

The Central Government must provide leadership to continue and sustain the present programme. The low level of educational resources of the central government for educational development should be improved. The capacity building of states along with a policy of encouraging man-power planning and vocational education at district level is urgently required to meet the demands of the 21st century. The local regional, grossroot level machinery to be strengthened to improve the quality of education and skill formation along with proper man-power utilisation in the proposed Tenth five Year Plan.

References

1. Natarajan; *"Introduction to Economics of Education"*, Sterling publishers, 1993, Madras, pp. 1.
2. M.S. Ramanujam; *"Man-power Development in India"*, Allied Publishers, Bombay, pp. 17, 64.
3. *"The Economic Challenger"*, No. 4, Issue 13, Oct-Dec. 2001, pp. 13.
4. Planning Commission, *"Eight Five Year Plan"*, Vol. II, 1992, New Delhi, p. 213.
5. Planning Commission, *"Seventh Five Year Plan"*, Vol. II, 1987, New Delhi, p. 283.

16

Gender–Related Issues of Urban Informal Labour Market

Prof. G. Raghava Reddy & J.M.J. Vinodini

Introduction

The role of the informal sector in the urban economy of the developing countries is well recognized and the literature on the subject is burgeoning. The informal sector of the urban economy provides an easy access to opportunities of work and thereby the means of livelihood for the deprived segments of the urban society as well as the migrants from the rural sector. The informal sector activity, its nature, character and structure has received greater attention than the labour component of it. It is also rather difficult to segregate the economic activities of persons who are self-employed such as petty traders, street-hawkers, piece-workers from their labour component. Since the informal sector is generally outside the regulatory framework to the government, labour laws are hardly enforced. Gender-discrimination and gender-gap in wages and earning are quite common. Issues of exploitation of women and child labour in the urban informal labour markets are receiving grater attention in recent years at all levels, because of the realization that they have been bypassed in the process of development. There is a reorientation in the developmental strategies and models being formulated at the national and global level.

Women's work escapes computation in home-based production, family concerns or on land owned by kin. World-wide estimates show that at least one-fourth of women are neither housewives nor in paid employment. Thus, a substantial number of women are invisible or at home in a sporadic and informal manner in unpaid jobs. Gender discrimination and gap in wage employment are widely reported in Human Development Report of the UNDP. The structural adjustment policies of the Fund-Bank being implemented in the developing world also seem to worsen segmentation and discrimination in the informal labour market. Due to the dynamics of the labour market over time and space there is a need for region/area specific studies to diagnose the labour situation and to formulate appropriate policy choice by those who are operating in such markets as well as policy makers.

Role of Women in the Urban Informal Sector

The role of women in economic activity has been underestimated in the past for a variety of reasons. However, the contribution of women to work at home as well as outside the home is receiving greater attention and recognition, especially since the advent of the Human Development Reports. The burden of work on the part of the women is higher in developing countries. The empirical literature suggests that there is a positive correlation between economic development and female labour force participation rates, however, the gender gap in labour force participation rates persists and it is significant in the Islamic countries. It is also noticed that economic development and urbanization go together due to inter linkage between industrialization and urbanization. It is widely reported that urban based industrialization and commercialization introduce the polarization and hirerarchisation of men's and women's role and relationships. In the informal labour market women's choice of activity is determined by norms of female seclusion and not by economic rationality. Poverty weakens traditional seclusion and strengthens economic rationality. In this sense poverty acts as an instrument of social change for economic betterment. No wonder, women workers in several developing countries are concentrated in non-wage employment. The persistence of discrimination in employment and disparity in wages and earnings tends to deprive women workers and marginalize their contribution. The concept of work participation rate has undergone a complete change in the Census Reports of India since 1961. A trichotomy of persons into mutually exclusive groups of main workers, marginal workers and non-workers was introduced in 1981 and continued in 1991 also. In 1981 as well as 1991 the gender gap in work participation rate hovered around 37 and 36 per cent respectively. Trends in usual status work participation rates indicate a remarkable stability highlighting the persistence of gender gap.

The size of the urban informal sector differs based on the concept followed and the size varies significantly across the major urban centres of the country ranging from a low of 28 per cent to a high of 75 per cent of labour in the respective locations. Among them more than 50 per cent of workers are women. Purely economic reasons account for nearly 1/3 of male migrants and hardly 2 per cent of female migrants. Among others the persistence of discrimination and disparity based on sex constraints mobility of female labour and thereby minimize their contribution to the world of work.

The Purpose of The Present Study

The purpose of the present study is to probe into some technical aspects of gender issues in the informal sector of Kavali town of Andhra Pradesh. In other words, it is proposed to comprehend and analyse the structure and working of the urban informal female labour market in terms of its segmentation and competitiveness. A wide variety of data were collected from different agencies and sources for fulfilling the specific objectives and testing the corresponding hypothesis.

As for as the primary data are concerned a 5 per cent stratified random sample was chosen covering 218 respondents. These 218 workers also represent 218 households wherever the household concept is applicable.

Employment, Earnings and Indebtendness

The average size of household of 122 residents and 96 migrants was found to be 5.7 and 5.5 respectively. This finding is in correspondence with the size of rural labour households. 56 per cent of workers among residents are married while this figure stands at 67 per cent in the case of migrants. Un-married workers constitute hardly 13 per cent among migrants which is understandable due to the vulnerability of un-married workers in the urban setting for different risks that are ever present.

The nexus between caste and occupation and religious seclusion is getting marginalized in the case of our respondents. In other words we notice "Extensity-refers to the total volume of goods and services available for sale and purchase. Purity refers to the market principle unhampered by non-market consideration such as, friendship, kinship, caste and class. The perfectly pure and extensive market is, of course, only an ideal one. It does not exist even in the most industrialized and commercialized societies, and purity is penetrating into the female labour market of our samples. Our analysis of the reasons for migration of our respondents enables us to accept the expected income model of Todar-Haris. Migrants are mostly (52 per cent) from within a radius of 15 to 20 kilometers of Kavali. Nearly 2/3 migrants entered the town during the past 4 to 7 years. The average duration of migration works out to 4.5 years. Surprisingly the correlation between level of education and average earnings of our respondents is negative though insignificant and in education. In migration and the link between education and earnings of our samples we reject our first hypothesis namely, there is no correlation between migration of male and female labour, level of education and earnings.

We incorporate the principal findings and statistical results of our empirical study regarding employment earnings and indebtedness and the causative and allied structural features in Table 1.

Our statistical analysis of work participation rates, labour force participation rates, work experience and earnings, work experience and mobility, wage levels of migrants and residents (serial No. 1 to 6 in Table 1) provide us enough evidence to partly accept our second hypothesis namely there is no significant difference in the participation rates between workers in different occupation, experience and mobility. Issues of poverty and indebtedness are inextricable of intertwined as well as the low economic status of women and their marginalisation in the household erena. We have incorporated the major statistical results on this front and these findings (serial no. 7 to 12 in table 1) enable us to reject the third hypothesis namely the incidence of poverty and indebtedness are not significantly different between categories of home-based and non-home based women labour households.

Effects of State Intervention on Labourers, and Living Conditions

The concern of the state for the poor is as old as the rise of utilitarianism. Welfare economics provides a strong foundation for advancing the cause of the poor on grounds of equity and efficiency. The directive principles of State policy of the Indian Constitution offer a tremendous challenge for the State to intervene in the labour market on behalf of women and child workers. In recent years, provision of micro credit for gainful employment and empowerment of

Table 1. Major Findings and Results

Sl. No.	*Variable*	*Reference Group/Category*	*Statistical measure/test*	*Finding/result*	*Remarks*
1.	Age of samples	*(a)* Residents	Chi-square test	Chi-square 26.80 Dg=6 Critical Value=12.592	Significant at 5 per cent level
		(b) Migrants	Chi-square test	Chi-sqare 9.9880 Dg=6 Critical Value=12	Not significant
2.	WPR of samples	*(a)* Residents	T-Test	T-Value=1.1854 T-critical value=2.0738	Not Significant
		(b) Migrants	T-Test	T-Value=2.53 T-critical value=2.0738	Significant at 1 per cent level
3.	LFPR samples	*(a)* Residents	T-test	T-Value=1.6655 T-critical value=2.0738	Not significant
		(b) Migrants	T-test	T-Value=1.0974 T-critical value=2.0738	Not significant
4.	Work experience and earnings	Respondents	R	0.9983	
5.	Work experience and mobility	Respondents	Chi-square test	Chi-square=15.14 Dg=g Critical Value=16.919	Not significant

(Cont...)

Table 1 (Contd...)

6.	Average wages and income	*(a)* Residents	ANOVA	F-value=87.9940	Significant at 1 per cent level
		(b) Migrants	ANOVA		Significant
7.	Income by Location of Occupation	Respondents	Chi-square Test	Chi-square=24.6951 DF=12 Critical Value=12.592	Significant at 1 per cent level
8.	Wage disparity between men and women workers	Respondents	t-test (paired t-test)	T-value=10.4354	significant at 1 per cent level
9.	Share of women's income in household income	Respondents	R	0.2817	Not Significant at 1 per cent level
10.	Indebtedness by location of Occupation	Respondents	Chi-square Test	Chi-square=27.6042 D>F.=12	Significant at 1 per cent level
11.	Incidence of Poverty	Respondents	Head Count ratio	71 per cent for home based workers 52 per cent for no-home based workers.	

Source: Table 4.4, 4.7, 4.8, 4.10, 4.11, 4.12, 4.13, 4.15, 4.16, 4.17 of the unpublished Ph. D. thesis of Vinodini, S.V. University, 2000.

women is widely followed. We notice that 26 per cent of current borrowings of our respondents are drawn from institutional agencies at an average rate of interest of 12.5 per cent annum. T-test and paired t-test indicate a significant difference in current borrowings from formal and informal sources by residents and migrants (Table-2).

The Child labour situation of our respondents and our statistical findings in this regard are indicated in Table 2 Child population and child labour, incidence of child labour among residents and migrants, disparity in earning are indicated. These results provide us arms and ammunition to hypothesis a significant positive relationship between child population and child labour and an insignificant association between the incidence of child labour and residential status of respondents as well as the persistence of disparity in their earnings. Child labourers contribution to household income stands at 16 per cent of our samples. The other elements of welfare promotion such as access to fair price shop, pucca houses with sanitation, access to electricity, health, water supply differ significantly across categories. We find that the proportion of household expenditure on food broadly in conformity with Engle's law of consumption.

Policy Choices

Women workers of our sample constitute the hard core of the informal female labour market of kavali town. Whether they are resident or migrants they are deprived of education and training and therefore, they are crowded in low income economic activities and burdened with household work. They are also constrained by seclusion in some cause and are therefore marginalized. They are hardly conscious of their fundamental rights let alone human rights. Their children are trapped in to the world of work and are deprived of education and therefore future earnings. Most of our respondents live in semi-permanent thatched houses without

Table 2. Effect of State Intervention on Selected Aspects of Samples

Sl. No.	*Variable*	*Reference Group/Category*	*Statistical measure/test*	*Finding/result*	*Remarks*
1.	Average borrowings	Respondents	T-Test (paired t-test)	T-Value-0.0779	Insignificant
2.	Child population and child labour	(a) Residents	R	0.9639	Significant at 1 per cent level
		(b) Migrants	R	0.8844	Significant at 1 per cent level
3.	Incidence of child labour	Respondents	Chi-Square Test	Chi-square=2.1932 D.F.=7	Not significant
4.	Disparity in earnings	Child labour	Percentage of girls earnings to boys	Lowest=71	In beverages
5.	Government subsidy for pucca houses owned	132 samples	Percentage subsidized	36	
6.	Income contribution to household	Child labour	Percentage	16	
7.	Access to fair price shop	(a) Residents	Percentage	62	There is a significant Price difference in the items between the FPS and open market
		(b) Migrants	Percentage	44	There is a significant Price difference in the items between the FPS and open market
8.	Income range level and proportion of expenditure on food	Respondents	R	-0.713	It is in line with Engel's law

Source: Tables 5.1, 5.4, 5.5, 5.7, 5.9, 5.10, 5.12, 5.14 Unpublished Ph. D. Thesis of Vinodini, S.V. University, 2000.

basic civic amenities. They are the cause as well as victims of urban pollution and insanitation. State intervention to improve the educational status of their children, provide health, sanitation and civil supplies to the respondents as well as housing amenities and work opportunities is necessary to alleviate the poverty and bring them into the mainstream of civil life. It must be noted as Mabub-ul-Haq stated that poverty is not due to lack of income but lack of opportunity to earn income.

A determined, purposeful, result-oriented goal directed, time-bound action is necessary to safeguard the interests of vulnerable groups like our samples in the era of market-driven, market-guided, market-friendly policies being pursued by the State in India. Economic policy without social content and labour-orientation might prove to be counter productive. Therefore, labour-oriented, equity-based, welfare-guided State policy is to be harmonized with growth-oriented, market-driven policies. The case for protection and promotion of the cause of the economically deprived, socially excluded and politically marginalized is as old as and as strong as welfare economics, which should be pursued at the micro level as well as at the macro level by the respective governments.

References

1. J.M.J. Vinodini's Ph.D. unpublished thesis, 'Role of Women in urban Informal Sector: A case study of kavali Town, A.P.' S.V. University, 2000.
2. The World Development Reports, Oxford, 1995-2000.
3. The World Bank, Women in Pakistan, 1989.
4. UNDP, Human Development Reports, Oxford 1990 to 2001.
5. ILO, World Labour, Reports, 1990-94.
6. GOI, Report of the committee on the Status of Women in India, 1974.
7. Malavika Karlekar, "Poverty and Women's work: A study of Sweeper women in Delhi", Shakti Bank, New Delhi, 1987.

8. World Bank country study, "India Reducing Poverty, Accelerating Development, Oxford, 2000.
9. World Bank Country Study, "Gender and poverty in India, Oxford, 1997.
10. UNICET, the progress of Nations, Oxford, 1997.

17

Impact of Economic Reforms on Industrial Workers

Dr. S. Indrakant & Rajat Kumar

Introduction

Economic Reforms were introduced in India in early 90's to overcome the economic crisis faced by the country at that time by improving the efficiency of the economic system and by introducing an element of competitiveness into the system. The available evidences indicate that the short-term objectives at least partially seem to have been achieved. Concerns have been voiced regarding medium and long-term implication of reforms. It is feared that reforms may adversely affect the conditions of people belonging to the lower rung of the society and this may widen the existing inequalities between the rich and the poor. In this context, it is worthwhile to examine the impact of reforms on the industrial workers in terms of employment opportunities and emoluments. The present study aims to throw some light on these issues.

To be more specific, this paper seeks to:

1. Compare growth in employment during pre and post reform periods.
2. Compare the growth in wages and salaries in nominal and real terms.
3. Examine the determinants of wage rates.

Data and Methodology

The study is based on the secondary data collected from the Annual Survey of Industries. The time frame of the study, keeping the objectives of the study and availability of data, has been taken to be the 17-year period from 1981 to 1998. For analytical purpose, the time-period has been divided into two sub-periods viz., (1) 1981-82 to 1990-91 i.e., pre-reform period and (2) 1991-92 to 1997-98 i.e., post-reform period. The data on employment and emoluments of workers and total number of employees for the manufacturing sector as a whole and selected industries of manufacturing sector have been collected. It may be note that total employees include both workers and supervisory staff. The strength of supervisory staff is obtained by subtracting the number of workers from number of total employees. Similarly, the earnings of supervisory staff have been arrived at by subtracting wages from total employments of all employees. Average wages per worker and average salary per supervisory staff have been worked out. In order to get an over-all impact of forces operating in manufacturing sectors of workers and supervisory staff for pre-reform period and post-reform period have been computed.

Nominal wages fail to reflect the levels of living of the workers while the economy is experiencing in prices of essentials. In such situation, nominal wages need to be deflated by cost of living index. As cost of living and wholesale price index are closely related, in the present study, the nominal wages are deflated by the wholesale price indices to obtain real wages. The average of real wages for the years 1981-82 to 1990-91 is taken as the average real wage for the pre-reform period. Similarly, the average of real wages for the years 1991-92 to 1997-98 is taken as the average real wages for the post-reform period.

Semi-logarithmic functions have been used to estimate the rate of growth in employment and emoluments of workers and supervisory staff. To accommodate the differences in growth rate during pre-reform period and post-reform period, a slope dummy variable has been incorporated in the equation. In case the estimated co-efficient of slope dummy variable was found to be statistically not significant, it was dropped and regression equation was re-estimated. In such cases, the estimated coefficient of time variable was taken as growth rate for both pre-reform as well as post-reform period. In cases, where estimated coefficient of slope dummy variable was significant, the estimated co-efficient of time variable was taken as growth rate for the pre-reform period and sum of estimates coefficient of time variable and slope dummy variable as growth rate for the post-reform period.

Wage rate is the outcome of the inter-action of demand and supply forces operating in the labour market. In organized sector, trade unions consider it their primary task to fight (and many times successfully) for enhancement of wages, in the face of inflation. Hence very often wages tend to increase more with price indices. There is also a tendency on the part of workers to take credit for improvement in labour productivity and expect, in return, a higher wage rate. Therefore, wage rate is likely to be influenced by labour productivity. It may be noted that demand for labour is a derived demand and whenever an industry faces an upward trend in demand for their product, the management is likely to try and increase its labour force by paying higher wages, though in a labour surplus economy this may not be a strong force. Therefore, in the regression exercise to explain the movement of wage rate three independent variable viz., (1) wholesale price indices (2) value added per worker (3) ratio of output of current year to the average of output of preceding two years have been used as independent variables. The third variable is expected to capture the growing demand intensity for the product of an industry. Simple and multiple regression equations have been estimated using ordinary least square method.

Discussion of Results

Generally impact on workers is examined in terms of level of employment of workers and their wages. The average employment level and emoluments of workers and supervisory staff for pre-reform and post-reform periods are presented in table 1.

The manufacturing sector provided jobs for 53 lakh workers during pre-reform period. Their number increased to 60 lakhs during post-reform period. During the same period, the supervisory staff increased from less than 14 lakhs to over 17 lakhs. There are some worth mentioning inter-industry differences. Food, Beverages and Chemicals have witnessed a substantial increase in employment. On the contrary, the employment of workers in cotton textiles has come down after the introduction of reforms.

The composition of employees in terms of workers and supervisory staff and changes therein have been analyzed in terms of ratio of worker to supervisory staff. It is observed that in the manufacturing sector for every four workers, there is one supervisor. The number of workers per supervisor is relatively high in Beverages (12) and Cotton Textiles (7) but low in Machinery and Equipment (2). After the reforms, the ratio of workers to supervisor has come down implying that growth in employment of workers in the manufacturing sector is relatively low.

The level of wage rate and changes therein greatly influence the conditions of workers. The workers of manufacturing sector in India earned on an average, Rs. 12,000 per annum, during the pre-reform period (see Table 2).

Wide inter-industry disparities in earning of workers are noticed ranging from Rs. 20,000 in Transport equipment industry to Rs. 5000 in Beverages. During post-reform period, the average earning of workers increased to Rs. 30,000 (from Rs. 12,000). Inter-industry variations continue to prevail.

Table 1. Employment in Manufacturing Sector

(In lakhs)

Sectors	*Average No. of Workers*		*Average No. of Supervisors*		*Average No. of Workers per Supervisor*		*Value Added per Worker*	
	Pre-Reforms	*Post-Reforms*	*Pre-Reforms*	*Post-Reforms*	*Pre-Reforms*	*Post-Reforms*	*Pre-Reforms*	*Post-Reforms*
Food Products	8.42	9.63	2.18	2.70	3.86	3.56	0.26	0.86
Beverages etc.	3.95	5.13	0.33	0.41	12.12	12.54	0.16	0.50
Cotton Textiles	8.06	7.12	1.09	1.10	7.38	6.47	0.22	0.55
Basic Chemicals	1.95	4.74	0.72	2.16	2.71	2.19	1.19	3.63
Non-Metallic Mineral Products	3.45	3.64	0.72	0.90	4.81	4.04	0.33	1.14
Basic Metal and Alloys	4.68	4.93	1.46	1.62	3.21	3.05	0.61	2.33
Machinery and Equipment	5.34	5.93	2.54	3.07	2.10	1.93	0.73	2.25
Transport Equipment	3.72	4.01	1.20	1.42	3.10	2.82	0.52	1.80
Aggregate Manufacturing Sector	53.05	60.21	13.93	17.33	3.81	3.47	0.44	1.47

Note: Pre-Reform—1981-82 to 1990-91, Post-Reform—1991-92 to 1997-98.

Table 2. Nominal Emoluments in Manufacturing Sector

Sectors	*Annual Wages per Labourer (in Rupees'000)*		*Annual Salary per Supervisor (in Rupees'000)*		*Ratio of Wages to Salaries*	
	Pre-Reform	*Post-Reform*	*Pre-Reform*	*Post-Reform*	*Pre-Reform*	*Post-Reform*
Food Products	6.86	18.17	15.11	39.79	2.20	2.19
Beverages etc.	4.78	11.25	20.49	40.65	4.29	3.61
Cotton Textiles	11.60	26.90	28.94	45.46	2.50	1.69
Basic Chemicals	16.15	40.12	31.43	83.11	1.95	2.07
Not-Metallic Mineral Products	8.80	22.32	20.92	50.18	2.38	2.25
Basic Metal and Alloys	18.50	43.24	29.95	77.87	1.62	1.80
Machinery and Equipment	17.26	41.80	30.42	76.13	1.76	1.82
Transport Equipment	19.58	46.79	31.83	78.94	1.63	1.69
Aggregate Manufacturing Sector	12.52	29.46	26.31	62.74	2.10	2.13

Note: Pre-Reform—1981-82 to 1990-91, Post-Reform—1991-92 to 1997-98.

Similarly, it can also be seen that the average annual salary of Supervisory staff increased from Rs. 21000 during pre-reform period to Rs. 62000 during post-reform period. It is observed that the average salary of Supervisory staff is twice that average wages of workers. It is noticed that the average salary of Supervisory staff in Beverage Industry is four times the average wages of workers. Another interesting finding is that the inter-industry variation in earnings of supervisory staff is relatively lower than the inter-industry variations in wages of workers.

As mentioned earlier, the trends in nominal wages do not reflect the levels of living of workers when prices are steadily increasing. Trends in real wages are obtained by deflating nominal wages by wholesale price indices. The results of the exercise are presented in Table-3.

In spite of inflation, the workers in manufacturing sector have managed to improve their real wages. The earnings of the workers, at 1981-82 prices, increased from 9000 rupees in pre-reform period to nearly 11000 rupees during post-reform period registering a growth of 16%. The growth is relatively high in Food products (35%), Chemicals (25%) and Non-metallic minerals (26%) but low in Cotton textiles (7%). It appears that reform process has not generated employment at desirable rate but it has hurt the living conditions of the already employed workers.

The earnings of supervisory staff in real terms have also increased. They increased from 19000 rupees per annum during pre-reform period to nearly 23000 rupees during post-reform period, registering a growth rate of 21%. The growth is relatively higher in food industry (33%), Chemicals (33%) and Basic metals (30%) but-low in Cotton textile (7%). It is disturbing to note that the earnings of supervisory staff in Beverages have declined in real terms.

Comparison of growth in earnings of workers and supervisors reveals that supervisory staff has experienced

Table 3. Real Emoluments in Manufacturing Sector

(In Rupees'000 per annum at 1981-82 Prices)

Sector	Wages per Worker			Salaries per Supervisor		
	Pre-Reforms	Post-Reforms	Post-Reforms / Pre-Reforms	Pre-Reforms	Post-Reforms	Post-Reforms. Pre-Reforms.
Food Products	4.91	6.64	1.35	10.86	14.47	1.33
Beverages etc.	3.46	4.11	1.19	16.04	14.71	0.92
Cotton Textiles	9.25	9.90	1.07	15.56	16.63	1.07
Basic Chemicals	11.63	14.68	1.26	22.87	30.31	1.33
Non-Metallic Mineral Products	6.44	8.11	1.26	15.39	18.16	1.18
Basic metal and Alloys	13.54	15.45	1.14	21.91	28.43	1.30
Machineryand Equipment	12.56	15.22	1.21	22.27	27.56	1.24
Transport Equipment	14.25	17.00	1.19	23.30	28.55	1.23
Aggregate Manufacturing Sector	9.23	10.73	1.16	18.81	22.80	1.21

Note: Pre-Reforms—1981-82 to 1990-91, Post-Reforms—1991-92 to 1997-98.

higher growth in real income. Some take it as an evidence of widening inequalities on account of reforms in the country.

As mentioned earlier, to examine the differences in growth rates of employment during pre and post-reform periods growth rates have been computed. The results are shown in Table-4.

Analysis of growth rates reveal that the employment of workers in manufacturing industry grew @ about 1 per cent per annum (1.25% to be precise). This is much below the natural population growth rate indicating that organized sector is not able to generate sufficient employment in order to reduce the magnitude of unorganized sector.

The process of reforms has not made impact on growth of employment. Inter-Industry analysis reveals that Chemical industry has been generating employment @ 11% per annum. The performance of Beverage industry is also better than the average for the manufacturing sector. On the other hand, the employment in Cotton industry has been declining though it is consoling note that rate of decline has come down during post-reform period.

Though employment in manufacturing sector has increased at a relatively low rate, the wages of workers are increasing at a high rate. Wages increased over 11% p.a. during pre-reform period. In post-reform period, the growth rate has marginally declined. Similar pattern is observed at industry level.

It is surprising to note that growth of supervisory staff (2.2%) is relatively higher than that of workers (1.25%). This may be because of increasing use of capital-intensive method of production in the manufacturing sector. The growth of supervisory staff is unaffected by reform process. The salaries of supervisory staff increased at 10% per annum, which is lower than the growth rate of wages of workers. Thus in the post-reform period the number of supervisory

Table 4. Compounded Annual Growth Rate in Employment and Emoluments

Sector	*Workers*				*Supervisors*			
	Employment		*Wage Rate*		*Employment*		*Salaries*	
	Pre-Reforms	*Post-Reforms*	*Pre-Reforms*	*Post-Reforms*	*Pre-Reforms*	*Post-Reforms*	*Pre-Reforms*	*Post-Reforms*
Food Products	1.07	1.07	14.66	13.10	1.70	1.70	12.42	12.42
Beverages etc.	2.80	2.80	12.53	11.32	3.30	3.30	7.36	7.36
Cotton Textiles	-2.57	-1.76	9.29	9.29	-2.54	-0.79	9.24	9.24
Basic Chemicals	10.82	10.82	11.46	11.46	14.04	14.04	11.57	11.57
Non-Matallic Mineral Products	0.62	0.62	10.30	15.51	2.56	2.56	10.20	10.20
Basic Metal and Alloys	0.60	0.60	10.40	10.40	0.90	0.90	11.10	11.10
Machinery and Equipment	1.10	1.10	10.80	10.80	2.20	2.20	10.90	10.90
Transport Equipment	0.71	0.71	10.70	10.70	1.58	1.58	10.80	10.80
Aggregate Manufacturing Sector	1.25	1.25	11.18	10.61	2.20	2.20	10.64	10.64

Note: Pre-Reforms—1981-82 to 1990-91, Post-Reforms— 1991-92 to 1997-98.

staff increased at relatively higher rate but their emoluments increased at marginally lower rate than that of workers.

As mentioned earlier, to examine the extent of influence of different factors on wage rate, the wholesale price indices, value added per worker and the ratio of output of current year to the average output of preceding two years have been taken as explanatory variables. Both single and multiple regression equation have been used. The results of the regression exercise are given in Table 5.

Table 5. Regression Results for Aggregate Manufacturing Sector

Eq. No.	*VAPW*	*DIVA*	*WPI*	*Adj.R^2*
1	0.6843 (22.792)			0.9698
2		10.794 (3.1212)		0.3471
3			0.1221 (25.699)	0.9761
4	0.6970 (17.750)	-0.5142 (-0.5277)		0.9679
5		1.5011 (2.1127)	0.1159 (22.723)	0.9800
6	0.2953 (2.6957)		0.0706 (3.3246)	0.9825
7	0.2282 (1.7929)	0.7408 (0.9598)	0.0793 (3.7844)	0.9821

Note:
1. Dependent variable is nominal wage rate Per Worker (in rupees thousands).
2. VAPW: Value added Per worker (in Rupees Lakhs).
3. DIVA: Ratio of Value Added of Current Year to Average of Value added of two preceding years.
4. WPI: Wholesale Price Indices.
5. Adj. R^2: Adjusted R-Square.
6. Figures in Parentheses represent t-ratios below, are very Illuminating.

The results of simple regression equation indicate that all the three explanatory variables individually influence the wage rate of a worker. The extent of influence differs. The regression of wage rate on wholesale price index reveals that for every one-point increase in wholesale price index the workers are likely to gain Rs. 122 in their wages. Similarly, the regression of wage rate on value added per worker shows that the workers manage to get Rs. 684 from whenever labour productivity increases by Rs. 1.00 lakh. The regression of wage rate on demand-intensity indicates that workers also benefit whenever an industry experiences an upswing in demand. When two of the three explanatory variables are combined, the coefficients become either insignificant or possess unexpected sign. This is due to the problem of multicollinearity. However, whole price index continues to posses expected sign and is statistically significant. Similarly, when all the three variables are used as independent variables, the results are distorted. Among all the equations, the regression of wage rate on wholesale price index and value added per worker yield the best results. The estimated regression-coefficients reveal that for every one point increase in wholesale price index, under given labour productivity, the wage rate of workers is likely to increase by Rs. 70. Similarly, workers tend to benefit by Rs. 300 in their wages in response to every 1 lakh rupee increase in labour productivity.

Conclusion

In conclusion it can be said that the economic reforms have not had any negative impact on the growth rate of employment for industrial workers and supervisors. Wage rates for both categories have also grown in real terms. In the post-reform period the salaries of the supervisors have grown marginally slower when compared to the wages of the workers. However, due to the lower base of wages, the absolute difference in the earnings of supervisors and workers has grown. An interesting funding has been that there are large inter-industry differences in all the variables described above. The wage rate of workers has been positively and significantly affected by the rise in the wholesale price indices and the labour productivity.

This study shows that contrary to what the critics of economic reforms had predicted, the Indian industrial workers in organized sector during the period under study have has not been adversely affected by the reforms. However, impact of unorganized sector seems to be different.

In days to come, the distinction between organized sector and unorganized sector is likely to disappear. Even in organized sector, the workers (including bank employees) are hired on daily wage basis. This trend would become stronger in the days to come.

It is true that no economic system can bear the burden of inefficiency forever. For the growth of a system, efficiency must be rewarded and inefficiency must be penalized. Objective criteria must be ensured a reasonable income (which serves as a base) and the increments in salary must be linked to performance.

The negative impact of reforms can be minimized with strong social security system. Reforms without social security are more harmful than no reforms. Therefore, it is the responsibility of the state to build a strong social security system along with the economic reforms.

References

1. Ahluwalia, I.J. (1992) "Productivity and Growth in Indian Manufacturing', New Delhi.
2. Bhalotra, Sonia R., (1998) 'Puzzle of Jobless Growth in Indian Manufacturing', Oxford Bulletin of Economics and Statistics, Vol. 60, No. 1.,
3. Fallon, P., and Robert E.B. Lucas, (1993) 'Job Security Regulation and the Dynamic Demand for Industrial Labour in India and Zimbabwe', Journal of Development Economics, Vol. 40, No. 2.

4. Goldar, Bishwanath (2000) -'Employment Growth in Organized Manufacturing in India' Economic and Political Weekly, Vol. 35, No. 14.

5. Goldar, Bishwanath (1998) 'Relative Efficiency of Modern Small Scale Industries in India', in K. B. Suri (ed.), Small Scale Enterprises in Industrial Development: The Indian Experience,: Sage Publications, New Delhi.

6. Little, IMD, D. Muzumdar and J.M.J. Page (1987), Small Manufacturing Enterprise, World Bank Research Publications, New York.

7. Nagraj, R., (1994) 'Employment and Wages in Manufacturing Industries: Trends, Hypotheses Evidence', Economic and Political Weekly, Vol. 29, No. 4, 22.

8. Nagraj, R. (2000) 'Organized Manufacturing Employment', Economic & Political Weekly, Vol. 35, No. 38.

9. Papola, T.S. (1989) 'Restructuring in India Industry: Implications for employment and Industrial Relations', in G. Edgren (ed.) Restructuring Employment and Industrial Relations: Adjustment Issues in Asian Industries, Geneva: ILO Publications.

10. Sandesara J.C. (1989) 'Performance & Change: A study of India's Industrial Sector since Independence', Centre for Advanced Study in Economics, Bombay (Mimeo).

18

Child Labour and Education Policy in India

Dr. M.C. Naidu

Any child out of school is a child labourer. The definition of child labourer therefore encompasses every non-school going child-irrespective of whether the child is engaged in wage or non-wage work or whether he or she is working for the family or others, employed in hazardous or non-hazardous occupations, employed on a day wage or on a contract basis is a child labourer. The Factories Act of 1948 defined that "a person below the age of 15 years is to be regarded as a child labourer. Therefore, any physical labour under taken by a child below 15 years either under compulsoion or voluntarily in an organized or unorganized sector qualifies to be called as child labourer.

Child labour became a global phenomenon today and is 'harsh reality'. The 'harsh reality' of child labour arises out of the fact that in the present state of development in the country, many parents on account of poverty, have to send their children to work in order to supplement their income and the income derived from the child labour, however meagre, is essential to sustain the family. This is the 'poverty' argument of child labour. The problem exists in almost all countries of the world but its scale varies from country to country. However, the predominance of child labour in many Third World countries continues to be quite pronounced, even though reliable data are limited. India has the largest population of child labourers who constitute nearly seven per cent of the work force and are contributing considerable amount of the Gross Domestic Product.

The term "child labour is at times used as a synonym for employed child". In this sense it is co-extensive with any work done by the child for a gain. But more commonly than not, the term 'child labour' is used in pejorative sense. It suggests something, which is hateful and exploitative. Thus, Homer Folks, the chairman of the United National Child Labour Committee, defined child labour "as work by children that interferes with their full physical development, their opportunities for desirable minimum of education or their needed recreation".

The prevalence of child labour is more or less seen in all periods of time, it varies in nature and dimension depending on the existing socio-economic structure of society. Children are the blooming flowers of the garden of society and valuable asset of a nation. They constitute a hidden treasure of potential development of a growing nation. Childhood has been considered as a most important period of life. During this period moulding and shaping of the life takes place and the behaviour, conduct and sentiments are developed. Paradoxically, it is unfortunate to say that tragically most of the child life is lost due to poverty, destitution, malnutrition and poor and unhygienic conditions, largely in the rural sector compared to the urban counterpart.

Child labour is mainly necessitated by economic compulsions of the parents in many cases. The main reasons which give rise to child labour are widespread of absolute poverty, unemployment and underemployment among the adult workers. Large families, lack of educational facilities, illiteracy and ignorance of parents about the importance of education as well as about the impact of labour on the health of their children are some of the reasons which breed child labour.

Diverting the child from work means the loss of income to the parents and as additional expenditure on education, however small. The economic benefits resulting from child employment are generally high as it generates an income, which is higher than what is consumed in the family. Probably this is one of the reasons where workers do not feel that it is useful to send their children to schools. Further, there are some factors due to which employers also favour child labourer. In the light of the above, a major reason for hiring children seems to be that non-economic are easier to manage because they are less aware of their rights, less trouble some, less prone to complaint, more trustworthy, less likely to absent themselves from work and no problem of unions.

The child labour continues to be a reality in almost all parts of the world. Although, the number of children working throughout the world is unknown. It is very large indeed and unquestionably in the hundreds of millions. In recent years the child labour problem and its impact have received increased attention. Undoubtedly this increased attention is due in part to the fact that child labour often has serious social, moral, economic and demographic implications for children, households, communities, societies and the world. Therefore, the elimination or reduction of child labour has been the aim of numerous fields in different parts of the world.

Over the years, however global consciousness about the seriousness of the problem has created several non-government organizations that are working towards the welfare of these children. The constitution of India is also committed to the protection and promotion of the welfare considerations over the economic ones. It was not surprising, therefore, that a series of committees and commissions have been appointed by the Government of either specifically on the question of child labor or on labour conditions in general which give us insights into the problem and suggestions to alleviate it. These are (1) The Royal Commission on Labour (1929); (ii) The Labour Investigation Committee (1944); (iii) The National Commission on Labour (1966); (iv) Gurupadaswamy Committee on Chid Labour (1966) and (v) Sanat Mehta Committee (1986) which deserves special attention to the Magnitude of the Problem.

The Constitution of India includes specific provisions against the use of child labour and seeks its ultimate elimination. In India, the problem of child labour in its nature and magnitude is complex and gigantic. Millions of children are working in large number of industries and occupations all over the country. To day, India is the home for the largest number of working children. According to the Government the number of working children estimated at 17.58 million, in the 43rd round of child labour estimates are 18.17 million in 1990 and 20.15 million in the year 2000. Whatever may be the actual figure of child labour, the important point is that the child labour phenomenon in India is on the rise and it shows that India has a substantial number of working children to be tackled.

Child Labour Policies

National Authority on the Elimination of Child Labour (NAECL) established by the Government of India in September, 1994 with Minister of State for Labour as Chariman and nine secretaries to the Government of India as members with the Secretary, Ministry of Labour working as the Member-Secretary of NAECL was a major initiative of the Government of India to orchestrate its policies dealing with the elimination of child labour. In view of its paramount concern for the elimination of child labour from hazards industries and activities culminating in the then Prime Minister of India, Sri P.V. Narasimha Rao, promising to have this component eliminated within a grossly unrealistic time-frame of only five years. This restricted the focus of NAECL to a small subset of child labour in India. ILO (1996) targeting the intolerable and its proposed Convention to be adopted in 1990 has again restricted itself to the so-called hazardous and intolerable forms of child labour.

UNICEF's views on child development and child labour, reports can be inferred from UNICEF (1994, 1995, 1996, 1997) some what broader than those of the narrowly targeted child labour policies of the Government of India. It deals with child labour as part of broader concerns of child development with a major emphasis on primary and middle school education and poverty eradication.

A number of initiatives and programmes have been undertaken in India over the last decade. The formulation of a New National Child Labour Policy, the enactment of Child Labour (Prohibition and Regulation) Act 1986, the setting up of a Task Force on Child Labour, the adoption of the Convention on the Rights of the Child and so on have all formed a part of this process. Corresponding initiatives were taken in the related area of education where a New Education Policy was formulated, which incorporated a separate component for working children.

This paper examined the role of the education policy in relation to child labour. It shows, how, in proposing Non-Formal Education as a major strategy for dealing with illiteracy among working children, the Government has failed to realize the potential of formal primary education as a powerful tool for withdrawing children from work.

As per the official estimate the percentage of children in the age group 6-14 attending school is around 49 per cent. The projected population in the age group for

1994-95 is 179 million, which implies that around 90 million children do not go to school. Even assuming that all working children do not go to school, there is an unexplained gap of at least 72 million children whose status is that of non-working, non-school going child.

In the rural situation the fact is that a child who does not go to a formal school is a working child. Collection of water, fuel, maintenance of the house and taking care of young siblings all constitute an important element of a child's life. While many of these activities do not necessarily fall under the definition of hazardous work, in as much as they interfere with the normal development of the child and in the child's ability to reach his/her true potential they constitute exploitation of the child. In the context of rural India, therefore, the concept of a non-working, non-school going child simply does not exist. Any effort to deal with the issue of child labour has to contend with this aspect.

Non-Formal Education

A related area, which has also been strongly influenced regarding child labour, is that of education. Under the action plan of the policy, National Child Labour Projects (NCLPs) have been set up in different areas to rehabilitate child labour. Major activities undertaken under the NCLP are the establishment of special schools to provide Non-Formal Education (NFE), vocational training, supplementary nutrition etc., to children withdrawn from employment. The New Education Policy which was to be closely coordinated with child labour policy incorporated a major effort to bring drop-outs and non-enrolled children into the education system through NFE. The NFE was put in place with the key objective of providing education for working children. It was proposed as an alternative to the formal education stream as it was argued that improving the facilities of primary schools would do little to help the poor who dropped out, whereas the system of NFE was targeted to meet the needs of the working children. The intended clientele included dropout children of weaker-sections, girls in the age group of 6-14 years and boys and girls who are employed in professions, like carpet weaving and so on. The NFE has prescribed to have a flexible curriculum according to the needs of the working children and the youth. Classes are to be held at hours taking into account the children's work schedule.

The NEF system has been the subject of much criticism in terms of its inherent limitations because of low-paid, ill-trained teachers, in an atmosphere not particularly conducive to learning for working children after a full day's work. However, NFE policy provides a clear example of the influence of acceptance of the poverty argument of child labour on the Elementary Education Policy.

Thus given the fact, that the poor have to send their children to work, the NFE provides a convention and framework of education, which does not interfere with the child's work. In the context of Article 32 what the NFE has done is that, in providing a solution to the problem of child labour interfering with the child's education, it has provided a system of child-education which does not interfere with child labour.

An Alternative Strategy

The starting point of any strategy dealing with the issue of child labour cannot lie in children engaged in hazardous occupations alone. While this section of children does constitute the most glaring example of the failure of our child Labour and education policies they too are only results of a larger phenomenon-taking place in the country side. 80 per cent of the child labour and consequently illiteracy exists in families engaged in agriculture work and we cannot afford to ignore this fact. Further, a significant proportion of the children engaged in hazardous occupations in the urban areas belongs to families who have migrated from the rural areas. It is essentially required to adopt Article 32 of the Convention in its true spirit and recognize the fact that any non-school going child is an exploited child. Given the facts, any plan to deal with child labour has to deal with the 90 million non-school going child labourers.

The Government has consistently been referring to programmes for providing education for all, raising the budgetary allocation to the Department of Education and Literacy is being enhanced from Rs. 4000- crores in 2001-2002 to Rs. 4900- crores for 2002-20003. What is required is a change in attitude and priorities rather than any ridical change in the programmes themselves. It also calls for a more effective coordination between the labour policies and education policies and a proper appreciation of the fact that such on-going programmes as Education for All are powerful means to bring about a qualifications-change in the child labour situation.

Compulsory Education Law

The issue of compulsory education has always been something of an enigma. At a theoretical level, very few find fault with the concept that all children should receive education, at least up to the primary stage or with the fact that children should not work. In fact, the State has committed it self not only to primary education but also the abolition of child labour through pronouncements. Inspite of all the general attitude of the policy planners that has been, the country cannot afford the distraction of a compulsory norm. A number of reasons are given for this, but the major objection is the non-implementability of such legislation which would remain only on paper.

It has been observed that in this country a large number of laws governing social issues have been passed which have never really been implemented. Although, the legislation set out to achieve laudable social goals, the State has not been able to put them to effect. A legislation to provide compulsory education, therefore, is most likely to meet a similar fate. Further, it is argued, as previous experience with legislation governing compulsory education has shown, there is a greater likelihood of the Act turning into an instrument of harassment against the parents.

These arguments view the issue from one perspective only, viz, that of the State apparatus. Notwithstanding the claims of the Government that more than 94 per cent of the children have been provided access to schools, the established infrastructure cannot cater to the full requirement of even the demand that exits. This is because infrastructure development has been a function of budgetary allocation rather than of demand. Once the logic of harsh reality of child labour is accepted, low allocation to the primary education sector especially in the rural areas can always be rationalized as being a response to the low projected demand for schools. Similarly, it is only when one accepts the absence of demand for education, legislation is an instrument for forcing unwilling parents to send their children to schools. Thus, any assessment which assumes the reality of child labour harsh or other wise is bound to lead not only to low per capita investment in the sector but also to the view that compulsory education laws are unimplementable.

Legislation of this nature has for long played the role of compelling the State to take action. The importance of this aspect would be fully appreciated when one considers the number of occasions the State has been compelled to act through the use of the Bonded Labour Abolition Act (1976), to release bonded children. A legislation to provide for compulsory education, therefore, would be of immense significance in situations where the State does respond to the requirements of the people. It has already been seen that the Government is response to the problem of illiteracy and child labour has been quite equivocal. A Legislation binding the State to provide compulsory education therefore is absolutely essential.

Conclusion and Policy Implications

A child labour policy, which defined the target group in the true spirit of Article 32 that all non-school going children (90 million) are child labourers in one form or the other. Agricultural child labour constitutes the core of the problem. Without tackling this issue, the issue of child labour in hazardous occupations cannot be handled.

Compulsory education has historically been one of the most effective instruments for eliminating child labour in practice. It is evident that children in school are less likely to be in full-time or close to full-time employment. Conversely, who are not obliged to attend school or who have no access to education have little alternative to working or falling into begging, delinquency or worse.

Child-labour policies and education policies have to be formulated and in tandem and not independent of each other. The relation between education and child work is complex, however, and seemingly obvious solutions may not always work. Shortcomings in the public education system can actually encourage the flow of children into work place. At least, schools must be available, accessible and affordable as far as possible free.

In the context of child labour it is important to emphasise about policies of population, education (primary and middle school education) investment, trade and labour productivity influence every aspect of economic growth as well as child labour.

A more positive attitude towards child labour, parents do want to be educated and poverty as a limiting factor is highly over rated. Recognised the fact that even today there are 'poor' parents sending their children to school instead of work. Motivation and availability of infrastructure rather than poverty are the key factors. Realised the fact cannot be a solution to either the problem of illiteracy or child labour. It is at best a temporary solution, which has no relevance unless simultaneously backed by adequate strengthening of the formal education structure.

References

1. GOI, Ministry of Labour, The Factories Act, 1948, Section 2(c), Vol. III, p. 412.
2. Stein, E. and Davis, J. 'Labour Problems in America, New York, 1940, p. 112.
3. Budged 2002, The Hindu, March, 2002, p. 10.

19

Economic Reforms and Organised Sector Employment in India

Dr. M. Devarajulu, R.S.V.N. Prasad

Introduction

Economic reforms may have given a boost for industrial productivity and brought in foreign investment in capital-intensive areas. Nevertheless, the boom has not created jobs. According to IPS, (Institution of Policy Studies) the combined sales of world's top 200 MNC's is now greater than the combined GDP of all but the world's nine largest national economies. Yet, the total direct employment generated by these multi-nationals is a mere 18.8 millions—one per cent of global work force. In India after economic reforms initiated in 1990-91, the growth in employment came down gradually and even registered negative growth in 1999 and 2000.

Structure of Employment in India:

Employment in India is divided into Organised and Un-organised sectors. Organised sector generally refers to employment in the public and private sectors employing more than 10 persons. It provides greater job security and yielding higher wages and other benefits. Un-organised sector, on the other hand refers to employment in unregistered small shops and organizations. The management determines wages and benefits in this sector and the scope for bargaining by the workers is meagre, as the employees in the unorganised sector are not united. Agricultural Workers, workers in construction, petty shops, etc. come under this sector. Un-organised sector employment comprises about 90 per cent of total employment in India. Thus, the organised sector employment is only 10 per cent of the total employment. Employment in organised sector has been further declining due to decline in the public sector employment in the wake of disinvestments in the public sector units and ban on recruitment in the public sector establishments.

Organised Sector Employment in India

Trends in organised sector employment in India are presented in Table 1. It reveals clearly that the growth rates of employment in organised sector declined in the period of 1994-2000 compared to the period of 1983-1994. The Table also reveals that the public sector employment declined drastically at -0.03 in 1994-2000 period compared with 1.52 per cent growth in 1983-1994 period. If we pursue private sector employment in the same period, it registered growth of 1.87 per cent in the liberalization period compared to 0.45 per cent in 1983-1994. We can infer that the decline in the organised sector employment is only due to decline in the public sector employment. The decline in the rate of growth of public sector employment is attributed to restructuring programmes of the public sector and the ban on recruitment in many departments and institutions as part of the economy drive to reduce government expenditure.

Growth of Employment in Public and Private sectors is presented in Table 2. It reveals that the major contribution in the overall growth of organised sector employment is made by the private sector after 1995. However, this growth in private sector employment did not offset the effect of the slow down in public sector employment since the share of private sector employment in the organised sector was only one-third. Growth in the organised sector employment is now depending on employment growth in the private sector.

Table 1. Total Employment and Organised Sector Employment in India

	Employment in (Millions)				*Growth rates*	
	1983	*1988*	*1994*	*1999-2K*	*1983-1994*	*1994-2000*
Total Population	718.21	790.00	895.05	1004.10	2.12	1.93
Total Labour Force	308.64	333.49	381.94	406.05	2.05	1.03
Total employment	302.75	324.29	374.45	397.00	2.04	0.98
Organised sector employment	24.01	25.71	27.37	28.11	1.20	0.53
Public sector	16.46	18.32	19.44	19.41	1.52	–0.03
Private sector	7.55	7.39	7.93	8.70	0.45	1.87

Source: Compiled and Computed from Planning Commission, Report of the Task Force on Employment Opportunities, 2000.

Note: 1. The Total Employment Figures are on Usual Status (UPSS) Basis.

2. The Organised Sector Employment figures are as reported in the Employment Market Information System of Ministry of Labour and Pertain to 1st March of 1983, 1988, 1994 and 1999.

Table 2. Growth Rates of Employment in Organised Sector

Year	*Public Sector*	*Private Sector*	*Total organised*
1991	1.52	1.24	1.44
1992	0.80	2.21	1.21
1993	0.60	0.06	0.44
1994	0.62	0.01	0.73
1995	0.11	1.63	0.55
1996	-0.19	5.62	1.51
1997	0.67	2.04	1.09
1998	-0.09	1.7	0.46
1999	0.002	0.11	0.04
2000*	-0.68	0.97	-0.17

Source: Economic Survey 2000-01, p. 192.

Note: *Quick estimates.

Trends in Organised Public Sector Employment

Employment in the organised public sector was 154 lakhs in 1981 and it rose to 190 lakhs in 1991 and further increased to 193 lakhs in 2000. It can be observed from the Table 3 that the absolute number of persons engaged in agriculture declined. Employment in Industry also showed declining trend after 1990. This was due to disinvestments and implementation of VRS in various public sector units. Employment in transport and trade though declined in 80's but found stable in 90's. It shows that there were no such disinvestments in public transport and trading but stagnation in further investments. Employment in finance and social services sector showed an increase in 90's but it is limited. Overall employment growth in all the sectors declined in 90's except in the finance and social service sectors.

Employment Trends in the Organised Private Sector

Employment in the organised private sector increased in the study period. Table 4 furnishes the employment trends in the organised private sector in 1990's. Agricultural

Table 3. Organised Public Sector Employment in India

(Persons in Lakhs)

Sector	*1981*	*1990*	*1991*	*1992*	*1993*	*1994*	*1995*	*1996*	*1997*	*1998*	*1999*	*2000*
Agriculture	12.81 (8.27)	15.15 (8.07)	15.55 (8.16)	15.60 (8.12)	15.57 (8.07)	15.60 (8.02)	16.05 (8.22)	15.33 (7.90)	15.11 (7.72)	14.67 (7.55)	14.41 (7.42)	14.38 (7.45)
Industry	32.74 (21.14)	39.01 (20.79)	39.06 (20.49)	39.28 (20.45)	39.36 (20.37)	38.89 (20.01)	36.55 (19.75)	38.43 (19.77)	37.51 (19.17)	36.79 (18.95)	36.28 (18.68)	35.69 (18.47)
Transport Trade	28.26 (18.26)	31.73 (16.92)	31.76 (16.67)	32.21 (16.7)	32.03 (30.15)	32.45 (16.68)	32.68 (16.75)	32.54 (16.75)	32.56 (16.64)	32.48 (16.73)	32.47 (16.73)	32.40 (16.77)
Finance Social service	81.00 (52.33)	101.73 (54.22)	104.21 (54.68)	105.01 (54.66)	106.29 (55.0)	107.51 (55.28)	107.87 (55.28)	108.0 (55.58)	110.41 (56.44)	110.25 (56.79)	110.89 (57.11)	110.67 (57.30)
Total	**154.84** ***(67.68)**	**187.62** ***(7.12)**	**190.58** ***(7.13)**	**192.10** ***(74.00)**	**193.26** ***(71.1)**	**194.45** ***(71.0)**	**195.15** ***(70.9)**	**194.29** ***(69.2)**	**195.5** ***(69.2)**	**194.12** ***(68.9)**	**194.10** ***(69.0)**	**193.14** ***(69.00)**

Source: 1. Ministry of Labour, DGET for Employment in Organised Sector.

2. NSSO, 55th Round of Employment and Unemployment in India. (1999-2000).

Note: 1. Figures in the Brackets are Percentages to Total Organised Public Sector Employment.

2. *Indicates Percentages to Total Organised Sector Employment.

Table 4. Organised Sector Employment in Private Sector

(Persons in Lakhs)

Sector	*1981*	*1990*	*1991*	*1992*	*1993*	*1994*	*1995*	*1996*	*1997*	*1998*	*1999*	*2000*
Agriculture	9.98 (13.36)	9.75 (12.88)	9.91 (12.92)	10.19 (12.98)	10.12 (12.89)	9.84 (12.33)	9.97 (12.37)	10.26 (12.05)	10.04 (11.55)	9.95 (11.37)	9.58 (11.01)	9.85 (11.39)
Industry	46.52 (62.90)	45.65 (60.21)	45.94 (59.84)	46.84 (59.69)	44.56 (56.75)	47.21 (59.16)	47.99 (59.54)	51.44 (60.43)	53.34 (61.40)	53.49 (61.14)	52.9 (60.81)	51.83 (59.94)
Transport Trade	3.37 (4.57)	3.43 (4.52)	3.53 (4.59)	3.5 (4.46)	3.56 (4.53)	3.58 (4.48)	3.66 (4.54)	3.77 (4.42)	3.8 (4.37)	3.86 (4.41)	3.92 ((4.50)	4.0 (4.62)
Finance & Social service	14.18 (19.17)	16.99 (22.40)	17.39 (22.65)	17.93 (22.85)	18.27 (23.27)	18.67 (23.39)	18.96 (23.52)	19.64 (23.07)	19.66 (22.63)	20.18 (23.06)	20.58 (23.66)	20.81 (24.02)
Total	**73.95 *(32.32)**	**75.82 *(28.8)**	**76.77 *(28.7)**	**78.46 *(29.00)**	**78.51 *(28.89)**	**79.80 *(29.0)**	**80.57 *(29.1)**	**85.12 *(30.5)**	**86.86 *(30.8)**	**87.48 *(31.1)**	**86.98 *(31.0)**	**86.46 *(31.0)**

Source: 1. Ministry of Labour, DGET for Employment in Organised Sector.

2. NSSO, 55th Round of Employment and Unemployment in India.

Notes. 1. Figures in the Brackets are Percentage to Total Organised Private Sector Employment.

2. *Indicates Percentage to Total Organised Sector Employment.

employment in the private organised sector started declining after 1996. Employment in the Industrial sector has shown small increase but with fluctuations. Employment in Transport, Trade and Financial Services has grown faster compared to other sectors. It reveals that during the Liberalization period much of investments made in service sectors like Power, Insurance that is why increasing trend in the employment in these sectors. Overall, there is an opportunity to increase employment in the private sector as most of the public sector units have been closed and investments diverted to the private sector.

Share of Public and Private Sectors in Employment

Table 5 presents the annual growth rates of employment in the organised public and private sectors by industry-wise in post-reform period and pre-reform period. It is important to note that the employment in the public sector decreased from 4.08 per cent to 0.13 per cent during pre-reform (1983-90) and post-reform period (1991-99) respectively. On the other hand, the contribution of private sector in post-reform period is 1.91 per cent compared to 1.13 per cent in pre-reform period. It can be observed that agriculture and allied activities in the public sector registered a negative growth in the post-reform period, which was 2.22 per cent during 1983-1990. In the private sector, also, the employment in agriculture and allied activities declined. In service sector, employment in the organised public sector also registered decelerated growth in post-reform period (0.63 per cent) compared to 4.48 per cent in the pre-reform period of 1983-1990. The highest growth achieved by the industrial sector in the post-reform period decelerated compared with pre-reform period. Overall, the growth of employment was high in the private sector compared to the public sector.

Sexwise Distribution of Employment in Economic Reform Period

If we observe employment in organised sector by sex, the share of female employment has shown growth in 1990's.

Table 6 Shows that employment of female in both public and private sectors increased year by year from 1990. It is also observed that female employment is high in private sector with compare to public sector. It also indicates the change in the structure of employment in India in post-reform period.

Table 5. Annual Growth of Employment in Organised Public and Private Sector

Sector	*1983-90*		*1991-99*	
	Public	*Private*	*Public*	*Private*
1. Agriculture	2.22	1.93	-1.21	-0.51
2. Industry	3.48	-0.34	-1.17	2.69
3. Transport & Trade	2.28	1.11	0.16	1.69
4. Financial & Social Service	5.20	4.96	0.77	1.99
(3+4)	4.48	4.27	0.63	1.94
Total	4.08	1.299	0.13	1.91

Source: Compiled and computed from planning commission (2000). Report of the Task Force on Employment Opportunities.

Conclusion

We may conclude that the employment in the organised sector has been declining because of the share of public sector employment has been declining. Employment in the private sector also declined compared to 80's but some growth is visible as compared with public sector. It is because of much investment fed into the private sector. Economic reforms also seem to have brought changes in female employment that is grown year by year in the liberalization period. This indicates that economic reforms exercised a favourable impact on employment generation in the private sector.

References

1. Bhattacharya B.B. and Mitra, A (2000), "Economic reforms and Emerging financial scenarios" in Dilip Dulta (Ed.) Economic liberalization and Institutional reforms in South Asia—Recent experiences and Future prospects, Atlantic publishers, Delhi.

Table 6. Sex wise Distribution of Employment in Organised Public and Private Sectors.

(Persons in lakhs)

Year	Public sector			Private sector			Public Private sector		
	Male	*Female*	*Total*	*Male*	*Female*	*Total*	*Male*	*Female*	*Total*
1990	165.22	22.50	187.72	61.88	13.94	75.82	227.09	36.44	263.53
	(88.01)	(11.99)		(81.62)	(18.38)		(82.18)	(13.82)	
1991	167.10	23.47	190.57	62.42	14.34	76.76	229.52	37.81	267.33
	(87.68)	(12.32)		(81.32)	(18.68)		(85.96)	(14.14)	
1992	167.81	24.29	192.10	63.67	14.79	78.46	231.48	39.08	270.56
	(37.35)	(12.65)		(81.15)	(18.85)		(83.56)	(14.44)	
1993	168.49	24.77	193.26	63.01	15.50	78.51	231.51	40.26	271.77
	(87.18)	(12.82)		(80.26)	(19.74)		(83.11)	(14.81)	
1994	168.8	25.65	194.45	63.41	15.89	79.30	232.21	41.54	273.75
	(86.80)	(13.20)		(79.97)	(20.03)		(84.33)	(15.17)	
1995	168.66	26.00	194.66	64.31	1628	80.59	232.97	42.28	275.25
	(86.64)	(13.36)		(79.80)	(20.20)		(84.64)	(15.36)	

(Cont...)

1996	167.94	26.35	194.29	67.20	17.92	85.12	235.14	44.26	279.41
	(86.44)	(13.56)		(78.95)	21.05		(84.18)	(15.82)	
1997	168.31	27.28	195.59	67.77	19.09	86.86	236.08	46.37	282.45
	(86.05)	(13.95)		(78.13)	(21.97)		(83.59)	(16.41)	
1998	166.55	27.63	194.18	67.37	20.11	87.48	233.92	47.74	281.66
	(85.77)	(14.33)		(77.02)	(22.98)		(83.06)	(16.94)	
1999	166.04	28.11	194.15	66.80	20.18	86.98	232.84	48.29	281.13
	(88.52)	(14.48)		(76.80)	(23.20)		(82.87)	(17.17)	
2000	164.57	28.57	193.14	65.80	20.66	86.46	230.37	49.23	279.60
	(85.20)	(14.80)		(76.11)	(23.89)		(82.40)	(17.60)	

Source: 1. Different Reports on Employment and Unemployment of NSSo, Government of India.

2. Planning Commission (2001), Report of the Task Force on Employment Opportunities.

Note: Figures in the brackets are Percentage to total Employment in the Concerned Sectors.

2. Chandra Sekhar and Jayathi Ghosh; "Disturbing Employment Trends", the Hindu-Business line, Jan. 23, 2001.
3. Gupta, S. (1995), "Economic Reforms and its impact on the poor", Economic and Political weekly, June, 1295-1313.
4. Planning Commission of India (1993), Report of the Expert group on Estimation of proportion and Number of poor, perspective planning division, New Delhi.
5. Planning Commission, Govt. of India (1990), Employment: Post trend and prospects for 1990s, working paper.
6. Planning Commission (2001), Report of the Task force on Employment Opportunities.
7. C.H. Hanumantha and H. Linneman (1996), Economic Reforms and Poverty Alleviation in India, Sage Publications, New Delhi.
8. Sen, A (1996) "Economic Reforms, Employment and Poverty Trends and Options", Economic and Political weekly, Vol. 1 (Sep.), 2459-78.
9. Sundaram, K. (2001a) "Employment-Unemployment situation in Nineties; Some results from NSS 55th round survey", Economic and Political weekly (March-17).

20

Role of Women Labour in Agriculture—A Case Study of Bethapudi Village of Guntur District

Dr. B.S. Rao, Dr. M.R.S. Babu

Agriculture is the mainstay of the Indian economy as over 70 per cent of our people depend on agricultural and allied occupations for their livelihood. Participation of women in economic activity is common in all countries developed as well as developing. The extent of their participation depends on factors too well-known to bear repetition. In developing countries, incomes by and large are low and the family requires the assistance of an additional earner. Where social conventions do not weigh oppressively against bringing women into paid employment, family income can be best supplemented by a draft on the female population in the working one group. A large number of women folk earn their daily wages as agricultural labourers. The rural women better called "farm women" who constitute almost 50 per cent of farm work force play a significant role in Indian agriculture. About 70 per cent of the farm work is performed by women. Thus it justifies "most farmers in India are women".

Role of Women in agriculture: Women played an important role because agriculture is largely a household enterprise. The largest avenue of employment for women in India, like other Asian countries is agriculture. According to the census data, women workers constituted 59.4 millions or 31.5 per cent of the total workers in the country in 1961. The number of male agricultural labourers increased from 3.47 Crores in 1981 to 4.55 crores in 1991. The number of female agricultural labourers increased from 2.08 crores in 1981 to 2.82 crores in 1991. According to 1991 census about 83 per cent women are illiterate and 90 per cent of the total female work force is in unorganized sector where social benefits and economic returns are low. The data clearly indicate that the women involvement in agriculture is very high and women are engaged in various agricultural activities. Inspite of this, they are discriminated in paying the wage rates etc. At this juncture, our paper attempts to study the (1) Socio-economic conditions of women-labourers, (2) the income earning capacity, (3) impact of women's income on family, and (4) the conditions of women labourers during the hours of work.

For this study 100 labourers are taken as sample from Bethapudi village in Mangalagiri Mandal of Guntur District where the entire population depends on agriculture for their livelihood. Majority of them are Agricultural labourers, out of 100 sample 50 are men and 50 are women.

Out of 100 sample beneficiaries, 50 per cent belong to SC and 30 per cent belong to Backward Classes, 15 per cent belong to Scheduled Tribes and 5 per cent belong to other community or Forward caste. With this, it is observed from Table 1 that majority of the agricultural labourers, are from the Scheduled Castes and Scheduled Tribes people. Among the Scheduled Caste 50 per cent are women. It reveals that women are equally participating in the work force along with men. Their labour plays a key role in the survival of millions of families. The problem of poverty cannot be tackled without providing opportunities for productive employment to rural women.

Table 1. Social Status of the Labourers

Community	*Men*	*Women*	*Total*
Scheduled Castes	25 (50.00)	25 (50.00)	50 (50.00)
Scheduled Tribes	5 (10.00)	10 (20.00)	15 (15.00)
Backward Classes	20 (40.00)	10 (20.00)	30 (30.00)
Other Castes	—	5 (10.00)	5 (5.00)
Total	**50 (100.00)**	**50 (100.00)**	**100 (100.00)**

N.B. Figures in brackets represents percentages top total.

Table 2 reveals the income earned by the agricultural labourers in that specified area. 60 per cent of the women are getting Rs. 1000-2000 per month, but 40 per cent of the male workers are getting Rs. 1000-2000 per month. However, 40 per cent of the male workers are in the range of Rs. 2000-3000, but a small percentage of women workers say 20 are in this income range. This clearly indicates that women are getting less income when compared to males. This is due to the fact that women are less paid by the land lord according to the work done-basis. In certain occupations despite the implementation of "Equal Remuneration Act," women workers are being paid lower

Table 2. Levels of Income (Per month)

Category	*0-1000*	*1000-2000*	*2000-3000*	*Total*
Men	10 (20.00	20 (40.00)	20 (40.00)	50 (100.00)
Women	10 (20.00)	30 (60.00)	10 (20.00)	50 (100.00)
Total	**50 (20.00)**	**50 (50.00)**	**30 (30.00)**	**100 (100.00)**

N.B. Figures in brackets represents percentages to total.

wages for similar jobs. A large number of women in rural areas, like other men folk, depend on daily wages earned in agricultural operations. Though they work hard for long hours, they get very less money leading to indebtedness. Yet they continue to depend on the land owners for employment and loans. Being illiterate, poor, needy and unorganised, they are almost at the mercy of the employers the middlemen and labour contractors.

Table 3 reveals about the betterment of the family with the income of the women in the family. As the women too are working along with men their income has been used for the purpose of the development of the family, i.e., education of children, purchasing of new assets and clearing of old debts. 70 per cent of the male labourers have expressed the opinion that they were benefited by the women's income to a greater extent. Whereas 30 per cent of them have said they are not benefited. 80 per cent of the female labours have expressed that their income has helped to increase their standard of living.

Table 3. Qualitative Assessment

Category	*Yes / Benefited*	*No / Not Benefited*	*Total*
Men	35 (70.00)	15 (30.00)	50 (50.00)
Women	40 (20.00)	10 (60.00)	50 (100.00)
Total	**75 (75.00)**	**25 (25.00)**	**100 (100.00)**

N.B. Figures in Brackets Represent Percentages to Total.

Table 4 depicts about the treatment given by the owners of the land towards the women-labourer who are working in agriculture. 60 per cent of the male workers expressed the opinion that the women are well treated by the owners. On the other, 50 per cent of the women labourers have expressed that they were ill-treated by the employers. This shows that even after 50 years of independence women-labourers are not treated well.

Table 4. Treatment by the Employers

Category	*Good*	*Medium*	*Worst*	*Total*
Men	30 (60.00)	20 (40.00)	—	50 (100.00)
Women	10 (20.00)	15 (30.00)	25 (50.00)	50 (100.00)
Total	**40** **(40.00)**	**35** **(35.00)**	**25** **(25.00)**	**100** **(100.00)**

N.B. Figures in Brackets represent Percentages to Total.

No separate trade union-organization has grown up in our country among the women-workers. They also do not stick to a job permanently and generally lack initiative and organizing capacity. As put by Sri V.V. Giri, "The traditional outlook that women are to take care of their health and home only, is slowly losing ground and today the services of women are equally reckoned with, when accounting the manpower potential of the country. Women labourers in agriculture through out India, irrespective of caste or religion, continue to have a subordinate status both within the home and outside. In the process of economic exploitation, the female agricultural labourers even become the targets of sexual harassment.

To conclude, the role of women in agriculture is increasing day by day. They are doing the work on par with men, inspite of that they are paid less. Although their income has been used as an additional income to the family to increase their standard of living, it is being increasingly realized that women's income in a family is very important in relation to the nutritional, economic and educational uplift of the family. For the socio-economic development of the family, women's contribution is significant in the domestic as well as economic front. Inspite of the constitutional safe guards, Article 30© about the equal pay for equal work and Article 42 for humance conditions, legislative measures, package of programmes by the government, no significant development took place in the socio-economic situation of women and they are still lagging behind men in their participation in the process of development. The Minimum Wages Act is not being implemented effectively and women are not paid equal wages for equal work. The following are the suggestions for the improvement of the women labourers' status.

1. Even though women work on par with men, they are less paid. So, the Government should take decision to remove this difference.
2. A separate women agricultural association should be formed to empower farm women activities.
3. It is necessary to increase awareness among women regarding their rights and responsibilities through education.

References

1. Report of the National Commission on Labour, p. 379.
2. Mehartag Begum, S. (2000): Women Rights and Rural Employment, Kurukshetra, p. 61.
3. Giri, V.V. Labour Problems in India Industry.
4. Beteille, A. (1974): Studies in Agrarian Social Structure, Oxford University Press, New Delhi.
5. Dantwala, M.L. (1949): Indian Agriculture: An Introduction to the Problem, National Information and Publications, Mumbai.
6. 1991 Census of India.
7. Viswanathan, M. (1994): "Women in Agriculture and Rural Development", Printwell, Jaipur, Rajasthan.

21

Agricultural Labourers in Rural Areas—Problems and Constraints

K. Santha Kumari

The Context

Inspite of crucial and pervasive role of agriculture in Indian economy, its two main partners—farmers and labourers are not paid that much attention as they deserve, while 75 per cent of farmers are marginal and small farmers with less than two hectares of holding, more than 50 per cent of agricultural labour are below the poverty line. Both of them are unorganised, voiceless and have no lobby. At the same time, they are victims of market forces, big farmers, Politicians and even the money-lenders. Specifically the agricultural labourers who account for 28 per cent of rural population have no access to land on which they work and there is little scope of acquiring any land of their own.[1] Early, due to religious sanction and practice, they are not only prohibited from acquiring land but also from using the public amenities like drinking Water Wells and roads. It is a matter of great concern for the Government and policy makers to bring them into the mainstream of the economy and to establish legislation to achieve better working conditions. This paper explores the socio-economic conditions of agricultural labourers and brings out their problems and constraints in the changing economic structure of India.

Poor Socio-economic Conditions

Agricultural Labourer is one who has no access to land on which he works and there is a little scope of acquiring any land of his own.' Agricultural labourers, predominantly belonging to the lower castes, are bereft of any ownership rights and have been living for the past several centuries at the merecy of an exploitative system based on caste and operated by combination of coercion and intimidation[2]. A majority of them belong to SCs. Due to religions sanction and practice they are not only prohibited from acquiring land but also from using the public amenities such as drinking water wells and roads. They are also subjected to several social disabilities such as not being allowed to wear shirts, footwear, ornaments, etc. Now, of course, these restrictions are Vanishing. But, on economic front, charges are not Significant[3].

Most of the agricultural labourers are living below poverty line due to low income, as they are poorly paid compared to any other workers. As they have very low level of staying power, they have very little option in the selection of jobs or terms and conditions of work[4]. Lack of assets, skills and basic capabilities such as education and health are responsible for the perpetual poverty of the labour households. Increasing mechanization, seasonal nature of work and illiteracy are further intensifying their poor living conditions in rural areas.

Classes of Agricultural Labour

Agricultural labourers could be divided into three types viz., casual labourers, attached and bonded labourers. There is a marked difference among these labourers. Casual labourer has the freedom to choose his work and his daily working hours are less. The casual labourers include ploughman, reapers, sowers, weeders and transplanters. The attached and bonded labourers do not have such freedom. Those labourers who pledge their person or sometimes a member of their families against a loan are known as attached or bonded labourers. It is hereditary and often transferred from father to son or from one member of the family to another. There may not be any interest on the amount borrowed by attached labourers but the bonded labourers have to pay interest also.

Reasons and Causes

The factors responsible for the continuous and steep rise in the number of agricultural labourers are many. Though the percentage of rural population in total population has declined from 82 in 1951 to 74 in 1991, the total number engaged in agriculture is now much larger than before. The fading of rural and cottage industries and ever increasing pressure on land has resulted in swelling the number of agricultural labourer. The law of inheritance has rendered a large number of holdings uneconomic. Due small holdings and low agricultural productivity, the Indian farmer has always lived in debt, to meet the consumption and other requirements, he has been approaching the village money lenders for loan. Taking the advantage of the illiteracy of the farmers the money lenders charge very high interest, which becomes a perpetual liability and ultimately many farmers passes to the landlords, turning the farmers into landless labourers.

The honest, illiterate and oppressed labourers think that repayment of debts with interest is their sacred duty. It is very difficult for them to lead life without loans as they are economically exploited and downtrodden. This forces them to get trapped into debt bondage. Further the eviction of tenants, who worked for landlords without having knowledge of their rights and privileges and the development of capitalist farming has led to large scale migration of agricultural labourers to wage employment in rural areas.

Growth and Structure

The growth and structure of Agricultural labourers in India is given in Table 1.

Table 1. Structure of Agricultural Labour in Indian Economy (1961-1991)

(in million)

Classification of Workers	*1961*	*1971*	*1981*	*1991*
Population	424.84	528.92	665.29	836.61
Cultivators	99.51	79.88	92.52	110.59
Agricultural Labourers	31.48	47.49	55.50	74.65
Total Agricultural Workers	130.99	126.67	148.02	185.24
Non-Agricultural Workers	57.43	54.71	74.49	100.19
Total Main Workers	188.42	181.37	222.52	285.42
Marginal Workers	—	—	22.09	29.48
Total Workers	**188.42**	**181.39**	**244.61**	**314.90**
Percentage of Cultivators to total main workers	52.81	43.65	41.58	38.75
Percentage of Agricultural Labourers to Total Main Workers	16.71	26.18	24.94	26.15
Percentage of total Agricultural Workers to total Main Workers	69.52	69.84	66.52	64.90
Percentage of non-Agricultural labourers to total Agricultural workers	30.48	30.16	33.48	35.10
Percentage of Agricultural labourers to total Agricultural workers	24.03	37.49	37.49	40.30
Percentage of Agricultural Workers to total workers	69.52	69.84	60.52	58.82
Percentage of agricultural works to total population	30.83	23.95	22.25	22.14
Percentage of Main Workers to total Population	44.35	34.29	33.45	34.12
Percentage of total Workers to total Population	44.35	34.29	36.77	37.64

Source: Statistical Abstracts of India, Directorate of Economics and Statistics, Ministry of Agriculture and Rural Development, Government of India, New Delhi.

The extent of agricultural labourers in Indian economy is given in Table 1 for the years 1961, 1971, 1981 and 1991. It could be seen from this Table, the total number of agricultural workers consisting of cultivators and agricultural labourers has gone up from nearly 131 millions in 1961 to 185 millions in 1991-an increase nearly of 50 per cent during the 30 years period. The percentage of agricultural labours to total agricultural workers had increased from 24.03 to 40.30 during the same period. Further the percentage of agricultural labours to total main workers had gone up from 16.71 in 1961 to 26.15 in 1991. All these figures invariably indicate that the size and proportion of agricultural labourers had increased significantly during the post independence period.

Further, the Sex-wise distribution of agricultural labourers in India shown in Table 2, indicates that the percentage of females had declined in respect of agricultural labourers.

Table 2. II. Sex-wise Distribution of Agricultural Labourers in India

(in million)

Classification of Agricultural Labourers	*1961*	*1971*	*1981*	*1991*	*DECE*	*NNIAL*	*Growth Rate*
					1971	*1981*	*1991*
Male	17.31	31.70	34.73	45.82	83.09	9.58	31.91
Female	14.17	15.79	20.77	28.83	11.45	31.49	38.83
Total	**31.48**	**47.49**	**55.50**	**74.65**	**50.85**	**16.87**	**34.50**

Note: Figures in Parenthesis Indicate the Percentage to Column Total.

Source: Census of India, 1991, Series-2, Andhra Pradesh, Paper-1 of 1991, Supplement Provisional Population Totals, Director of Census Operations, 1992.

Table 3 furnishes the State-wise estimates of agricultural labourers in India.

Table 3. Changing Production of Agricultural Labour Households in Major States: 1974-75 to 1993-94

State	Number of agricultural labour households (000)					Proportion of agricultural labour households to total labour house holds				
	1974-75	*1977-78*	*1983*	*1987-88*	*1993-94*	*1974-75*	*1977-78*	*1983*	*1987-88*	*1993-94*
Andhra Pradesh	2668	3520	3929	4007	4583	35.78	41.45	41.55	39.49	41.56
Assam	202	500	463	548	816	13.06	17.01	19.45	19.76	22.98
Bihar	2960	3898	4028	4334	4844	33.27	36.08	37.11	36.06	39.22
Gujarat	759	1229	1267	1582	1959	22.30	31.08	30.69	34.35	34.83
Haryana	125	275	512	405	364	9.11	18.19	20.24	19.73	15.87
Himachal Pradesh	10	35	17	41	26	1.78	5.22	2.19	4.83	2.85
Jammu & Kashmir	12	24	52	51	11	1.83	3.11	6.35	5.57	3.33
Karnataka	1252	1710	1762	2069	2180	30.78	37.92	36.59	39.34	37.73
Kerala	886	1030	1148	1179	1102	27.40	26.99	31.70	30.13	28.22
Madhya Pradesh	1325	2169	2302	2714	3332	21.79	2790	30.15	31.43	34.85
Maharashtra	1945	3029	3031	3308	3937	31.96	38.64	38.55	38.64	41.17
Orissa	1249	1713	1725	1826	1516	30.12	37.09	36.41	35.22	25.46

Table 3. (Contd...)

Punjab	380	507	561	683	706	20.88	24.10	25.26	28.11	27.69
Rajasthan	157	432	545	686	576	3.96	10.08	11.10	12.66	9.97
Tamil Nadu	2399	2627	3117	3088	3761	38.06	39.34	42.24	40.17	42.08
Uttar Pradesh	2395	2906	3040	3636	3061	15.81	18.11	18.01	20.08	15.31
West Bengal	1824	2772	3139	2989	3252	30.94	41.95	38.50	35.98	32.57
All-India	20739	28587	30867	33305	36262	25.27	29.88	30.70	30.74	30.34

Source:
1. Rural Labour Enquiry, 1974-75: Final Report on Wages and Earning, Labour Bureau, Shimla.
2. Rural Labour Enquiry, 1977-78: Report on Wages and Earnings, Labour Bureau, Shimla.
3. Rural Labour Enquiry, 1983: Report on Consumption Expenditure, Labour Bureau, Shimla.
4. Rural Labour Enquiry, 1987-88: Report on Consumption Expenditure, Labour Bureau, Shimla.
5. Rural Labour Enquiry, 1993-94: Report on General Characteristics of Rural Labour Households, Labour Bureau, Shimla.

It shows that as many as 11 major states viz Andhra Pradesh, Assam, Bihar, Gujarat, Haryana, Karnataka, Madhya Pradesh, Maharashtra, Punjab, Rajasthan and Tamil Nadu recorded a Significant increase in the proportion of agricultural labourers during the 20 year period 1974-75 to 1993-94. Among the remaining states, while the increase was marginal in Himachal Pradesh and Jammu & Kashmir), in Kerala and Uttar Pradesh their proportion remained unchanged. In Orissa, it actually declined.

Hours, Wages and Income

The hours of work of agricultural labour, unlike in the industrial sector, are not regulated by legislation. Hours of work vary from place to place, season to season and from crop to crop. The working hours are generally from sunrise to sunset. Sometimes, they are made to work during the nights for irrigation, threshing etc. In fact the terms are dictated to them and they have absolutely no purchasing power.5

Since agricultural labour is highly unorganised and the nature of employment is highly seasonal, their wages and family incomes are very low in India. The changes in the daily real wage earnings of adult male and female labour in agricultural and non-agricultural Occupations during the 20-years period since 1974-75 are brought out in Table 4 and 5. The Tables show that daily real wage earnings of adult male labour increased continuously over the period both in agricultural and non-agricultural occupations, except during 1983 when these declined in most of the states. Over the years, daily real wage earnings in agricultural occupations increased between 1987-88 and 1993-94, by varying degree in all states. While in some states, the increase was indeed substantial.

The real wage earnings of adult female labour also increased continuously, again except for 1983, both in agricultural and non-agricultural occupations in all states

Table 4. Trends in Daily Real Wage Earnings of Agricultural Labour in Agricultural Occupations in Major States: 1974-75 to 1993-94 (1980-81 = 100)

State	*Adult male*					*Adult female*				
	1974-75	*1977-78*	*1983*	*1987-88*	*1993-94*	*1974-75*	*1977-78*	*1983*	*1987-88*	*1993-94*
Andhra Pradesh	2.98	4.18	4.01	5.99	7.24	2.21	2.92	3.12	4.18	5.20
Assam	4.77	6.02	6.61	7.41	8.72	3.63	5.21	3.52	6.83	7.32
Bihar	3.52	4.42	3.73	5.59	5.99	2.99	3.98	3.18	4.91	5.24
Gujarat	3.61	5.09	4.60	5.52	6.81	2.81	4.53	3.63	5.47	6.62
Haryana	6.29	7.58	5.58	6.57	9.72	5.12	6.31	4.50	4.81	8.29
Himachal Pradesh	6.57	7.56	3.54	8.71	10.82	4.27	6.30	2.51	7.99	8.85
Jammu & Kashmir	6.10	6.99	5.16	6.61	11.66	4.29	4.98	4.87	4.19	8.35
Karnataka	3.30	4.01	3.23	5.39	6.84	2.09	2.70	2.70	3.90	5.10
Kerala	5.96	8.15	7.98	9.83	12.46	4.24	5.60	6.51	7.23	8.65
Madhya Pradesh	2.57	3.40	3.09	5.05	6.27	2.85	2.77	2.65	4.47	5.24

(Cont...)

Table 4. **(Contd...)**

Maharashtra	2.93	3.97	3.64	5.85	7.38	1.70	2.49	2.50	3.84	4.60
Orissa	3.40	3.87	2.76	4.86	6.27	2.03	2.94	2.47	3.74	4.62
Punjab	8.32	9.59	8.36	10.26	14.07	4.42	6.01	4.12	5.97	11.99
Rajasthan	4.19	5.89	2.88	6.17	9.78	2.97	4.09	2.79	5.87	8.17
Tamil Nadu	3.53	4.94	2.54	6.07	9.22	2.25	2.99	2.73	3.83	5.57
Uttar Pradesh	3.85	4.86	3.71	5.89	7.49	3.01	3.54	2.75	4.57	5.70
West Bengal	4.13	5.28	3.91	7.32	8.56	3.35	4.61	3.64	6.60	7.42
All-India	3.60	4.74	4.03	5.96	7.62	2.52	3.36	3.04	4.40	5.42

Note: The Money Wage Earnings have been Deflated Using Consumer Price Index for Agricultural Labourers (CPIAL). The Base of CPIAL has been Shifted from 1960-61 to 1980-81.

Source: Rural Labour Enquiry: Report on Wages and Earnings, 1974-75; 1977-78; 1983; 1987-88; 1993-94 Labour Bureau, Chandigarh/Shimla.

Table 5. Trends in Daily Real Wage Earnings of Agricultural Labour in Non-agricultural Occupation in Major States: 1974-75 to 1993-94 (1980-81 = 100)

State	Adult male					Adult female				
	1974-75	*1977-78*	*1983*	*1987-88*	*1993-94*	*1974-75*	*1977-78*	*1983*	*1987-88*	*1993-94*
Andhra Pradesh	3.15	4.99	3.11	6.60	8.84	2.49	3.43	2.30	4.60	5.34
Assam	3.88	5.73	5.80	8.40	11.55	3.08	5.16	3.71	7.25	4.60
Bihar	3.69	5.72	2.74	6.68	7.26	2.53	4.22	2.07	5.08	2.28
Gujarat	3.59	7.38	4.85	5.68	9.45	3.20	4.21	3.34	5.20	6.51
Haryana	5.42	7.25	5.27	8.35	12.87	3.77	4.03	1.35	6.41	6.18
Himachal Pradesh	5.75	6.49	4.87	10.92	12.75	3.17	6.80	1.83	-	-
Jammu & Kashmir	6.33	5.34	6.09	7.46	15.09	3.49	4.48	5.32	1.40	—
Karnataka	3.66	4.66	4.25	5.66	9.19	2.77	3.40	2.51	4.99	6.55
Kerala	5.42	7.30	7.22	7.55	13.40	2.75	4.16	2.43	5.49	6.52
Madhya Pradesh	2.58	4.27	4.11	6.38	8.53	1.87	2.74	2.72	5.76	6.55

(Cont...)

Table 5. (Contd...)

Maharashtra	3.20	6.38	7.59	6.42	8.86	2.09	2.97	3.18	4.93	6.58
Orissa	2.78	5.14	2.05	5.73	7.36	1.98	2.74	1.46	4.24	5.30
Punjab	7.60	8.91	6.58	8.38	14.33	2.47	2.97	1.75	5.06	5.86
Rajasthan	3.76	6.34	5.99	6.71	10.97	2.22	3.68	4.40	5.70	4.08
Tamil Nadu	3.46	5.95	5.35	5.66	10.03	1.95	3.05	2.99	3.73	4.57
Uttar Pradesh	4.42	6.66	5.05	7.02	10.37	2.59	4.18	2.11	4.58	6.15
West Bengal	3.87	6.59	3.31	7.35	9.26	2.20	2.89	1.98	4.63	5.69
All-India	3.63	5.99	4.38	6.43	9.63	2.36	3.36	2.54	5.01	5.79

Note : The Money Wage Earnings have been Deflated Using Consumer Price Index for Agricultural Labourers (CPIAL). The Base of CPIAL has been Shifted from 1960-61 to 1980-81.

Source : Sharma H.R. "Employment and Wage earnings of Agricultural Labourers—A State Wise Analysis", The Indian Journal of Labour Economics, Vol. 44, No. 1, Jan-March 2001, p. 34.

barring Assam, Haryana & Rajasthan, where these declined between 1987-88 and 1993-94. Looking over a long period, the gender wage differentials have declined in most of the states, while in Kerala, Madhya Pradesh, Tamil Nadu and Uttar Pradesh, these have become pronounced. In non-agricultural occupations male and female wage disparities have widened in states like Andhra Pradesh, Assam, Gujarat, Haryana, Karnataka, Kerala and Rajasthan.

It may also be pointed out that agricultural labourers are often denied their Wages in the event of natural calamities such as floods, droughts, etc. They have to work in all conditions and in all weathers in order to survive. They, being Sick, unfit for work due to some family tragedy are not entittled to any sympathy or leniency from their masters. Give them any name, they still carry the yoke of serfdom on their shoulders.

Government Measures of Assistance

In order to ameliorate the conditions of agricultural labour, the Government, both at the central and State level, passed many Acts and started various welfare programmes.

Legislative Controls

Statutory legislations such as The Minimum Wages Act 1948, The Equal Remuneration Act, 1976. The Contract Labour system Abolition Act, 1970, The Bonded Labour system (Abolition) Act, 1976; The Inter-State Migrant Workmen (Regulation, Employment and conditions of Service) Act, 1979 have been enacted at the States initiative to ensure the minimum subsistence level of income to labourers.[6] Among them, the Minimum Wage Act, 1948 assumes special significance. It authorised state governments to fix minimum rates of wages and regulate daily, weekly hours of work, overtime wages, weekly off etc. But unfortunately the implementation of these minimum wages is practically absent. The bureaucracy is not so genuinely interested. The wage rates differ in different areas and seasons. As the labourers are spread over the length and breadth of the country, the effective enforcement of Minimum Wages Act was proved to be inconvenient and cumbersome.

Land Reforms

The concept of land-reforms has been conceived and implemented by the Indian Government to achieve an egalitarian society. Priority has been given to the landless agricultural labourers while distributing the surplus land through land reform legislations. The national guidelines drawn up in 1972, recommended that while distributing surplus and waste lands priority should be given to the agricultural labourers, particularly those belonging to the SCs and STs.

But the report of the commission for SCs and STs 1984, shows that at all-India level 22,64415 acres of land was redistributed which constitutes only 2.64 per cent of the total land operated in 1985-86[7]. Thus the data unmistakably show that the land reform legislation has not sufficiently altered the agrarian structure. Thus the land reform legislations have to be amended in such a way that the tiller should own the land and those who do not till the land should not be allowed to own the land.

Rural Industrialisation

In order to provide subsidiary employment of land less laboruers, the Government of India has encouraged occupations like dairying, animal husbandry, poultry fisheries, etc., to accommodate those who cannot find adequate work in the land based occupations. Massive rural works programmes were also started connecting them to markets through approach roads. Steps were also taken to rehabilitate the bonded labourers and to acquire suitable income-generating assets and skills. However, there is a need for broad-based, regionally balanced pattern of industrialisation and removal of imperfections of credit markets and ignorance about new technologies.[8]

Rural Employment Generation Programme

Right from the implementation of Five Year Plans, India had tried to tackle the problem of rural unemployment through various anti-poverty projects and employment generation programmes. These programmes aimed at providing additional and seasonal employment to rural poor and also a source of supplement to their income. Food for Works programme, and Community Development Programme attempted to augment employment resources. A series of programmes viz., DPAP, SEDA, IRDP, NREP, RLEGP, JRY, etc., were launched to reduce regional disparities in providing rural employment. But these programmes were not successful in achieving their goals. People's participation was almost negligible, huge amounts allowed were being cornered by middlemen.[9] and the fruits of the programmes that percolated down to the beneficiaries were ignorable. Thus the unemployment problem continues to be colossal and pervasive as ever.

Unionism

Labour Unions consisting of poor peasants, tenants and agricultural labourer are formed to fight against exploitation and low wage rates. These organisations are enabling the implementation of various development programmes by ensuring benefits to the rural poor. The implementation of land reforms was successful in Kerala, and West Bengal mainly due to caste Hindu agricultural labourers do not join with the depressed class laboruers in the matter of strikes. Another problem of unionisation of agricultural laboruers is the employees preference of non-member by the union and submissive nature of person for employment in agriculture.

A strong case for the unionisation of agricultural labourers was started early in 1931 'The Kisan Sabhas,

Krishak Sabhas, Peasant Unions etc., were spread to different parts of the country to protect the interests of landless labourers.[10]

The organisation is also taking in terms of rapid political movements, popularly known as the Naxalite groups, who are organising the rural labouring poor by engaging in what they believed in class struggle. This has led to violent confrontations and challenges to the Government. Although they have some successes, in mitigating the labour poor they have only limited appeal under prevailing civilised society. Trade Unions of political parties like All India Agricultural Workers Union of Communist party of India (Marxist) 1964 and the Bharatiya Khet Mazdoor 1968, Union of Communist Party of India which are working to increase the staying power of labour and to narrow the gap in earning and working conditions between the organised and unorganised sectors. A number of empowerment groups (NGOs) constituting religions and charitable institutions and development organisations are conducting micro-credit programmes for the rural poor.

Issues and Concern

In order to protect the interest of rural labourers, certain conditions need to be improved in the rural areas. Rural areas are deprived of proper education, health care and sanitation facilities. Eighty five per cent of Child labour exists in rural areas, which is bad for the economy of the country.[11] Few options are available for employment generation in the organised sectors. Alternative strategies have to be worked out to tackle poverty in rural areas by creating self employment. The government should support policies and projects that offer loans to poor people in the villages. It may be necessary to find out the cost effectiveness, replicability and sustainability of various self-employment schemes in the prevailing economic structure. Suitable and attractive incentives like house sites, agricultural lands etc., may be offered to encourage the man power to move from surplus areas to deficit areas which will have favourable effect on demand-Supply relationship and consequently on wage rates.

The strategy for large employment opportunities in rural areas has to be multi-pronged. The potential of employment in non-agricultural rural jobs should be fully explored in order to accommodate the surplus labour in agriculture. Rural industrialisation with agro-based industries and other non-farm activities might solve the problem of agricultural underemployment and unemployment. Added to this, the cropping pattern has to be changed and intensive farming be promoted.

There should be a separate organisation at the state level dealing exclusively with the problems of agricultural labourers and a committee at the block level to implement the minimum wages and solve the wage disputes. For the development of skills, institutions should be set up and adequate training be imparted by qualified persons. This would necessitate the development of a well-designed and broad-based support-system, capable of assisting the new class of artisans and craftsmen at all crucial states like the formation of projects for procurement of finance, machinery and equipment. The role of Panchyat Raj bodies, voluntary agencies. Cooperatives and workers' organisations should be recognised in the planning process and mechanism should be evolved to strengthen them.

Finally, social mobilisation through motivation and awareness building, has to precede any training programme on rural employment. There is a need for sustained campaign for enlisting active participation of people in their development. It is important to carry awareness-campaigns through conferences, seminars, Village meetings and distribution of leaflets through colleges and Schools in rural areas.

People's participation is the only effective way so that the poor can overcome their difficulties. All campaigns aim at encouraging peopole's participation in rural development programmes—from planning and implementation to monitoring. All efforts should be made to sensitise officials and educate the people about the need and virtues of self-employment as key to rural development.

Summary

Agricultural labourers constitute the single most important segment of the rural proletariat. Over decades their number is rapidly growing. The efforts made during Five Year Plans have not significantly improved their economic position. There were 185.24 million agricultural workers in India in 1991. As many as 11 major states Viz., Andhra Pradesh, Assam, Bihar, Gujarat, Haryana, Karnataka, Madhya Pradesh, Maharashtra, Punjab, Rajasthan and Tamil Nadu recorded a significant increase in the proportion of agricultural labourers. Continuous subdivision of landholdings, lack of alternative employment opportunities, poverty and other seasons compel many of the small and marginal landholders to participate in agricultural labour market. Regulation of wage rates, rural industrialisation, trade unionism, skill formation and people participation are the powerful instruments to fight against problems of agricultural labour in rural areas.

References

1. K.P. Kannan, "Changing Economic Structure' and Labour Institutions in India "The Indian Journal of Labour Economics, Vol. 42, No. 4, Octo,—December, 1999, p. 762.
2. Ani Lukose, "Labour Movements and Agrarian Relations", Raw at Publications, 1991, Jaipur, p. VII.
3. M. Thangaraj; "Socio-economic Conditions and Problems of Agricultural Labourers" Social Change, Vol. 25, No. 4, December, 1995, p. 44.
4. K.P. Kannan, Op. cit.

5. Amarjit Singh and A.N. Sadhu, "Agricultural Problems in India", Himalaya Publishing House, Bombay, p. 157.

6. S. Mohan Kumar and R.K. Sharma, "Mnimum Wage Legislation and its Impact on Rural Wage Formation" The Indian Journal of Labour Economics, Vol. 43, No. 2, April June, 2000, p. 247.

7. M. Thangaraj, Op. cit.

8. Navin Chandra Joshi; "Evolving Strategies for Rural Employment" Kurukshetra Vol. 48, No. 7, April, 2000, p. 31.

9. D. Sunder Raj, "Rural employment Generation Programmes", Kurukshetra, op. cit. p. 42.

10. K. Sivaramakrishna, K. Ramesh and M. Gangadhara Rao, "Human Resource Management in Agriculture" Discovery Publishing House, New Delhi, 1995, p. 193.

11. D.K. Giri; "Reflecting on Rural Self-employment, Kurukshetra, Op. cit, p. 50.

22

Male and Female Labour Productivity in Agriculture: A Comparative Analysis

Smt T. Naga Prasuna & Prof V.K. Reddy

Introduction

Agriculture is the first culture that man has learnt to practise as a means of livelihood and a way of life. It is the most important sector in all countries. In India more than 70% of the population are engaged in this sector.

Among the various inputs to agriculture, labour plays a crucial part with both male and female labour being employed. Male labour participation is quite high in some of the crop operations like irrigation, ploughing, etc., while female labour participation is high in crop operations like transplanting, weeding, etc.

The term "Agricultural Labour" is used to denote all individuals, employed for carrying out different agricultural operations, either on permanent or temporary basis. The demarcation of labour (i.e., into male and female activities) is based on the effort required for the work. If the effort required is more (ploughing, irrigation, etc.,) males are employed. On the contrary if the effort required is less (transplanting, weeding, etc.,) women are employed. Thus as the effort and jobs vary, so does productivity.

'Productivity' is a ratio of output. Thus productivity varies from men to women, from agriculture to allied activities. The present investigation was taken up with the following objectives.

1. To examine the resource-use productivities of various resources on farm.
2. To compare the resource productivities of male and female labour on farm.
3. To examine the substitutability of male and female labour on farm.

Methodology

The study pertains to Cuddapah district of Andhra Pradesh. Six villages were selected at random. The villages are Machupalli, Jangalapalli, Mulapalli, Jyothi, Onethatipalli, Onethiripalli. The cultivators in these selected villages were classified into three categories viz., marginal farms (< 1 acre), small farms (1-2 acres) and large farms (> 2 acres). A sample of 150 farm households was selected by simple random sampling through proportional allocation method. In all 50 marginal, 50 small and 50 large cultivators were selected for detailed analysis. The primary data were collected through survey method for the year 2000-2001.

The log-linear production function was fitted for the farm enterprise. The functional form of the model was as

$$Y = b_o X_1^{b1} X_2^{b2} X_3^{b3} X_4^{b4} X_5^{b5} e^u$$

where

Y = Per acre income from the whole farm in rupees

b_o = Constant term

b_i = Elasticity coefficients

X_1 = Capital in rupees (which included per acre expenditure on seed, bullock labour and plant protection measures)

X_2 = Per acre expenditure in rupees on fertilizers and farm yard manure.

X_3 = Per acre requirement of male labour in days.

X_4 = Per acre requirement of female labour in days.

X_5 = Per cent irrigated to total area under all crops.

e^u = Random term

The marginal value productivities for various factors of production was worked out as follows:

$$MVP_{(xi)} = b_i \frac{\overline{Y}}{\overline{X}_i}$$

Where

$MVP_{(xi)}$ = The marginal value productivity of X_i.

$\overline{Y}$ = The value of output at its geometric mean level.

$\overline{X}_i$ = The value of ith input at its geometric mean level.

b_i = Elasticity coefficient of ith input.

The standard way to examine such efficiency is to compare marginal value products (MVPs) with the marginal factor cost (MFC) of each variable input. The optimum use of a particular input would be indicated by the condition of equality of marginal value products and marginal factor cost i.e., MVP/MFC=1. Deviating MVP to MFC indicates the degree of resource use inefficiency.

The efficiencies of male and female labour were compared by using the following formula:

$$b^1{}_i = b_{iF} \frac{\overline{X}_{iM}}{\overline{X}_{iF}}$$

and the significance was computed using t-test.

$$t = \frac{b_i - b^1{}_i}{\sqrt{s^2(b_i) + \left(\frac{\overline{X}_{iM}}{\overline{X}_{iF}}\right)^2 s^2(b^1{}_i)}}$$

Where

b_i	is the elasticity coefficient for male labour in the ith farm size.
b_i^1	is the elasticity coefficient necessary to yield marginal employment of male labour equal to that of female labour in ith farm size.
b_{iF}	is the elasticity coefficient of female labour in the ith farm size.
$\overline{X}_{iM}$	is the average number of male days in the ith farm size
$\overline{X}_{iF}$	is the average number of female days in the ith farm size
$S^2(b_i)$	is variance of b.in the ith farm size
$S^2(b^1{}_i)$	is variance of b^1 in the ith farm size

Results and Discussion

Input-output Relationship

To examine the input-output relationship for the farm with respect to crops, the total annual income for all the enterprises (major and minor) was taken together. The expenditure incurred on all the factors of production involved in the production of crops grown throughout the year was considered and then the relationship of various factors with the value of output was worked out. The results thus obtained are presented in Table 1. The explanatory variables are explained about 30 per cent (large farms) to 38 per cent (all-farms) of total variation in the farm enterprise.

Table 1. Input-Output Relationship for Farms

Explanatory Variables	*Regression Coefficients Farm-Size*			*All-Farms*
	Marginal	*Small*	*Large*	
X_1	0.3961 (0.2185)	0.4513 (0.2589)	0.3907** (0.1160)	0.4155** (0.1011)
X_2	0.2921 (0.2124)	0.2378 (0.2906)	0.1357 (0.1157)	0.2112* (0.1037)
X_3	0.0209 (0.1437)	0.1949 (0.1589)	0.0553 (0.0952)	0.1229 (0.0705)
X_4	–0.0431 (0.2213)	–0.1319 (0.1460)	–0.1202 (0.1282)	–0.0298 (0.0807)
X_5	–0.4473 (0.2468)	–0.1744 (0.3472)	–0.2209 0.1301)	–0.1303* (0.0475)
Constant term	1.6759	1.5772	2.3457	1.4995
Σb_i	0.2187	0.5777	0.2406	0.5895
$\overline{R}_2$	0.3624*	0.3343*	0.3008*	0.3886*

Note: Figures given in parentheses represent standard errors.

*Shows significance at 5 per cent probability level.

**Shows significance at 1 per cent probability level.

The returns to scale measured in terms of the sum of elasticity coefficients (Σb_i) were less than unity under all the categories under discussion.

On marginal farms, the elasticity coefficients of the variables capital (X_1), expenditure (X_2), male labour (X_3) are positive but not significant. The elasticity coefficients of the variables female labour (X_4), and irrigated area (X_5) are negative and non-significant. This might be due to the surplus availability.

In the case of small farms the elasticity coefficients of the variables capital (X_1), expenditure on fertilizers and farm yard manure (X_2) and male labour (X_3) are positive, whereas the coefficients of female labour (X_4) and irrigated area (X_5) are negative. None of the variables are found to be statistically significant.

In case of large farms the elasticity coefficient of the variable capital (X_1) is found to be positive and significant, while all other variables are found to be insignificant. This indicates that one per cent increase in capital would increase output by 0.39 per cent.

When the pooled data were analysed, the regression coefficients for capital (X_1), expenditure (X_2), male labour (X_3) were positive, and capital and expenditure are significant. The female labour input (X_4), irrigated area (X_5) were negative and non-significant. This might be due to the surplus availability. The magnitude of elasticity coefficient for capital (X_1) was maximum and that for female labour (X_4) was minimum. Thus the capital input (X_1) was found to be the most effective input whereas, the female labour (X_4) was found to be the least effective input. The sum of the elasticities (0.5895) is less than unity implying that there was decreasing returns to scale on pooled farm group. The coefficient of multiple determination ($\bar{R}^2$) was 0.3886 which implies that the explanatory variables used in the model explained only 38% of the variation in the output. The F-value was significant implying that all the included variables were important for explaining the variation in pooled farms.

Resource-Use Efficiency

Marginal value product (MVP) to factor cost ratio is the measure of resource use efficiency. This ratio of MVP to factor cost indicates the optimum resource use efficiency of a particular input. Deviation of MVP to factor cost ratio indicates the degree of resource use inefficiency.

The marginal value productivity of each input factor was worked out and the results are presented in Table 2.

The MVP ratio of irrigated area is positive and greater than unity in marginal farms and thus there is scope to increase the level of this input for increasing the production.

This ratio is found to be negative but greater than unity in small farms and less than unity in large farms.

Table 2. Marginal Value Products (MVPS) to Factor-Cost Ratios (MFC)

Explanatory Variables	*Regression Coefficients Farm-Size*			*All-Farms*
	Marginal	*Small*	*Large*	
X_1	0.6685	0.7904	0.6727	0.7143
X_2	0.7022	0.5968	0.3757	0.0405
X_3	0.0149	0.1419	0.0382	0.0874
	(0.003)	(0.0028)	(0.0008)	(0.0017)
X_4	-0.0314	-0.0899	-0.0751	-0.0202
	(-0.0010)	(-0.0029)	(-0.0025)	(0.0007)
X_5	2.2603	-1.8452	-0.0436	-1.0936

Note: *(i)* MVP's and MVP to Factor-cost ratios are same for all inputs except male and female labour.

(ii) MVP to factor-cost ratios for male and female labour are given in brackets.

The MVP ratios of all the variables except irrigated area (X_5) in all situations are less than unity. Further the ratios are negative for female labour (X_4). This implies that capital, expenditure on fertilizers and male labour are over utilized whereas female labour is underutilized in all the categories of farms.

Comparison of Male and Female Labour Efficiency

The results shown in Table 3 indicates that the marginal value productivities of male labour were higher in small farms. Further the marginal value productivities of male labour are found to be higher than female labour in all categories of farms. The differences in marginal value productivities between male labour and female labour are found to be positive but not significant. This indicates that the marginal employment was higher for male labour compared to female labour in the farms but not significant. On comparison of male and female labour efficiency for the farm as a whole, the male labour efficiency is found to be greater than the female labour efficiency.

Table 3. Comparison of Male and Female Labour Efficiencies

Farm-size	b_i	b^1_i	b_i-b^1_i
Marginal	0.0209	-0.0439	0.0648
Small	0.1949	-0.1234	0.3183
Large	0.0553	-0.1089	0.1642
All-Farms	0.1229	-0.0284	0.1513

Note: b_i Elasticity coefficient for male labour.

b^1_i Elasticity coefficient necessary to yield marginal employment of male labour equal to that of female labour.

b_i-b^1_i When +ve Indicates that marginal employment was higher for male labour and reverse was true for-ve sign.

* Shows significance at 5 per cent probability level.

** Shows significance at 1 per cent probability level.

Conclusion

The comparison of male and female labour efficiencies indicated that the productivity of male labour was higher than female labour in farm enterprise. The results indicated that the inputs were overutilized and the farmers were operating in decreasing returns to scale. Therefore, efforts should be made to use these resources efficiently through relocation and timely-use of resources along with their balanced and enhanced use.

Decreasing returns to scale were experienced in all categories of farmers in farm enterprise. The marginal value productivities of all explanatory variables in all categories are found to be less than unity. This implies that the resources are overutilized. The MVP ratios for male labour is found to be greater than the female labour because of comparatively efficient performance by male labour in farm enterprise.

The labour input was found surplus which needs immediate withdrawal. This may be made possible by diverting the labour from agriculture to non-agricultural sector for which non-farm enterprises within the villages should be created particularly in small scale industries. As the male labour was efficient in farm enterprise, the extension workers must organise demonstrations and training camps, especially for women in order to enhance their knowledge and awareness. The women should be made aware of their capabilities and opportunities around them which they might explore to engage themselves in non-farm jobs to increase their overall productivities. This will lead to economic independence of women.

References

1. Alam, Q.M. (1989), "Resource Use Efficiency of Irrigated and Non-Irrigated Farms in a Selected Area of Bangladesh", Economic Affairs, 34(4):271-277.
2. Banerjee, B.N. (1985), "Concepts of Farm Size, Resource Use and Productivity in Agriculture", Economic Affairs-30(1):17-22.
3. Das, K.K. and Banerjee, B.N. (2000), "Farm Size and Labour Use pattern-A study of Attached Labour based on Farms in West Bengal", Economic Affairs, 45(3):187-192.
4. Inder Sain and Singh, A.J. (1994), "Labour Productivity and Use Efficiency on the Punjab Farms", Economic Affairs, 39(4):159-208.

23

Transition Era and Its Impact on Social Security

Prof. S.V. Raju & P. Purnachandra Rao

Introduction

A citizen who has contributed or is likely to contribute something to his country's welfare, should be given protection against certain hazards. Social security envisages that the members of a community shall be protected by collective action against social risks causing undue hardship and privation to individuals whose private resources can seldom be adequate to meet them. In India, all the Five-Year Plans emphasized the need for social security schemes. Social security measures are usually divided into two categories, (1) Social Insurance, (2) Social Assistance. Social Insurance schemes are usually financed through contribution by the employers, employees and the state. Social Assistance schemes seek to provide assistance to the poor and needy persons.

The concept of social security is based on the ideals of human dignity and social justice. It represents only one of the measures to be taken by the state to achieve the general objective of providing a certain minimum standard of living of its people through maintaining a continuous flow of adequate income to their families.

Need

Social security is an instrument of social and economic justice as it works for horizontal and vertical redistribution of incomes in the society. First, for at least two reasons; an adjustment of the distribution of personal income still seems to be even more urgent due to inequality in developing countries than in Industrialised countries. And also the absolute poverty is generally more widespread in rural areas than in urban areas. Secondly, the body of redistribution machinery needs to be strengthened for the above purpose.

Significance of the Social Security

Social Security is one of the finest contributions of mankind because the principle of the society stepping in to help persons who are not able to earn due to no fault of their's be it due to sickness, work injury, voluntary unemployment or old age etc., was accepted universally by the United Nations Organizations, the I.L.O. (International Labour Organization) and the constitutions of most of the countries.

The International Labour Conference (ILO) held in Philadelphia in 1944, decided that all social security plans should attempt to provide curative and/or preventive medical care, income insecurity in case of voluntary loss of income and a grant of additional income to persons with dependants.

According to Beveridge, the idea of Social Security is that, "The state shall make itself responsible for ensuing a minimum standard of material welfare to all its citizen on the basis wide enough to cover all the contingencies of life form Womb to Tomb. It is the Social Security that designed to eliminate five giants of Beveridge viz., Want, Disease, Ignorance, Squalor and Idleness.

The Directive Principle of State Policy' as embodied in the Constitution by special stress on the goal of the welfare state envisages under Article 41 that the state shall within limits of its economic capacity and development make effective provisions for securing the right to work, education and public assistance in case of unemployment, old age, sickness and disablement. The underlying idea is, for the contributions of the country's welfare by the people, should be given protection against certain risks.

Labour Reforms

The Group of Ministers (GOM) was set-up in February 2000 and was reconstituted in October 2001. It was chaired by Planning Commission Deputy Chairman, K.C. Pant and its recommendations were as follows:

- The amendment to the Industrial Disputes Act proposes to enhance the limit of workers from 100 to 1000 of establishments that can go in for closure and retrenchment without seeking the Government permission. According to some estimates, 95% of the Indian enterprises will benefit from the amendment.
- The amendment to the contract labour (Abolition & Regulation) Act, 1970, proposes free use of contract labour in a large number of establishments. The thrust is, to facilitate the process of casing workers out of presently permanent and secure employment. It is to create a redefined framework where in labour can be engaged on terms that are flexible, time-bound and can be easily terminated. The stated objective of the amendment is to encourage private sector investment in labour intensive and export-oriented industries. It is easier for prospective employers to hire and fire. The highly exploitative and insecure nature of contract labour is widely recognized.
- The Payment of Wages Act' changes have also been approved to the upper wage ceiling for workers who get protection under this Act. This wage ceiling is now proposed to be increased from Rs. 1,600/- per month to Rs. 6,500/-.

Process of Globalisation

Since 1970s, even in Industrialised countries, employment relations, have become increasingly fragmented. The form, this takes, varies from country to country. In some cases, such as Spain, the main feature has been a growth in temporary work. In others such as the U.K., the most notable development has been in part-time work and in low-income casual jobs, in many countries the wage differentials between the skilled and the unskilled workers have grown. There have been a widespread growth in home working and self employment of one sort or another. As a result, the share of employment which can be described as regular, permanent, full-time and with adequate social protection, has tended to decline.

After liberalization of Indian Economy (1991 July 24th), the signals of labour reforms, amendment to the existing Acts are being made towards the interest of the private sector. The amendments are being made to the existing laws by the Government of India to scrap the enjoying legislative protection of the Government staff and public sector employees and workers so far. Such as

New Pension Scheme

Group Insurance Scheme

Company (Amendment) Bill

Contract Labour Act, 1970

VRS/Golden Shake hand scheme

Trade Unions (Amendment) Act

Factories Act, 1948

Budget Proposal of 2002-03

A new pension scheme for fresh employees in government sector has been announced by the Union Finance Ministers, Yashwant Sinha, in his fifth budget presentation on 28th February 2002.

Clause of Labour Standards

The issue of labour standards to trade is being debated in various fora (recent Doha) and ground realities are changing drastically. Already a number of leading international retailers and brands have developed 'Code of Conduct' for their suppliers world-wide. Some call it 'Vendor Compliance Monitoring Programme' others call it 'Responsible Manufacturing' and so on.

The issue relating to trade and labour standards is highly sensitive. There is no mention of inclusion of social clause or labour standards in WTO. However, some industrialized nations have raised this issue now, and are instating that the subject should be studied by WTO to bring the matter of labour standards into the organisation's purview. There is a great division between most of the Industrialised nations on the one hand and developing countries on the other. The developing countries like India are looking at it as a ploy of developed nations to annihilate their comparative advantage of labour costs and argue that ILO is the right forum to discuss these issues. It is not enough to say that labour standards can't be linked to trade.

A Case

Krishna Milk Union is a District Milk Producers' Co-operative Society came into existence in July 1983. It was registered as Krishna District Milk Producers' Co-operative Union Limited (KDMPC). Krishna milk union currently has 515 functional dairy co-operatives in villages with about one lakh farmer members organized on the lines of Anand pattern. It is affiliated to A.P.D.D.C.F., head-quarters at Hyderabad. The union operates individually procuring surplus milk from about 900 villages in the district, processes the milk, supplies pasterurised milk to all the urban consumers of Krishna district. It also manufactures various premium dairy products and markets across the country through Federation. It also manufactures pre-mixed cattle feed, mineral mixture and supplies to dairy farmers of the district. It has annual turn-over of over Rs. 93 crores with an established Vijaya' brand. It has annual wage bill of Rs. 15 crores. It has one of the best Aspetic Packing Stations of India.

Manpower

The union has a solid manpower strength of 1035 on regular basis, having vast experience of over 3 decades and 400 contract labourers.

We have collected primary data from the regular employees through questionnaire with a sample size of 10 per cent i.e., 100 respondents. The opinions of the respondents regarding New Pension Scheme and Voluntary Retirement Scheme (VRS) are as follows:

Table 1. Openions of Respondents

Sl. No.	*Provision*	*Satisfied*	*So-So*	*Not satisfied*	*Others (Unable to tell)*
1	New Pension Scheme	–	–	91	9
2	V.R.S.	3	11	73	13

- About New Pension Scheme, since 1995, they have expressed their dissatisfaction over the execution of the scheme which provides Rs. 400/- to 500/- per month on the retirement. They feel that the share of pension amount is less than their accumulated contributions and interest throughout the career.
- About 600 employees have availed the VRS so far, but most of the respondents opined their unwillingness and dissatisfaction over the scheme due to the numerous troubles which are being faced by the seniors in their practical life and uncertainty of the future, happening laziness etc.
- Predicament of Contract Labour: The Contract labourers are being paid Rs. 50/- per day and

having neither welfare facilities nor social security provisions. They are not allowed in canteen on par with regular staff, co-operative credit facility, recreation facility etc. Their duty is only confined to the stipulated work and timings, after completion of work they have to get permission from the concerned authority to leave the organization. Therefore, the contract labour system is nothing but the state has to give up the responsibility of welfare and security of the employees whereas it tends to pave the easy path towards the objectives of the corporate sector.

Conclusion

India, having more than I billion population got Independence over 50 years, but not yet eradicated social evils such as poverty, illiteracy, unemployment and inequality. Significant percentage of people (over 30) are still below poverty line (BPL). So it is inevitable to the state that should not give up the social responsibility, labour welfare and social security.

It is an ideal that performance based, productivity based provision of welfare and security to be made to set right the problems and loopholes of the public sector employees and regular staff of various departments. Thereby, the state has to take such required measures to be implemented to protect the morality and humanity of the employees.

References

1. Oskar Gans, 'The Economics of Social Security in Developing Countries', The Economics of Social Security, Vol. 54, p. 45.
2. Approaches to Social Security, International Labour Office, 1948, p. 1.
3. Cole G.D.H. Beveridge.
4. Malviya Committee Report on Labour Welfare, 1969, p. 1172.
5. Supriya Roy Chowdhury, 'The Law and Labour', The Hindu, January 20, 2002, p. 13.

6. Johannes Jutting. "Social Security System in low Income Countries', The Indian Journal of Labour Economics, Vol. 42, No. 3 1999, p. 330.

7. Rajesh Bhada, National Institute of Fashion Technbology (NIFT), New Delhi, 'Beware, Labour Standards are already here', Economics Times, p. 4.

Part III

Policy Choice and Emerging Perspectives for India

24

Labour for Development in 21st Century: Challenges and Perspectives

Prof. P. Murali

The global workforce has grown massively in recent decades. In 1995 there are an estimated 2.5 billion men and women of working age in the world's labour force almost twice as many as in 1965. Estimates projects a further world wide increase of 1-2 billion by 2025. Economic growth is good for workers. As such the demand for higher growth is more now than ever before in the history of world economic growth. Growth has reduced poverty through rising employment, increase labour productivity and higher real wages. World Development Report emphasized that problems of low incomes, poor working conditions, and insecurity affecting many of the world's workers can be effectively tackled in ways that reduce poverty and regional inequality. Better economic performance demands sound domestic policy and a supportive international environment. This implies that government must:

1. Pursue market-based growth paths that generate rapid growth demand for labour, expansion in the skills of the work force, and rising productivity.
2. Take advantage of new opportunities at the international level, by opening up to trade and attracting capital-but manage the dislocations that international changes sometimes bring.

3. Construct a framework for labour policy, the complements informal and rural labour markets, supports collective bargaining in the formal sector, provides safeguards for the vulnerable, and avoids biases that favour relatively well-off workers, and
4. In those countries struggling with the transition to a more market-based and internationally integrated pattern of development, try to design the transition to make it as rapid as possible without excessive or permanent costs for labour.

Market-based development, which encourages firms and workers to invest in physical capital, new technologies and skills, is the best way to deliver growth and rising living of workers. Labour policy in low and middle income countries has a crucial role in promoting cardial atmosphere for proper labour management relations. Labour policy through public action can complement. Community arrangements enhance the welfare of informal workers by improving the environment in which they operate. Labour plays a dominant role in the economic development of developing economics. This postulates the development of an efficient, committed and promotable working class in industry. An accelerated tempo of economic development is the final result of the actions and interactions of the three major participants in industrial relations i.e., labour, management and state.

The recent trends of globalization, liberalization and privatizations have created several challenges and emphasizing the need for second generation economic reforms specially on the labour front which sparked off a great deal of public interest and a real threat of opposition from labour unions, and national labour union federations.

The twentieth century has witnessed more divergence than convergence in the fortunes of workers in different parts of the world. Can the twenty first century be different? Will it bring in an era of inclusion in which economic integration continues and speeds up, rising substantially the employment opportunities and incomes of workers in all regions-and particularly the poorest and the vulnerable? Labour policy is in need of reform in South Asia (India/ and China). Infact, to transform these economics, the new forms of governance are advancing fast. China and India, the two giants of the region, have to face internal difficulties. These countries have to work with the legacies of past policies and development structures for both government and workers, that is just the starting point. Both are agents of change. It is the task of these developing economies to design the required policy choices, economics reforms, structural adjustment and to reverse the marked features of the last century, and bring new hope and opportunities, and horizon to millions currently trapped in poverty. All these certainly would set the stage for a truly global golden age in the twenty first century.

25

"Labour and Development in the 21st Century: Challenges and Perspectives"

N. Sampath

Introduction

All India Bank Employees' Association which represents 5 lack bank employees in this country, is an organization which has membership throughout our country in Public Sector Banks, Private Sector Banks, Exchange Banks, Gramin Banks and Cooperative Banks. Our organization a premier one, started in 1946 is the largest organization of bank employees in our country. Our organization which fought endlessly for nationalization of Banks in sixties is at present campaigning for defending public sector banking and for defeating the moves of the government for privatization of banks. Our organization which struggled for removing the ills in the banking industry in seventies and eighties is spearheading a campaign for exposing the defaulters of the Industry. Our organization which is, as any other trade union, striving to improve the wages and service conditions of its members is more utilizing its energies to see that the Banking Industry serves better for National Development and for improving the Rural Economy. Friends, as I represent Labour, the present scenario, both global and domestic, will be looked at by me in the context of its effect on Labour and Human Resources. Since I am connected more with Banking, my approach will also be centred around it.

In general, it is being told that Economic Reforms are the products of Globalisation and Liberalisation and that the Globalisation will bring prosperity and benefits to all. It is with this area, specific economic programmes are being foisted on the basis of such claims and theories that Capitalism is the sole monarch of all its surveys, though in reality, the benefits of the process are caused by a select few among the various countries, for example goods from the industrial countries enjoyed much greater tariff reductions than those from developing countries. Similarly a major part of the world with 70 per cent total population gets only 10 per cent of the financial flow from FDI (Foreign direct investment) In the same way there is tremendous pressure on the developing nations to cut down agriculture and food subsidies. This unequal competition has destroyed the livelihood of many in developing countries.

Again in the area of Technology, the cost of technology transfers of developing countries have increased and consequently those countries cannot take advantage of the opportunities the globalisation is supposed to offer. Similarly the growth of Transnational Corporations is based only on the Developed countries. These Corporations with nearly 2.5 lac foreign affiliates dominate entire worldwide exports of goods and services. The Concept of 'World Trade' has become very significant. They even manage to bypass the market regulation and competition. Because of this trend, riches are being cornered in a handful of countries, while billions of people are suffering under poverty in underdeveloped and developing countries.

Same is the position in currency markets. Because of the free and unfettered movement of Capital, many countries are shaken by economic crisis. Because of the concentration of Billions of Dollars in a few hands, they tend to influence the currencies with their investment and disinvestments and their profits come from the impoverishment of others. All these happen because speculators have a field day.

It is in this background, we witnessed in the closing years of last century, many large mills, factories, establishments were closed down in many countries. Many workers were sent out. Many families were uprooted. Unemployment was on the increase, Workers everywhere fought bigger battles and prolonged struggles.

The philosophy of Globalisation is maximizing profit, reduction in the cost of production, flexible labour, cheap labour, dominant power to employer to accomplish them. Thus what we witness today is a jobless growth every where.

Let us look at what is happening in our country. Industrial production has gone down from 6.5% to 2.3% in the last decade. The growth rate in Agriculture has slided down. Even though there are enough food stocks, farmers are unable to purchase. Many of the farmers are not getting remunerative prices. Many families are breaking down. In some places they are selling their organs and Children. Artisans are marginalized. There are nearly 260 million children in streets. 12 million people engaged in fishing industry, are suffering, even though we have a very long coast line compared to any other country. Textile Industry is collapsing. Handloom workers are on the streets fighting for survival. Our exports are dwindling. Because of foreign inflow, our domestic units are ruined. Small industries are closed down.

The external debt has gone up from Rs. 16,300 crores to Rs. 4,30,000 crores. The exchange rate of Indian Rupee depreciated from Rs. 18/- to Rs 48.75/- at present. Thus the performance of Indian economy cannot take credit on any major account such as employment, poverty alleviation, growth rate of external fronts. We are also facing stiff competition from foreign goods, foreign banks, foreign Insurance and Foreign communication companies. Core industries in Public Sector are handed over to private sector.

Steel, coal, mines, telecommunication, port, many government departments in postal, railways and airports are privatized. Disinvestments is taking place in a fast pace in profit making public sector units. Many units are merged.

In the name of VRS and Golden Handshake, thousands of workers are sent out. Downsizing and right sizing are taking place in industries, establishments of government offices. Contract system is being introduced everywhere.

As far as workers are concerned, attacks are being mounted in the name of Labour Reforms. Registration of Trade Unions will be made rigid. Strikes will be indirectly prohibited. Industrial Disputes Act is being amended. Retrenchment will be made simpler. Hire and fire policy will be brought back. Wages will be linked to productivity. Service conditions can be changed at the whims of the employer. More contract jobs will be encouraged.

Downsizing will be allowed in government offices and establishments, employees will be retired at 55. No DA increase for next 5 years. Withdrawal from PF will not be allowed. There will not be any Pay Commission in future.

More than 10,000 post offices will be closed. 50,000 postmen will be rendered jobless. Public will be asked to go to post offices to collect their tapals. 3 lac extra departmental staff will be denied regularization of jobs.

Provident fund rates are already reduced. Taxes on perks are introduced, Bonus Act is virtually on the paper. Maternity benefits and minimum wages are not implemented in many establishments.

Thus in the Globalisation era, we face an uncertain future. This system is affecting us all. We are passing from crisis to deeper crisis. We are losing the spirit of Nationalism. Human Resources, which is the 'Capital' for India is losing its potential. Even though we have capacity and efficiency we are marginalized. Self-reliance concept is being eliminated. Indian money is being robbed.

In the Banking Industry, we have today nearly Rs. 70,000 crores as Non-Performing Assets, together with interest it may cross Rs. 1 lac crores. It is the unscrupulous big tycoons who have defrauded the banks by not repaying their loans. They have siphoned off the money they borrowed. They have no intention to repay. They are willful defaulters. Their names have to be published and criminal actions have to be taken against them, but the government is in no mood to do that. Instead they are thinking of setting up a new mechanism by which these non-performing assets will be purchased on a Discount and the entire amount will be taken out of the banks. How they will recover subsequently is a wild guess. We do not have strict legal remedy to recover the amounts. Because of this, the Public Sector banks are being labled as inefficient and attempts are to reduce the stakes of the government to 33% from 100% and allow private participations. Slowly the government will lose control over public sector banks Foreign holding is allowed up to 98%. Thus the World Bank's dictum will be implemented in the next few years. With this, the misery of Indian people will be full. Thus the Reform process will be a death knell to our country's economy.

As the World bank is insisting for free market and privatization of public enterprises, our government has started in right earnest to implement the dictates of their foreign masters and in doing so it has targeted the key economic sector i.e. Banking. It is every body's knowledge that 85% of the commercial banking at present belongs to public Sector. The progress and performance of public sector banks since Nationalisation in 1969 have been phenomenal. The net work of branches form 8200 to the present level of 67100 is the largest in the world. It has tapped deposits of Rs 10,75,000 crores from mere Rs. 4600 crores in 1969. The development of credit is around Rs 4,80,000 crores as compared to mere Rs. 3600 crores in 1969. For every 15000 population we have one office as against one for 64000 population. We have branches in 33000 rural areas, whereas in 1969 we had our presence only in 1830 rural stations. Agriculture sector which was neglected prior to 1969 has been given over Rs. 30000 crores, even through it is a very small amount compared to total credit deployed. For the present, developments of country's economy, build up of huge industries and self sufficiency in so many segments, the public sector banking industry have played a big and due role. But in the recent decade 18 private sector banks collapsed and all of them have been taken over by Public Sector Banks. Now, because of the new economic policy, consequent to Globalisation, the government is deciding to the public sector banks by diluting its stake. If, unfortunately this happens, entire economy of our country will come under the control of Private Corporate houses and slowly by foreign private business houses and MNCs. Worst hit will be the rural economy. At present it is the public sector banks, RRBs, cooperative banks which are helping the rural poor, agriculture, small and marginal farmers, artisans etc., and in short the Rural economy. If public sector banks are privatized, the rural economy will be in doldrums. Of course there are some weak spots in public sector banks. Several suggestions have been made for revamping them. But privatization is not panacea for the current ills of the banks. If all loans given by public sector banks are recovered and banks are managed effectively and professionally, these banks will gain necessary momentum to move on their own effectively.

As per the Globalisation policy, our government has introduced the exit policy and has started shedding the so called surplus labour thereby putting lot of untold sufferings and difficulties to the work force. 4 lac jobs have lost in public sector enterprises. Same is the position in small private and foreign enterpirses. In the Banking Industry nearly 1.2 lac jobs have gone out. In Information Technology front several thousands of jobs have been axed. Downsizing has been effected in textiles, Air India, Port Trust, VSNL, HMT, Hindustan Motors, Crompton Greaves, Bajaj Auto, Tata Tea, Glaxo India, Modern Foods, Shipping Corporation of India, SAIL, BHEL etc.

Again because of new economic policies several industrial units and 2.75 small units have become sick and unable to recover from their fall. Winding up of BIFR and SICA will result in economic death of 12 lacs families who are working those sick industries.

But as against exodus of human resources there is virtually a ban on recruitments, there is heavy work load on existing employees. There is multipronged attack on workers. The various Labour Reforms proposals will adversely affect the working class and in short a total offensive war against Trade Unions in the country.

Thus the impact of the Globalisation can be summarized as under.

- No preference of Domestic Industry
- Paves way for more and more privatization
- Small Scale Industries are ruined
- Human Development has been completely ignored
- There is insecurity among society
- Poverty has been aggravated
- There is deterioration in employment generation
- There are large scale, closures, Retrenchment and loss of jobs
- There is increase in outsourcing of work and employment of more contract labour
- There is economic slowdown
- Purchasing power of people has declined
- Health and Education are neglected

- Private Sector is nor participating in infrastructure development
- Exports have taken a beating'
- Social tension increases and explodes
- Educated youth remain unemployed
- MNCs corner production and wealth
- Social programmes and expenditure are cut.

The net result is increase of human distress and poverty. Thus the labour has become a victim of globalisation and economic ruthlessness

Hence there is no way out other than to fight untidily the globalisation concept.

26

Trends in Quantum, Employment and Wage Rates of Agricultural Labourers (A State-Wise Analysis)

Dr. C. Srinivasulu

The study of agricultural labour assumes importance, as they constitute a vulnerable segment of rural population, whose proportion has increased significantly in almost all the States of India. They constitute the historically deprived social groups, displaced handicraftsmen and dispossessed peasantry. Assetlessness, unemployment, low wages, under-nutrition, illiteracy and social backwardness constitute the poverty syndrome among agricultural labourers, these reinforce one another as to constitute a vicious circle of poverty (Parathasarathy, 1996, p. 145). Some studies have shown that the incidence of poverty was highest among agricultural labour households as compared to rural households and self-employed in agriculture and those employed in non-agricultural occupations (Mahendra Dev, 1988; Sharma, 1995; Alok Kumar, 1994; Unni Jeemol, 1997.

There are many factors which determine the economic status of agriculture labour. Out of which, two important factors are taken into consideration for this study i.e., nature and trends in the employment days available to agricultural labourers and trends in wage rates (money wage and real wage rates) in major States of India.

The present study was undertaken with three objectives. First to study the changing proportion of agricultural labour households in total rural households and changing proportion of agricultural labour households with land in major States (Part-II). Secondly, to study the trends in the number of employment days available to both male and female agricultural labourers and also examine the changes in the relative importance of different sources of employment. (Part-III) Thirdly, to examine the trends in money wage rates and real wage rates of male agricultural labourers. (Part-IV). Part V gives summary and conclusions.

Sources of Data and Methodology

Relevant data for this study was collected through secondary data. Various Rural Labour Enquiry Committee Reports were used to study the quantum of agricultural labourers households and changing structure of employment days available to male and female agricultural labourers. The various issues of "Agricultural Wages in India" and Indian Labours Journals were used to study the trends in money and real wages.

The trends were analysed through simple growth rate using formula

$$\frac{Y_t - Y_{t-1}}{Y_{t-1}} \times 100,$$

Where Y_t is the current year and Y_{t-1} is the preceding year value.

PART II

Growth of Agricultural Labour

According to Census Report 1881, in India, the total labourers were 7.5 millions and they were magnified to a level of 74.65 millions in 1991. According to Rural Labour Inquiry Committee Reports, the number of agricultural labour households swelled from 15.34 millions to 36.26 millions in between 1964-65 and 1993-94 with a growth rate of 136 per cent. With the help of estimates of Rural Labour Enquiry Committee Reports the agricultural labours households multiplies with wage earners per family, the total number of agricultural labourers are increased from 30.8 millions to 66.3 millions in between 1964-65 and 1994-94.

In India, before Independence, there were two types of arguments with regard to origin of agricultural labour. According to one argument (Mukherji 1957; Rama Krishna Mukherji 1969; Kosambi 1965) the caste hierarchy of Hindu society was responsible for the origin of agricultural labour. The lowest category of the society, shudras or serving castes remained at the bottom of the society with landlessness. The second argument (Dharma Kumar, 1965; Utsa Patnaik, 1999; Srinivasulu, 1998;) reveals that the British colonial administration and its policies of exploitation pauperized the peasants through changes in land systems and tenancy systems, rigid revenue collections, creation of money lenders, which resulted in creation and the growth of agricultural labourers in India.

Regional Variations in the Growth of Agricultural Labour Households

According to Table 1, the growth of agricultural labours households has increased from 22 per cent to 30 per cent in between 1964-65 and 1993-94. State wise data reveals that as many as fourteen major States, Bihar (125 per cent), Jammu & Kashmir (120 per cent), Karnataka (129 per cent) Tamil Nadu (117 per cent), Andhra Pradesh (136 per cent) Assam (777 per cent), Gujarat (301 per cent), Haryana (191 per cent), Himachal Pradesh (160 per cent), Madhya Pradesh (175 per cent), Maharashtra (155 per cent), Rajasthan (195 per cent) and West Bengal (166 per cent) recorded a significant increase, more than cent per cent during the period of thirty years since 1964-65. The highest growth rate was recorded in Assam (777 per cent) and lowest growth rate was recorded in Kerala (58 per cent).

Table 1. Agricultural Labour Households in Major States: 1964-65 to 1993-94

State	*No. of Agricultural Labour households (000)*						*Growth*
	1964-65	*1974-75*	*1977-78*	*1983*	*1987-88*	*1993-94*	*between 1964-65 and 1993-94*
Andhra Pradesh	1939 (31.42)	2668 (35.78)	3520 (41.45)	3929 (41.55)	4007 (39.49)	4583 (41.56)	136
Assam	93 (4.92)	282 (13.06)	500 (17.01)	463 (19.45)	548 (19.76)	816 (22.98)	777
Bihar	2150 (27.96)	2960 (33.27)	3898 (36.08)	4028 (37.11)	4334 (36.06)	4844 (39.22)	125
Gujarat	489 16.70)	759 (22.30)	1229 (31.08)	1267 (30.69)	1582 (34.35)	1959 (37.83)	301
Haryana	—	125 (9.15)	275 (18.19)	512 (20.24)	405 (19.73)	364 (15.87)	191
Himachal Pradesh	NA NA	10 (1.78)	35 (5.22)	17 (2.19)	41 (4.83)	26 (2.85)	160
Jammu & Kashmir	5 (0.90)	12 (1.77)	24 (3.11)	52 (6.35)	51 (5.57)	11 (3.33)	120
Karnataka	954 (27.22)	1252 (30.76)	1710 (37.92)	1762 (36.59)	2069 (39.34)	2180 (37.73)	129

(Cont...)

Table 1. (Contd...)

Kerala	696 (28.14)	886 (27.40)	1030 (26.99)	1148 (31.70)	1179 (30.13)	1102 (28.22)	58
Madhya Pradesh	1213 (20.33)	1325 (21.79)	2169 (27.90)	2302 (30.15)	2714 (31.43)	3332 (34.85)	175
Maharashtra	1545 (31.07)	1945 (31.96)	3029 (38.64)	3031 (38.55)	3308 (38.64)	3937 (41.17)	155
Orissa	861 (24.71)	1249 (30.12)	1713 (37.09)	1725 (36.41)	1826 (35.22)	1516 (25.46)	76
Punjab	366 (14.32)	380 (20.88)	507 (24.10)	561 (25.26)	683 (28.11)	706 (27.69)	93
Rajasthan	195 (5.47)	157 (3.96)	432 (10.08)	545 (11.10)	686 (12.66)	576 (9.97)	195
Tamil Nadu	1735 (28.02)	2399 (38.06)	2627 (39.34)	3117 (42.24)	3088 (40.17)	3761 (42.08)	117
Uttar Pradesh	1779 (13.88)	2395 (15.81)	2906 (18.11)	3040 (18.01)	3636 (20.08)	3061 (15.31)	72
West Bengal	1222 (25.42)	1824 (30.94)	2772 (41.95)	3139 (38.50)	2989 (35.98)	3252 (32.57)	166
All-India	15337 (21.79)	20739 (25.27)	28587 (29.88)	30867 (30.70)	33305 (30.74)	36262 (30.34)	136

(Cont...)

State	Percentage of Agriculture Labour Household with Land					
	1964-65	*1974-75*	*1977-78*	*1983*	*1987-88*	*1993-94*
Andhra Pradesh	33.03	39.10	41.17	39.43	84.30	41.91
Assam	56.85	55.80	46.58	43.23	93.80	50.95
Bihar	62.48	58.20	60.03	47.93	80.30	37.81
Gujarat	25.46	34.50	40.20	26.45	66.20	39.13
Haryana	—	16.60	7.64	4.55	88.50	14.97
Himachal Pradesh	NA	76.70	80.00	77.83	73.40	72.27
Jammu & Kashmir	57.83	2.70	70.84	66.00	92.20	57.96
Karnataka	35.15	46.70	45.62	45.76	85.50	47.63
Kerala	70.26	86.70	87.48	82.12	94.00	24.30
Madhya Pradesh	46.23	52.80	49.66	49.17	78.90	56.68
Maharashtra	31.55	47.00	42.32	41.90	67.10	42.16
Orissa	54.65	62.60	53.42	55.83	93.70	58.00
Punjab	12.29	8.30	7.10	4.76	49.70	5.41
Rajasthan	49.03	46.40	60.56	53.60	79.80	51.85
Tamil Nadu	31.55	36.20	36.36	28.39	75.00	24.89
Uttar Pradesh	53.97	56.80	60.80	53.62	79.10	62.14
West Bengal	41.95	45.80	45.66	47.00	81.60	49.28
All-India	45.60	49.20	48.63	44.05	79.40	43.03

Note: 1. *Included in Punjab 2. Figures in Brackets Denotes Proportion of Agricultural Labour Households to Total Rural Households

Source: Various Report of Rural Labour Enquiry Labour Bureau Ministry of Labours Government of India Simla/ Chandigarh.

Proportion of Agricultural Labours Households to Total Rural Households

The Table shows over 1964-65 and 1993-94 period, the percentage of agricultural households to total rural households had increased by 8.55 per cent at all India level. Across the States Assam, Jammu & Kashmir, Gujarat, Rajasthan, shows a substantial rise in the percentage of agricultural Labour Households in total rural household and in remaining States, the marginal increase was recorded except in Kerala (28 per cent), where the proportion of agricultural labour households to total rural households remained constant over the period of thirty years with some periodical fluctuations.

Proportion of Agricultural Labour Households with Land

Further, as is well known, continues sub division of land holdings as consequence of unrelenting population pressure, coupled with lack of alternative employment opportunities, compel many of the small and marginal landholders to participate in agricultural labour market (Sharma, 2001, p. 29). Therefore it is necessary to examine the proportion of agricultural labour households with land among total number of agricultural labour households. According to Table 1, except in 1987-88 (1), the percentage of agricultural labour household with land increased in most of the States except in Assam, Bihar, Haryana, Kerala and Punjab and constant in Jammu & Kashmir, with slight fluctuations in the middle of the study. Drastic reduction was recorded in Kerala where the agricultural labour households with land decreased from 70 per cent in 1964-65 to 24 per cent in 1993-94.

Part III

Structure and Sources of Employment

Table 2 reveals the structure and trends in the total number of employment days available to male agricultural labourers and different sources of employment self-

Table 2. Structure of Employment of Male Agricultural Labourers in Major States: 1964-65 to 1993-94

	W.E.					
State	*1964-65*	*1974-75*	*1977-78*	*1983*	*1987-88*	*1993-94*
Andhra Pradesh	207 (80.20)	219 (88.31)	219 (77.12)	214 (76.98)	207 (72.89)	231 (76.74)
Assam	NA	307 (94.46)	295 (87.02)	320 (92.75)	290 (87.88)	294 (84.73)
Bihar	213 (85.70)	201 (89.33)	266 (87.79)	257 (85.38)	267 (83.70)	287 (86.97)
Gujarat	286 (95.10)	231 (87.17)	227 (77.21)	243 (83.22)	248 (84.64)	278 (82.01)
Haryana	*	224 (88.54)	230 (80.42)	224 (82.05)	250 (82.51)	228 (84.13)
Himachal Pradesh	NA	282 (87.04)	175 (57.75)	190 59.19)	212 (61.99)	226 (64.20)
Jammu & Kashmir	NA	189 (84.75)	215 (63.05)	182 (62.54)	146 (49.83)	185 (56.75)
Karnataka	236 (84.20)	221 (81.55)	—	220 (76.92)	242 (79.08)	247 (79.94)
Kerala	179 (89.70)	143 (83.63)	163 (74.09)	183 (81.33)	180 (77.92)	218 (79.56)
Madhya Pradesh	240 (82.60)	228 (88.37)	252 (81.03)	243 (77.39)	229 (74.35)	241 (77.49)
Maharashtra	251 (85.50)	239 (86.28)	238 (78.81)	222 (76.55)	235 (76.55)	223 (75.34)
Orissa	244 (81.10)	191 (79.25)	227 (77.21)	216 (72.48)	211 (71.04)	213 (70.07)
Punjab	232 (73.50)	235 (87.69)	252 (83.44)	234 (82.69)	239 (79.40)	308 (91.12)
Rajasthan	198 (73.00)	250 (85.32)	187 (66.78)	228 (76.25)	207 (69.00)	247 (76.47)
Tamilnadu	203 (88.80)	167 (84.34)	190 (78.51)	192 (82.05)	176 (72.43)	216 (83.08)
Uttar Pradesh	212 (75.30)	215 (80.52)	208 (69.33)	228 (74.75)	217 (70.68)	221 (71.29)
West Bengal	286 (95.10)	232 (90.27)	247 (84.30)	218 (82.89)	241 (80.87)	230 (78.50)
All India	230 (84.80)	211 (84.74)	230 (79.31)	225 (79.23)	227 (76.95)	240 (79.21)

(Cont...)

State	SE					
	1964-65	*1974-75*	*1977-78*	*1983*	*1987-88*	*1993-94*
Andhra Pradesh	51 (19.8)	25 (10.08)	62 (21.83)	58 (20.86)	70 (24.65)	66 (21.93)
Assam	NA	18 (5.54)	35 (10.32)	22 (6.38)	32 (9.70)	50 (14.41)
Bihar	36 (14.30)	22 (9.78)	35 (11.55)	40 (13.29)	42 (13.17)	34 (10.30)
Gujarat	15 (4.90)	30 (11.32)	59 (20.07)	46 (15.75)	41 (13.99)	51 (15.04)
Haryana	-	24 (9.49)	45 (15.73)	47 (17.22)	22 (7.26)	42 (15.50)
Himachal	NA	42 (12.96)	126 (41.58)	122 (38.07)	72 (21.05)	72 (20.45)
Jammu & Kashmir	NA	30 (13.45)	116 (36.95)	95 (32.65)	112 (38.22)	112 (34.35)
Karnataka	44 (15.8)	48 (17.71)	—	62 (21.68)	58 (18.95)	57 (18.45)
Kerala	20 (10.3)	26 (15.20)	55 (25.00)	37 (16.44)	35 (15.15)	47 (17.15)
Madhya Pradesh	50 (17.40)	27 (10.46)	54 (17.36)	66 (21.02)	67 (21.75)	66 (21.22)
Maharashtra	43 (14.50)	32 (11.55)	59 (19.54)	63 (21.72)	65 (21.17)	65 (21.96)
Orissa	57 (18.90)	46 (19.09)	64 (21.77)	68 (22.82)	69 (23.23)	88 (28.95)
Punjab	84 (26.50)	30 (11.19)	44 (14.57)	40 (14.13)	48 (15.95)	20 (5.92)
Rajasthan	73 (-27.00)	42 (14.33)	92 (32.86)	68 (22.74)	76 (25.33)	61 (18.88)
Tamilnadu	26 (11.20)	27 (13.64)	48 (19.83)	38 (16.24)	59 (24.28)	39 (15.00)
Uttar	70 (24.70)	51 (19.10)	89 (29.67)	74 (24.26)	76 (24.76)	84 (27.10)
West Bengal	15 (4.90)	22 (8.56)	42 (14.33)	42 (15.97)	48 (16.11)	58 (19.79)
All India	42 (15.20)	33 (13.25)	56 (19.31)	54 (19.01)	58 (19.66)	57 (18.81)

(Cont...)

State	E.S.B 1964-65	1974-75	1977-78	1983	1987-88	1993-94
Andhra Pradesh	*	4 (1.61)	3 (1.05)	6 (2.16)	7 (2.46)	4 (1.33)
Assam	NA	0	9 (2.66)	3 (0.87)	8 (2.42)	3 (6.86)
Bihar	*	2 (0.89)	2 (0.66)	4 (1.33)	10 (3.13)	9 (2.73)
Gujarat	*	4 (1.51)	8 (2.72)	7 (1.03)	4 (1.37)	10 (2.95)
Haryana	*	5 (1.97)	11 (3.85)	2 (0.73)	31 (10.23)	1 (0.37)
Himachal	NA	0	2 (0.67)	9 (2.80)	58 (16.96)	54 (15.35)
Jammu Kashmir	NA	4 (1.80)	—	14 (4.81)	35 (11.95)	29 (8.90)
Karnataka	*	2 (0.74)	—	4 (1.40)	6 (1.97)	5 (1.61)
Kerala	* *	2 (1.17)	2 (0.91)	5 (2.23)	16 (6.63)	9 (3.29)
Madhya Pradesh	* *	3 (1.17)	5 (1.61)	5 (1.59)	12 (3.90)	4 (1.29)
Maharashtra	* *	6 (2.17)	5 (1.65)	5 (1.73)	7 (2.28)	8 (2.70)
Orissa	* *	4 (1.62)	3 (1.02)	14 (4.70)	17 (5.73)	3 (0.98)
Punjab	* *	3 (1.12)	6 (1.99)	9 (3.18)	14 (4.65)	10 (2.96)
Rajasthan	* *	1 (0.35)	1 (0.36)	3 (1.01)	17 (5.67)	15 (4.65)
Tamilnadu	*	4 (2.02)	4 (1.66)	4 (1.71)	8 (3.29)	5 (1.92)
Uttar Pradesh	* *	1 (0.38)	3 (1.00)	3 (0.99)	14 (4.56)	5 (1.61)
West Bengal	* *	3 (1.17)	4 (1.37)	3 (1.14)	9 (3.02)	5 (1.71)
All India	* *	3 (2.01)	4 (1.38)	5 (1.76)	10 (3.39)	6 (1.98)

(Cont...)

State	Total					
	1964-65	1974-75	1977-78	1983	1987-88	1993-94
Andhra Pradesh	258 (100)	248 (100)	284 (100)	278 (100)	284 (100)	301 (100)
Assam	308 (100)	325 (100)	339 (100)	345 (100)	330 (100)	347 (100)
Bihar	249 (100)	225 (100)	303 (100)	301 (100)	319 (100)	330 (100)
Gujarat	301 (100)	265 (100)	294 (100)	296 (100)	293 (100)	339 (100)
Haryana	* *	253 (100)	286 (100)	273 (100)	303 (100)	271 (100)
Himachal Pradesh	NA NA	324 (100)	303 (100)	321 (100)	342 (100)	352 (100)
Jammu & Kashmir	NA NA	223 (100)	331 (100)	291 (100)	293 (100)	326 (100)
Karnataka	280 (100)	271 (100)	— —	286 (100)	306 (100)	309 (100)
Kerala	199 (100)	171 (100)	220 (100)	225 (100)	231 (100)	274 (100)
Madhya Pradesh	290 (100)	258 (100)	311 (100)	314 (100)	308 (100)	311 (100)
Maharashtra	294 (100)	277 (100)	302 (100)	290 (100)	307 (100)	296 (100)
Orissa	301 (100)	241 (100)	294 (100)	298 (100)	297 (100)	304 (100)
Punjab	316 (100)	268 (100)	302 (100)	283 (100)	301 (100)	338 (100)
Rajasthan	271 (73)	293 (100)	280 (100)	299 (100)	300 (100)	323 (100)
Tamilnadu	229 (100)	198 (100)	242 (100)	234 (100)	243 (100)	260 (100)
Uttar Pradesh	282 (100)	267 (100)	300 (100)	305 (100)	307 (100)	310 (100)
West Bengal	301 (100)	257 (100)	293 (100)	263 (100)	298 (100)	293 (100)
All India	272 (100)	247 (100)	290 (100)	284 (100)	295 (100)	303 (100)

Note: 1. WE = Wage Employment, SE=Self Employment, ESB = Employment on Salary
2. Figures in Parentheses are Percentages.
3. Stars Indicates ESB Included in S.E.

Source: As Per Table 1.

employment like wage paid employment and employment on salary basis from 1964-65 to 1993-94. Despite periodic fluctuations, the number of employment days was increased in all the States in these thirty years except in West Bengal, where total employment days available to male agricultural labourers was decreased from 301 days to 293 days in between 1964-65 and 1993-94. Some of the States, particularly Bihar (80 days) Jammu & Kashmir (100 days), Kerala (100 days) and Rajasthan (52 days) recorded a significant increase in available employment days to male agricultural labourers.

Male Wage Paid Employment

This Table further explains the relative importance of wage-paid employment days (in percentage terms) in total employment days, which declined in all States except in Punjab, (where it was increased to 13 per cent), followed by Rajasthan (3 per cent) and Bihar (1 per cent) in between 1964-65 and 1993-94. If it is examined in absolute terms, the wage paid employment days of male agricultural labourers was increased in all States except in Assam, Gujarat Jammu and Kashmir, Maharashtra, Orissa and West Bengal.

Male Self Employment

Table 2 also reveals that the proportion of self employment days in total employment days was decreased in Bihar (4 per cent) and Punjab (21 per cent) Rajasthan (8 per cent). And in the remaining States, the proportion of self-employment was increased. In terms of number of self employment days, most of the States recorded moving upward trend except in Punjab, where the number of self employment days was decreased from 84 days in 1964-65 to 20 days in 1993-94 and in Bihar, some marginal decrease was recorded.

Male Employment on Salary Basis

This Table also reveals the employment on salary basis of male agricultural labour, which remained very low in all the States. According to 1993-94, data employment on salary basis significant proportion was recognized in Himachal Pradesh (15 per cent), Jammu & Kashmir (9 per cent) Assam (7 per cent) and Rajasthan (5 per cent)

Employment Days of Female Agricultural Labour

Table 3 shows the trends in the total number of employment days available to female labourers and the changing importance of different sources of employment. With regard to total employment days available to female labour was increased in all States except in Maharashtra and West Bengal.

Female Wage Paid Employment

The proportion of wage-paid employment in total employment days of female labour was increased in Assam, Bihar, Haryana, Jammu & Kashmir, Rajasthan and Uttar Pradesh. This proportion declined in other States. In terms of number of days in wage paid employment days of female labour was increased in most of the States except in Himachal Pradesh, Jammu & Kashmir, Maharashtra and West Bengal.

Female Self Employment

The proportion of Self-employment days in total employment days declined in seven States (Assam, Bihar, Haryana, Jammu & Kashmir, Orissa, Rajasthan, Uttar Pradesh) and it was increased in remaining States. It is important to note that the proportion of self-employment days in total employment days is very significant in Himachal Pradesh and Jammu & Kashmir, where more than 70 per cent to total employment days are available in self employment. This increase in the percentage-share of self-employment was associated with a decrease in the wage paid employment.

Female Employment on Salary Basis

The Table 3 also reveals that the employment days on salary basis is very negligible in all the States (less than 3 per cent) except in Himachal Pradesh and Rajasthan.

Table 3. Structure of Employment of Female Agricultural Labourers in Major States: 1964-65 to 1993-94

	W.E.					
State	*1964-65*	*1974-75*	*1977-78*	*1983*	*1987-88*	*1993-94*
Andhra Pradesh	122 (89.50)	148 (92.12)	185 (84.86)	187 (84.23)	190 (78.19)	208 (79.89)
Assam	NA NA	274 (97.86)	287 (91.99)	310 (95.97)	315 (96.92)	307 (98.08)
Bihar	119 (-6.50)	119 (79.86)	202 (88.60)	209 (87.00)	234 (88.40)	255 (90.43)
Gujarat	243 (97.20)	176 (86.70)	185 (78.39)	192 (79.34)	197 (79.43)	271 (83.90)
Haryana	—	117 (56.25)	140 (61.95)	191 (88.44)	271 (89.40)	200 (90.91)
Himachal Pradesh	NA NA	114 (35.90)	43 (19.03)	109 (43.60)	82 (28.95)	— (22.98)
Jammu & Kashmir	NA NA	46 (18.47)	90 (38.30)	226 (100)	22 (10.48)	67 (21.34)
Karnataka	194 (90.60)	178 (85.58)	—	217 (85.43)	213 (85.20)	237 (87.13)
Kerala	150 (88.80)	106 (78.52)	159 (83.25)	164 (83.25)	168 (78.14)	196 (81.67)
Madhya Pradesh	166 (81.50)	145 (86.31)	203 (84.94)	207 (79.01)	198 (76.15)	201 (76.13)
Maharashtra	239 (87.50)	145 (86.31)	203 (84.94)	207 (79.01)	198 (76.15)	201 (76.13)
Orissa	166 (78.10)	192 (88.88)	194 (82.20)	180 (82.10)	208 (78.49)	212 (80.61)
Punjab	160 (75.20)	124 (74.69)	163 (78.36)	166 (74.11)	162 (65.85)	181 (68.30)
Rajasthan	116 (55.90)	103 (36.65)	157 (59.25)	150 (55.97)	220 (70.97)	285 (86.10)
Tamilnadu	146 (90.70)	170 (76.58)	156 (63.16)	184 (69.43)	140 (56.22)	193 (65.20)
Uttar Pradesh	94 (54.00)	124 (85.52)	172 (83.09)	169 (86.22)	165 (73.99)	196 (81.67)
West Bengal	221 (87.90)	145 (74.36)	219 (85.88)	195 (84.05)	219 (79.06)	167 (73.89)
All India	154 (83.90)	143 (79.89)	184 (81.06)	188 (81.74)	190 (77.07)	212 (80.30)

(Cont...)

State	SE					
	1964-65	1974-75	1977-78	1983	1987-88	1993-94
Andhra	14 (10.50)	21 (7.88)	32 (14.68)	33 (14.86)	51 (20.99)	51 (19.54)
Assam	NA NA	6 (2.14)	10 (3.21)	9 (2.79)	8 (2.46)	6 (1.92)
Bihar	37 (23.50)	30 (20.14)	24 (10.53)	30 (12.50)	35 (12.77)	24 (5.51)
Gujarat	8 (2.80)	28 (12.81)	48 (20.34)	48 (18.59)	49 (16.76)	47 (14.55)
Haryana	*	87 (41.83)	69 (30.63)	28 (11.11)	9 (6.29)	26 (8.09)
Himachal Pradesh	NA NA	203 (64.04)	183 (80.97)	135 (54.00)	228 (72.15)	239 (71.34)
Jammu & Kashmir	NA NA	203 (81.53)	145 (61.70)	0	171 (81.43)	247 (78.66)
Karnataka	20 (9.40)	30 (14.42)	—	35 (13.78)	31 (12.40)	32 (11.76)
Kerala	19 (1.12)	29 (21.48)	31 (16.23)	30 (15.23)	36 (16.74)	39 (16.25)
Madhya Pradesh	38 (18.50)	22 (13.09)	34 (14.23)	53 (20.23)	54 (20.77)	60 (22.73)
Maharashtra	34 (12.50)	22 (13.09)	34 (14.23)	53 (20.23)	54 (20.77)	60 (22.73)
Orissa	47 (21.90)	23 (10.65)	41 (17.37)	36 (16.44)	53 (20.00)	45 (17.11)
Punjab	53 (24.80)	42 (25.31)	43 (20.67)	45 (20.09)	69 (28.05)	84 (31.70)
Rajasthan	92 (44.10)	177 (62.99)	103 (38.87)	104 (38.80)	72 (23.22)	35 (10.57)
Tamilnadu	15 (9.30)	52 (23.42)	91 (36.84)	78 (29.43)	99 (39.76)	95 (32.09)
Uttar Pradesh	80 (46.00)	20 (13.79)	34 (16.42)	25 (12.76)	50 (22.42)	41 (17.08)
West Bengal	31 (12.10)	48 (24.62)	34 (13.33)	35 (15.09)	49 (17.69)	38 (16.81)
All India	29 (16.10)	35 (19.55)	41 (18.06)	39 (16.96)	52 (20.55)	48 (18.18)

(Cont...)

	E.S.B					
State	*1964-65*	*1974-75*	*1977-78*	*1983*	*1987-88*	*1993-94*
Andhra Pradesh	* *	0	1 (0.46)	2 (0.90)	2 (0.82)	2 (0.77)
Assam	NA NA	0	15 (4.80)	4 (1.24)	2 (0.62)	0
Bihar	* *	0	2 (0.87)	1 (0.42)	5 (1.82)	3 (1.06)
Gujarat	* *	1 (0.40)	3 (1.27)	5 (2.07)	2 (0.81)	5 (1.55)
Haryana	* *	4 (1.92)	17 (7.52)	1 (0.45)	13 (4.31)	0
Himachal Pradesh	NA NA	0	0	6 (2.40)	6 (1.90)	19 (5.68)
Jammu & Kashmir	NA NA	0	0	0	17 (8.09)	0
Karnataka	* *	0	—	2 (0.79)	6 (2.40)	3 (1.11)
Kerala	* *	0	1 (0.52)	3 3(1.52)	11 (5.12)	5 (2.08)
Madhya Pradesh	* *	1 (0.60)	2 (0.83)	2 (0.76)	8 (3.08)	3 (1.14)
Maharashtra	* *	1 (0.60)	2 (0.83)	2 (0.76)	8 (3.08)	3 (1.14)
Orissa	* *	1 (0.47)	1 (0.43)	3 (1.37)	4 (1.51)	6 (2.28)
Punjab	* *	0	2 (0.97)	13 (5.80)	15 (6.10)	0
Rajasthan	* *	1 (0.36)	5 (1.88)	14 (5.23)	18 (5.81)	11 (3.33)
Tamilnadu	* *	0	0	3 (1.14)	10 (4.02)	8 (2.71)
Uttar	* *	1 (0.69)	1 (0.49)	2 (1.02)	8 (3.59)	3 (1.25)
West Bengal	* *	2 (1.02)	2 (0.86)	2 (0.79)	9 (3.25)	21 (9.93)
All India	* *	1 (0.56)	2 (0.88)	3 (1.30)	6 (2.38)	4 (1.52)

(Cont...)

State	Total					
	1964-65	*1974-75*	*1977-78*	*1983*	*1987-88*	*1993-94*
Andhra Pradesh	136 (100)	169 (100)	218 (100)	222 (100)	243 (100)	261 (100)
Assam	243 (100)	280 (100)	312 (100)	323 (100)	325 (100)	313 (100)
Bihar	156 (100)	149 (100)	228 (100)	240 (100)	274 (100)	282 (100)
Gujarat	251 (100)	203 (100)	236 (100)	242 (100)	248 (100)	323 (100)
Haryana	* *	208 (100)	226 (100)	225 (100)	302 (100)	220 (100)
Himachal Pradesh	NA NA	317 (100)	226 (100)	250 (100)	316 (100)	335 (100)
Jammu & Kashmir	365 (100)	249 (100)	235 (100)	226 (100)	210 (100)	314 (100)
Karnataka	214 (100)	208 (100)	— 0	254 (100)	250 (100)	272 (100)
Kerala	169 (100)	135 (100)	191 (100)	197 (100)	215 (100)	240 (100)
Madhya Pradesh	204 (100)	168 (100)	239 (100)	262 (100)	260 (100)	264 (100)
Maharashtra	273 (100)	168 (100)	239 (100)	262 (100)	260 (100)	264 (100)
Orissa	213 (100)	216 (100)	236 (100)	219 (100)	265 (100)	263 (100)
Punjab	213 (100)	166 (100)	208 (100)	224 (100)	246 (100)	265 (100)
Rajasthan	208 (100)	281 (100)	265 (100)	268 (100)	310 (100)	331 (100)
Tamilnadu	161 (100)	222 (100)	247 (100)	265 (100)	249 (100)	296 (100)
Uttar	174 (100)	145 (100)	207 (100)	196 (100)	223 (100)	240 (100)
West Bengal	252 (100)	195 (100)	255 (100)	232 (100)	277 (100)	226 (100)
All India	183 (100)	179 (100)	227 (100)	230 (100)	253 (100)	264 (100)

Note:
1. WE = Wage Employment, SE=Self Employment, ESB = Employment on Salary.
2. Figures in Parentheses are Percentages.
3. Stars Indicates ESB Included in S.E.

Source: As Per Table 1.

Unemployment

With the help of Table 3, it can be estimated the unemployed days of male and female labourers in a year. According to 1993-94 Rural Labour Enquiry Report, the proportion of unemployed days of male labourers in a year was more in Tamilnadu (29 per cent), Haryana (26 per cent), and Kerala (25 per cent), and more than 10 per cent unemployment days was recorded in Andhra Pradesh (18 per cent), Orissa (17 per cent) Karnataka, Madhya Pradesh, Uttar Pradesh (15 per cent), Rajasthan (12 per cent) and Jammu & Kashmir (10 per cent).

The proportion of employment days of female labourers was more in Haryana (40 per cent), West Bengal (38 per cent), Kerala and Uttar Pradesh (34 per cent), Andhra Pradesh and Orissa (29 per cent), Madhya Pradesh, Maharashtra and Punjab (28 per cent).

The above Table (2 & 3) brings out five further points. First, that in general, despite periodical fluctuations, average employment days of male and female agricultural labourers was increased in all States except in West Bengal. Secondly, that employment days of male agricultural labourers was more than female laboruers in all States except in Rajasthan where male and female employment days was more or less equal. Thirdly, that the proportion of wage-paid employment days in total employment days of male and female labourers decreased and it was associated with an increase in the self-employment days. Fourthly, that employment days on salary basis is negligible in all States for both male and female labourers except in Himachal Pradesh. Fifthly, that the proportion of unemployed days of male and female labourers was more in highly developed agricultural States i.e., Haryana and strongly unionized (agricultural labour) State i.e., Kerala.

PART IV

Trends in Money Wage Rates and Real Wage Rates of Agricultural Labourers

A large number of scholars studied the trends of money wages and real wages of 'Sweated' agricultural labourers for different periods and for different States. Parthasarathy (1987) covered the period from 1974-75 to 1984-85 and 1985-86 to 1993-94 (1996). Jose (1988) and Acharya (1988) observed the trends for the period 1970-71 to 1984-85. Krishnana (1991) computed real wages for the years of 1960, 1970, 1980, 1984 and 1987. Haque (1998) also analysed the trends in Money wages and real wages for the years of 1970-71, 1980-81, 1985-86, 1990-91 to 1994-95. Dash (1996) studied the trends of Money wages for a long period from 1958-59 to 1993-94. Sharma (2001) studied the trends with the help of Rural Labour Enquiry Reports for the years of 1974-75, 1977-78, 1983, 1987-88 and 1993-94. But are found largely limited to pre and post green revolution periods or pre and post liberalization periods.

To fill the gaps, this study deals with the trends of money wages and real wages of agricultural labourers of major States for the period of forty one years i.e. from 1960-61 to 2001-02. This period of forty one years i.e. from 1960-61 to 2001-02 was divided into four sub-periods, such as, Pre-green revolution period (1960-61 to 1966-67), Post-green revolution Period (1967-68 to 1980-81), Pre-liberalisation period (1981-82 to 1990-91) and Post-liberalisation period (1991-92 to 2001-2002).

Trends in Money Wages Rates

According to Table 4, despite some marginal fluctuations in one or two years, the money wage rates of male agricultural labourers are increased in all States during four decades of this study (1960-61 to 2001-2002). Highest increase was recorded in Kerala from R. 1.72 in 1960-61 to Rs. 177.56 in 2001-02. The very number of studies reveals that the unionization of agricultural labour and their campaigns are responsible for the highest wage rates in Kerala (2). Next to Kerala, Himachal Pradesh Haryana, Rajasthan recorded significant increase in money wages, while Madhya Pradesh, Tripura, Bihar, Orissa and Andhra Pradesh, the agricultural labourers are getting low wages compared to other States.

Table 4. Money Wage Rates of Unskilled Male Agricultural Labour (Rs. per day)

Year	*A.P.*	*A.S.*	*BI*	*GU*	*HA*	*H.P.*	*KA*	*KE*	*M.P.*	*MA*	*OR*	*PU*	*RA*	*T.N.*	*TR*	*U.P.*	*W.B.*
1960-61	1.26	2.29	1.31	1.91	*	2.30	1.53	1.72	1.23	1.42	1.18	2.45	NA	1.43	2.00	1.27	1.81
1961-62	1.48	2.30	1.32	1.99	*	2.39	1.65	2.09	1.29	1.48	1.24	2.52	NA	1.50	2.00	1.35	1.89
1962-63	1.50	2.27	1.25	1.99	*	2.62	1.63	2.28	1.34	1.56	1.27	2.82	NA	1.64	2.00	1.34	1.85
1963-64	1.55	2.49	1.42	1.81	*	2.72	1.79	2.33	1.38	1.64	1.45	2.69	NA	1.52	2.00	1.17	2.01
1964-65	1.64	2.75	1.73	2.25	*	2.86	1.94	2.60	1.49	1.91	1.51	3.24	NA	1.87	2.00	1.78	2.27
1965-66	1.79	3.09	2.11	2.35	*	2.92	2.81	2.97	1.70	2.20	1.87	3.18	NA	1.96	2.04	1.53	2.50
1966-67	2.14	3.00	2.59	2.51	3.78	3.14	2.81	3.45	1.88	2.47	2.13	3.53	NA	2.20	2.50	2.04	2.81
A.A.G. Rate	8.09	4.10	10.80	4.39	###	4.59	9.95	10.68	6.34	8.38	9.08	5.68	#VALUE!	6.71	3.51	9.19	6.63
1967-68	2.26	2.89	2.64	2.79	4.74	3.33	2.81	4.22	2.01	2.52	2.21	4.35	2.83	2.37	3.00	2.28	3.12
1968-69	2.38	3.55	2.57	2.84	5.44	3.53	2.12	4.47	2.02	2.63	2.17	6.69	3.08	3.54	3.00	2.47	2.96
1969-70	2.45	3.83	2.59	2.91	6.15	3.63	2.56	4.64	2.11	2.67	2.13	6.45	3.03	2.66	3.00	2.73	2.96
1970-71	2.63	4.02	2.69	3.29	6.66	3.97	2.61	4.97	2.17	2.94	2.16	6.51	3.48	2.73	3.00	2.78	3.05
1971-72	2.78	3.79	2.75	3.66	6.99	4.41	2.86	5.11	2.28	2.98	2.26	6.89	3.57	2.70	3.75	2.98	3.41
1972-73	2.88	4.12	2.92	3.52	7.09	4.58	2.92	5.15	2.56	2.93	2.34	7.14	3.94	2.96	4.00	3.31	3.56
1973-74	3.26	4.63	3.85	3.87	7.18	5.06	3.31	5.74	2.81	3.28	2.60	7.46	4.27	3.38	4.00	3.93	4.01
1974-75	3.37	5.10	4.16	3.91	8.16	5.44	3.58	6.78	3.32	3.68	3.12	8.61	4.56	4.78	4.00	4.81	4.20

(Cont...)

Year	A.P.	A.S.	BI	GU	HA	H.P.	KA	KE	M.P.	MA	OR	PU	RA	T.N.	TR	U.P.	W.B.
1975-76	4.02	5.58	4.68	5.87	8.53	5.85	4.31	7.25	3.98	3.74	3.56	8.64	5.68	4.86	4.00	4.85	4.54
1976-77	4.56	5.59	5.01	5.99	8.99	6.42	4.92	7.03	4.25	3.81	4.11	9.87	7.16	4.18	4.00	5.27	5.48
1977-78	4.76	5.98	5.13	8.33	10.81	6.62	5.24	7.05	4.24	3.95	4.15	9.86	6.52	4.43	4.33	5.63	5.90
1978-79	4.97	6.27	5.31	6.45	11.07	6.79	5.11	7.49	4.30	4.20	4.32	10.32	7.21	4.81	5.04	5.64	6.13
1979-80	5.49	6.37	5.18	6.87	11.97	7.21	5.55	8.14	4.45	5.11	4.50	10.85	7.68	5.15	6.36	6.07	6.74
1980-81	5.96	7.26	5.83	7.28	12.55	8.07	6.02	11.88	4.76	5.22	4.77	11.74	8.58	5.62	7.46	6.66	6.97
A.A.G. Rate	8.28	7.27	6.75	9.85	9.87	7.56	6.69	10.57	7.56	6.09	6.58	10.48	9.28	9.03	9.22	9.67	7.40
1981-82	6.85	8.48	7.21	7.86	14.48	8.53	6.55	12.91	5.36	5.79	5.30	12.32	10.32	6.61	8.16	8.12	7.43
1982-83	7.95	9.54	7.93	10.73	16.23	11.52	6.64	14.55	6.87	6.52	6.89	13.58	13.61	6.74	9.17	8.52	7.87
1983-84	9.28	11.16	8.84	12.39	18.46	14.88	6.93	15.31	8.16	7.81	7.89	15.71	14.15	8.86	9.75	9.38	8.40
1984-85	10.26	12.35	9.57	13.56	19.83	16.59	7.21	17.91	9.00	10.66	8.07	18.64	10.95	8.62	11.08	10.39	12.00
1985-86	11.09	14.03	10.68	14.13	20.73	17.41	9.55	19.93	9.75	11.36	8.32	19.97	14.50	9.22	12.96	11.72	16.00
1986-87	12.21	15.81	12.13	14.71	22.59	20.21	9.09	22.88	10.64	10.97	9.02	21.43	16.72	9.92	11.50	12.95	18.25
1987-88	13.34	17.43	13.39	14.86	23.72	22.97	9.83	24.98	11.46	11.96	10.06	24.57	23.33	10.54	11.44	14.04	19.50
1988-89	14.70	19.07	15.86	16.40	27.69	27.13	13.46	27.47	13.06	13.43	11.01	28.58	22.67	11.89	19.79	15.71	23.24
1989-90	17.01	21.71	17.04	17.17	31.93	27.64	15.02	29.37	15.04	17.58	12.23	31.70	22.01	13.90	23.00	18.69	24.05
1990-91	18.42	25.09	19.23	19.04	35.15	29.40	15.57	34.30	17.46	20.12	14.48	37.11	25.18	15.41	23.21	21.34	25.86
A.A.G. Rate	11.99	13.23	12.77	10.47	10.93	14.25	10.65	11.25	14.02	14.75	11.99	12.29	12.94	10.97	13.70	12.45	14.65

(Cont...)

Year	*A.P.*	*A.S.*	*BI*	*GU*	*HA*	*H.P.*	*KA*	*KE*	*M.P.*	*MA*	*OR*	*PU*	*RA*	*T.N.*	*TR*	*U.P.*	*W.B.*
1991-92	21.14	27.19	22.20	22.64	41.75	34.03	16.84	39.61	20.13	22.86	17.37	43.18	31.10	17.58	23.91	25.15	28.16
1992-93	24.50	29.72	22.74	26.34	50.12	39.53	16.33	48.64	23.91	23.83	19.77	49.12	30.78	21.76	24.21	26.93	35.06
1993-94	26.06	30.36	25.49	28.51	55.62	42.89	22.29	53.34	24.82	28.87	21.34	57.17	33.21	25.16	24.50	29.52	37.07
1994-95	25.66	32.95	27.95	32.68	60.87	51.70	21.81	62.45	28.86	35.74	23.28	61.51	38.45	29.48	23.92	31.83	37.71
1995-96	32.56	36.37	29.75	35.65	64.88	66.71	22.86	86.46	32.07	36.55	25.63	62.07	46.88	34.67	25.92	38.77	41.68
1996-97	36.78	39.18	32.38	40.49	74.76	71.16	29.19	101.95	35.87	40.15	27.60	67.44	56.69	39.53	31.83	41.18	49.75
1997-98	41.95	40.55	36.48	44.52	75.91	75.32	36.21	125.65	38.89	45.25	35.72	67.45	66.71	42.55	45.35	51.21	56.25
1998-99	42.51	49.22	39.21	49.66	78.62	79.65	41.62	130.72	40.92	50.32	41.35	70.55	78.12	49.65	49.25	59.31	65.85
1999-00	44.11	52.55	42.26	58.32	78.91	83.12	49.28	170.75	41.84	56.82	43.45	74.75	85.41	51.32	53.55	61.85	69.35
2000-01	57.14	65.22	47.36	59.90	79.11	89.12	51.27	190.49	43.78	58.13	46.38	77.83	96.31	54.56	56.38	69.14	72.18
2001-02	55.16	69.65	51.18	64.30	85.46	101.12	57.88	177.56	45.45	60.95	52.23	79.95	82.94	72.50	55.60	72.63	78.32
A.A.G. Rate	10.96	9.91	9.36	11.80	8.63	12.12	13.30	16.73	9.22	10.81	12.56	7.37	12.00	15.38	8.91	11.97	10.80

Note: A.P. Andhra Pradesh; AS-Assam; BI-Bihar; GU-Gujarat; HA-Haryana; H.P.-Himachal Pradesh; KE-Kerala; KA-Karnataka, M.P.-Madhya Pradesh, MA-Maharasthra; OR-Orissa; PU-Punjab; RA-Rajasthan, T.N.-Tamil Nadu; TR-Tripura; U.P.-Uttar Pradesh; W.B.-West Bengal.

Source: 1. Various issues of Agricultural Wages in India Directorate of 1. Economics & Statistics. Ministry of Agriculture & Cooperation Government of India, New Delhi.

2. Various Issues of Indian Labour Journal, Labour Bureau. Ministry of Labour, Govt. of India, Simla/Chandigarh.

The average annual growth rate of money wage rates of male agricultural labourers of major States (Rank-Wise) in four sub-period can be observed from Table 4. It is evident from the Table that highest growth rate was recorded in Kerala (12.3 per cent), Rajasthan (11.4 per cent) and Uttar Pradesh (10.8 per cent) and lowest growth rate was recorded in Assam (8.6 per cent) Tripura (8.8 per cent) and Punjab (9.0 per cent). Out of seventeen major States, ten States recorded more than 10 per cent and remaining seven States recorded less than 10 per cent over a period of 41 years of this study. Most striking point is that the experience of Punjab and Haryana, those States are known as highly developed agricultural States in India, where annual growth rate of money wages is very low.

The data of growth rates of money-wage rates for the period of 1960-61 to 1966-67 (pre-green revolution period) reveals the fact that Bihar followed by Kerala and Karnataka registered the highest growth rate in the money-wages of agricultural labourers. The States in which growth of agricultural wages had been comparatively low in Tripura, Assam, Gujarat and Himachal Pradesh.

In comparison of post-green revolution period with pre-green revolution period, the growth rate of money-wages rates was increased in all the States in post green revolution period except in five States (Bihar, Karnataka, Maharasthra, Orissa and Kerala). In Kerala, even after small decline in growth rate, the highest growth rate was recorded among all the States in Post-green revolution period followed by Punjab and Haryana. But in the pre-liberalisation period and in post-liberalisation period, this trend was to sustain in Punjab and Haryana. Most important and higher growth rate than post-green revolution period and surprisingly, all the States registered more than ten per cent growth rate in this pre-liberalisation period. During post-liberalisation period the growth rate of money wages declined in all the

States except in Gujarat, Karnataka, Kerala, Orissa and Tamilnadu. But more than 10 per cent growth rate was discontinued in six States (Assam, Bihar, Haryana, Madhya Pradesh, Punjab and Tripura).

Trends in Real Wage Rates(3)

Practically, the real wages of agricultural labourers will indicate the real economic conditions of this section. It is observed, as per Table 5, that there has been a moderate increase in real wage rates (more than two times) in all the States except in Kerala where real wage rates were increased more than five times and Rajasthan also registered more than three times during forty one years of study.

According to Table 5, it is also a fact that there is no continuous increase in real wages in all the States and in all the sub periods of this study. Steep increasing trends and declining trends can be seen in every state. This significant variations is due to steep and slow increase in CPIAL indices.

With regard to growth rate of real wages, Table 5 shows that Rajasthan (only 33 years of data) registered highest growth rate in real wage rates followed by Kerala and Andhra Pradesh in four decades of this study. In some other States, which registered a comparatively moderate growth rates (2 to 3 per cent) are Maharasthra, Uttar Pradesh, Karnataka, Bihar, Tripura, West Bengal, Orissa, Himachal Pradesh, Haryana and Gujarat. The States in which growth rate of real wages had been comparatively low are Tamil Nadu, Madhya Pradesh, Punjab and Assam.

During pre-green revolution period (1960-61 to 1966-67) only three States registered positive growth rate, such as Kerala (3.3 per cent), Andhra Pradesh (1.5 per cent) and Karnataka (0.4 per cent) remaining States registered negative (-) growth rates particularly, the agricultural labourers of Assam, Tamil Nadu, are the worst sufferers.

Table 5. Trends in Real Wages of Male Agricultural Labourers (In Paisa)

Year	*A.P.*	*A.S.*	*BI*	*GU*	*HA*	*H.P.*	*KA*	*KE*	*M.P.*	*MA*	*OR*	*PU*	*RA*	*T.R.*	*TN*	*U.P.*	*W.B.*
1960-61	126	229	116	191	*	230	153	172	123	142	118	245	NA	200	143	127	181
1961-62	146	232	128	195	*	230	165	197	125	151	122	242	NA	200	150	130	180
1962-63	138	240	135	190	*	235	170	195	129	141	125	248	NA	175	145	120	175
1963-64	120	245	120	180	*	220	165	196	130	142	128	240	NA	165	140	110	165
1964-65	128	210	116	178	*	210	166	195	110	139	120	235	NA	150	139	100	145
1965-66	131	213	118	173	*	211	164	198	109	138	115	230	150	140	137	93	147
1966-67	136	158	113	164	217	180	157	214	93	141	116	203	158	131	126	97	143
A.A.G. Rate	1.45	-4.55	-0.16	-2.12		-3.28	0.44	3.31	-3.62	-0.03	-0.19	-2.56		-5.77	-1.72	-3.64	-3.22
1967-68	140	147	120	174	260	172	156	233	98	143	111	192	165	137	135	120	158
1968-69	143	171	137	178	281	183	116	229	104	149	100	347	169	144	200	138	148
1969-70	139	206	128	171	313	185	145	230	102	146	100	329	155	161	140	139	150
1970-71	154	198	130	190	343	204	139	232	110	153	102	336	201	147	157	152	148
1971-72	152	179	133	200	340	215	149	242	110	144	101	336	203	177	144	155	162
1972-73	140	192	122	156	310	201	134	233	107	120	94	313	173	186	154	141	164
1973-74	135	178	114	157	263	185	120	208	91	119	92	273	150	154	140	130	145
1974-75	105	149	106	123	242	161	104	177	80	101	79	255	124	117	118	127	124

(Cont…)

Year	A.P.	A.S.	BI	GU	HA	H.P.	KA	KE	M.P.	MA	OR	PU	RA	T.N.	TR	U.P.	W.B.
1975-76	138	185	153	202	276	190	134	198	115	107	92	280	195	133	146	168	149
1976-77	162	190	168	225	292	210	159	216	133	123	119	324	258	136	140	190	168
1977-78	160	190	150	292	325	199	170	222	123	123	118	297	200	137	145	168	184
1978-79	176	189	169	225	329	202	174	231	128	133	123	307	227	152	162	172	186
1979-80	178	167	139	214	320	192	166	236	116	141	108	290	213	166	154	162	179
1980-81	169	180	136	205	287	184	151	313	110	129	108	269	202	184	144	146	174
A.A.G. Rate	2.44	1.73	2.46	3.94	2.72	0.53	0.85	3.54	2.23	-0.28	0.05	4.14	4.08	3.44	2.68	4.01	1.98
1981-82	168	199	153	198	312	184	141	308	117	126	106	266	224	191	153	182	165
1982-83	191	199	151	264	338	240	146	304	141	143	113	283	304	191	145	174	158
1983-84	213	208	157	275	359	289	132	262	155	153	131	306	300	181	168	179	160
1984-85	226	225	181	290	350	293	133	301	166	205	140	330	209	201	168	192	231
185-86	239	249	191	273	343	288	174	332	164	209	140	331	243	229	172	198	284
1986-87	252	260	204	278	375	335	163	344	182	189	146	356	296	189	173	218	301
1987-88	248	263	194	249	347	336	159	354	176	189	140	360	351	172	165	199	300
1988-89	237	261	212	267	350	343	182	349	173	190	146	361	299	271	172	196	336
1989-90	277	279	216	259	386	334	198	347	190	235	159	384	283	296	192	231	327
1990-91	280	294	224	256	377	316	193	366	203	251	174	399	285	271	197	222	307
A.A.G. Rate	5.38	5.10	5.28	2.82	2.94	6.12	3.09	1.85	6.53	7.56	5.04	4.08	5.22	5.54	3.37	4.74	6.80

(Cont...)

Year	A.P.	A.S.	BI	GU	HA	H.P.	KA	KE	M.P.	MA	OR	PU	RA	T.N.	TR	U.P.	W.B.
1991-92	248	268	214	246	399	325	167	380	195	214	168	414	302	235	187	225	288
1992-93	252	270	204	265	429	339	143	417	219	215	186	421	291	219	212	242	353
1993-94	274	252	210	273	426	328	202	405	211	271	186	438	269	203	236	225	335
1994-95	242	248	219	276	428	363	170	426	214	268	179	432	271	180	238	220	317
1995-96	276	249	215	277	458	503	156	508	224	252	179	422	320	179	248	267	316
1996-97	284	253	208	298	468	492	188	553	227	268	179	425	353	206	267	235	361
1997-98	307	242	233	308	453	485	221	655	235	290	225	402	404	271	282	289	379
1998-99	284	265	221	311	426	467	234	653	225	295	236	382	437	266	301	301	373
1990-00	287	272	226	316	417	469	268	834	221	316	227	395	447	279	299	312	399
2000-01	366	337	262	348	404	501	290	904	232	328	244	402	498	292	317	345	415
A.A.G. Rate	3.34	1.74	1.81	3.19	0.79	5.31	5.60	9.82	1.46	3.19	3.78	0.13	6.02	3.51	5.00	5.05	3.42

Note:
1 Included in Punjab.
2 X Included in Assam.
3 To Determine Real Wage Rates the Average Money Wage Rates of Various States have been Deflated with Consumer Price Index for Agricultural Labour (CPIAL 1961-91 = 700) of Respective States.

Source: As Per table 3.

There was a sharp increase during post-green revolution period (1967-68 to 1980-81) in all States except in Maharashtra, which registered negative growth rate (-0.3 per cent). In this period the highest growth rate was recorded in Punjab (4.1 per cent), followed by Rajasthan (4.1 per cent) and Uttar Pradesh (3.9 per cent) and lowest in Orissa (0.1 per cent), Himachal Pradesh (0.5 per cent) and Karnataka (0.9 per cent).

During the pre-liberalisation period (1981-82 to 1990-91) the growth rate of real wage rates increased in all the States except in Gujarat, the highest growth rate was recorded in Maharasthra (7.6 per cent), West Bengal (6.8 per cent), Madhya Pradesh (6.5 per cent) and Himachal Pradesh (6.1 per cent) and lowest Kerala (1.9 per cent), Gujarat (2.8 per cent) and Haryana (2.9 per cent).

In comparison with previous period, the growth rate of real wage rates declined in post liberalization period in most of the states except in Gujarat, Karnataka, Kerala, Rajasthan, Tripura and Uttar Pradesh. Accordingly, the ranks also changed drastically during this period. Highest growth rate was registered in Kerala, Rajasthan, Karnataka, Himachal Pradesh and Uttar pradesh and gained highest ranks too. Punjab, Haryana, Madhya Pradesh, Assam and Bihar show the lowest growth rates.

In some States particularly in Punjab, Haryana, Kerala and Rajasthan some abnormal trends in real wage rates (increase/decrease over the previous periods) can be observed with the help of ranks, which are depicted in Table 6.

Punjab

According to the Table 5 and 6, Punjab showed highest average annual growth rate of real wage rates during post-green revolution period i.e., 4.1 per cent (Ist rank) and the same growth rate was continued in pre-liberalisation period but rank was decreased to 12th rank. During the post-liberalisation period, the growth rate was came down to

Table 6. Average Annual Growth Rates of Money Wages and Real Wages

Rank	Money Wages					Real Wages				
	1960-61 to 1966-67	*1967-68to 1980-81*	*1981-82 to 1990-91*	*1991-92 to 2001-02*	*1960-61 to 2001-02*	*1960-61 to 1966-67*	*1967-68 to 1980-81*	*1981-82 to 1990-91*	*1991-92 to 2001-02*	*1960-61 to 2001-02*
1	BI(10.8)	KE(10.6)	MA(14.8)	KE(16.7)	KE(12.3)	KE(3.3)	PU(4.1)	MA(7.6)	KE(9.8)	RA(5.1)
2	KE(10.7)	PU(10.5)	WB(14.7)	TN(15.4)	RA(11.4)	AP(1.5)	RA(4.1)	WB(6.8)	RA(6.0)	KE(4.6)
3	KA(10.0)	HA(9.9)	HP(14.3)	KA(13.3)	UP(10.8)	KA(0.4)	UP(4.0)	MP(6.5)	KA(5.6)	AP(3.2)
4	UP(9.2)	GU(9.9)	MP(14.0)	DA(12.6)	TN(10.5)	MA(-0.1)	GU(3.9)	HP(6.1)	HP(5.3)	MA(2.6)
5	OR(9.1)	UP(9.7)	TR(13.7)	HP(21.1)	KA(10.2)	BI(-0.2)	KE(3.9)	TN(5.5)	UP(5.1)	UP(2.6)
6	MA (8.4)	RA(9.3)	AS(13.2)	RA(12.0)	OR(10.1)	OR(-0.2)	TN(3.4)	AP(5.4)	TR(5.0)	KA(2.5)
7	AP(8.1)	TR(9.2)	RA(12.9)	UP(12.0)	MA(10.0)	TR(-1.7)	HA(2.7)	BI(5.3)	OR(3.8)	BI(2.4)
8	TN(6.7)	TN(9.0)	BI(12.8)	GU(11.8)	WB(10.0)	GU(-2.1)	TR(2.7)	RA(5.2)	TN(3.5)	TR(2.4)
9	WB(6.6)	AP(8.3)	UP(12.5)	AP(11.0)	BI(10.0)	PU(-2.6)	BI(2.5)	AS(5.1)	WB(3.4)	WB(2.3)
10	MP(6.3)	HP(7.6)	PU(12.3)	MA(10.8)	AP(10.0)	WB(-3.2)	AP(2.4)	OR(5.0)	AP(3.3)	OR(2.2)
11	PU(5.7)	MP(7.6)	OR(12.0)	WB(10.8)	HA(9.8)	KE(-3.3)	MP(2.2)	UP(4.7)	GU(3.2)	HP(2.2)
12	HP(4.6)	WB(7.4)	AP(12.0)	AS(9.9)	HP(9.7)	UP(-3.6)	WB(2.0)	PU(4.1)	MA(3.2)	HA(2.1)
13	GU(4.4)	AS(7.3)	KE(11.3)	BI(9.4)	MP(9.3)	MP(-3.6)	AS(1.7)	TR(3.4)	BI(1.8)	GU(2.0)
14	AS(4.1)	BI(6.8)	TN(11.0)	MP(9.2)	GU(9.2)	AS(-4.6)	KA(0.9)	KA(3.1)	AS(1.7)	TN(1.7)
15	TR(3.5)	KA(6.7)	HA(10.9)	TR(8.9)	PU(9.0)	TN(-5.8)	HP(0.5)	HA(2.9)	MP(1.4)	MP(1.6)
16	HA(*)	OR(6.6)	KA(10.7)	HA(8.6)	TP(8.8)	HA(*)	OR(0.1)	GU(2.8)	HA(0.8)	PU(1.4)
17	RA(NA)	MA(6.1)	GU(10.5)	PU(7.4)	AS(8.6)	RA(NA)	MA(-0.3)	KE(1.9)	PU(0.1)	AS(1.0)

Note: 1. Figures in Bracket show percentages. 2. *Included in Punjab.

0.1 per cent which leads to further decline in the ranks to 17th rank.

Kerala

This state registered the highest growth rate in pre-green revolution period among all the States. During the second period, there was a slight increase in the growth rate of real wages, but not as equal to some other States and declined its rank from 1st to 5th rank. In Pre-liberalisation period, surprisingly lowest growth rate was recorded and its rank was moved to the last (17th) rank. But in the post-liberalisation period, it showed sudden rise of about 9.8 per cent and climbed to the 1st rank.

Haryana

This State also showed and annual growth rate of 2.7 per cent (7th rank) in post-green revolution period, which was slightly increased to 2.9 per cent (15th rank) in pre-liberalization period and suddenly decreased to 0.8 per cent (16th rank) in post-liberalisation.

Rajasthan

This state also registered the highest growth rate (4.1 per cent) in post-green revolution period on par with the agriculturally advanced state of Punjab. During pre-liberalisation period, this state had not sustained its rank, but more growth rate was registered (5.0 per cent) than previous period. In the subsequent period, this state registered 6.0 per cent growth rate and reached the second rank among all the States. The long term growth rate, from 1960-61 to 2001-2002, also showed 5.1 per cent per annum which was the highest among all the States.

It is a surprise to note that the growth rates of real wages rates of male agricultural labourers declined in the most agriculturally advanced States like Punjab & Haryana and increased in Rajasthan, which being agriculturally backward state.

Part V

Summary and Conclusions

The total number of agricultural labour households was increased significantly in all States during 30 years since 1964-65. But growth rate of agricultural labour households was different from State to State. The highest growth rate was recorded in Assam and Gujarat and the lowest in Kerala and Uttar Pradesh. Over 1964-65 to 1993-94 period, the percentage of agricultural labour households to totals rural households increased by 8.5 per cent at all India level. Across the States, some States show substantial rise and some show marginal increase. The percentage of agricultural labour households with land was also increased in most of the States, which resulted in the dependence on wage paid employment was decreasing and self-employment was increasing.

The structure and trends in the total number of employment days available to male and female labourers reveal that over all employment days were available to male and female agricultural labourers were increasing in all the States. The sources of employment were also changed significantly, particularly, self-employment days increased in every state but incremental variations are different.

It gave an indication that the diversification of economic activity is taking place in rural side. But this change was not remarkable in most agriculturally advanced States like Punjab, Haryana and some other States like Karnataka, Kerala and Uttar Pradesh.

Despite some fluctuations in one or two years, the money wage rates of male agricultural labourers are increased in all States during forty one years of this study. With regard to growth rates in different periods, some States recorded continuous increasing trends, particularly in Kerala, Karnataka, Tamil Nadu and Gujarat. Sudden jumps and downs also are found in between sub periods of this study.

The state-wise data on growth rates of real wage rates for different periods also reveals that sudden jumps and downs are found. There are only four States (Karnataka, Rajasthan, Tripura and Uttar Pradesh) recorded contentious increasing trends. This study reveals some abnormal trends in real wage rates, increase/decrease, in certain States like Punjab, Haryana, Kerala and Rajasthan, which need further in depth probe.

In general, the rise in the total employment days together with an increase of real wages of male and female labourers across the states, suggests an improvement in the economic status of agricultural labour households. But the incidence of poverty among the agricultural labour is higher. This reveals that whatever improvement in income generation is taking place through increase in employment days and real wages are not sufficient to live above the poverty line. Because of rising trends of the wages are lagging behind the price-rise. The unemployed days of male and female labour is also significant.

To fill these gaps, policies must be designed in such a way to improve access of the poor labour to employment and wage earnings through effective implementation of Employment Guarantee Programmes & land reforms, more public investment in agricultural infrastructure development Programmes and timely revision & effective implementation of minimum wages. Nevertheless, without effective organization of agricultural labourers, the pauper levels will not be ameliorated. Therefore, even after several constraints, they should organize united campaigns for their upliftment.

Notes

1. During 1987-88 more than 50 per cent of agricultural household with land, did not reported to the Enquiry Committee and in some States it is exceeded to 90 per cent. Rural Labour Enquiry Committee Report-1987-88.

2. For more details see (a) Omvedt. Gail, 1977, Women and Rural Revolt in India, Social Scientist, Vol. 6(6), September; (b) Jose. George, 1984, Politicization of Agricultural workers in Kerala, A study of Kuttanand, K.P. Bagchi & Company Calcutta; (c) Alexander, K.C., 1981 Peasant Organizations in South India, Indian Social Institute, New Delhi (d) Jose. A.V., 1973, Wage Rates of Agricultural Labourers in Kerala, Economic and Political Weekly, Vol. 1. 8(4-6) Annual Number; (e) Ani Lukose, 1991, Labour Movements and Agrarian Relations, Rawal Publishers, Jaipur.
3. To determine the real wage rates, the average money wage rates have been deflated with Consumer Price Index for Agricultural Labourers (CPIAL Base Year 1960-61=100) of respective States, those are constructed by the Labour Bureau, Minister of Labour, Government of India. The data from 1986-87, the CPIAL of 1986-87 = 100 was converted into CPIAL of 1960-61 = 100 with the deflators of respective States.

References

1. Acharya Sarthi (1989), Agricultural Wages in India Desegregated Analysis, Indian Journal of Agricultural Economics, Vol. 44 No. 2.
2. Alok Kumar (1994), Determinants of the Incidence of Poverty among Rural Labour; A cross-Sectional Study, Indian Journal of Labour Economics, Vol. 37, No. 4.
3. Dash, J. (1996), Minimum Wages Law, Agricultural Labour and Uniform Minimum Wages, Indian Journal of Labour Economics, Vol. 39, No. 2.
4. Dharam Kumar (1965), Land and Caste in South India, A study of agricultural Labour in the Nineteenth Century, Cambridge University Press, London.
5. Hanumanth Rao, V, Acharya. N.K. & Swami Nathan M.C. (1998), (eds.) Andhra Pradesh at 50, A Data News Features Publication, Hyderabad.
6. Haque. T (1998), Regional Trends Patterns and Determinants of Agricultural Wages in India, India Journal of Labour Economics, Vol. 41 No. 4.
7. Jose A.V. (1988), Agricultural wages in India, Economic and Political Weekly, V. XXIII No. 26.
8. Kosambi (1965).

9. Krishnan, T.N. (1991), Wages, Employment and Output in Interrelated Labour Markets in an Agrarian Economy: A Study of Kerala, Economic and Political Weekly, Vol. 26 No. 26.

10. Mahendra Dev. S. (1988), Poverty of Agricultural a Labour Households in India: A State Level Analysis, Indian Journal of Agricultural Economics, Vol. 43, No. 1.

11. Parthasarathy G. Adiseshu. K. (1982), Real Wages of Agricultural Labour in Andhra Pradesh, Economic and Political Weekly, Vol. XVII, No. 31.

12. ...... (1987), Changes in the Incidence of Rural Poverty and Recent Trends in some Aspects of Agrarian Economy, Indian Journal of Agricultural economics, Vol. 42, No. 1.

13. ..... (1996). Recent Trends in Wages and Employment of Agricultural Labour, The Indian Journal of Agricultural Economics, Vol. 51, No. 1 & 2.

14. ..... (1997), Minimum Wages with in Agriculture, The Indian Journal of Labour Economics, Vol. 40, No. 4.

15. Rama Krishna Mukherji (1969), Rural Class Structure in West Bengal, in Edi Desai A.R. (1969), Rural Sociology in India, Popular Prakasan, Bombay.

16. Sharma, H.R. (2002), Employment and Wage Earning of Agricultural Labourers; A State—Wise Analysis, Indian Journal of Labour Economics Vol. 44, No. 1.

17. Srinivasan, M.V. (1977) Minimum Wages in Agricultural, The Indian Journal of Labour Economics, Vol. 40, No. 4.

18. Srinivasulu. C. (1988), Unionization of Agricultural Labour in Andhra Pradesh, Spellbound Publications, Rohtaka.

19. Unni, Jeemol (1977), Employment and Wages among Rural; Labourers; some Recent Rends, Indian Journal of agricultural Economics, Vol. 52, No. 1.

20. Utsa Patnaik (1999), The Long Transition, Tulika Publications, New Delhi.

27

Social Security and Labour Welfare Measures in Karnataka State Road Transport Corporation

Prof. R.G. Desai, Dr. (Smt) M. Madhumathi

Introduction

Labour welfare plays a vital role in any industrial society. Provision of welfare measures to the workers and other employees receives much importance to maintain good industrial relations. Welfare facilities influence the workers' motivation when they feel that the employer and the government are interested in welfare and happiness, their tendency to grouse and grumble will steadily disappear. From this the industrial peace will develop and ultimately higher development will be achieved.

Welfare does not mean amenities but the right atmosphere where the worker can breathe an air of growth and development and think constructively so as to understand the play and interplay of his subconscious instincts and conscious emotions.

Welfare concept refers to a state of living of an individual or a group in a desirable relationship with the total environment. Welfare could be viewed from economic, social, psychological and other dimensions. In India, the framework of providing welfare measures to workers consists of statutory and voluntary measures, the former being taken by the management, and the latter being achieved through collective bargaining agreements. In addition to the statutory framework, the collective bargaining agreements reached at industry and company level also and extent of welfare measures. The statutory framework and collective agreements prescribe the minimum targets to be achieved regarding welfare measures.

The efficiency of workers increases by providing more and more labour welfare facilities. The efficiency of workers increases the productivity while cheap food, free medical aid, education, housing, etc., increase the real income of workers. If the workers go on strike, they will be deprived of all these facilities. That is why, the workers try to avoid the industrial disputes, strikes, etc., if they are provided good welfare facilities.

In this paper, in general, an attempt has been made to examine the social security and labour welfare facilities in Karnataka State Road Transport Corporation and in particular, following objectives have been put forth.

Objectives

1. To reveal the existing social security and labour welfare measures in Karnataka State Road Transport Corporation.
2. To assess the use and abuse of such facilities.
3. To study the changing outlook and emerging perspectives in the Karnataka State Road Transport Corporation.

Material and Method

Material is collected from the secondary sources such, as, official records, annual administrative reports of the organisation. Simple tabular analysis and annual percentage growth rate and linear growth rates are followed in this paper. The study covers the time series data over a period of 10 years from 1988-89 to 1997-98. One of the objectives of this paper is to reveal the existing social security and labour welfare measures in Karnataka State Road Transport Corporation. Several measures of social security are extended. They are medical facilities, compensation under workmen's compensation Act, Motor Transport Worker's Act of 1961, Leave Salary, Festival advance, Bonus, encashment of leave, workers' education scheme, canteen facilities, co-operative societies, sports and cultural activities, call bus facility, housing facility, Retirement benefits like Provident Fund and Death cum Retirement Benefit Fund, Rehabilitation centre and De-addiction Programme etc. Among all facilities, we have discussed very important facilities extended by Karnataka State Road Transport Corporation in this paper are due to time and other constraints.

Medical Facilities

Medical care for workers forms an integral part of labour welfare programme for all the countries of the world. This facility not only provides protection against sickness but also ensures availability of a physically fit and stable manpower for economic development.

Health of the industrial workers assumes great importance in the modern industry. As ill health of workers would lead to wide spread absenteeism, low morale and bad time keeping take place. It also leads to decreased production, spoiled work and ultimately results in bad labour management relations. In India, the health of the workers is adversely affected due to bad climatic condition ignorance, poverty, long hours of work, low wages etc. Therefore, provision of medical facilities for the workers is of great importance in the country.

The Karnataka State Road Transport Corporation has made provision for medical facilities for its employees and their families. It has maintained dispensaries in all the divisional Headquarters except in the new divisions formed recently.

The Corporation has constructed its own hospitals at Bangalore, Hubli, Bijapur and Gulbarga. Full time Doctors at Bangalore and Hubli and part time Doctors in all the divisions are provided. Under the KSRTC employees (Medical Attendance) Regulation 1970, there is a provision for reimbursement of medical claims. Apart from this in-patient facilities are provided to the employees and their families. It has reserved 80 capitation beds at Government hospitals at various places in the state by paying Rs. 25/- per day per bed.

Table 1 presents detailed information relating to the number of patients and the amount spent by the corporation in the sphere of medical and towards the medical reimbursement to employees from 1988-89 to 1997-98. It also shows the number of employees received medical claims and reimbursement made to them. The amount spent by the organisation depends upon the number of patients and the type of treatment required by them. In 1988-89, number of patients treated were, 1,16,898 and amount spent on medicine and upkeep was Rs. 10,11,487 Per capita average expenditure was Rs. 8.6. In the same year 18,947 employees claimed medical reimbursement to the tune of Rs. 21,93,203 which works to Rs. 115.7 per capita average medical reimbursement in 1988-89. In 1997-98 the number of patients treated was 45,335 and amount spent on medicine and upkeep was Rs. 15 lakhs and per capita average expenditure was Rs. 33. However, 51,136 employees claimed medical reimbursement and received Rs. 4,20,32,412 towards medical claims, and Rs. 412 was per capita average medical reimbursement in that year.

If we go by the number of patients treated vis-a-vis per capita medical Reimbursement, there is a strong negative relation. The number of patients treated is decreasing where as the amount of reimbursement is increasing. This may be due to either the Medicine charges might have increased, or the employees might have claimed false medical bills. If

Table 1. Medical Aid in KSRTC from 1988-89 to 1997-98

Year	*No. of Patients Treated*	*Amount Spent on medicine and upkeep*	*Per Capita expenditure on patients*	*No. of employees received medical claims*	*Amount Reimbursed towards medical claims*	*Per Capita medical reimburse reimbursement*
1988-89	1,16,898	10,11,487	8.6	18,947	21,93,203	115.7
1989-90	1,39,808	7,67,078	5.4	25,647	33,67,678	131.3
1990-91	1,11,663	9,50,790	8.5	23,669	30,71,465	129.7
1991-92	62,546	13,06,073	20.8	41,080	58,53,741	142.4
1992-93	1,07,004	8,04,156	7.5	32,384	81,10,235	247.0
1993-94	1,25,033	10,26,577	8.2	38,346	1,18,64,361	309.4
1994-95	97,656	14,80,348	15.1	41,563	70,07,764	168.6
1995-96	49,238	7,90,489	16.0	19,354	67,32,946	347.8
1996-97	49,538	15,00,000	30.2	13,161	72,67,025	552.1
1997-98	45,335	15,00,000	33.0	51,136	4,20,32,312	821.9

Source: Compiled from Administrative Reports, Various Issues.

we compare the per capita expenditure on patient and per capita Medical reimbursement there is a direct relation between the two.

Rehabilitation Centre

Under the auspices of family welfare Association, the Corporation has established Rehabilitation Centre. The objective is to provide employment to the dependants of the deceased employees who are denied employment opportunities for want of educational qualification and age as per Cadre and Recruitment Regulations of the Organisation.

The Rehabilitation Centre is entrusted with the responsibility of imparting training in tailoring, knitting and envelop-making. It also undertakes jobs such as stitching uniforms, knitting jerseys, manufacturing envelopes and manufacturing conductors cash bags. The Corporation has provided Rs. 10 lakhs to the Centre to equip itself with plant and machinery.

De-Addiction Programme

Alcoholism is one of the menaces of the workers affecting the productivity and the public sectors are not an exception to it. Addiction to alcohol has affected the physical, mental, social, psychological and economic status of an individual employee. It also causes less productivity, loss of image, rude behaviour, insubordination, increase in absenteeism and serious accidents, some times fatal and affect the performance of the Corporation adversely.

A pilot study showed that two per cent of the employees of the Corporation were found to have consumed alcohol while on duty, which posed serious problems for road safety. There are many cases, in which the drunken drivers have caused serious fatal accidents leading to heavy Corporation outflow from corpus. In order to reduce absenteeism, increase the productivity, improve operational efficiency and road safety, a project of the De-Addiction Programme in the organisation was launched during the year 1997-98.

Two senior officers of KSRTC attended a workshop conducted by the ILO during May 1997 at Bangalore on "Prevention of Alcohol and Drug Abuse at Workplace". During the workshop, the magnitude of the problem in the organisation was explained. The ILO was requested to extend financial and other assistance regarding training, prevention, treatment, etc., and to take up KSRTC on experimental basis as a project in the industrial sector in the State. Later a reference was made to the National Project Coordinator, ILO, New Delhi, to extend necessary assistance in this regard. A Memorandum of understanding was signed in this direction.

Analysis of all the Welfare Measures of KSRTC

Having discussed the nature and extent of two or three welfare measures provided by the Organisation, it is now proposed to examine the trends in the amounts spent on these welfare measures.

The annual percentage growth rate is calculated by taking the present year expenditure on labour welfare and divided by the previous years expenditure on labour welfare multiplied by 100, i.e.,

$$\frac{Y_t - Y_{t-1}}{Y_{t-1}} \times 100$$

Y_t = Present year (1989-90)

Y_{t-1} = Previous year (1988-89)

$$\text{E.g.:} \frac{2329.53 - 2179.00}{2179.00} \times 100$$

$$= 6.90\%$$

Table 2. Annual Percentage Growth Rate Labour Welfare Expenditure of KSRTC from 1988-89 to 1997-98 (Rs. in lakhs)

Year	*Total expenditure on Labour Welfare*	*% Growth Rate*
1988-89	2179.00	6.4
1989-90	2329.53	6.9
1990-91	2783.41	19.4
1991-92	2812.66	1.0
1992-93	3018.54	7.3
1993-94	3514.81	16.4
1994-95	3708.15	5.5
1995-96	4879.19	31.5
1996-97	5606.48	14.9
1997-98	6336.82	13.0
Total	**37168.59**	**12.19**

Source: Compiled from Administrative Reports KSRTC, Various Issue.

The above Table shows the annual percentage growth rate of Labour Welfare Expenditure of KSRTC from 1988-89 to 1997-98. In 1989-1990, the total labour welfare expenditure of KSRTC was 2329.53 and the annual percentage growth rate was 6.90. In 1990-91 it was increased to 19.4. The annual percentage growth rate of labour expenditure of KSRTC was very high in 1995-96 i.e., 31.5 and very low in 1991-92, i.e., 1.0. In 1997-98 it was 13.0 and the total expenditure on labour welfare was Rs. 6336.82. Annual average percentage growth rate was 12.19. It reveals that the labour welfare expenditure in KSRTC is growing year after year.

Linear Growth Rates were computed for the three sub-periods and as well as for the entire period of study. These growth rates are presented in the above Table. During the period I, the Labour Welfare expenditure increased at the rate of 10.9% per annum. This rate decreased to 8.2% during period II, and it was increased to 16.2% during period III. On the whole, labour welfare expenditure in KSRTC was increased to 12.19% per annum during the entire period of study.

Table 3. Linear Growth Rate of Labour Welfare Expenditure in KSRTC from 1988-89 to 1997-98

Period	*Labour Welfare expenditure (% per annum)*
Period I (1988-89 to 1990-91) (3 years)	10.9
Period II (1991-1992 to 1993-94) (3 years)	8.2
Period III (1994-95 to 1997-98) (4 years)	16.2
Entire Period	12.19

Note: The Linear Growth Rates are Calculated by Using the Previous Table.

Table 4. Per Capita Labour Welfare Expenditure in KSRTC from 1988-89 to 1997-98

Year	*Total Staff*	*Total expenditure on Labour Welfare*	*Per Capita Expenditure on Labour Welfare*
1988-89	50,169	2,17,90,000	434
1989-90	54,315	2,32,95,300	428
1990-91	54,844	2,78,34,100	507
1991-92	55,296	2,81,26,600	508
1992-93	56,465	3,01,85,400	534
1993-94	58,911	3,51,48,100	596
1994-95	57,512	3,70,81,500	644
1995-96	57,806	4,84,91,900	844
1996-97	58,603	5,60,64,800	956
1997-98	58,807	6,33,68,200	1077

Source: Compiled from Administrative Reports KSRTC, Various Issues.

The Table shows the per capita expenditure on labour welfare in KSRTC from 1988-89 to 1997-98. The per capita expenditure is obtained by dividing the total expenditure on labour welfare by the total staff employed in KSRTC during a year. In 1988-89, the total staff was 50,169 and the total expenditure on labour welfare was Rs. 2,17,90,000. The per capita labour welfare expenditure during the period was Rs. 434. The per capita labour welfare expenditure was very low in 1989-90 i.e., Rs. 428 and very high in 1997-98, i.e., Rs. 1,077.

Table 5. Linear Growth Rate of Per Capita Labour Welfare Expenditure in KSRTC from 1988-89 to 1997-98

Period	*Per Capita Labour Welfare expenditure (in rupees)*
Period I (1988-89 to 1990-91) (3 years)	456.3
Period II (1991-1992 to 1993-94) (3 years)	546.0
Period III (1994-95 to 1997-98) (4 years)	880.5
Entire Period	652.8

Per capita labour welfare expenditure of all the facilities in KSRTC was calculated year wise in the previous Table. The present Table explains the linear growth rates for three sub-periods and as well as for the entire period of study as shown in the table.

During period I, the per capita labour welfare expenditure increased at the rate of Rs. 456.3 per annum. This rate increased to Rs. 737 during period II, and further it was increased to Rs. 880.25 during period. III. On the whole the per capita labour welfare expenditure increased at Rs. 652.8 per annum during the entire period of study.

Major findings

1. If we go by the number of patients treated vis-a-ais per capita Medical Reimbursement, there is a strong negative relation between number of patients treated and the amount of reimbursement.

2. If we compare the per capita expenditure on patient and per capita Medical reimbursement there is a direct relation between the two.
3. Important finding of the study is that the KSRTC established Rehabilitation Centre to provide employment to the dependants of the deceased employees, who were denied employment opportunities for want of educational qualification and age as per Cadre and Recruitment Regulations of the organisation. In this respect KSRTC is a model to other organisations.
4. In order to reduce absenteeism and increase the productivity, to improve operational efficiency and road safety, KSRTC launched De-Addiction Programme during the year 1997-98. It was another milestone of KSRTC to put an end to addiction of Alcohol among its employees.

References

1. Moulvi M.M. (1997): "Impact of Social Security-cum-Labour Welfare Measures on Production, Absenteeism and Attitudes of Industrial Workers—A Comparative Study of KSRTC Regional Workshops of Hubli and Bangalore" unpublished thesis, Karnataka University, Dharwad.
2. Note on the working of Karnataka State Road Transport Corporation.
3. "Sarige Sampada" Monthly Magazine of KSRTC various issues.

28

The Contours of Labour Sector Reforms in India

Dr. D.S. Leelavathi

Introduction

Globalization has called for a series of serious economic reforms in of the labour sector. The major objectives of economic reform are to create transparency, competitiveness and flexibility by minimizing bureaucratic shackles. These reforms actually paved the way for integrating Indian economy with the rest of the world. The last decade of the 20th century witnessed the formation of a large number of commissions in different areas in order to suggest a roadmap for smoothening the process of structural transformation in the economy. These commissions have given us a definite framework for economic reforms in different sectors.

Ever since 1990, the government has been trying to conceptualize the need mechanism of labour sector reforms. (LSR). Of all these attempts, mention may be made of Ramanujan committee (1990), National Commission on labour standards (1995) a twelve member committee to address the issues pertaining to structural adjustment in labour sector (1966), apart from the regular labour law committees. Besides, many of the industrial reforms commissions like that of Disinvestment Commission (1966) also have dealt with LSRs. However, the most significant effort in this context is the setting up of II National Commission on Labour (II NCL) under the chairmanship of Mr. Ravindra Verma in 1999. This commission has actually shouldered the responsibility of preparing an agenda for LSR keeping in view the incomplete task in the first generation of economic reforms and challenges in the next generation. The commission is expected to submit its report by the end of 2001.

Going ahead with the second generation of reforms seems to be high on the NDA Government, particularly in the budget of new millennium. The constitution of the II NCL is a welcoming decision, after a gap of exactly 30 years. (The first NCL was set up in 1969) because in the entire Phase of the first generation, LSRs were virtually by passed. The mandate of the second commission now is to rationalize the existing laws relating to labour in the organized sector and to suggest umbrella legislation for ensuring a minimum labour protection to the unorganized sector.

Objectives

The paper attempts to discuss the contours of LSR in the background of major events in this sector during 90s. Also, the paper intends to analyse the LSR keeping in view the three fundamentals namely labour market flexibility, wage flexibility, and employment security. The Economic survey 2001-2000 which has set the tone for the next round of reforms stated that New Delhi is alarmed by industrial growth rate touching a ten-year low rate during the current fiscal year. Among many other things, which have contributed to industrial declaration, lack of reforms in the labour sector is one of the most significant reasons. It is in this background that the paper assumes special attention.

PART I

Genesis of LSR

The recent history of LSR can be traced back to 21st July 1991, on the Government of India, which constituted the main plank of the New Economic Policy, announced the

New Industrial Policy. It gave a new twist to the history of labour movement in India as well as the LSR. For the first time it gave common forum for all trade unions to unite for a common cause forgetting their political and personal differences. Both the trade unions and opposition political parties persuaded the government to adopt a human approach in the SAP. It is in this context that the Government has introduced the Exit Policy to provide a safety net to workers in order to minimize the adverse effects of globalisation on labour. This exist policy gradually became a policy of 'downsizing' or 'right sizing' of labour in order to ensure greater efficiency and flexibility in the labour market. Besides, competitive efficiency, globalisation demanded the simplification and integration of labour laws in order to ensure transparency and reduce rent seeking-behaviour. All these developments paved the way for LSRs in India.

Major LSRs in the First Generation

In the beginning of 90s some bold attempts were made to flexibalise market so as to ensure efficiency in both industry and labour of which mention may be made of-

1. Articulation of exit policy to right size the labour force and to allow the employer to hire and fire the work force.
2. Introduction of the Voluntary Retirement Scheme (VRS) with golden hand shake.
3. Setting up of National Renewal Fund (NRF) in February 1992 to protect the interest of workers affected by industrial restructuring.
4. Although certain modification in BIFR, MRTP Act, Trade union Act, SICA etc are primarily concerned with industrial restructuring, have lot of implications for labour as well.

However, even with all these drastic measures, nothing could be done to reform the labour market. Infact, throughout

90s, the demand for a well defined and feasible exit policy has remained as a fundamental demand by the foreign direct investors. Thus the incomplete and half-hearted LSR could not hold the key for successful reforms during the first generation of economic reforms. Therefore at present the II NCL is trying to fill this vacuum and is gathering a lot of information from cross sections of both employers, employees and the public.

Ninth Plan Approach to LSR

The 9th plan approach to LSR provides a broad perspective of in the labour sector. The plan document states that one of the major concerns of the governments has been the improvement of labour welfare with increasing emphasis on productivity and provision of a reasonable level of social security. Many of the initiatives taken by the government in the labour sector have to be reviewed regularly in the context of an evolving economic and social background. The labour laws aim at creating a safe work environment and better incentives to work and productivity. The document also states that simplification and integration of labour laws so as to reach a greater proportion of the workforce would be the priority factor in the area of economic reform. However, the myths and realities of LSR in the first generation paved the way for certain bold reforms announced in the first union budget of the new millennium.

Union Budget 2001-2002 and the LSR

The budget has proposed a series of LSRs to pave the way for flexibility. The previous finance ministers have given us the impression that movement towards LSRs would be political suicidal. But Mr. Yashwant Sinha has not only made lay-offs and closures easier for a large number of industrial units but also removed some of the constraints on using contract labour. He insisted that good economics is also good politics and also that unionized labour must be forced to come to terms with a free labour market.

The finance minister reiterates that Indian labour laws have road block to industrial competitiveness adversely affecting growth. Mr. Shinha has regularized an existing phenomenon when he proposed legislation to facilitate unrestricted outsourcing of activities and often contract employment. These measures will provide the private sector the much needed flexibility to increase the number of jobs in their industrial establishment.

Major LSR Proposed in the Union Budget Includes

1. Factories employing upto 1000 workers will no longer need prior government approval to layoff or retrench workers and to close units.
2. Separate compensation to be increased from 15 days wages to 45 days wages for every completed year of service.
3. Companies allowed to outsource employees without restrictions. All such employees to enjoy health, safety, social security and retrenchment benefits.
4. Workers' interests to be safeguarded while promoting industrial investment in labour intensive import-oriented activities.
5. Workers' wage ceiling for coverage under employee provident fund enhanced from Rs. 5000/- to 6500.
6. Adequate social security coverage for workers in unorganized sector IRDA.
7. Ashraya Bhima Yojana, a group insurance was announced for the benefit of those workers affected by liberalization.
8. The government would not distinguish between core and non-core sector while protecting the outsourced individuals.

The LSR promises in the budget are going to open the k in several areas of the labour sector so as to create the much desired labour market flexibility. At the same time it is equal to that these reforms also create some new challenges in the labour sector.

Agenda for LSR

A recent report entitled "unshackling Indian industry" submitted to Ministers council on Trade and Industry', by a group of industrialists argues that only with LSR, we can move on to the second generation of economic reforms. The report further states that LSR should address the following-

1. The firms' right to retrench irrespective of its size.
2. Appropriately uniform rights conforming to the international practice should be established for all workers irrespective of whether they are employed in small or big group and
3. Finally to give substance to these provisions, proper enforcement mechanism must be initiated.

In a similar tone, Professor J.N. Bhjagawath one of the foremost international Trade, a Development and Migration theorist of his generation says "...If I am not working, yet being protected and not being disciplined or fined... that is not good for progress". That means hiring and firing of workers should be a major agenda for LSRs. However, the leading issues, which constitute the agenda for LSR, centre on three aspects namely labour market flexibility (LMF) wage flexibility and employment security.

Labour Market Flexibility

LMF is an important prerequisite in order to achieve competitiveness the very purpose of LSR is to create what is called LMF, which means quick adjustment of labour costs in enterprises. It implies freedom to enterprises in recruitment, retrenchment and lay-off. It ensures an additional right to hire and fire the work force. This calls for deregulation of labour market so as to overcome the rigidities in the labour market. The proponents of LMF view institutional interventions in the labour market basically as distortions in otherwise perfectly functioning competitive market. Liberalization calls for removing such distortions by ensuring LMF.

Wages Flexibility

Wages for public sector employees are virtually set by the government led bodies and in India nearly 20 boards decide wages. Although, they are tripartite in nature, recommendations are not statutorily binding and hence there is more scope for conflicts. Wages are hardly linked to productivity.

Further, although trade unions are very strong in India, wage increase is comparatively less when compared to weak unions in East Asian countries, where wage increase is substantial. This stands to reason that wages cannot be increased unless productivity also increases.

The wage packet in the organized sector is composed of three main parts name is basic wages, dearness allowance and bonus. Basic wages are fixed by pay commissions and are revised periodically. However, there is no mechanism for adjusting wage in response to changes in productivity and profitability and wage growth tends to be exogenously given to enterprises. Similarly dearness allowance is only a compensatory finance and not linked to either productivity or profitability. Also, with regard to bonus, a minimum of 8.33% of the basic is fixed, without regard to the financial viability of the unit.

Employment Flexibility

In India, workers in the public sector which account for nearly 70% force, enjoy maximum security. It is difficult for the employers to dismiss employees even on grounds like unjustified absence, misconduct, dereliction of duty, redundancy etc. Even in private sector, hiring and firing of labour is almost impossible owning to protective labour laws, strong trade unions, human rights dimension etc. This has become a stumbling block in achieving LMF.

Employment security in the organized sector is governed by Industries 1947. This regulation has made labour adjustment relatively cumbersome. Even the sick industries are rarely granted permission to close down due to various considerations particularly the adverse impact on employment.

It is in this background, that we have got to discuss the emerging challenges in the LSR.

PART II

EMERGING CHALLENGE IN THE LSR

Major challenges in the LSR can be conveniently discussed under the following heads.

Integration of Labour Laws

Integration of labour laws is one of the fundamental challenges in the LSR. Indian labour sector has a law heavy system. Since labour is in the concurrent list, both central and state governments have enacted quite a good number of labour laws. Infact, there are 167 central labour legislations and another 57 state labour legislations to protect the interest of labour. However, they reach only a small segment of labour force, which is in the organized sector and a vast labour force which is in the unorganized sector and which actually needs more protection is left out. Besides, the administration of the labour laws has led to a lot of bureaucratic shackles, delays and rent seeking activities. Moreover, these labour laws were formulated under an altogether different situation and hence they need to be thoroughly reviewed in the context of liberalization.

With regard to enforcement of labour laws the machinery in the state severe strain and hence miscarriage of justice is difficult to avoid. Therefore, to avoid these complications, devising a single code is necessary. But this task itself is a complicated challenge in the prevailing labour market dualism. Integrating labour laws in such a way as to maximize efficiency productivity, employment, wage etc. irrespective of the their nature of employment, is going to be a tough task, which is now entrusted to the II NCL. The challenges now before the commission are:

1. To identify the laws which are no longer needed and repeal them.
2. To identify the laws which even in harmony with the climate of economic liberalization and hence need no change and
3. To amend the laws which require changes.

The already expressed second line of thought with regard to the establishment of II NCL, has of course, made us little skeptical towards the output.

Amendments to IDA-1947

Employment security in the organized sector is governed by the Industries Disputes Act 1947. The amendments to the Act in 1976 and 1982 have almost made retrenchment impossible. Although originally the provisions were means to apply only to industrial workers, interpretations by the courts of law effectively extended the coverage to service sector employees also. This regulation has made the labour adjustment relatively cumbersome.

The union budget 2001-2002 has proposed 5B of the I D A which stipulates that employers in specified industrial establishment must obtain prior permission from the appropriate authority for effecting lay-off retrenchment and closure, will now apply to industries employing not more than 1,000 workers, instead of 100. According to the latest figures available, over 99% of units registered in this country would be given freedom to lay off employees by this change in the threshold. This is against 13.95% of units which enjoyed this freedom until now. Also, only large units, accounting for 0.82% of the units registered in this country would continue to seek government approval to hire and fire their staff after the new legislation comes into force.

This amendment to IDA has created a few challenges also. For eg: once the new IDA is executed, nearly 55% of the work force in registered units could automatically go out of job security net and only 24.61% of the workers working in large units would continue to enjoy job security. Thus the overall magnitude of unprotected labour could increase significantly, for which a different social security net needs to be provided. At the same time, lay-off will become dearer to employees since they have to pay 45 days separate pay for every year of completed service as against 15 days salary earlier.

Contact Labour (Regulation) and Abolitions Act-1970

The major objective of the Act is protection of workers on contract and abolition of contractual work to prevent the exploitation of Labour. All these days, what has happened is, even if there is scope for creating a permanent job, deliberately the employers preferred contract labour, as this would reduce the cost of labour.

There has been a long standing demand from employers, especially SCOPE, to amend this Act so as to only regulate the contract labour. Also, the changing business environment, which expects a more flexible labour market, makes it impossible to do away with the practice of contract labour. However, regulating their employment and protecting the interest of such workers are equally important, therefore employers have requested that the Act be renamed as contract Labour Regulation Act.

As per the growing demand, now section 10 of the Act which envisaged prohibition of contract labour, if the nature of the job is perennial and also which enabled the contract labour engaged in prohibited jobs to become direct employees of the principal employer, will be changed. The finance minister has proposed an amendment to the Act to facilitate outsourcing of activities without any restrictions as well as to offer contract appointments. The amendment has also reduced the formalities to obtain a licence by a job contractor. However, he has to meet the provisions pertaining to welfare, health, safety, wages and other facilities. Provision for wage may also form part of the amended law. A gratuity fund for contract workers has also been proposed apart from penalty for the violation of the Act. Also, contract workers could be entitled to wage party with regular workers, working in similar jobs. On retrenchment, each worker would have to be paid compensation for every year of service and part thereof rendered in excess of six months.

However, certain gray areas of the Act which may create new challenges are:

(a) Implementation aspect of amended Act,

(b) Financial burden of protection and welfare of the vast magnitude of contract labour,

(c) Regulatory provisions may need a further review,

(d) Judiciary demands more clarity with regard to contract labour. Well, if these are taken care of, the future will be a smooth sail.

Stream Lining of SICA, BIFR, MRTP and Trade Union Act

In this context, an attempt would be made to highlight a few challenges created on account of some amendments/ modifications in the respective Acts.

SICA: Special provision Act was enacted in 1985 to look into the revival of sick companies. The recent amendment of the Act defines sickness not interns of erosion of net worth, but in terms of default in repayment of loans in secured creditors like bank and financial institutions. Thus the emphasis is on recovery of loans of secured creditors rather than on rehabilitation. Naturally, willful avail of several benefits meant for sick units and thus employers will have a free hand to swindle the public funds.

BIFR: was set up in 1986 under the statutes to implement the provisions of SICA. The Government entrusted some powers to BIFR in order to facilitate the exit of sick units. However, even BIFR became more busy in liquidating the assets of sick units rather than reviving sick units. On the one hand it provides for monetary settlement of workers and at the same time adversely affects new job creation.

MRPT: Act, (1970), which was enacted with the intention of controlling monopoly and restrictive trade practice, has been scrapped beyond recognition, monopoly clause is gone completely and restrictive and unfair trade practices are to be considėred both in private and public sector. The proposed replacement of the MRTP commission by the competition commission, with a view to increase competitive efficiency, further flexibilities the labour market and create new dimensions to LSR. To substantiate this, we can mention the recent high court judgment, upholding employers' right to refuse to pay for union work, which has become a landmark while checking the undue right of workers.

Amendments to Trade Union Act (1926)

On the basis of recommendations of Ramanujan Committee on industrial relations, in a move to remove labour market rigidity and to increase the comfort level of industrial establishment, the amendments to the T U Act increased the number members ferrous to register a T U in an industry from just 7 to 10% of labour force. The other amendments include curb on the participation of outsiders, mandatory elections through secret ballot, compulsory auditing of T U accounts, compulsory submission of annual reports, promotion of internal democracy...etc evoke very strong responses from the T Us, which in turn may block LSR from different directions.

V. Revival of the Fading Exit Policy

The exit policy was formulated in the early 90s to provide a human face to the SAP, by providing safety net to the affected workers. The policy aimed at maximizing efficiency of the economy through the flexibilization of labour market. The policy manifested itself with the so-called 'right sizing' or down sizing' or labour. However, gradually the exit policy faded away not only due to pressure from the trade unions but also the opposition political parties. Equally true is the fact that a lot of internal inconsistencies along with confusing interpretations by the then ruling party prominent, led to the disappearance of exit policy. To quote a few instances for example- P.V. Narasimha Rao, under whose regime new policy was introduced, himself has told in the international business meet at Davos, Switzerland that India has not plants to permit employers to freely retrench their workers. Similarly, Mr. Manmohan Singh, the then Finance Minister, stated that the western type of hire and fire policy is not possible in India. On similar grounds, Mr. Montek Singh Ahluwaliya, the then finance secretary mentioned that the Government had not plans to amend IDA and lack of an exit policy was no determinent to industrial growth and investment. Mr. P.A. Sangma, the then labour minister stated that the objective of exit policy is to discipline the workers and not to displace them. But the ground reality is, unless we have a well defined, feasible exit policy, the flow of FDI would be adversely affected.

National Renewal Fund (NRF) was setup in Feb. 1992 to act as a social security measure to protect the interest of workers in the wake of industrial restructuring. The fund operates through National renewal Grant Fund, Employment Generation Fund and Insurance fund for Employees. However the working of NRF shows that, it is concerned more or less with financing the VRS, rather than encouraging, retraining and redeployment of workers. However, in 1996, a major revamping of the Fund was taken up to streamline its activities in tune with the modern industry and labour requirements. There is also a proposal to merge the Disinvestments Fund with NRF. Since LSR renders more workers jobless, NRF has to prepare itself for imparting new training so as to make them re-employable and has to learn from the experience of other countries.

Growing Magnitude of Unorganised Labour

One of the biggest challenges with regard to LSR is protecting the interest of unorganized labour which constitutes nearly 90% of the total work force. This trend is also significantly increasing. This labour force is mostly outside the purview of the labour laws and their protection demands a prior attention whatever piece meal efforts we have for the unorganized labour needs to be integrated properly. Institutional arrangements for providing group insurance to the rural poor/labour across the country need to be made more effective and their coverage increased.

Any scheme that has to benefit the working population in the unorganized sector has to be employed friendly. The problem of the National Scheme of Social Security is to explore the most appropriate institutional mechanism for distributing among working population, what has been earned by labour, rather than financing the full cost of social security has to be promoted on a location specific basis. Resources for social security raised primarily by the employees and employer and Government can provide a token support, but cannot meet the full expenditure incurred on social security.

Moreover, the social security setup as it exists in industrial countries is not applicable to India, where informal sector employs the bulk of labour force and a significant proportion of the employed poor is also significantly increasing. Therefore in this context the question is how to extend the coverage of National Social Assistance Programme introduced during the Eighth plan period to benefit the casual and self-employed workers in informal sector both a rural and urban areas.

Changing Trends in Employment Generation

Since 90s, certain distinctive trends have started emerging in the employment scenario. The diversification of the economy away from agriculture as measured by the sectoral pattern of employment has been much lower than expected. The share of the organized sector in employment has continued to below and has been declining, accounting for 7.82% of total employment in 1991. Within the organized sector, the share of the private sector in employment is reduced from 42% in 1991 to 30% in 1995. However, since 1995, the rate of expansion of employment in the private sector has been higher than in the public sector. The proportion of casual labour has increased from 19.7% in 1972-73 to 28% in 94-95. Similarly the proportion of self-employed in employment had reduced but still accounted for 56% of those employed in 1992. Employment per enterprise has also been declining. Also, with 70% or organized employment being in the public sector, a peculiar situation has developed in which the government assumes the role of an employer as also of an arbitrator. All these trends reveal that the implications of LSR would be wide and varied and hence the countervailing measures also need to be varied and effective.

The most significant trend in employment generation however, is the declining employment elasticity of growth, not only in India but also in the rest of the World. Employment intensity of growth speaks of employment content of growth. Therefore, the modern growth has been branded as 'jobless growth'. The challenge in this context would be, whatever LSR we propose in the second generation should keep in mind this declining trend in employment elasticity.

International Labour Standards and Social Clause

Revival of interest in the International labour standards is one of the most important impacts of globalization. International labour standards are those formulated by ILO by a consensus of 3 parties, employers, employees and government. It covers many areas of labour policy of relevance to member countries and ought to be seen as a set of goals for achievement. They emphasize human rights and the related workers' freedom of association, the right to collective bargaining, the prohibition of forced labour, equality of treatment and non-discrimination in employment, minimum age etc. ILS constitutes fundamental framework for the exercise of labour rights and provides stimulus to national action in formulating labour welfare and social security laws.

The most controversial issue, however, relates to ILO convention No. 138, which is concerned with minimum age of employment to protect children from working which amounts to a complete ban on child labour. But this convention has been ratified by a relatively few governments and none of the countries of South Asia, including India, has approved this because banning child labour in one stroke in these countries would almost be impossible.

However, globalization, has given rise to a number of interrelated concerns with respect to its social repercussions. These include its impact on employment environment, distribution of income and the role of labour standards. Globalisation's pressure for cost efficiency and economy increases the pains and sufferings of labour and therefore, the argument is labour standards should be set in the light of a more liberalized international trade policy.

At present U.S.A. is championing the cause of labour and pressurizing WTO for introducing 'social clause' to be followed by the member countries. The term social clause refers to a link between the international trade agreements and the observance of minimum labour standards and has become a non-tariff protection measure.

Despite the fact that India has enacted the Child Labour (Regulation) And abolition Act (1986), even today nearly 20% of the GDP is being contributed by child labour. This speaks of the difficulty in abolishing child labour in India. Naturally India opposed the social clause in WTO at Seattle negotiation. Moreover, child labour is a deep-rooted socio-economic problem in the country and cannot be done away with, by mere legislations and inserting social clause in WTO.

True, that any attempts to use to alter labour standards would necessarily affect developing countries. At the same time, blind opposition to link WTO and labour standards, would in the longrun hurt our interests. The more we oppose, the stronger will be the impression among consumers in the west that Indian goods are manufactured under abysmal labour standards and this affects the brand equity of Indian products.

In the background of all these developments, LSR in India creates new challenges say for eg., what should be or stand with regard to ILS and social clause, what modifications are necessary in the existing Child labour Act, how to reduce the magnitude of child labour how to protect their interest in the globalisation context etc. However the biggest challenge would be how to tackle the non-tariff barriers.

Policy Implications

The experience of LSRs in India and abroad reveal certain policy implications for this field.

1. Minimizing labour market rigidities is the need of the hour. However, in this context, detailed understanding of the challenges through case-by-case method is necessary. That is to say, the impact of the amendments/modifications of each one of the labour laws on labour market and their social security network needs a thorough study.
2. Removing the constraints on the implementation of exit policy.

3. There is the need for Government intervention altogether in a different role so as to counteract the adverse effects on LSR and the human face approach is absolutely necessary.
4. However, the entire social security network cannot be expected to be provided only by the Government, the role of employers and employees is equally important.
5. There is again a need for revamping the NRF for the second time so as to enable more training and redeployment of affected workers than merely financing VRS.
6. Educating the workers, trade unionists and even the politicians is necessary in order to mobilize their support for LSR.
7. The ILO can play a very effective role in smoothening the labour transition since it has the knowledge of bank to disseminate information to its member nations in order to enable them to take proper policy initiatives.
8. The role of Human Resource Management in respective industries in guiding and monitoring VRS and in counselling and advising the fruitful Investment of VRS amount can never be underestimated.

Conclusion

LSRs hold the key for successful transformation of the economy. Infact, globalisation effort would be paralysed in the absence of effective LSRs. The labour market rigidities in India have been a major road block to industrial competition. Some of the reforms introduced in the first generation were indeed bold but could not be implemented effectively due to various reasons. However, better prospects of economic reforms during the second generation, presupposes a competent and strict LSRs. It is quite satisfying to note that the latest union budget has outlined certain bold LSRs, pending since a decade, along with a well defined safety net for workers. Similarly the setting up of the second national commission on labour is also a welcoming development as the commission is busy in providing a road map to LSRs. The ground reality is that the labour policy needs to be returned in accordance with the requirements of globalization, if not the labour sufferings become much more serious.

It is true that LSR, creates a series of new challenges, but they have to be studied and understood in the right economic as well as human perspective. Although globalization intends to keep state intervention at a low profile, what is actually required is a changed role of the state, which formulates a series of countervailing measures to set right the adverse impact of globalization on labour. Streamlining and integrating scattered labour laws is a tough task. But the toughest challenge would be to educate the workers and trade union leaders in order to mobilize their support for LSR. Our labour problems are unique and hence demand a strong political will and determination. The golden solution of course, depends on converting the challenges into opportunities.

References

1. Horton, Kambar S.R. & Majundar D: Labour markets in the era of adjustment INL Review Vol. 130, No. 5-6, 1991.
2. Ratnam C.S.V. Managing people in a global business, New Delhi, 1992.
3. Seema Singh: New Economic Policy: Some implications for employment and labour market I.J.I.R., Vol. 28, No. 4, April 1993.
4. Sunil Guha: towards industrial dynamism and harmony, Oxford and I.B.H., New Delhi.
5. Rizwanul Islam: Social dynamism of economic reform in Asia ILO-SAAT, New Delhi, 1994.
6. G.S. Batia and Narendra: Globalisation strategies and economic liberalization, Anmol Pvt., New Delhi, 1995.

7. G.S. Saxena & J.S. Narayana Rao: Restructuring and surplus labour rehabilitation, Fredrich Best Stifstung, Delta Pub, New Delhi, 1995.
8. ILO: World Employment Report, Geneva, 1997.
9. Kirit S Parek (ed): India Development Report, 1999-2000 Oxford University Press, New Delhi.
10. Government of India: Ninth Plan Document.
11. K.R. Shyam Sundar: Second National Commission on Labour: Not up to the task EPW, July 22, 2000.
12. Leelavathi D.S.: Second National Commission on Labour: Agenda for Labour Sector Reforms, Southern Economist, May 1, 2001.
13. Sudha Deshponde and Lalit Deshponde: Impact of liberalization of labour market in India, EPW, Vol. XXXIII, No. 22, May 30, 1998.
14. Arunkumar; Major issues before trade unions in India, Indian Journal of Labour Economics, Vol. 42, No. 4, 1999.
15. Union Budget, 2002-2003.

Economics Times

1.	Labour laws still a far cry	20-05-2000
2.	A special report on labour reforms	01-07-2000
3.	Agenda for labour market reforms	08-08-2000
4.	How to enter the exit policy?	19-07-2000
5.	Labour flexibility for comparative edge	04-03-2001
6.	Amends to Act may ease contract licensing	06-03-2001
7.	Political dimensions of labour reforms	09-01-2002

29

Child Labour in India—A Micro Analysis of Mopidevi Mandal, Krishana District, A.P.

Prof N. Sudhakar Rao, Dr. P. Narasimha Rao & Sri. P.B.K. Prasad

Introduction

Labour in economics implies physical or mental exertion in anticipation of remuneration either in cash or in kind. The prevalence of child labour is one of the most important problems confronting the world at large, especially developing countries such as India. In spite of the several legalizations made to eliminate child labour, child labour almost in all the major countries in the world. Elimination of child labour is associated with social problems since many families in developing economics depend on children for their day-to-day livelihood. In the absence of child labour, these families will fall on street and their living is at stake. In spite of these hard realities, there is every need to eliminate child labour since it is associated with many social and economic issues. The present child is the future citizen of any country. Unless and otherwise children are sound, healthy and happy and the nation cannot progress well. Thus, child labour occupies an important position in the context of economic development of any country

Concept of Child/Child Labour

The census of India defines persons below the age of fourteen as children. As per the factories Act 1948, a child below fourteen years of age is not allowed to work in any factory. Rights of the child find a prominent place in the chapter of rights and guaranteed under the Indian constitution. Child labour means "The employment of children under a specified legal age. The United States department of labour defines child labour as "The employment of boys and girls when they are too young to work for hire, or when they are employed at jobs unsuitable or unsafe for children of their ages and under conditions injurious to their welfare". It is important and helpful to separate child work from child exploitation. The internationally recognized definition of exploitative child labour (under ILO Convention 138) focuses on labour that is likely to jeopardize the health, safety or morals of young persons less than 18 years or 16 tears where the health, safety and morals of young persons are fully protected. Accordingly to ILO child labour means full time work at too early an age; to many hours spent working; work that exerts under physical, social or psychological stress; work and life on streets in bad conditions; work that entails to much responsibility; work which hampers access to education and is detrimental to full social and psychological development, and work that undermines dignity and self esteem.

All most all countries in the world have unanimously resolved to end the exploitative practice of extracting labour from children. No nation can risk its children's lives. Child labour can be viewed as an economic practice and as a social evil as well. Exploitative child labour is undeniably a social evil. It hampers the mental, physical and psychological growth of children. Child labour robs the essential qualities of childhood, the child's future is doomed and the nation's future, depends upon, the health of children.

"Child labour" means according to the New Encyclopedia Britannica, Micropedia Vol. II, 15th edition (1978) p. 329 "the employment of children under a specified legal age". But the term 'child labour' is more meaningfully defined by the United States Department of Labour as "the employment of boys and girls when they are too young to work for hire, or when they are employed at jobs unsuitable or unsafe for children of their ages and under conditions injurious to their welfare."

"The term 'Child labour' is commonly interpreted in two different ways: First as an economic practice and secondly, as a social evil. In the first context it signifies employment of children in gainful occupations with a view to adding to the labour income of the family. It is in the second context that the term child labour is more generally used. In assessing the nature and extent of the social evil, it is necessary to take into account the character of the jobs on which they are exposed and the opportunities of development which they have been denied."

Need for the Study

There is a genuine need to reexamine the economics of child labour and children's contribution to their families by straining their nerves when they are supposed to study in schools. Would their families really crumble when the child is withdrawn from work and rehabilitated in schools? Could the employer be satisfied with comparatively low skills and old technological base of the child labourers in the context of globalization, which calls for high degree of efficiency to outweigh competition from abroad with highly advanced sophisticated methods of production? These questions are to be answered. Undoubtedly child labour is a serious multidimensional problem related to the poverty of the masses and their development. It should be approached in a comprehensive way. It has become clear that hast abolition would entail serious adverse economic effect, which can be described as cure worse than disease. The present study is an attempt to examine the incidence of child labour in the selected area exploring the different dimensions of the problem.

Child Labour A Global View

The accurate estimate of child labour, either from a qualitative or quantitative point of view is not possible. Children have been working in the houses and field from the advent of human civilization at an incredibly early age. Modern industry has exposed them to new challenges and total hazards.

Child labour is not confined to less developed countries alone. Even in advanced industrialized countries children work in hazardous as well as in the less exploitative occupations. Today children form a sizeable section of the labour force in several areas of employment. Though child labour is a global phenomenon, its incidence is more acute in the less developed countries.

The ILO report said some as young as 5 and as many as 25 per cent of all children between the ages of 10 and 14 are estimated to be working. Although it is difficult to pinpoint exactly how many are working, since so many are working illegally, the numbers have swelled especially in the developing world. According to recent report of the US Labour Department, more than 50 per cent of the world's estimated 100 million child labourers are in Asia and also constitute a large part of the work force in parts of Latin America and Africa. According to the US-Labour Department Report, in India 17.5 million, in Bangladesh 5.7 million, in Indonesia 2.2 million, in Nepal 3 million in Pakistan 2 million, in Philippines between 21 million and 5.7 million, in Thailand 4 million and in Egypt 4 million children are working. More than 80 million children in the Indian subcontinent are languishing in bondage today, working 14 to 16 hours a day in inhuman, unhygienic conditions as voiceless non-beings' said a report submitted to the United Nations Human Rights Conference in Vienna.

The UNICEF report dated 23rd May, 1995 revealed that horror stories of child trafficking and prostitution, forced labour and physical abuse in sweet shops, mines, factories, brick yards and domestic service in all regions. It also states that as many as 200 million of the world's children under 15 years of age spend most of their waking hours at work. They work at the risk of their survival, physical and mental development.

Child Labour in India

Incidence of child labour is very high in India. It is estimated that 1/3 of the child workers of Asia are in India. What is disquieting is that the number of child workers in labour force is increasing in India while it is declining world wide. Largest number of child labourers are found in agriculture. Its a paradox that high level of adult employment coexist with high incidence of child labour in India.

It has been assumed that a certain amount of child labour will persist in family enterprise, which is non-exploitative. Every third house in India has a working child, every fourth child in age of 5-15 is employed. At the same time there are other forms of child employment in hazardous trades, factories and other organized establishments, which should not be allowed to continue.

In 1971 census estimated child workers below the age of 15 year at 10.74 million. According to the global labour force estimates of the ILO every fifth child in the age group of 10-14 years was part of the country's active labour force. The number of child workers in India was estimated at 15.1 million in 1975. The NSS-32nd Round (1977-78) estimated child workers in the age group 5-14 at 16.25 million in 1978. According to 1981 census 13.6 million children are in the labour force (11.2 million as main workers and 2.4 million as marginal workers). As per the census of India 1981, activity wise distribution of main and marginal workers reveals that in all categories 11.17% children are main child workers. The per cent age of total child workers to total workers was 5.02%. The distribution of main workers to the total workers in the cultivators category was 4.34% in agriculture, 8.60% livestock, 14.10% mining and quarrying, 2.14% manufacturing, (households 3.50% and non-households 3.10%) construction 2.24%, Trade and commerce 1.76%, Transport, Storage and Communication 0.56% and others 1.67%.

In 1983, the planning commission had projected the number of child workers at 17.36 million.

According to the 43rd round of the National Sample Survey (1987), the number of working children was estimated to be 17 million. According to the 1991 census, there were 13.59 million working children in India. While the national sample survey revealed that the number is 17.36 million. According to O.R.G., working children in our country are around 44.0 million. Out of these about 21.0 per cent are in urban areas and the rest are in rural areas. The government of India announced that there are at present 20 million child labourers in India and 2 million are in hazardous occupations. Child labourers are increasing with increase in towns and cities due to globalization and urbanization. Child labour continues to concentrate in rural areas with nine out of ten working children living in villages. Thus child labour constitutes a major component in our population and there is a need for a study of child labour despite a number of earlier studies in the light of earlier studies and in the light of conflicting and changing views on child labour.

Policies and Programmes of Govt. of India

The constitution contains provisions for protection of children from work which is beyond their capacity, or involves long hours of work interfering with their education, recreation, rest and overall physical and mental development. Is also available under various industrial Acts and labour laws enacted from time to time. A number of other initiatives and programmes have been undertaken during the last decade or so, with the basic objective of dealing with the problem of child labourers.

The formulation of a National Child Labour Policy, 1987, the enactment of the Child Labour (prohibition and regulation) Act 1986, the setting up of a Task Force on child labour and the ratification of the child have all formed a part of this process. The National policy on Child Labour was formulated in 1987 which, apart from requiring enforcement of legal provisions to protect the interest of children, envisages focusing of general development programmes for the benefit of child labour and project-based plans of action in areas of high concentration of child labour. The drive for the elimination of child labour has received further impetus after the announcement of a new programme in August 1994 for the rehabilitation of children working in hazardous occupations. Under the programme an estimated 2 million children are to be withdrawn from employment and put in special schools to enable them to become productive members of the society. India has been participating in the International programme on Elimination of child Labour (IPEC) launched by the ILO on 1991. Recently the Government has announced the commitment for the elimination of child labour from all occupations and industries and makes primary education a fundamental right.

Thus, the Government of India has strongly committed to the elimination of child labour in hazardous occupations. It has set fourth the goals and practical plans of action. A child labour cell has been set up in the National Labour Institute, Noida with the assistance of the UNICEF. The cell would function as a national focal agency and undertakes functions of documentation, advocacy, public awareness, education, studies and training. In many under developed countries and especially in tribal economics, children contribute substantially to their family incomes. Children who are neither in school nor in work places are drawn into anti-social activities by selfish elements. Children are engaged in drug trafficking, child prostitution and child pornography. Thus child labour assumes many dimensions

All child work is not as hazardously exploitative as it is in industries like match-stick manufacturing, carpet weaving, glass-bangle-making, gem-polishing and diamond-cutting. But in many economic activities undertaken by the children, children are outrageously exploited. The bangle industry at Ferozpur exploits boys and girls paying a pittance of wage ranging from Rs. 3 to Rs. 4 a day. Their work continues for over 18 hours a day. India needs $5 billion to abolish. The depravation in the lives of the female children and the grinding labour of their working hours merits the attention of researchers, experts and policy makers.

Child Labour in Mopidevi Mandal-Sample Study

The main objective of the present study is to examine the nature of child labour through a sample study. In the present study an attempt has been made to conduct a survey through an interview schedule to elicit information on child labour; with regard to their socio-economic conditions in Mopidevi Mandal, Krishna Dist. A.P. The selection of the sample area is purposive. The study covered 5405 households in different villages of the mandal. The data was collected during July, 2000 to December 2000. All the villages in the mandal are taken for study. The village elders, senior adult workers and middlemen who supply child labour to the needy were contacted.

To select the sample, the entire Mandal was divided into 3 main clusters of villages. No. of households in the village and concentration of child labour in the village are given importance in arriving at the proportion of the sample to be taken.

Ten villages in the Mopidevi Mandal were selected for the study. Table 1 provides information on the number of households, number of child labour estimated and number of child labourers taken for study. 400 child labourers were considered for study. The estimated child labourers are 2000. Thus, study covered 20% of the population.

Table 1. Number of Villages in Households, and Estimated Child Labour

Sl.	*Name of the village*	*No. of*	*%*	*Estimated child*	*Labour*	*%*
No.		*Households*		*Child Labour*	*taken*	*7*
1.	Mopidevi	2011	37	500	100	25
2.	Mopidevi Lanka	159	3	-	-	-
3.	K.G. Kothapalem	1129	20	300	60	15
4.	North Cheruvu Lanka	473	10	250	50	12.5
5.	Nagayathippa	424	8	200	40	10
6.	Kokkuligadda	285	5	150	30	7.5
7.	Merakanapalli	281	5	150	30	7.5
8.	Porrurivaripalem	217	4	150	30	7.5
9.		215	4	150	30	7.5
	Total	**5405**	**100**	**2000**	**400**	**100**

Source: Computed.

Prohibited to work out of the four hundred child labourers 258 (64.5) are boys and 142 (35.5) are girls. It implies that boys outnumber girls in child labourers. The analysis of age distribution respondents reveal that most (54.4) of the child workers are in the age group of 8-11 i.e., 216 out of 400 are in these age groups. In the age group 8-11, 116 are boys and 110 are girls. Again, in the age group 11-14 out of 131 only 7 are girls. It implies that child labour prevalence is higher among girls when they are young, as age advances because of social factors, their prevalence is less. The more number of boys working in the age group 11-14 implies that economic necessities of the families sending children for work.

Table 2. Age and Sex Distribution of Child Labour

Sl. No.	*Name of the Village Labour*		*age & sex*			*Distribution*				*Total No. child*
			5-8			*8-11*				*11-14*
1.	Mopidevi	04	14	18	30	09	02	31	46	77
2.	Mopidevi Lanka	01	00	15	05	02	00	18	05	23
3.	K.G. Kothapalem	05	08	26	16	05	00	36	24	60
4.	NC Lanka	01	01	12	16	20	00	33	17	50
5.	Nagayathippa	02	01	13	12	12	00	27	13	40
6.	Kokkuligadda	02	04	04	10	10	00	27	13	40
7.	Merakanapalli	00	02	02	06	20	00	22	08	30
8.	Porrurivaripalem	01	02	03	04	20	00	24	06	30
9.	M.M. Lanka	02	03	03	04	18	00	23	07	30
10.	Bobbaralanka	00	00	10	07	08	05	18	12	30
	Total	**18**	**35**	**106**	**110**	**124**	**07**	**258**	**142**	**400**

Source: Computed.

Causes of Child Labour

Inadequate legislation, inefficient enforcement of child labour laws, poverty, illiteracy, unemployment, large number of children in poor families, single parent families, high school dropout rates especially in rural areas, repellent school atmosphere, illiteracy of parents, dependence of the poor on the income of their children, non committal official dom incharge of elimination of child labour and compulsory primary education, paucity of Government funds, all these factors are responsible for the continuation of the evil of exploitative child labour. This has been provided with statistical evidence by different researchers.

The neglect of rural areas changes in agricultural practices, marginalisation of traditional occupations, the displacement of huge populations by large-scale contributed to the pauperization of the countryside and rural people. This led to the migration of rural population including to the cities for survival. Unplanned, uncontrolled urbanization adds to the enormous increase in the number of slum dwellers whose children are left with no option other than earning their livelihood themselves. The economic distress suffered by the poor and larger sections of the population paved way to growing commercialization of child work, which is the evil outcome of under-development. Low level of development and misdistribution increases the incident of poverty and unemployment. These two evils are the principal causes of child labour in both rural and urban areas.

The causes of child labour are many and interrelated. Generally it may be said that children are compelled to work because of their poor socio-economic conditions. Though poverty is said to be the major cause of child labour it is not the only cause. The extent and nature of child labour are also influenced by the structure of the economy and the level and pace of development. Child labour in India is necessitated primarily by economic compulsions. Poverty and unemployment are the root cause of child labour in our country. Inequitable distribution of land and assets in our country has resulted in economic disparities.

Table 3. Occupational Structure of Respondents

S. No.	*Occupation*	*No. of Child Labour*					
		Boys	*%*	*Girls*	*%*	*Total*	
1.	Agriculture	192	69.5	84	30.5	276	100
2.	Hotel work	08	50.0	08	50.0	16	100
3.	Mechanics	22	100	00	-	22	100
4.	Cycle shops	08	100	00	-	08	100
5.	Domestic Servants	04	33.3	08	36.7	12	100
6.	Automobile	04	100	00	-	04	100
7.	Sweepers	04	33.3	08	36.7	12	100
8.	Cattle rearing	08	60.0	12	60.0	20	100
9.	Tailoring	02	16.6	10	83.4	12	100
10.	Hackers	06	33.3	12	66.7	18	100
	Total	**258**	**64.5**	**242**	**35.5**	**400**	**100**

Occupational Status

Children working in industries are not only child workers, child workers in all form of non-industrial occupations which are harmful to their physical, mental, moral and social development constitute the child labour force. Children work as bonded labourers, domestic labourers (including own household labourers) street and farm labourers.

Table 3 Provides information on the occupational status of the respondents. Most (69%) of the child labour work in agriculture. 276 out of 400 are working in agriculture. The next occupations are, automobile (5.5%) and cattle rearing (5%).

Table 4. Causes of Child Work Among Respondents

S. No.	*Cause*	*No. of Child Respondents*					
		Boys	*%*	*Girls*	*%*	*Total*	*%*
1.	Poverty	162	71.4	65	28.6	227	100
2.	Parental work	07	18.9	30	87.1	37	100
3.	Self Reliance	20	100	00	-	20	100
4.	Ignorance	23	47.9	25	52.1	48	100
5.	Death of Bre Winner	07	25.9	20	74.1	27	100
6.	Lack of interest in Education	26	100	00	-	26	100
7.	Repellent School atmosphere	13	86.7	02	13.3	15	100
	Total	**258**	**64.5**	**142**	**35.5**	**400**	**100**

Source: Computed

Table 4 provides information on causes of child labour to work. Poverty is the main cause. Out of 400 child labourers 227 (69%) are working because of poverty. These is so among both the sexes. The girls working because of parental force are more.

Income Status

Table 5 provides information on the income earned by the child labour per month. Most of the child labourers earn less than 300 per month. i.e., 220 out of 400 get less than 300-600 per month. Hardly three members that too boys are earning more than 900. This clearly shows that child labourers are exploited and paid very low wages.

Table 5. Income Distribution of the Respondents

S. No.	*Income per Month*	*No. of Child Labouer*					
		Boys	*%*	*Girls*	*%*	*Total*	*%*
1.	Less than	160	72.7	60	27.3	220	100
2.	Rs. 300-600	85	54.8	70	45.2	155	100
3.	Rs. 600-900	10	45.5	12	54.5	22	100
4.	Rs. 900 and above	03	100	00	-	03	100
	Total	**258**	**64.5**	**142**	**35.5**	**400**	**100**

Source: Computed.

Impact of Child Labour

Child labour effects physical, biological, psychological, social and economic development of a child. Practice of child labour jeopardizes the possibilities of their becoming productive adults and to take their legitimate place in the society. Putting children to work may be temporarily beneficial to the family, but costs heavily to the child as an individual, its family and the society at large. Unhappy and disturbed childhood experiences do not offer sound foundation for their future growth and development. Tender physique and biology of children are vulnerable to the hazardous tasks performed by them. Working children are easily esposed to biological disorders. Unclean, unhealthy working conditions prevailing in unorganized manufacturing units, contaminated drinking water and polluted air cost immune competency and debility in the Working children due to premature and underdeveloped biology. Viruses, bacteria and parasites easily enter into tender and pre-matured body system, affect digestive system and cause biological growth of children costing functional disorders in the organism resulting in reduced life span.

The basic requirements for normal psychological development of child are warm and accepting environment, stable parents who can understand child' emotional needs, conversational interchange, opportunities to play, discipline, supervision and support. Psychological development of child also needs increasing autonomy, independence, interaction with other children may take to nightmares, ill temper, lying and stealing habits. Consumption of drugs and tobacco smoking/alcohol are often some of the ways they choose to ward off despair and feeling of inadequacy.

Child labour costs a great loss of the society in terms of diminished value of human resource for future development of the society. Child labour practice means greater loss to the society in the form of diminishing contribution of adults, whose health, education and energies have been sacrificed during their childhood.

The net life-time earnings of a worker who starts working as a child labourer is likely to be much lower than that of a worker who joins the labour force as an adult after having gone through normal childhood, education and vocational training. Since child labourers are easily available at low wages with less personal problems to the employers, they are preferred to adult workers. A good number of children, street children in particular, are used for smuggling of contraband goods, sale or distribution of liquor and poisonous drugs. Such activities of children increase criminalisation of society and creates law and order problem for the law enforcing authorities. Thus child labour effects child's growth in many dimensions and there is every need to curb it.

Policy Measures to Compact Child Labour

In a civilized society child welfare needs to be given prominence, because the welfare of the entire community, it growth and development, depends on the health and well-being of its children. Children must be brought up in an atmosphere of love and affection and under the tender care and attention of parents, so that they may be able to attain full emotional, intellectual and spiritual stability and maturity and acquire self-confidence and self respect and a balanced view of life with full appreciation and realization of the role which they have to play in the nation building process without which the nation cannot develop and attain full prosperity because a large segment of the society would then be left out of the development process.

Policies of modern governments in relation to child labour and child development must be pragmatic and comprehensive. New and more down-to-earth ways of dealing with the multifactor problem of child labour are to be examined in the light of specific problems of specified regions. Areas differ in social, economic and cultural values and development.

Main causes of child labour are poverty, illiteracy among parents, large family and demand from employees because child labour is cheap and reliable. So, there is need for legislative measures for their improvement. Schooling for learning, child development programmes make the child work more creatively by making child an agent of social change through self esteem.

Summary and Conclusion

It is generally observed that child labour is a serious problem all over the world. It affects the development of a child in many dimentions. The prevalence of child labour is very high in India. It is estimated at 20 million in 2001. The Government of India has taken several measures to combat child labour.

The sample study conducted with the help of 400 child labourers in Mopidevi Mandal, Krishna Dist., Andhra Pradesh most of the child labourers are boys. The prevalence of child labour is high among girls in the age group of 5-8 and very low in 1-14 age group. Most (69%) of the child labourers are working in agriculture and allied activities. Poverty is the main reason for the child to work. The income earned by child labourers is very low. Most of them (55%) earn less than Rs. 300 per month. Hardly less than one per cent are earning more than Rs. 900.

Combating child labour is not an easy task. As it is a social evil, a social movement should be generated against this evil. Both Governments and non-governmental organizations need to develop a joint strategy and a comprehensive and pragmatic approach towards protection of working children of the world. The problem can be dealt with only through a series of short and long-term measures.

The study suggests that there is every need to eliminate child labour by adopting anti-poverty programmes in India. The immediate task of the Government should be to build a strong political will to discourage child labour.

30

Indian Economic Reforms, Labour Market Mechanisms and the Twenty-First Century Policy Imperatives

M.R. Khurana

In the wake of Indian economic reforms since June 1991, adequate research interest has not as yet begun to appear in matters pertaining to the evolving labour market mechanism(s). In view of such an important research lacuna, our primary focus, in the present paper, is on the issues as are of utmost importance in the context of workforce in India. In this regard, it is argued that the ongoing controversial labour market reforms as also the ones in the offing do not seem to be auguring well for the numerically growing Indian workforce, a segment of which has had the privilege of enjoying the benefits of a protected labour market throughout the post-independence growth experience. The paper also warns that in the absence of adequate, timely and appropriate safety nets, the forces of competition would unleash a reign of uncertainty so much so that the process of ongoing reforms may prove to be counter-productive or even backfire culminating into an environment in which development itself would become unsustainable. And with that happening, it is bound to spell doom not only for the workforce, but for the overall emerging scenario itself as well. To cope with such eventualities, the paper proposes an alternative focus that would offer better growth prospects together with increased employability of the growing workforce in India in the new millennium. What is actually desired is to have a thoughtful re-look at the various policy drives as are being presently contemplated. The local of real and robust policy imperatives in the twenty-first century, in our considered opinion, necessarily lie elsewhere.

The Concerns

Concerns have been expressed in some quarter in recent years with regard to the high incidence of unemployment/ underemployment[1] and low earnings of socially and economically disadvantaged groups of our society both in the rural and urban areas. These two segments of the Indian labour market, it needs to be noted in particular, operate side by side, and as such, the possibility of movement of the workers, across these areas cannot be ruled out altogether. A characteristic feature of the Indian labour market, inter alia, has been that while it is characterized by shortages in one segment of the market; there is continuing irregularity of employment coupled with low levels of earnings in the other, implying thereby that in an overall sense labour market clearing mechanism does not operate in the two. This, the relatively poor performance of Indian labour market(s) in terms of high incidence of unemployment/ underemployment in a particular sector (or even in the economy as a whole), has been attributed to the process of various institutions and regulations, which have prevented the functioning of the labour market clearing mechanism.'

It is being apprehended in these quarters that the impending adverse impact of economic reforms on the functioning of the labour market(s) is inevitable. Labelling the policy changes as economic turmoil rather than reforms, some well-meaning analysts of the ongoing process argue that the so called labour market reforms in vogue as also the ones[2] proposed to be undertaken in the near future do not seem to augur well for the Indian labour force. The forces of globalisation, in their opinion, would unleash a reign of uncertainty and great socio-economic deprivation on the workforce in India and, as such, would spell doom for it. It may not be altogether impertinent to point out here that in the emerging economic scenario, we will be developing as part of the global capitalist system. Viewed from this angle, recurring spells of business oscillations of increasing amplitude are bound to become an integral component of the envisaged capitalistic process of growth. This, coupled with growing volume of chronic unemployment/ underemployment that presently characterized our economy, the decline in domestic public sector outlets and outlays, and the emergence of absolute and relative immiserization of the proletariat in India, is not without foundations. Rather these are the inevitable ground level starkest realities, which seem to be staring us in the face. In view of this, therefore, it is quite likely that under the emerging dispensation, while the real wages might experience an upward escalation for a small segment of our working class as a whole would experience too notable a decline to be glossed over in view of its far reaching repercussions for the national economy in general, and for the working class as a whole in particular. Moreover, it is also being apprehended that the emerging process of capitalist growth, in addition to possibly causing the conditions of work to deteriorate and destroying the demand for skills together with its inherent tendency of reducing the workers to mechanical naught through the progressive penetration of mechanization, may be accompanied by acute pauperization, growing misery and mental degradation of the Indian working class, and finally also culminate into worsening of its socio-economic lot.

It is now being contended that the deliberate and conscious action taken by the state over the past couple of decades in the post-independence pre-reform period in India in regard to redistribution of income in favour of labour through a wide variety of ameliorative measures as assume critical significance from the viewpoint of socio-economic well-being of the working class, is bound to witness considerable erosion in the emerging scenario. With this happening, the protective character of the labour markets in India will, over the period of time, come under tremendous pressure with far reaching social and economic repercussions. In the ultimate analysis, one might come across a situation in which with the growing dilution of the state together with the heavy pressures of labour organizations getting eroded, there might be a reassertion of the famous classical basic economic tendency of wages to hover around the subsistence level. It is also being emphatically argued that the high standard of living which a small segment of the Indian populace belonging to the elite class in general and aristocracy of labour in particular will come to enjoy in the emerging scenario, would somehow be due to the ruthless exploitation of masses at the lower rung of the socio-economic ladder.

In sharp contract to the above, emphasis is being laid on the need to suitably amend the existing labour laws so as to fine-tune them in line with the practice, prevalent in other advanced capitalist economies of the world. The underlying argument in this regard, is that the existing laws cover only the organized labour force, which barely accounts for about 8.0 per cent of the total labour force in India. In other words, as high as 92.0 per cent of our working population in India does not derive virtually any benefit from the existing outdated laws, according to these sources. In fact, these laws, it is argued, actually constrain the growth of high quality employment in the organized sector, and to that extent are also detrimental to the interests of prospective job seekers in the labour market.[3] In view of this, therefore, some optimist observers of the process have come to believe that the perceived adverse effects of labour market reforms are somewhat over exaggerated. In support of their contention, they argue that historically, employment opportunities have expanded mani-fold and there is no reason to believe that this trend would now get reversed. Moreover, the workers are now becoming increasingly conscious of the fact that more children are a bane rather than a boon in respect of managing the household economy. This would lead to slowing down of the population growth at the lower rung of the socio-economic ladder and, coupled with their becoming increasingly education-conscious, would culminate into a situation in which the absolute number of workers would not swell as much as has hitherto been the case. The envisaged process of socio-economic modernization as is sought to be attained through the various policy drives underway, under such circumstances, they argue, would, in turn, bring about substantial gains to the working class in India. Furthermore, it is also observed that India's existing labour laws make firms bereft of the flexibility which otherwise is needed by them to operate successfully in the emerging highly competitive market[4]. To substantiate this line of thinking, it is being contended in some well-meaning circles that as of now, without getting the prior government permission, the firms scarcely have the flexibility in regard to retrenching of the labour force or close down a particular unit-establishment in the company even if the changing market conditions so warrant. Moreover, without following an expensive and time consuming cumbersome procedure, it is not possible to bring in the required changed in respect of the existing labour laws government employment and earnings of workers particularly in the organized sector of our economy. Consequently, the redeployment of the workers in diverse set of economic activities in times of need becomes an exceedingly difficult, if not an altogether impossible, proposition[5]. In addition, it is also being maintained that while the concerned laws principally aimed at providing protected employment/earnings to the workforce in the country experiencing great socio-economic deprivation owing to a wide variety of factors, yet in trying to do so these laws actually have, more often than not, tended to discourage the growth of new employment. Furthermore, while the emergence of such trend did not seem to be posing so serious a problem in the earlier period of post-independence planning particularly when the economy was ridden with controls owning to its more closed character, domestic competition was exceedingly limited, and also that the additional costs could simply be passed on to the consumers in the form of higher prices; this, nonetheless, does not seem to be compatible with the emerging situation when our economy is progressively opening up and is also gearing itself to face, inter alia, the onslaught of global competition. Under these circumstances, it seems quite plausible to argue that to cope with the emerging challenges of globalisation, the industrial sector in the country needs considerable flexibility in terms of downsizing the workforce when required to do so, and various other such measures.[6] To put the record straight, this viewpoint maintains that the existing labour laws in this regard act as a serious impediment to do the needful in respect of formidable emerging challenges. The resulting inflexibility proves detrimental from the viewpoint of free expansion of the business firms. Besides, it also prevents restructuring on their part which otherwise is imperatively needed by them improves upon their operational efficiency and also for creating a basis for future expansion of employment by them[7].

In addition, it is also being emphatically opined that since the existing provisions relating to the contract labour make it is difficult for establishment to outsource services, which have to be performed on the premises, these laws, therefore, also need to be appropriately amended. In this regard, it is felt that increased flexibility in this area would lead to a proliferation of smaller businesses that would provide economically useful services to the existing firms, which are otherwise unwilling to increase their own labour force. This, in turn, in addition to resulting into tremendous growth of small enterprises, would also make a significant contribution towards total employment generation in the economy[8].

Viewed in terms of the above, the ongoing process of reforms, underway in India since June 1991, constitutes an important event in the history of post-independence economic development of the country in that the national economic, since its very unfolding, has been experiencing some perceptible changes. The diverse set of reforms, undertaken as for now in the wake of economic reforms and the ones as are being currently contemplated to be introduced in respect of the functioning of the labour maket(s) in particular in the near future, have evoked a lot of interest among observers and analysts belonging to various disciplines. Accordingly, the possible socio-economic effects of various measures have, very rightly, tended to become issues of a lively debate and discussion. It is more so following the changes as currently and would be sweeping through the labour market(s) in the wake of the ongoing process under reference.

The preceding discussion makes it abundantly clear that polarized opinion has emerged in India in respect of actual and proposed labour sector reforms. The existence and accentuation of these aforementioned diametrically opposite viewpoints do indicate that the present and the proposed labour market reform(s) in India have many far-reaching socio-economic implications. Therefore, both from the academic and policy implications viewpoints, it unambiguously calls forth the need to examine the issues involved threadbare, spell out the various policy implications emanating from our discussion, and also, to pinpoint the policy imperatives to cope with the emerging challenges in respect of the functioning of the labour markets(s).

In view of the above, the main objectives of this study are, first, to understand the functioning of the labour market mechanism as it has tended to evolve itself during the pre- and post-economic reforms era since the dawn of independence and, second to focus on various policy imperatives to cope with the emerging challenges being and likely to be thrown by the ongoing process under reference. The paper is organized as follows. The preceding section I, focuses on the concerns taken up for examination in the paper. In section II, we describe the pre-reforms labour market scenario in India during the post independence era. An attempt has been made in section III to portray the labour market scenario as has tended to evolve itself in the post-economic reforms period. Section IV of the paper is devoted to an analysis of policy imperatives from the twenty-first century. And finally, section V of the paper presents a few concluding remarks.

An Overview of Pre-reform Indian Labour Market

In the preceding section, we focused on the concerns being expressed in various academic circles in respect of the evolving labour markets in India in the emerging scenario. It was observed that the high incidence of unemployment/underemployment in one sector of the economy and scarcity of workforce in the other signifies the manifestation of the non-functioning of the labour market clearing mechanism. With the objective of getting the necessary feedback to our study, we attempt below in this section a brief overview of the pre-reform study, we attempt below in this section a brief overview of the pre-reform Indian labour market of the post-independence period. Before doing so, it is nevertheless important to note in passing that throughout the post independence period, the generation of adequate and gainful employment opportunities in the economy to absorb the existing unemployed/underemployed as well as the increase in labour force has been one of the major and continuing concerns of national planners and policy makers. In this regard, employment policy as pursued from plan to plan, inter alia, has been focusing incessantly on the need for comprehensive programme of rural development having large employment creation potential, reducing underemployment for the majority of labour force, cutting down of long-term unemployment through the launching of several employment generation schemes, labour intensive public works programmes, adopting a suitable structure of investment and production envisaging promotion of appropriate types of technology and products (for domestic and foreign markets) in industries, and organizational support which would help to promote the growth of productive employment the idea underlying all these efforts has been the growing realization that in the absence of growth and diversification of the economic base of our economy, full employment at rising levels of productivity and incomes would, in any case, be feasible. Besides, the concerted efforts made by the government over the past couple of decades in the post-independence pre-reform period in India in regard to the redistribution of income in favour of the working class(or at least professedly so) have also appeared in various protective manifestations such as land reforms measures, factory acts, minimum was legislation, growth of the social services, progressive income tax, rise of inheritance tax, growth of trade unions, and a wide variety of such other ameliorative measures as assume critical significance from the viewpoint of its socio-economic well-being.

In view of the above, an important feature of the Indian labour market worth underlining in the 1970s is that it was characterized by the fact that unemployment/unemployment of workforce had already emerged as a major concern during the 1970s when it was recognized, for the first time in the post-independence period that poverty and unemployment were intertwined with each other[10]. This was indeed a great recognition in that prior to this, it had come to be commonly contended that there did not exist such a correlation between the two[11]. As against this, the prevalent viewpoint is that unemployment tends to breed unemployment and job displacement is followed by a lower trajectory for future earning after re-engagement. The combined effect of the two efforts will be particularly damaging not only in terms of exacerbating lifetime inequality, but also in bringing the threat of poverty and social exclusion.

The upshot of our discussion in this section is that in the economic development as experienced in the post independence pre-reforms period in India has been beneficial to the working class in more than one way. For instance, not only has the money wage rate per unit of time/work done recorded a notable increase during the period under reference, gains have also accrued to the workers in terms of several other manifestations mainly due to government intervention. The government, through various regulations and other protective devices has probably obstructed wage and earnings flexibility to some extent in the relatively small sized sectors of the economy. The unorganized sector workers have, in spite of their having constituted an overwhelmingly high proportion in the total workforce, remained largely uncovered. Apart from the government intervention, the other potentially important factor is, of course, the trade union movement. It is generally contended that the growth of union power has led not only to a higher rate of growth of real wages in the organized sector than elsewhere, but also to increased inflexibility of nominal and real wages in the concerned sector. The existing pre-reform legislation on hiring and firing, under these circumstances, is a more serious impediment to flexibility of adjustment and, as such, needs to be amended suitably to permit labour market mechanism(s) act uninterruptedly.

The Post-Reforms Scenario

The proposed reform seeks to target the existing labour market(s) and employment opportunities in the secondary and tertiary sectors, which were basically due to the adoption of the labour intensive industrialization as well as the rapid expansion of the public sector intervention in the period following immediately the post-independence. In the present section, we make an attempt to look at the evolving labour market(s) and various implications thereof.

What needs to be born in mind at the very outset of this section is that it is largely the degree of wage flexibility which, inter alia, conditions the ability of an economy to make those adjustments to its productive structure that are necessitated by exogenous events, without minimum damage to output and to employment. Accordingly, our discussion of Indian labour market is guided by this consideration and, as such, does not therefore examine the way in which relative wages or earnings are determined, or the extent to which they may fail to reflect the scarcity/abundance of labour of different kinds and in different sectors of the economy. Nevertheless, the view that the flexibility of relative wages is of utmost importance when the economy has to adjust itself to external events that cause a change in its terms of trade or balance of payments is not completely unknown to any curious observer of the functioning of the labour market, and least to an economist with a formal training inhuman resource development. But desirable adjustments of productive structure, regardless of underlying forces, also become easier of some flexibility does exist across sectors that permits and encourages the transfer of labour. What is also further required to be underlined is the fact that the existing pre-reform regulations regarding hiring and firing may also block the process of adjustment. As regards the factors accounting for the said inflexibility, institutional intervention in the market, according to the pro-reformers, thus far remains the major cause. While the process of evolution of our economy in the 40 years period preceding the process of economic reforms attempted to transfer many functions elsewhere, the responsibilities in regard to the social security of workers and educational functions had, directly or otherwise, largely been assumed by the state. Also, with the new economic policy in place, we are moving towards a new paradigm of development, which is significantly at variance with the earlier one. In view of this therefore labour market mechanism(s) in India, in the growlingly emerging process of progressive integration of the Indian economy with that of the global economy in general and labour sector reforms in particular, should be discussed in conjunction with the dynamics of employment and unemployment. Two important points, in this regard, in particular need to be noted here.

First, there is growing apprehension that labour market(s), in the emerging scenario, is (are) bound to experience important shocks owing basically to the fact that with the implementation of the proposed policy of hiring and firing of workers gathering momentum in the times to come, it is bound to make it exceedingly difficult on the part of the firms to continue to persist with the existing levels of employment[13]. This, in turn, is bound to generate a sort of hysteria in the labour market. The degree of incidence of unemployment/unemployment persistence may be asymmetric across various regions of the country. Any Second, the effect of incidence of unemployment on the level of earning would not be evenly spread across space. Some analysts of this type of labour market situation contend that employment interruption has no direct effect on future earning the young workers. Furthermore, although emergence of these effects on relatively young workers from extended duration of their unemployment cannot be ruled out altogether by any stretch of imagination, yet it is basically the class of middle aged workers, particularly in the group of 35 to 50 years and in higher level occupations, who would be bearing most of the brunt on this count[14].

At this stage, it certainly would be too presumptuous on our part to think that all unemployment could be eliminated in a fire labour market, which is sought to be evolved over the period of time. We must not obliterate an important fact that the functioning of the real labour market(s) across the country is characterized by imperfections that play important roles in system-evolution. There is no denial of the fact that competitive labour market should be capable of bringing about ex-post allocational efficiencies. As against this, these markets, in actual practice, fail because of uncertainty and the cost of collecting and analyzing relevant information. The presence of market imperfections implies that the efficiency of market mechanism in terms of labour force allocation efficiency cannot be guaranteed. Such a viewpoint obviously has far reaching welfare implications. What this implies in plain language is that regulations and government interventions are imperatively needed to ward off against market failures.

Another important point which ought to be noted in particular in respect of the emerging labour markets is that these markets would not adjust to changing conditions as rapidly as the markets for some other factors and commodities with which labour markets are often compared. It is owing to the fact that in comparison to other markets, information about relevant alternatives in labour markets would not be as widespread. This, together with other factors, would make the adjustment in labour markets quite sluggish. In view of this, therefore, while attempting to evaluate the efficiency of labour markets, it is imperatively important to examine the cause of sluggish adjustment in more details as also the appropriate necessary correctives in this regard.

In the emerging environment, it is quite likely that the firms requiring additional workers will hire job seekers, thereby reducing the community's pool of unemployment workers. In view of this, there is every possibility that some of the new jobs created might get filled up through promoting workers who are currently employed in the firm at less desirable jobs or at the relatively lower rung of the job ladder. It is quite possible that some workers will not change because of an improvement in alternative employment opportunities. In the event of firms' favouring to promote from within for manual workers, workers would be left with no choice except to enter at relatively low paid jobs, and earn promotions to a better job in due course of time through some combination of merit, experience and seniority. Also, as jobs would be created and destroyed, and employers and workers would attempt to seek suitable job matches, incidence of unemployment is bound to become a part of the ongoing process of workforce reallocation. The viewers of the macroeconomic efficiency gains as are expected to percolate from the process of economic reforms, however, seem to be too preoccupied with other considerations for reasons best-known to them that they seem to have become totally oblivious of the likely adverse effects on individuals, temporarily or permanently, from the reallocation process or from intervening spells of unemployment. It is not irrelevant to point out here that work experience cannot be accumulated during unemployment. There is therefore every likelihood that in the emerging scenario, the skills acquired previously may get substantially eroded or become totally redundant, or even the process of acquisition of the required new skills may get hampered to a considerable extent. Ultimately, there might emerge a situation in which the resulting unemployment/underemployment will be inevitably leading to lower earnings in future.

A distinctive feature of the Indian labour market has been in terms of the emergence, existence and persistence of dualism, it has been observed, becomes manifest in that owing to excessive pressure of population on land, wages in the agricultural sector tend to be considerably lower in comparison to those prevailing in the modern capitalist industrial sector. Furthermore, this dualism is explained by the fact that despite low wage due either to ignorance of better opportunities outside agriculture, or to their inability to obtain a modern sector job despite wishing to do so, or to the cost of moving being unacceptably high in relation to the expected wage premium, a preponderant majority of workers in the countryside, in spite of low prospects of eking out a reasonable living, remain confined to the traditional agricultural sector. Needless to over-emphasize, these low wages in the agricultural sector lead to low per capita income and this, in turn, results in low labour productivity. What needs to be underlined here is that it is the cheapness of the labour in the traditional agricultural sector that causes it to be employed extensively here in this sector, particularly to perform the tasks, which would be unprofitable at the modern wage rate, given the traditional mode of production.

It scarcely needs to be overemphasized here that the current and proposed process of reforms has a number of important implications for the emerging nature of labour market segmentation. First, in terms of duration of employment also, the workers in the farm sector will have significantly higher probability of retaining their employments than their secondary second counterparts. Also, in terms of avenues of promotion, while such opportunities do seem to exist, albeit on a limited scale, for the secondary sector workers; the agricultural sector, in the other hand, would operate more like an auction market. To put it pithily, while employers in the secondary sector use their wage offers to stimulate their workers' productivity; their agricultural sector counterparts, on the other hand, are prevented to do so for the obvious reasons. This has important implications in terms of labour turnover costs. As such, these costs assume significance mainly in the secondary sector and not in the agricultural sector. Owing to these reasons perhaps, one finds that while the secondary sector workers wield some market power, agricultural sector workers, on the other hand, do not seem to be fortunate enough in this regard. The latter sector workers, from this angle, are more competitive.

In tune with what has been observed above, it is quite likely that in the emerging scenario some firms would pay their workers higher wages than others would do, regardless of the occupations, age, and tenure groups from which the workers are drawn. Numerous studies conducted on this aspect of the functioning of the labour market(s) from time to time in the past have invariably shown that firm that pay comparatively high wages tend to have relatively high profits, high concentration ratios in product markets, high capital-labour ratios, and high density.

An important implication which follows from the preceding discussion is that in the emerging labour market environment, economic discrimination, in spite of its constituting an untidy area of analysis and also being characterized by controversy and a lack of consensus, will appear as one on its key features. More importantly, this discrimination would discern itself a variety of guises assuming different forms for different groups in terms of wage rate, employment opportunities, occupations/jobs and human capital formations. Needless to overemphasize, this discrimination, in whatever forms it occurs, will, it seems, be self-reinforcing and, as such, also tend to perpetuate itself. Imagining, that if the disadvantaged groups of the Indian workforce anticipated that the said discrimination would be exposed to frequent and prolonged spells of unemployment/underemployment, they would then rationally choose to invest less than otherwise in human capital formation. To put the record straight, the expectation of post-market discrimination will reduce the rate of return expected in investments in education and training, which will aggravate the compounding of the pre-market condition of inadequate preparation for many jobs. The disruption as also the very large social costs being currently witnessed in the aftermath of economic reforms in India also point towards growing social vulnerability. The loss of jobs and the resultant decline in wages will lead to huge decline in the standard of living of the workers. This, in turn, will have two important implications. First, the labour market mechanism(s) as would be emerging in the wake of economic reforms in India tends to suggest that the net outcome might be that of social exclusion on the part of individuals, families or even social groups. This, in turn, would growingly push them to sub-human conditions in slums, whose number, in any case, is on the rise. The socio-economic fallout of such a development is bound to witness considerable accentuation with many a deleterious consequence for the society as a whole. And Second, with certain industries' experiencing unusually large fluctuations in demand, their workers would, by every stretch of imagination, become peculiarly subject to frequent spells of unemployment/underemployment. Such fluctuations may be seasonal or they may get synchronized with the level of general economic activity. When most of a worker's job experience is in only one of these industries, he may resist moonlighting[22] elsewhere, which usually would be at lower wages than he is accustomed to earning, and remain unemployed for quite some time. And in view of the fact that certain firms and industries would become unusually prone to fluctuations in demand, large numbers of very desirable workers would, under these circumstances, often fall into the pool of unemployed labour while those clearly with inferior skills and capabilities would remain at work. This obviously, will have many socio-economic implications.

In sum, it can be maintained that since the number of unemployed/underemployed has been on the increase throughout the period of planning and given the underlying demographic factors, unemployment and poverty are bound to have increased in the years since the economic reforms were introduced. And the situation will probably worsen further, given the sort of economic scenario that is evolving.

The Policy Imperatives

In view of the fact that the pressing challenges for our national planners and policymakers at the moment, among other things, remain the acceleration of economic growth together with generation of gainful employment for the numerically growing workforce, what are then the various policy imperatives in respect of labour market mechanisms in the twenty-first century India? Before exploring this important policy matter, we must bear in mind that the envisaged labour market reforms attempting to change policy parameters to the advantage of the capitalist class are likely to further aggravate the overall unemployment/unemployment situation in the country. This situation in the labour market(s), therefore, would in all probability become somewhat more fluid. Under these circumstances, there is therefore a strong case of combining vision and wisdom with growing focus on expansionary labour demand management with such social meaningful reforms as might ensure the stimulation of employment in the times to come on a regular basis. Accordingly, the need of setting up the fostering of the pro-labour institutions as also the strengthening of the existing such institutions in the twenty-first century can scarcely be overemphasized. In out viewpoint promotion, providing resources that facilitate faster economic growth, creating a more pro-labour policy environment, improve the domestic institutions, and also act as innovations unemployment/underemployment reduction which normally characterizes the workforce. The real challenge, therefore, is to design mechanisms that will ensure that these very cherished objectives are translated into practice. While doing so, what must necessarily be borne in mind by planners and policymakers is that functioning of the labour market(s), unlike that of ordinary markets, is (are) governed as well as affected by customs, traditions and other such prevailing notions. It is also equally important to underline that institutional structures have a historical and social contact and what may work in one country/situation need not necessarily work in another, due to the existence of considerable degree of interdependence between labour market institutions on the one hand, and other social and economic structures of a country, on the other. In plain language, there is the need for building better safety nets for the poor. The alternative to this would be abroad to the disaster in that it would lead to utter imponderables in diverse spheres of our socio-economic lives. The policymakers, labour economists and social scientists in other related disciplines must realize that the problem of unemployment/underemployment in India is multi-dimensional in character. In view of this, what actually needs to be objectively appreciated before embarking on any strategy of sustainable employment generation, however, is that there are some key elements underlying all initiatives in this regard. Some such elements are achieving and sustaining of high economic growth rate as well as ensuring that majority of the prospective employment generating sectors are involved and benefit from the perceived economic growth. To this end, great focus needs to be laid on a process of manpower planning both at the macro and micro levels. While at the former level, it envisages to match an economy's overall requirements and availabilities of manpower; at the latter, on the other hand, it intends to assure an organization that it will have the proper number of properly qualified and motivated employees in its work force at some specified future time to carry on the work that will have to be done. There is, however, no denying the fact that depending upon a variety of objectives underlying the process of manpower planning by the individual firms, their manpower plan activities, in general, might considerably across firms, space and time. Any well-meaning manpower planning attempt at the firm or micro level, therefore, must necessarily encompass in its fold, forecasting, inventorying, determining problem areas and planning for future needs[23]. As regards the appropriate necessary correctives, which specifically merit serious consideration in outlining the blueprint of any strategy of employment generation to cope with emerging challenges of the twenty-first century, we feel the following can help the planners and policymakers to a considerable extent.

First, in view of the existence of mutually supportive relationship between economic growth and education, the provision of better and more efficient services in education and accelerated creation of productive employment opportunities in the primary, secondary and tertiary sectors are the important strategies to tackle the problem of unemployment/underemployment. The role of education in raising labour productivity and income levels has long been recognized. In fact, education or knowledge, through its impact on human capita formation, seems to be increasingly emerging as the mainspring of economic growth in modern times. There is, therefore, the need for the formulation and implementation of highly meaningful programme, which simultaneously raises labour productivity, provides gainful employment to their workforce on a sustained basis, raised its current income and also stimulates investment in the human capital of workers, and particularly their children, thereby raising their potential income. In fact, the belief that expanding education promotes economic growth has been a fundamental tenet of development strategy during the large part of the post-Second World War period. The basic institutional framework and the incentives that are built into education, undoubtedly, play a decisive role both in development and shaping the kinds of skills and knowledge that pay off. In this regard, the planners and policymakers in India have, nonetheless, to ensure that knowledge based skills to be created by education are in demand for doing the right kind of things. Such a need arises presumably, because it is quite possible that the bad institutional environment might produce a situation in which these skills would prove to be remunerative for individual workers but socially directed towards socially wasteful activities, signifying thereby a trade-off between individual and collective choice. We must take note of the fact that depending upon a wide variety of factors, the rate of growth of demand for educated labour would vary across regions. As a consequence, the regions with the same initial individual returns and equal subsequent expansion in the supply of educated labour would experience a situation in which the marginal returns to education would be falling dramatically, staying constant, or escalating upward. Again, while in some regions, the education would turn out to be essentially worthless and creates no skills whatsoever; in others, on the other hand, it is likely to become significantly effective in transmitting knowledge and skills.

Second, there is ample evidence which suggests that to begin with India's battle against poverty is to be fought in the rural sector in general and the agricultural sector in particular. Appropriate areas specific strategies in this regard need to be designed ensuring the forging and, strengthening of important inter-sectoral linkages on the one hand, and participation and empowerment of the women-folk in particular, on the other. This latter tasks can be accomplished through the expansion of job opportunities, particularly for women belonging to the poor labour households. The necessary correctives in this regard will have to be brought about by appropriate structural changes in our socio-economic set up so that they also become a party to the sharing of fruits of the resultant socio-economic transformation. Besides, adequate special measures would be required to be designed to provide sufficient safety nets in respect of the working children who have been, are and would continue to be subject to high degree of exploitation in diverse forms. In precise terms, increasing the demand for unskilled labour relative to its supply could be expected to be the major means of employment generation in the economy. This apart, there is, nevertheless, no denying the fact that agricultural development alone would be inadequate to significantly reduce unemployment/underemployment and its other various correlates. It must be supplemented by rural industrialization, creation of non-farm employment; time-bound effective population control programmes, community development and rural urbanisation. These rural development programmes, together with the provision of infrastructure, basic needs and welfare programmes, would serve to better the quality of life and well-being of the rural population as well as bring about greater integration between the rural sector and the national economy. In fact, it is the growth of the non-farm sector in the interior of the Indian countryside as also in the periphery of the urban areas, which assumes critical significance from the viewpoint of sustained employment generation. A remarkable increase in the non-farm employment as supplementary sources to agriculture employment opportunities can play a critical role in meeting the emerging challenge of overall employment generation on a lasting basis. For this purpose, growingly concerted efforts are needed to be directed towards the development of appropriate infra-structural, institutional and technological factors the synchronization of which would condition the pace and pattern of growth in the future. Needless to over emphasis, in view of considerable diversity across various regions of the country, area specific plans in terms of decentralized planning need to be drawn and implemented through participatory development mechanism and embodying the involvement of Self-Help groups in this regard.

Third, we must become oblivious of the fact that an overwhelmingly high proportion of our workforce is and would also continue to work in the unorganized sector as attached and non-attached farm servants, construction workers, rickshaw pullers, porters, hawkers in restaurants and shops, and such other diverse set of economic activities in the informal sector economy. The workers engaged in the unorganized sector have been, are and would also continue to be deprived of even a barest minimum possible social security support. The lack of reliable social security system for them, it needs to be pointed out, would not only be their loss, it would, rather, also be the loss of their employers as well as that of our national economy presumably because their sickness and absenteeism would have a direct telling effect on their productivity and hence of the financial bottom lines of their employers. In view of this, nation's commitment to ensuring social security for workers in general and the ones in the unorganized sector in particular can scarcely be overemphasized. What, however, needs to be emphasized is that social security need not necessarily be exclusively state-funded in the emerging scenario. To cut the matter short, it can be argued that there is no need for relying solely on bureaucracy and the government agencies for implementing/enforcing the social security schemes both in respect of the organized and unorganized sectors. Ample incentives and disincentives are therefore required to be created so that employers of unorganized workers themselves come forward to provide for social security of their workforce. The state at best, in such case, should play the role of a regulator and facilitator. It should, however, continue to contribute generously to various social security schemes for the poorest of the poor. These schemes may be run by various government agencies, private companies and social organizations, ensuring proper enforceability, transparency and accountability. Concerted efforts therefore are required to be made to strengthen and activate all the non-government providers of social security to the workers who, in turn, can become an excellent interface between the vast unorganized sectors on the one hand, and the state and other organized providers of social security on the other.

Fourth, a world for the union as well. What would be required of them in the emerging scenario is that they will have to do serious introduction and also make a serious attempt to rid themselves of their tainted members so that they become socially more acceptable. It would not be impertinent to mention here that to us, particularly from a longer-term viewpoint, certain labour force trends that are likely to restrict the growth of unions are discernible owing to several reasons. First, the white-coolar jobs would be shrinking to the labour force. Second, it is quite likely that the workers in these jobs, particularly those at the upper rung of the wages ladder, would resist unionization. And finally, likewise trend would be discerned in respect of female workers, whose proportion, in any case, is going to remain substantial in relation to the overall labour force.

Fifth, in any strategy of employment generation on sustainable basis, the importance of education, health, nutrition and sanitation cannot be overemphasized at all. The programmes relating to these socio-economic activities, in fact, are considered to be the main levers for raising the level of well being of the people in general. There is need for intensifying the development efforts with special focus on economic infrastructure such as education, health, nutrition and sanitation and a host of other such activities. The economy must however, over the period of time, begin to learn to develop its capacity to finance programmes, which tend to promote the social welfare of the masses in terms of cost effectiveness and their optimal use.

And finally, as regards the implementation of the policy measures, we are of the firm opinion that the haphazard and inappropriate implementation of labour market reforms, whereby policy parameters attempted to be changed inadequately and inappropriately in haste, would prove to be counterproductive in overcoming the problems being thrown by the process of economic reforms. The main reason is that the socio-economic fabric of tour society is not as simple as it seems to be. Any solution, sought to be attained through adhoc measures, is bound to add to our complacency and prove suicidal for the economy. Many of the labour market adjustments may not turn out to be complementary as in being contemplated by our present breed of planners and policymakers. Under these circumstances, therefore, a judicious-mix of policy measures must ensure a thoughtful and well-planned combination of expansionary labour demand management with bold policy initiative to stimulate employment generation together with a growing focus on skill formation and effective control of numerically rapidly growing population at the lower rung of our socio-economic ladder. An imminent alternative to this is, in our considered opinion, sheer chaos and disaster in terms of indicators of social and economic development.

The Concluding Remarks

We are aware of the fact we have crossed the threshold into the twenty-first century. As such, we find ourselves at that juncture of the new millennium where, we have to tread a very long as well as an arduous path. Accordingly, we shall not attempt to summarize the main point of this paper. Instead, for putting the discussion in perspective, we prefer to make a few concluding remarks.

First, we have not been particularly successful in identifying the strategies that lead to accelerated economic growth together with gainful employment generation for the existing as well as additions to the workforce either in the pre-post-reforms periods throughout the post independence era. While, we have some important accomplishments to gloat over, we have several failures too in this regard. To be more specific, while formulating strategies to cope with the future emerging challenges, reasons underlying our failures must not be glossed over.

Second, it must be amply clear to our planners and policymakers that half-backed and adhoc solutions to the multi-dimensional problem of unemployment/ underemployment and its other correlated, as has largely hitherto been the case, would lead us nowhere. These would rather compound our problems future. It is time that the unemployed/underemployed are made more productive through a well-conceived and equally well-implemented strategy aiming at cognitive skill formation.

Third, because of the predominantly rural base of our economy, all future strategies of gainful employment generation must essentially begin to focus on rural development is general with agricultural development as their essential kingpin, primarily because roughly three-forth of our total population and nearly three-fifth of our working population continue to be in one way or another, closely tied with these areas in socio-economic terms. Neglecting rural areas, in any perceived strategy of socio-economic development, implies excluding an overwhelmingly high proportion of our population form the mainstream process. Besides focusing on the sector, priority also needs to be accorded to the development of a sound and enduring non-farm sector for the creation of gainful employment in the rural areas.

While financial institutions can be roped in to meet the credit requirements of non-farm sector; Self-Help Groups, on the other hand, can also be involved as financial intermediaries to promote the sustainable growth of this sector. In brief, in sharp contrast to realization of the urban areas as presently in the case, concerted efforts are required to be made in regard to urbanization of rural areas through the provision of necessary area specific-structural and other amenities of socio-economic betterment of the masses. It should be amply clear to our planners and policy makers that any deviation from this would tantamount to groping in the dark.

Fourth, whether the disparate experience of the controlled population growth can be effectively combined with indicators of perceived socio-economic transformation with working class becoming willing partner in it will, in all probability, continue to remain a daunting challenge for Indian planners and policymakers of the country. This issues will require utmost and urgent attention in terms of formulation and implementation of innovative strategies of generation of gainful employment. As such, it will indeed be a testing time for them.

Finally, as of now, much seems to be at stake in the future in view of the emerging socio-economic trends in our society on the one hand, and our options becoming increasingly limited on this count on the other. We have to choose between sustained egalitarian set up in terms of indicators of scio-economic transformation or imminent disaster which, in view of the recent Gujarat events involving communal frenzy and catching up of the unfortunate process of withering away of the Indian nation, seems to be very clearly staring at us in the face. Choice obviously is our own.

Bibliography

1. Acemoglu, D. (2000), "Technical Change, Inequality, and the Labour market", National Bureau of Economic Research, Working Paper No. 7800.

2. Aghion, P. and Howitt, P. (1996), "Research and Development in the Growth Process", Journal of Economic Growth, Vol. 1, pp. 49-74.

3. Ahluwalia, Montek S (2001), 'Economic Reforms- a Policy Agenda for the Future", in Uma Kapila and Raj eds. (2001), "India's Economy in the 21st Century", Academic Foundation, Delhi, pp. 70-91.

4. Allen, Tim and Alan, Thomas (2000), "Poverty and Development", Oxford University Press, New York.

5. Arulampalam, W, Booth, A.L. and Taylor, M.P. (2000), "Unemployment Persistence", Oxford Economic Papers, Vol. 52, pp. 24-50.

6. Becker, Gary S (1957), "The Economics of Discrimination", University of Chicago Press, Chicago.

31

Reforms and Social Security in India

Prof. K.M. Naidu, Prof. K.S. Naidu & P. Manjushree

In the context of implementation of economic reforms, the experts on labour studies began to know the impact of reforms on social security of workers, more so on the labour working in the unorganized sector. So much so, the study in this direction has received higher attention from academics, policy makers, multilateral organizations and non-governmental organizations. It has gained the status of a growth industry (see Van Ginnerkan 1997, 1998, Jhabwala and Subramanya 2000, Seeta Prabhu 2001.)

As the economy undergoes change and as societies develop, there emerges a need for social security to those who lack an income due to disability, old age, death of main earner, maternity, unemployment, injury at work place etc. The Government of India as in other developing countries have small programmes and not very extensive and hence cover only a small part of working population not exceeding 10% the organized sector. Even here the amounts allotted, are meagre and being reduced every year since 1990 when even the government experienced resource crunch. The interest in this subject of social security gained much significance after the award of Noble Prize in Economics to Prof. Amartya K. Sen in 1998 for his outstanding contributions in the field of welfare economics and his stress on capability, empowerment, entitlement, efficient allocation of resources, poverty, unemployment etc. Social Security is used in a broader sense in developing countries than that is observed in developed countries. The content of social security measures differ, depending on country's economic development. On the whole, the social security made available by government or private effort helps in raising the living standards of the people that are covered. The paper attempts to analyse the spread and impact of social security in India after implementation of economic reforms. The definition and issues on social security of labour are covered in section 2, how the growth promoting policies help the labour is explained is section 3, the supported social security programmes are analysed in section 4 and last section (5) examines effectiveness of social security programmes.

Definition and Issues

Beveridge committee Report (1942) defines social security as "Freedom from want". But in practice its provision was confined to only three aspects-Children's allowances, comprehensive health and rehabilitation services and maintenance, of employment to avoid mass unemployment. The most authoritative definition on social security emerged from the efforts of the ILO (Parott 1992) and led to identification of costs of social security provisions (with the heads on which the social security departments of public bodies incurred expenditures and the costs in different countries were published in 1952 at the 35th session of International Labour Conference of the Social security (Minimum standards) convention (102). According to the ILO the term social security has been used to refer to "the result achieved by a comprehensive and successful series of measures for protecting the public (or a large sector of it) from the economic distress that, in the absence of such measures, would be caused by the stoppage of earnings in sickness, unemployment or old age and after death, for making available to the same public, medical care as needed and for subsidizing families bringing up young children". The above definitions aim is provision of relief mainly to workers from particular contingencies and action. The circumstances which forced the adoption of definition were forgotten and the institutional definition was accepted as the official definition of the ILO. In this process the emphasis by Beveridge committee Report on freedom from Want was sidelined. The net result is that the social security measures are mostly confined to the organized sector workers only. Even here the record of government of India by way of budgetary allocation as well as legislative measures and its implementation leave much to be desired as they are inadequate and less than needed. Moreover in India 90% of the Indian workers are to be found working in unorganized sector whose coverage was completely neglected. The economic reforms initiated by government were mainly meant to benefit elite and richer section of social and hence mostly neglected poor and weaker sections in the society and labour markets in India. The suffering of these people instead of reducing, steadily increases after the implementation of economic reforms.

Increasing interest in economic globalisation led to increasing interest envinced by developing countries and development organization like UNDP and the world Bank resulting in new concepts and approaches in social security. The Western idea about social security does not cover high degree of deprivation and vulnerability of the majority of population seen in developing countries. Discussion on social security began to emphasize social risk management and human security. This necessitated public measures to help individual, households, communities and groups in managing income risks to reduce vulnerability, improve consumption, and enhance equity while making efforts to develop the economy, while income security and human security to over come deprivation so as to ensure the safety of all people (through better standard of living) and this led to thinking on social structures and practices. Social security has to be seen, therefore, in terms of safety from chronic threats like hunger, disease and protection from sudden and hurtful descriptions in the regular daily life-may be in homes, in jobs or in communities (UNDP, 1994). It took security to mean methods to promote human development and defined it in terms of protection against human deprivation. Human development is taken as a social security measure. But the latter mainly aims at removing vulnerability by preventing a decline in living standards in general and promoting basic living standards during economic failures.

As per the scientific view the concern with social security is mainly related to direct role that public action can play in reducing human deprivation and eliminating vulnerability in developing countries. The emphasis is on the use of efficient means (publication) to follow necessary objectives (reduction of deprivation and vulnerability). This action is justified because "many developing countries have large shares of employment in unorganized/informal section and workers in this sector do not have access to the benefits of traditional social security measures".

The Issues

The organized sector covers the Government sector, the public sector and the private organized section. The workers in this three categories have the facility of conventional types of social security schemes. In the nineties nearly 26 million workers were organized out of 262.3 million workers (10%) in India. Social security schemes in the organized sector are divided into three types (a) employee liability scheme, (b) Social relevance schemes and (c) Provident funds. Even these schemes are not working well as found in the government report; eg. The Maharashtra's Employment State Insurance Scheme reported that the ESIS is not helping the beneficiaries. The schemes suffer from corruption and the facilities in the hospitals are very poor besides the negligence of those concerned. Moreover the workers are dissatisfied with ESIS Scheme due to its inadequate funds, insufficient medicines, improper care etc.

Table 1. Organised and Unorganised Workers and Percentage Share of Unorganised Workers in the Total: 1999-2000

Sector	*Organised Workers (millions)*	*Unorganised workers (millions)*	*Total workers (millions)*	*Share of Unorganised sector (per cent)*
Ag. allied activities	1.39	236.11	237.61	99.42
Mining quarrying	1.01	1.25	2.26	55.31
Manufacturing incl. Repair services	6.79	37.27	44.02	84.67
Electricity, gas and water	1.00	0.05	1.05	4.76
Construction	1.18	16.41	17.59	93.29
Trade, hotel & restaurants	0.49	40.77	41.26	98.81
Transport, Storage & Communication	3.15	11.59	14.74	78.63
Financial Services	1.65	3.37	5.02	67.13
Community, social & personal services	11.49	21.95	33.44	65.64
All Sectors (Total)	**28.11**	**368.89**	**397.00**	**92.92**

Source: Computed from GOI (2001).

Inspite of these difficulties, there is some help from government for organized workers, but one can see total negligence or workers in the unorganized sector.

There are six types of unorganized rural labour (Sankaran 1996) like agricultural labours, weavers, rural artisans. Fishermen, salt workers, construction workers etc., besides workers in urban informal sector, in which majority form migrants from rural labour in search of employment in urban are as nearly 93% of workers were in unorganized sector in 1999-2000. Even in manufacturing sector, more than 80% of total workers were in the unorganized sector. Likewise service sector has large share of unorganized workers.

Inspite of shift to non-form sector in rural areas, agriculture has 71% of males and 85% of females. After inclusion of urban areas, agriculture accounts for 60% of workers in 1999-2000 (see table No. 2). This points to dominance of unorganized sector in agriculture.

In the case of organized workers, there is need for measures to protect their income in the circumstances that deprive them of income or to reduce it. But in the case of unorganized labour with no regular employment and assured income, the need is for employment security and improvement in quality of employment. In both the cases, the primary concern is protection of regular income so as to make them live a better quality life.

However major issues are:

(a) low employment growth inspite of high GDP growth, as growth of employment dropped from 2% per annum during 1983 to 1993-94 to less than one per cent per annum between 1993-94 to 1999-2000. It means that post-reforms period witnessed jobless growth, putting unemployed (including workers in closed units) to severe deprivation and low levels of living.

Table 2. Sectoral Distribution of Workers at One Digit Level: Rural India, 1977-78 to 1999-00

Sectors	*1977-78*	*1983*	*1987-88*	*1993-94*	*1999-00*
		Rural Persons			
Agriculture & Allied	83.4	81.5	78.3	78.4	76.3
Mining & Quarrying	0.4	0.5	0.6	0.6	0.5
Manufacturing	6.2	6.8	7.2	7.0	7.4
Electricity, gas & water	0.1	0.1	0.2	0.2	0.2
Construction	1.3	1.6	3.3	2.4	3.3
Trade, hotels and restaurants	3.3	3.4	4.0	4.3	5.1
Transport, storage, communication	0.8	1.1	1.3	1.4	2.1
Services	4.5	4.9	5.1	5.7	5.2
All	100.0	100.0	100.0	100.0	100.0
		Rural Males			
Agriculture & Allied	80.7	77.8	74.6	74.0	71.4
Mining & Quarrying	0.5	0.6	0.7	0.7	0.6
Manufacturing	6.4	7.0	7.4	7.0	7.3
Electricity, gas & water	0.2	0.2	0.3	0.3	0.2
Construction	1.7	2.2	3.7	3.2	4.5
Trade, hotels and restaurants	4.0	4.4	5.1	5.5	6.8
Transport, storage, communication	1.2	1.7	2.0	2.2	3.2
Service	5.3	6.1	6.2	7.1	6.1
All	100.0	100.0	100.0	100.0	100.0
		Rural Females			
Agriculture & Allied	88.2	87.5	84.7	86.2	85.4
Mining & Quarrying	0.2	0.3	0.4	0.4	0.7
Manufacturing	5.9	6.4	6.9	7.1	7.6
Electricity, gas & water	-	-	-	-	-
Construction	0.6	0.7	2.7	0.8	1.1
Trade, hotels and restaurants	2.0	1.9	2.1	2.1	2.0
Transport, storage, communication	0.1	0.1	0.1	0.1	0.1
Services	3.0	2.8	3.0	3.4	3.7
All	100.0	100.0	100.0	100.0	100.0

Source: Visaria, 1999 and NSSO 2000.

(b) The other important issue faced by workers is actualization and marginalisation of workers, for eg. the percentage of casual labourers for males and females in rural areas rose by 11.8% (22 to 33.8%) and 7.3%. (31.4 to 38.7%) respectively between 1972-73 and 1993-94. Similarly due to closure of many units substantial percent of workers (20 to 50%) have become marginalized pushing them to low levels of living and into social problems.

(c) The effect of jobless growth has been neutralized by self-employment process which is without heavy burden on the poor and weaker sections of society. No doubt the proportion of self-employed declined, yet their percentage is very high at 53% in India in 1999-2000 and the same was 58%, 40% and 48% respectively in agriculture, secondary sector and tertiary sector.

(d) The sufferings of poor workers and the nature and quality of employment. Unemployment as such is not a problem in India. Workers in organized sector are thrown out of employment suddenly and face problem in finding alternative job simultaneously or after some time. This forces them to seek work in urorganized sector. Naturally many people are forced to work in unorganized sector whose nature and quality are: low earnings, poor working conditions, lack of (social security) protection, contract nature of work etc. On account of these characteristics, the incidence of poverty is highest for casual labour in both rural and urban areas. In 1993-94 (and even 1994-2000 as per world Bank study) 50% of workers were below poverty line (49.4% in rural areas and 57% in urban areas). As per NSS data latest round (43) the incidence of poverty declined during the last decade (Table No. 3). But the World Bank Study estimated for 1999-2000 that 50% of people are living below poverty line which applies equally to workers. The only saving point is that rate of decline in poverty in share, was the lowest for casual workers and highest for regular workers. It is therefore to be inferred that casualisation be related to marginalisation and immiseration in the form of low income and poor living. The other observation is that suffering from poverty for casual labourers and self employed was more than that experienced by the unemployed.

Table 3. Incidence of Poverty by for Workers and Unemployed: 1993 to 1993-94 (%)

Worker Types	*Rural*			*Urban*		
	1983	*1987-88*	*1993-94*	*1983*	*1987-88*	*1993-94*
Self Employed	38.5	32.4	28.3	44.3	41.2	34.0
Regular Employed	32.7	26.5	17.5	26.9	24.5	18.3
Casual Labourers	59.3	52.0	49.4	62.9	63.9	57.0
Total Workers	44.8	38.4	35.2	40.8	38.4	32.0
Unemployed	33.0	38.5	21.1	40.1	36.0	27.1

Source: Estimated by the Author Based on NSS data.

Growth Promoting Policies

Based on the economic strength of the economy, a country adopts a programme. To suit their convenience different schemes are advocated. Two approaches have been suggested by Dreze and Sen (1989) for raising the living standards of workers. The first approach emphasizes promotion of economic growth to raise private and public incomes. This they called 'Growth mediated security". The second is named by them as 'Support led-security'. In the latter higher support is extended to areas like employment provision, income redistribution, health care, education and social assistance to help improve distribution without waiting for a change in the level of general efficiency. Government effort alone is sufficient to provide social and economic security to the poor. Hence there is need for public and private co-operation to effectively implement growth-mediated and support-led security measures. Private effort means steps taken by private business firms, NGO's community based organization etc.

Broadly the government followed a dual policy strategy in providing social security for the organized workers (10% of work force) 7% as on March 2002 as out of 40 crores workers the organized sector has only 2.8 crores. In this 86 lakhs workers are in private sector (3%) and the balance 97% are employed in public sector. Bharat Junjunwala (the Eenadu March 23, 2002 p. 3) the government implemented many social security schemes through different legislations. These schemes are mostly, funded by employment and some by employees. Employers liability is for accident relief and maternity benefits, social insurance for health benefits through contributions from employers and employees; social assistance through welfare fund legislations funded through taxes on employers, retired benefits like provident funds, pension and gratuity, which are saving schemes made available with joint contributions from employees and employers. Excepting gratuity, all these schemes are mostly funded by employers and administered by government. Eg. 12% of wages on provident fund, 4.81% by way of gratuity, 4% by way of ESI contribution, and 8.33% (loss making units) upto 20% (profit making units) by way of loans are contributed by employers. The total cost to companies on social security and welfare benefits accounts for 40% of the wage bill. Apart from these benefits, employees run mutual benefit thrift societies, consumer cooperatives with support from employers.

India depended on both growth promoting and support led policies to help the unorganized workers. In the case of support-led policies the country relied on promotional measures like self-employment and wage employment programmes, general health, education etc. It is practically impossible financially unfeasible to cover with social security benefits for all the poor workers as the poor are so large and their problems so massive. Even the programme of unemployment benefit in India would be highly costly and administrative complex. Hence India relied on promotional forms, direct anti-poverty programmes, as against protective interventions.

Growth promoting policies emphasize and aim at increasing employment opportunities and quality of employment with are expected to improve social and economic security for the unorganized workers. This means policy thrust for growth as well as structural changes in the economy as a whole (GOI 2001) the task force on employment opportunities (GOI 2001) identified five areas which form the strategy for employment generation. They are 1) accelerating the rate of growth of GDP particularly the sectors whose spread will help low income segments of labour force 2) appropriate sectorial policies in individual sectors. 3) implementation of particular special programmes for creating additional employment, helping vulnerable groups (by passed by general growth policies, 4) adopting appropriate policies fro education and skill development to upgrade quality of labour force so as to create high quality-jobs, 5) ensuring that the policy and legal conditions relating to labour market encourage labour absorption, particularly in the organized sector (GOI 2001). In these 1,2 and 4 relate to growth promoting and skill improvement policies and 3 relates to support led policies, but 5 pertains only to organized sector. In the growth promoting security policy, the government role is limited to as facilitator or motivator for private investment and for skill improvements.

The growth promoting policies need support form removal of anti-poor laws, setting right market failures and adoption of appropriate macro and micro strategies.

Anti-poor laws have to be rectified to help the poor person, farmer, small trader to establish units of their own.

Eg. Tribal should cultivate land with the support of forest laws, a farmer and a trader should be able to establish without a licence a brick plant, a rice shelling plant, cold storage etc to increase non-farm activities in the rural areas.

Macro strategies should concentrate on growth of agriculture particularly in rainfed areas so that labour force may move from agriculture to rural non-farm activities which would also reduce rural poverty. The sub or allied sectors like poultry, dairy, fisheries and forestry be promoted to increase employment.

Relating to micro strategies, there is need to concentrate on a few selected growth engines. Infrastructure facilities in rural areas be sufficiently improved to help rural growth.

Labour market failures be avoided by shortage of agricultural labour in coastal region and in urban manual activities coexist with a large amount of seasonal unemployment in dry areas; unemployment for powerlooms and handloom workers coexist with a shortage of garment workers at Approach export parks. Such failures be eliminated.

Even credit market failure, commodity and product market failure be removed. Infrastructure constraints like of power, communication facilities hamper growth activities. Here government and private effort in unison remove the failures to create more jobs for the benefit of the poor and unemployed.

Support Led Social Security Programmes

India adopted the following schemes as support led security programmes.

1. Land reforms and its equitable distribution to help the poor residing in rural areas.
2. Promotional social security programmes like:

(a) Wage employment programmes like EGS, JRY

(b) Self employment programmes like IRDP and SGSY.

(c) Providing basic needs: primary education, basic health services etc.

(d) Public distribution system, PDS, and nutrition programmes such as Integrated Development Services (ICDS) and midday meal schemes.

(e) Elimination of social exclusion: Reservation for some Classes. Some of the above programmes may also be taken as protective measures.

3. Protective social security measures: These are provided both at the National and State level with the aim of giving financial cushion against unexpected poverty suffered by the poor that seriously affects them like sickness, accidents, old age and maturity, flood damage etc. Table 4 gives various social security and welfare schemes implemented at the state level. Prasad in 1985 (p. 794) presented a review of these social security schemes (relating to unorganized labour) in different states in India, Broadly observation are:

   (a) All states implemented old age pension schemes. Some states like Andhra Pradesh, Gujarat, Kerala, and Tamil Nadu have special pension schemes for agricultural labour.

   (b) Tamil Nadu, Kerala, Gujarat and Orissa have pension schemes for poor widows and the physically handicapped.

   (c) Maharashtra is unique in the introduction of an employment guarantee scheme, but

Table 4. List of Various Social Security and Welfare Schemes at the State Level

1. **Old Age pension**
   - Andhra Pradesh (1960)
   - Assam (1983)
   - Bihar (1970)
   - Gujarat (1978)
   - Haryana
   - Himachal Pradesh (1968)
   - Jammu & Kashmir (1976)
   - Karnataka (1965)
   - Kerala (1960)
   - Madhya Pradesh (1970)
   - Maharashtra (1980)
   - Orissa (1975)
   - Punjab (1968)
   - Rajasthan (1964)
   - Tamil Nadu (1962)
   - Uttar Pradesh (1957)
   - West Bengal (1964)
2. **Pension for agricultural landless labourers**
   - Andhra Pradesh (1984)
   - Gujarat (1981)
   - Kerala (1982)
   - Tamil Nadu (1981)
3. **Destitute women**
   - Tamil Nadu (1975, 1986)
4. **Maternity benefit**
   - Gujarat (1975, 1986)
   - Karnataka (1984)
   - Kerala
5. **Physically disabled**
   - Haryana
   - Gujarat (1978)
   - Kerala (1982)
   - Tamil Nadu (1974)
   - West Bengal
6. **Health and Medical under voluntary agencies**
   - Maharasthra
   - Tamil Nadu
   - Voluntary health services (1963)
7. **Employment**
   - Maharasthra (EGS)
8. **Relief for the educated unemployed**
   - Gujarat (1979)
   - Kerala (1982)
   - Maharashtra (1979)
   - Tamil Nadu (1980)
   - West Bengal (1985)
9. **Self employment**
   - Kerala (1982)
   - Maharashtra (1980)
   - Tamil Nadu (1985-86)
   - Gujarat (1981)
10. **Group insurance schemes**
    - Gujarat
    - Kerala
    - Maharashtra
    - Orissa
    - Tamil Nadu
    - Bihar
    - West Bengal
    - Karnataka

Source: Statistical Abstract and Economic Surveys at State Level, Various Issues.

States like Tamil Nadu, Kerala and Gujarat have unemployment relief schemes.

(d) Maternity benefits for landless agricultural labour have been implemented in Gujarat, Karnataka and Kerala to balance loss of wage due to absence at work allowance, though paid for first and second issues only.

(e) Health care is not extended to workers is any state

(f) Gujarat, Tamil Nadu and Maharashtra have some welfare schemes only for women and children, while many states provide welfare benefits for different types of population below poverty line.

Table 5 presents a picture of coverage of schemes for selected states. It is to be inferred that the beneficiaries covered are very meagre and expenditure incurred is quite small compared to the magnitude. Despite this drawback, the attempt made by some states to provide social security to unorganized labour is laudable and worthy of emulation by other states. Among the states listed in the Table, Kerala extends all types of benefits (five) during 1989-90 to 1990-92, Orissa offered three schemes, old age pension, assistance to workers, assistance to the disabled between 1989-90 and 1991-92 and pension to agricultural workers only for 1991-92 and for 1991-92; Tamil Nadu provided help only for two schemes old age pension and assistance to workers during 1989-90 and 1991-92 -Old age pension scheme, assistance to workers and assistance to the disabled; and Maharastra adopted during the same period only two schemes old age pension and unemployment relief, the latter earned name at the all India level and recommended for implementation by other states.

The Union budget 1995-96 for the first time initiated 4 schemes to help the unorganized and vulnerable sections

Table 5. Beneficiaries and Expenditure[A] for Various Social Security Schemes

Year/State Scheme	*Old Age Pension (OAP)*		*Assistance to Widows*		*Assistance to Disabled*		*Pension to Agricultural Workers*		*Unemployment Relief*	
	Benefici-aries	*Expen-diture*	*Benefici-aries*	*Expen-diture*	*Benefici-aries*	*Expen-diture*	*Benefici-aries*	*Expen-diture*	*Benefici-aries*	*Expen-diture*
					Gujarat					
1989-90	56,470	5.63	1,813	20,96	865	6.35				
1990-91	58,622	9.05	2,437	33.33	1,445	1.09				
1991-92	63,658	9.04	2,883	66.24	1,088	1.31				
					Kerala					
1988-89	57,321	13.47	1,20,244		66,764	69.84	30,06,347		2,15,456	23.54
1989-90	58,115	11.79	1,24,355		73,835	69.86	3,02,312		2,46,040	19.96
1990-91	27,795	12.77	1,33,401		77,372	87.52	3,23,781		2,64,314	19.35

(Cont...)

Table 5. (Contd...)

					Maharashtra					
1989-90	3,21,5767	41.57	-						14,183	4.96
1990-91	3,40,557	41.46	-						12,206	5.29
1991-92	3,28,592	50.17	-						12,140	5.51
					Orissa					
1989-90	1,00,000	7.57	40,000	3.03	20.000	113				
1990-91	89,847	9.07	62,994	6.36	20,000	202				
1991-92	1,30,422	16.45	1,93,026	24,34	30,000	292	76,707	9.67		
					Tamil Nadu					
1989-90	1,71,9722	103.1	1,28,820	90.9(e)						
1990-91	2,13,213	122.3	1,60,997	105.3(e)						
1991-93	2,32,821	133.7	1,91,140	205.9(e)						

Note: (a) Expenditure Shown is in Rupees Lakh, (b) Data not Available for all the Districts. (c) Data Includes Widows also as Maharashtra has no Special Schemes for this. (d) Scheme for Agricultural Labour Introduced During 1991-92. (e) Includes Pension to Physically Handicapped Destitutes and Destitute Labour.

Source: Prasad (1995).

1) NABARD was authorized to open credit cooperative and RRB's were asked to meet the credit needs of STs. 2) Loans to Khadi and village industries through banks; 3) NABARD extends refinancing to commercial banks for providing credit to cooperative handloom institutions; and 4) programmes only for rural are as a) building one million houses in 1995-96; b) introduced natural social assistance scheme under which a) minimum old age pension of Rs. 75 PM will be paid to people above 65 years of age, and below poverty line; b) one time settlement amount of Rs. 5 thousand in the case of sudden death of primary bread winner in the poor households, c) pre and postnatal monetary care to poor women; d) group LIC. Some of these schemes have been continued in the subsequent and the latest budget for 2002-2003. In this way protective measures introduced in 1995-96 were continued at the National level. It would help the deprived and vulnerable sections of society if the allocation of funds are increased depending upon the success of implementation.

Effectiveness of Social Security Programmes

As discussed in the earlier pages, India adopted many promotional and protective social security schemes. The main problems are insufficient allocation of funds and its inefficient utilization of funds by the governments (both state and central and also by NGO's.) There is need for more funds for social security programmes in a poor country like India, compared to rich western countries and rich developing countries in Asia (Singapore, Malaysia). The State Governments should allot more funds particularly poorer states like MP, Bihar, UP, Rajasthan and Orissa (BIMARU states).

Besides higher allocation of funds, emphasis should be placed on effectiveness of the schemes touching upon efficient utilization of funds and the reach of the same to poorer sections. The record of Kerala and Tamil Nadu bears this out amply. Kerala success story, inspite of being poor state in economic growth relates to efficient public action on health and education (basic needs) which enhanced standard of living of poor people. The efficiency lies in effective utilization rather than in allocation of resources. Keral's success owes partly to historical reasons. But the Malabar region, a part of Kerala, was much behind Travencore and Cochin when the state was formed in 1956; but this region levelled with other regions by 1980's (in social development) mainly due to state action and peoples' own interest, besides public participation and local leadership (Ramachandran 1997). According to Kannan (1992), the Vigilance of different political parties and their unions and the adoption of strict measures in the village offices, have contributed to the success of social security measures and in particular payment of pensions to the poor. Perhaps some protective social security schemes might have helped remove the contingent poverty of some deprived sections of the people in the unorganized sector.

Tamil Nadu is a pioneer state in the implementation of nutrition scheme (midday meal programme) and protective social security measures. The two successful security schemes are a) C.M's Nutrition Meal Programme (CMNMP) and TN Integration Nutrition Project (TNIP); the first one, largest in the World, helped in the increase of nutrition of may school going children; the second one, a health-linked nutrition intervention scheme; was implemented in rural areas in a cost effective manner. There may be some faults in implementation in some areas of the Tamil Nadu, but the State did well in these social security schemes. Other States can learn from the success experience of Kerala and Tamil Nadu in the area of protective social security measures at affordable cost to help the vulnerable poor, avoiding the drawbacks found.

A few states also have taken initiatives in this direction. Eg. Employment Guarantee Schemes in Maharashtra, primary education scheme in Himachal Pradesh and Madya

Pradesh public distribution schemes in Andhra Pradesh and land reforms in West Bengal. However the less developed states like Bihar, UP and Rajasthan have not shown, for reasons unknown, interest to adopt social security programmes.

There is every need for the promotional and protective programmes of the government to reach the needy poor. This is possible through decentralization access to information and social mobilization on the top of active peoples' participation.

Financing of Social Sector

Since the introduction of economic reforms, allocation on social services and poverty alleviation programmes have been declining (social sector expenditure) i.e., spending on Social Services and Rural development). Tables 6,7 and 8 reveal this tendency very clearly.

As a share of GDP, Social sector expenditure has not shown increase during the reform period (first generation reforms) except in 1999-2000 for the states and centre taken together (Table 6), the share in 1990 was lower than in 1980's. But as proportion of total expenditure, the share of social sector clearly indicated rise since mid 1990s.

Since 1993-94 the share of GDP pertaining to social sector was higher compared to 1990-91 (first year of reform thought not much different viewed from 1980's (Table 7). It is a fact that as a proportion of public expenditure and as real per capital expenditure we observe a substantial rise in social sector spending since mid 1990s and higher compared to 1980s.

State expenditure as a proportion GSDP and aggregate expenditure, on social sector spending has declined (Table-8) no doubt in per real expenditure, there has been some rise, but not in the half of 1990s and also not much for rural development.

Table 6. Social Sector (Social Services+Rural Development) Expenditure by Centre and States

Year	*Social Sector Exp. (Revenue+Capital)*			*Social Sector Exp. (Revenue)*	
	As % of GDP	*As % of Agg. Pub. (Rev.+Capital)*	*Per capita exp.(in Rs.) In 1993-94 prices*	*As % of GDP*	*As % of Agg. Pub. Exp. (Revenue)*
1987-88	7.74	25.29	562	7.23	31.53
1988-89	7.40	25.22	583	6.95	30.97
1989-90	7.64	25.19	633	7.23	30.98
1990-91	6.78	24.85	623	6.43	30.00
1991-92	6.58	24.28	599	6.21	28.54
1992-93	6.39	24.06	594	6.06	28.83
1993-94	6.46	24.58	623	6.16	29.09
1994-95	6.41	25.01	633	6.06	28.74
1995-96	6.40	25.95	675	6.10	29.51
1996-97	6.48	27.22	739	6.15	29.13
1997-98	6.60	26.95	789	6.29	30.01
1998-99	6.94	27.36	890	6.60	30.41
1999-00(R)	7.55	27.69	1027	7.11	30.27
2000-01(B)	6.97	26.61	959	6.54	29.29

R: revised; B: budget.

Source: Estimates Based on Data from *Indian Public Finance Statistics*, GOI, 1995 and 2000-01.

Table 7. Social Sector (Social Services+ Rural Development) Expenditure by Central Government

Year	*As % of GDP*	*As % of Agg. Exp.*	*Per captial exp (in Rs.) in 1993-94 prices*
1986-87	1.61	7.47	113
1988-89	1.59	7.90	124
1990-91	1.42	7.55	130
1991-92	1.25	7.23	114
1992-93	1.29	7.70	119
1993-94	1.49	8.92	144
1994-95	1.49	9.26	147
1995-96	1.54	9.97	162
1996-97	1.56	10.48	177
1997-98	1.60	10.35	191
1998-99	1.67	10.39	213
1999-00	1.59	10.22	216
2000-01(R)	1.58	10.24	217

R: revised; B: budget.

Source: Expenditure Budgets of GOI, Vol. 1.

It appears that Centre has done better than the states in post reform period; one caveat has to be added. Centre has withheld money from the States. The central schemes increased during 1990s and even in 2002 at the expense of allocation (from overall plan outlay) to the states. In the social sector, however, the responsibility of the states are increasing compared to the central government.

These is a visible change in the composition of social sector spending both the States and the Centre from 1996-97, a shift away from rural development. Even within rural development outlay at the centre, the government moved from rural employment schemes to rural housing, water, rural roads etc and on to basic minimum services. This indicates a shift from traditional ways (removal of poverty) to human development or improvement of basic needs.

Table 8. Social Sector Expenditure (Social Services+Rural Development) of 25 States Excl. NCT Delhi

Year	*As % of GSDP*	*As % of Aggregate Exp.*
1990-91	5.98	39.20
1991-92	5.85	37.20
1992-93	5.72	37.60
1993-94	5.57	35.64
1994-95	5.27	34.82
1995-96	5.33	37.31
1996-97	5.13	36.21
1997-98	5.18	36.52
1998-99	5.41	38.07
1999-00	6.06	38.60
2000-01	5.46	35.80

Source: RBI Bulletins, 1991-92 to 2001.

Another fact to be known is that expenditure on health not changed much both at the centre and states. From 1990 to 1995 there is no change and after 1995 the per capita real expenditure on health by the States increased. The percentage spending on education declined from 4.1% in 1990-91 to 3.8% in 1998-99 (at the centre) and the trend is to be seen in the States.

In most states expenditure on social sector spending has not increased upto 1995, but in the second half increase is observed in terms of per capita real expenditure. The rich state (Goa) and middle income (West Bengal) states have shown better performance than the poor states. Within the proper state, spending on social sector is better in MP, Orissa and Rajasthan and very poor in Bihar and UP.

International aid has shown increase on children. There has been underutilization to the extent of 10% of plan expenditure during end of the 1990s decade due to absence of matching funds, lack of local infrastructure or skills, lack of interest, delays in release of funds.

Compared to other countries, social sector spending in India is low; to other developing countries, to east Asian countries and also even low compared to UNDP prescribed rations.

Whether the reform process causes withdrawal of the state from some economic activities. The answer is yes. But it is to be admitted that after 1995, more amounts have been allocated to social sector, yet as a shares of GDP, spending has not shown increase; even if there is an improvement, it is only marginal.

The above analysis leads to two desirable statements. One, there is an immediate necessity to hike social sector spending by government, particularly in the context of 93rd Amendment to the constitution by Lock Sabha regarding right to education for children between 6-7 years of age which needs only a rise of one per cent of GDP per annum in the next ten years. Financial commitment amounts to Rs. 9800 crores every year. The Hindu dated December 1, 2001 p. 10. State and Central Government should evince interest (overcoming cuts in education spending as the first step) in allocating more amounts in budgets in the Tenth Five Year Plan Period. Public vigilance and demand is the only remedy that could achieve this aim.

The effectiveness of many Central and State sector schemes is poor. The mid-term appraisal of the Ninth Plan has critically commented on this negligence and lapse of governments (GOI, 2000). The Planning Commission also never hides this fact of deterioration about the quality of governance of these schemes. The remedy lies in decentralization, devolution, daring attitude of people at the grass roots level, supported by young dynamic leadership both in the administration and in the political parties.

The above analysis drives to one significant conclusion. The country like India can ill afford to reduce expenditure and in the Tenth Five Year Plan, Government of India should increase the allocation in every year budget. There is need for better and efficient utilization of allotted money for social sector. The Planning Commission and GOI (2000) admit failures in the implementation (poor quality). The remedy lies in decentralization, grass roots level vigilance, participatory approach by people, commitment by government officials and political power for helping the poor workers (both in organized and unorganized sectors) to overcome deprivation and vulnerability so as to lead better quality of life.

1. Beveridge Committee Report, 1942, p. 120
2. International Labour Organisation Report, 1958, p. 11
3. Ahmed E, Jean Dreze, J Hills and A. Sen (1996): "Social Security in Developing Countries". Oxford University Press, Oxford.
4. Some parts and date in this section are taken from Mahendradev (2001)
5. Dreze Jean and A. Sen (1989) "Hunger and Public Action", Oxford, Clarondon Press, p. 183.
6. C. P. Thakur and C.S. Venkataratnam (2001) "Social Security for Organised labour" in Social and Economic Security in India" ed. By S. Mahendradev and others by IFHD, New Delhi, p. 64.
7. Taken from Mahendra Dev (1999)
8. See the Union Budget for 2002-2003
9. Drawn from S. Mahendradev (Dec. 2001)
10. The Hindu, December 1, 2001, p. 10

References

1. Guhan S (1992): Social Security Initiatives in Tamil Nadu 1989, in S. Subramanian (ed. Themes in Development Economics, Essays in honour of M. Adiseshaiah, Oxford University Press, Delhi.
2. Guhan, S (1993); "Social Security for the Poor in the Unorganised Sector: A Feasible Blue Print for India", (Eds.) Parikh K.S. and R. Sudarshan (1999).
3. Ginnekan W. (1998): "Social Security for all Indians", Oxford University Press, New Delhi.

4. Prabhu Seetha (2001): Economic Reforms and Social Development, Sage Publications, New Delhi.

5. S. Mahendra Dev and Other (Eds) 2001: Social and Economic Security in India: IFHD, New Delhi.

6. The Indian Journal of Labour Economics (2001), Conference Issue, No. 4, October-December.

32

Implementation of National Child Labour Project: Some Issues

Prof. G. Savaraiah, Dr. M. Devarajulu

Introduction

Child labour is a pernicious practice, a denial of joy of Childhood and access to school opportunities which eventually impair the holistic development of the personality of children—their creativity and enabling them to grow into a full-being. The existence of Child Labour in hazardous industries is a grave problem in India. Within the broad ambit of child labour, the plight of girl children (irrespective of whether they are working at home or outside) is worse. Such a practice which is abhorrent to our social conscience should, therefore, be eradicated from our social and economic milieu. It is in this perspective that elimination of child labour and integrated development of children have been important objectives of all our developmental plans. There are about 250 million child workers aged 5 to 14 in the world without taking into account those who work with their families in domestic activities. The Asian Countries accounted for 73 per cent of the child working population. According to the 43rd Round of National Sample Survey (1987), the number of working Children was estimated to be 12 million and the present figure is estimated to be more than 20 million. As per the CACL (Campaign Against Child Labour) Estimates, this number may be in between 70 to 80 million in India. There is no accurate estimates of child labour in India.

Plight of Child Labourers

Child Labour is rampant and many of them are withering away in factories, quarries, home—based industries, explosive manufacturing units, and lime kilns. More often than one would find little nimble fingers cleaning bowels in the backyard of hotels or wrenching the nuts of a wheel in a motor workshop. Young children work alongside their parents on tea plantations, picking the leaves to add to their mothers baskets. The small children mostly girls are involved in assembling the stock match boxes, crackers, explosives/firework in manufacturing units at Sivakasi where the children are also met with fire accidents. The general tendency of the owners or the managements of such units is to provide lower wages with longer working hours without any public holidays. In many instances, girls work longer hours than boys. Child labourers in hazardous and other industrial activities lead lives of degradation and hardship, deprived of their rights as children. The majority are involved in farming and are routinely exposed to harsh estimate, sharpened tools, heavy loads and increasingly to toxic chemicals and motorized equipment. Some child labourers are either knowingly or unknowingly, involved in risks at work places particularly in mining, construction work and explosive factories. In the farm sector, most of the child labourers are affected with respiratory track infections diseases caused by chemical pesticides, insecticides and other harmful chemical fertilizers used on the farms. Young girl working as domestic servants away from their homes, are the frequent victims of physical, mental and sexual abuse. The tourism industry has also encouraged the young girls into prostitution. The ILO Report on Child Labour (Dec. 1999) mentioned categorically about forced postitution of girls who are mostly the dropouts of schools and child labour.

Apathy of The Government Towards Eradication of Child Labour

Kuldip Nayar has opined that the governments policy seems to promote the employment of the children. It is evident from the fact that the small scale industries are legally permitted to use child labour directly or to subcontract with the so called family owned workshops/industries "In fact, there is no statutory protection for children in factories which employ not more than 10 workers. The government support to cottage and tiny industries indirectly promotes the employment of children in unregulated hazardous work. And through its centres for training children weavers in the carpet industry, the government competes with schools to attract children. In fact, child labour helps sustain the otherwise uneconomic small industries by keeping the cost down so that the carpet industry, gem and brassware industries can expand their exports.

As good profits all assured with low wages, the child labour has been increasing at an alarming rate and creating social problems. The European Community has also banned the imports of goods like carpets from India as these goods are made with the help of child labour. The European Countries have also threatened India to stop the Aid as it is employing the children in industries and as a result the children are losing their human rights and with all these pressures and consequences, the government of India has concentrated its efforts to prevent children from exploitation at work and to improve the working conditions. The policy of the government is to avoid the employment of children below the age of 14 years in factories, mines and hazardous employment.

Eradication and Rehabilitation of Child Labour

The Government of India has announced the National Policy on Child Labour in August 1987 with a view to eradicating and rehabilitating the child labour in the country with an action plan which comprises, viz.,

1. A legislative action plan;
2. Functioning of general development programmes for benefiting children, wherever possible, and
3. Project-based action plans in areas of high concentration of child labour engaged in wage/ quasi-wage employment.

The governments have been passing many laws for eliminating the child labour. But there are no concrete efforts made by the different State Governments to enforce these laws even to reduce the child labour in hazardous occupations.

The government of India has also introduced many schemes through NGO's to eliminate the child labour. But there is no headway in these programmes. However, the Government of India has given much priority to the project-based action plans to eliminate and rehabilitate the child labour in the country.

Under the project based action plan, 12 National child labour projects (NCLP) were started in Andhra Pradesh (Jaggampeta and Markapur), Bihar (Garwah), Madya Pradesh (Mandsavr), Maharastra (Thane), Orissa (Sambalpur), Rajasthan (Jaipur), Tamil Nadu (Sivakasi) and Uttar pradesh (Varanasi, Mirzapur, Bhadori, Moradabad, Aligarh and Ferozabad). The number of child labour projects (NCLP) has been increased to 100 during 2001-2002.

The present phase of NCLP was launched in 1994 to eliminate/reduce and rehabilitate, over a five year period, 20 lakhs (2 million) of children working in hazardous occupations in 132 problematic districts throughout the country. A budget of Rs. 850 crores was allocated to the programme to implement in the special schools. Which would incorporate non-formal education and provide vocational training, stipends (Rs. 100 per child) health check ups and nutritional benefits i.e. the One noon meal a day scheme. The ultimate objective of the NCCP is to convert working children into productive and participative members of the society. A modest beginning has been made in terms of conceptualization, planning and operationalisation of few NCL projects during the year 1994-95 and 1995-96. Under this programme 76 projects have been sanctioned and covering a mere 1.5 lakhs working children upto 1999 in the child labour endemic states of Andhra Pradesh, Madya Pradesh, Gujarat, Orissa, West Bengal, Bihar, Rajasthan, Uttar Pradesh, Maharastra, Karnataka and Tamil Nadu. During 2000-2001, 96 National child labour projects have been sanctioned in the above child labour endemic states for rehabilitation of about 2.00 lakh children removed from work. The state-wize coverage of special schools and working children under NCLP is shown in the Table 1

Table 1. Coverage Under National Child Labour Project Year 2000-2001

Sl. No	*States*	*Sanctioned of*		*Actual coverage*	
		Schools	*Children*	*Schools*	*Children*
1.	Andhra Pradesh (22)	975	61050	984	63991
2.	Bihar including Jharkhand (8)	194	12200	187	11268
3.	Karnataka (3)	110	5500	69	3018
4.	Madhya Pradesh including Chattingarh (8)	237	14500	119	6309
5.	Maharashtra (2)	74	3700	61	3184
6.	Orissa (18)	614	36750	580	34620
7.	Rajasthan (6)	180	9000	136	6800
8.	Tamil Nadu (9)	425	21900	407	20986
9.	Uttar Pradesh (11)	370	22500	270	16987
10.	West Bengal (8)	346	17350	277	13841
11.	Punjab	27	1350	-	-
	Grand Total (96)	**3552**	**205800**	**3090**	**181004**

Source: GOI: Annual Report 2000-2001, Ministry of Labour New Delhi, p. 127.

The Table above reveals that the sanctioned level has not fulfilled in actual coverage of number of schools and children at national level. About 87 per cent of the special schools are started, covering only 88 per cent of the working children as against their sanctioned number during the year 2000-2001. With regard to the state-wise performance of NCLP, only the state of Andhra Pradesh has surpassed the sanctioned number of special schools and coverage of the working children. In the states of Madhya Pradesh and Karnataka the targeted level was achieved below 55 per cent; whereas it was 75 per cent in Uttar Pradesh and Rajasthan respectively. But it is disheartening to note that the NCLP has not been implemented in Punjab. Further, the NCLP programme has not covered all the 132 problematic districts throughout the country. Besides, even one million working children have not been covered under this programme during the span of five years, as stipulated by the government. While on one hand, the child labour has been continuously increasing in India, and on the other, the child labourers who have completed their learning (both vocational and general study) in the special schools are not properly rehabilitated. It has been recognized that the allocation of two rupees and fifty paise per day per child for mid-day-meal is extremely inadequate to nourish a child. Generally, a street child or working child with the age of 14 years can eat rice of 300 grams which costs about Rs. 3 or 3.50 and excluding curry/sambar etc. In such conditions, it is difficult to run the special schools by the small NGO's. The poor attendance of child labourers is found in many schools in Andhra Pradesh. Many of these schools have now closed down due to delayed disbursement of financial resources.

Inadequate Allocation of Funds

Inadequate allocation of funds has resulted in poor implementation of the NCLP in the country. The actual utilization of funds for the project of Rs. 4.93 crores (12 projects) during the seventh plan and Rs. 15 crores (i.e. 82

projects) for the Eight five Year Plan as against the budgetary allocation of Rs. 850 crores. It indicates that the programme is inadequately funded. Hence it did not reach the target level of rehabilitating of 2.00 million child labourers. Further, for the Ninth Five Year Plan, Rs. 249.60 crores have been allocated for the implementation of NCLP. And National Agenda for Governance—1998 states that the aim is to ensure that no child remains illiterate, hungry or lacks medical care and that measures will be taken to eliminate child labour. However ambitious the target of eliminating/ rehabilitating the child labour, might be, NCLP can't be effectively implemented unless Government ensures, with a sense of genuine political commitment of that adequate and timely financial support is promoted, without bureaucratic hassles, to all NGO's in bringing cheer and light into the lives of the exploited and innocent children.

Awareness Campaign Against Child Labour

The awareness-generation programmes have a positive impact on preventing the growth of child labour. The Ministry of labour (GOI) had released meagre amounts of Rs. 6.65 crores during 1996-97 to the project societies at District level to undertake awareness-generation programmes. The total funds were not utilized for the said purpose, only Rs. 750/- was given to each school in Andhra Pradesh for Identification of the Child Labourer during 1996-97, the rest of the funds were diverted by the state governments (Project Directors of project societies) for other purposes. The NGO's at gross root level did not conduct the awareness campaign against child labour. The national level NGO like the Campaign Against child labour has been organizing the awareness gencration camps to eradicate child labour.

The employment of child labour Acts are not properly implemented in India. Infact, the Supreme Court Judgement on child labour (10-12-96) has given fresh impacts to take steps for the eradication of child labour.

India is significant exception to the global trend towards removal of child labour from the labour force and is providing compulsory universal primary school education. As compared to India, many countries of Africa like Zambia, Ghana, Libya, Zimbabwe have performed well in this respect despite their low income levels. Evidently eradication of child labour persists not due to dearth of resources but lack of political will and commitment. Owing to the continuous efforts made by the enlightened and committed Governments of Kerala in respect of Universalization of primary education and effective implementation of social and extension services, which have made the people aware of the rights of the child to get educated and lead a decent life, the presence of child labour is not felt in the state. If every state in India could emulate the 'Kerala Model', the goal of elimination of child labour could be effectively realized.

33

Agricultural Labourers of Andhra Pradesh During 1951-2001 and Policy Perspectives for the 21st Century

Prof. M. Atchi Reddy, Sneha Nalla

Agricultural labourers in India are disadvantaged in two ways. The first is their low productivity leading to low wages and so they are in chronic poverty. Second is the meagre scope for unionism and collective bargaining as they are dispersed over too wide an area that they can not form and operate any strong trade unions. And they are to weak a section of the Indian labourers that they cannot successfully bargain for higher wages even in the regions of agricultural prosperity like Punjab, Haryana, Western Uttar Pradesh or even in coastal belt of Andhra Pradesh. Adding to this miserable situation, their numbers had been increasing in India both in absolute terms as well as their proportion to the total agricultural population. Their poverty and miserable conditions of living could not be solved by the land reforms and the green revolution, which are the two major development events that marked the Indian agricultural sector during the past five decades or so. Are there any reasonable hopes at least in the 21st century to change the fate of this largest chunk of the unorganized rural working population? An attempt is made in the present paper to provide a few reasonable solutions.

Agriculturally employed workers in India showed a slower growth in the last two decades. They increased from 207.23 in 1983 to 237.56 million in 1999-2000. The annual growth rate of agriculture Workers decreased from 2.04% in 1983 to 0.98 in 1994-2000 (GOI, 2001-2002). This decline is a result of water shortage along with unfavourable monsoon. A few farmers are left unemployed and keep on looking out for better employment, and there was even a shift from cultivators to agricultural labourers which is a result of the inability of the farmers in paying debts that are a result of buying essential inputs for production purposes.

The size of the GDP, the annual growth rates and the levels of economic developments of the nations have surfaced as the all-pervasive issues in the present globalisation. All of us agree that economic development is basically about people. The aim should be to make India a modern and technologically progressive economy with expanding capacity to provide the basic material and cultural requisites of well-being for the people (VII Plan Draft, p. 8). Therefore, the human factor is of supreme value in any pattern of economic development. More so, are the agricultural labourers of India, the country's largest unorganized section comprising the poorest workers, toiling on the vast sunny fields of India. Most of them hail from the socially disadvantaged sections of our society and a large chunk of them continue to live under the poverty line as leftovers in the development process.

A large working force of about 193 million or about 67.53% of the Indian total active work force of about 286 million are employed in the agricultural sector in 1991 (Census Atlas, 1991, p. 57). But the gross national product of this sector is only about 24.5% of the GDP for the year of 1999-2000 (Economic Survey, 199-2000, Table 2). It indicates the low levels of the average per-capita productivity of the agricultural workers leading to the very low rates of wage being paid to the hired workers, most of whom continue to live below the poverty line in the villages or add to the growth of the urban slums of the already crowded cities creating serious environmental problems. Most of them are yet to partake the fruits of the modern economic development and its trickle down effects.

Most of these problems are common to India as a whole though their nature and extent vary from state to state and from region to region depending mainly on the agrarian conditions of the region. Andhra Pradesh is one such state where agricultural labourers constitute about 34% (Census Atlas, 1991, Series II India, Part III, B Series p. 191) of its total main workers in 1991 while the corresponding figure for India was only 26.09% (Census Atlas, 1991, p. 59). It is ironical that their proportion in the total workers had increased steeply during the post-Independence period. There is no major study on the nature and extent of their growth in spite of the multiple problems arising from their underemployment and low wages often leading to disorders, violence and loss of property. The present study, though brief, tries to fill this gap. Main sources of data are the decennial population censuses, a number of other published and unpublished studies that are referred to. Changes in the growth of agricultural labourers can be measured either in absolute numbers or as a proportion to the total population, to agricultural population, to total workers and so on. Growth in their absolute numbers in any given period depends upon the net growth rate in their numbers, i.e., births minus deaths and occupational migration into or out of this group. The combined effect of all these factors determine the direction and extent of variation in the growth rates of the agricultural labourers in any decade or period in any given region or area of the country. Thus the chief source is high rates of growth of population in different regions.

II

The population in Andhra Pradesh grew by an unpresciently large percentage of about 143% during the period of 1951 to 2001 and added a huge burden to the already crowded employment market. The agricultural economy with its 'Hindu rate of growth' could not provide them enough work and income, nor the growth of modern industry could absorb them in any large numbers. While the organized sector enjoyed the freedom of selecting its personnel requirements mostly from the literate market, the rural economy is forced to maintain the rest by providing subsistence to each one leading to a sort of redistribution of the available opportunities.

The population of Andhra Pradesh grew by about 143% between 1951 and 2001 (see Table 1). Most of the Telangana districts had registered a very high rate of growth, and a considerable portion of this growth can be attributed to the geographical migration. The three urban agglomeration centres are Hyderabad, Vishkhapatnam and Vijayawada. Large influx of population into Nizambad district was due to the attraction of its irrigation facilities while the large tracts of culturable waste in the district of Khammam attracted the entrepreneurial farmers from the coastal belt of the state. Also, the newly irrigated tracts under Nagarjunsagar and Sriramsagar projects attracted a sizeable number of workers and settlers in the 1970's and 1980s into the districts of Guntur, Nalgonda and Karimnagar. The geographical movement of population was mainly from the rural tracts to the urban concentrations on one hand and from dry belts to the irrigated tracts on the other. They can be termed as ruro-urban and ruro-rural migrations after the direction of their movement.

The rates of growth varied over decades in the same district, and over districts in the same decade (see table 2). The highest rate of about 30.88% was recorded by Khammam in the first decade, by Hyderabad of 35.33% in the second decade and 42.43% in the third decade and by Ranga Reddy with 60.32% in the fourth decade and by a lesser 37.41% in the final decade. The city of Hyderabad including the present district of Rangareddy kept at a low level in the

Table 1. Variation of Population in Different Districts of Andhra Pradesh, 1951-2001

District	*1951*	*2001*	*Variation*
Adilabad	831600	2479347	198.14
Nizamabad	835243	2342803	180.49
Karimnagar	1428168	3477079	143.46
Medak	110971	2662296	2299.09
Hyderabad	1821711	3686460	102.36
Rangareddy		3506670	
Mahbubnagar	1447132	3506876	142.33
Nalgonda	1287169	3238449	151.59
Warangal	1329836	3231174	142.98
Khammam	802002	2565412	219.88
Srikakulam	2123136	2528491	19.09
Vizianagaram		2245103	
Vishakhapatnam	2072698	3789823	82.84
East Godavari	2301822	4872622	111.69
West Godavari	1697727	3796144	123.60
Krishna	1736429	4218416	142.94
Guntur	2560064	4405521	72.09
Prakasam		3054941	
Nellore	1794552	2659661	48.21
Cuddpah	1162888	2573481	121.30
Kurnool	1617464	3512266	117.15
Anantapur	1483591	2629304	145.30
Chittoor	1666266	3735202	124.17
Andhra Pradesh	31115259	75277541	143.38

Source: Census Reports, Government of India, India.

first decade, but recorded progressively high rates during the next decades mainly due to the influx of migrants.

The average rate of growth of the state of Andhra Pradesh increased from 15.65% in the first decade to about 24.2% in the fourth decade and then declined to 13.86% in the final decade (see Table 2). It is notable that the decennial rates have been progressively increasing in spite of the numerous measures of population control whether poverty breeds population growth, or high growth rates result in poverty is an issue to be debated. The latter is the common notion while the former is a new but important point when one looks into the macro-picture of poverty.

Table 2. Decennial Rates of Growth of Total Population in Different Districts of Andhra Pradesh, 1951-2001

District and State total	*1951-61*	*1961-71*	*1971-81*	*1981-91*	*1991-2001*
Adilabad	21.37	27.65	27.15	26.95	19.06
Nizamabad	22.36	28.5	27.87	21.31	14.98
Karimnagar	13.54	21.12	24.04	24.68	14.47
Medak	10.6	19.6	24.5	25.6	17.29
Hyderabad	13.24	35.33	42.43	39.76	17.18
Rangareddy			33.16	60.32	37.41
Mahbubnaagar	9.92	21.46	20.63	25.87	13.97
Nalgonda	22.36	15.54	25.04	25.11	13.5
Warangal	16.21	21.06	23.01	22.54	14.63
Khammam	30.88	29.54	27.38	26.5	15.78
Srikakulam	10.26	13.82	7.51	18.46	8.93
Vizianagaram			14	17	6.35
Vishakhapatnam	10.52	22.46	23.76	27.5	15.36
East Godavari	13.32	18.36	19.9	22.7	7.3
West Godavari	16.52	20.02	20.33	22.39	7.92
Krishna	19.61	20.06	21.99	21.33	14.05
Guntur	17.57	22.23	20.48	19.57	7.27
Prakasam		14.85	27.95	18.44	10.72
Nellore	13.5	15.06	23.27	18.73	11.18
Cuddpah	15.4	17.54	22.22	17.47	13.48
Kumool	18.01	26.17	21.3	23.5	18.14
Anantapur	1913	19.68	23.78	24.81	14.31
Chittoor	14.91	19.37	21.14	19.14	14.54
Andhra Pradesh	15.65	20.9	23.19	24.2	13.86

Source: Census Reports, Government of India, India.

The density of population shows their concentration and its variation over time revealing the preference of the people to different places or districts. The density of population was already high around 200 per sq. km. In 1951 in the irrigated coastal belt stretching from East Godavari to Guntur and the same belt continued with the high density of above 450 people per sq. km. in 2001 too (see Table 3). The density of the various districts was more evenly spread in 2001 than 1951, even though the range was still high even in 1981, 1991 and 2001.

It would be interesting to desegregate the growth of population into occupational rates of growth. However, here we analyse mainly the growth of the agricultural labourers with reference to the total agricultural workers. The serious problem is that the agricultural population registered a higher rate of growth than the general rate. It grew by about 306% while general rise was about 113% during four decades from 1951 to 1991 implying that there was occupational migration into agriculture. Whether the workers were pushed out from the non-agricultural rural pursuits that declined overtime, or agriculture could absorb extra numbers by providing same sort of subsistence wages is too large an issue to be analysed here; and we confine our attention to the rates of growth of cultivators and agricultural labourers in the different regions and districts of Andhra Pradesh in each of these decades i.e. 1951 to 1991.

The cultivators of the state of Andhra Pradesh increased by about 55% between 1951 and 1991. The highest growth of about 204% is in the Rangareddy district around Hyderabad city while the lowest figure of only 24.89% is in the district of Nellore. The average percentage of the growth of cultivators in the irrigated coastal belt is very low and it is as low as 9.56% in the East Godavari district (see Table 4). It can be explained that the very high rate of growth in the Rangareddy district is mainly due to the fact that a number of small cultivators took to the small

Table 3. Density of Population in Each District of Andhra Pradesh, 1951-1991

District and State Geographic Density of population Variation

District and State total		*1951*		*2001*
Adilabad	16128	52	154	196.15
Nizamabad	7956	105	294	180.00
Karimnagar	11823	121	294	142.98
Medak	9699	114	274	140.35
Hyderabad	217		16988	
Rangareddy	7493		468	
Mahbubnagar	18432	133	190	42.86
Nalgonda	14240	90	227	152.22
Warangal	12846	104	252	142.31
Khammam	16029	50	160	220.00
Srikakulam	5837		433	
Vizianagaram	6539		343	
Vishakhapatnam	11161		340	
East Godavari	10807	213	451	111.74
West Godavari	7742	219	490	123.74
Krishna	8727	199	483	142.71
Guntur	11391	225	387	72.00
Prakasam	17626		173	
Nellore	13076	87	203	133.33
Cuddpah	15359	76	168	121.05
Kurnool	17658	92	199	116.30
Anantapur	19130	78	190	143.59
Chittoor	15152	110	247	124.55
Andhra Pradesh	275068	196	275	40.31

Source: Census Reports, Government of India, India.

scale commercial farming of vegetables and fruits to meet the needs of the expanding markets in the city of Hyderabad. A number of cultivators that got the status of a cultivator in Nalgonda between 1941-1951 due to the land reforms had emigrated to the city of Hyderabad due to the prolonged

Table 4. Variation of Agricultural Cultivators in the Districts of Andhra Pradesh, 1951-1991

District	*1951*	*1991*	*Variation*
Adilabad	171003	294493	72.22
Nizamabad	231513	457958	41.20
Karimnagar	281421	457958	62.73
Medak	338581	419894	24.02
Hyderabad		2050	
Rangareddy	84259	256505	204.42
Mahbubnagar	319951	586403	83.28
Nalgonda	372664	416879	11.86
Warangal	327307	413934	26.47
Khammam	327307	261090	-20.23
Srikakulam	321265	333823	3.91
Vizianagaram		368490	
Vishakhapatnam	232351	477441	105.48
East Godavari	275430	249094	-9.56
West Godavari	216949	219955	1.39
Krishna	225261	243322	8.02
Guntur	354954	384353	8.28
Prakasam		337328	
Nellore	290206	217978	44.88
Cuddpah	188119	272545	44.88
Kurnool	150354	331821	120.69
Anantapur	254210	490385	92.91
Chittoor	339513	528514	55.67
Andhra Pradesh	4975311	7891167	58.61

Source: Census Reports, Government of India, India.

periods of dry spells in these areas. Explanation for the irrigated tracts as to elevate the labourers into cultivators. The pieces of land distribution among the agricultural labourers could not elevate them into full pledged or cultivators and most of them continue to derive a major part of their livelihood income from agricultural labour. Infact, this phenomena had undermined the effects of the reforms measured by occupational shifts.

III

Given growth rates of the population general, the growth rate of agricultural labourers in any region is the function of two chief variables. The first and the major addition is the result of the high birth rates in these poverty stricken families. Next and important factor is that the agricultural labour market serves as an 'informal social security net.'

Those that are pushed out of other livelihood classes enter into this ever open and free entry market. In other words, the additions to the labour force had far exceeded those that left it in favour of better avenues. Most of the additions seem to be from the other occupations, Agricultural labourers for obvious reasons.

The growth of agricultural labourers is very high in the Rayalaseema districts and Rangareddy. Migrants are registered in Rangareddy district while occupational deterioration is responsible for high growth of agricultural labourers in the Rayalaseema. The occupational Tables of the four decennial censuses show that non-agricultural occupations in the Rayalaseema declined faster than the same in the other two regions of the state; the deterioration in the district of Cuddapah being the worst case notably among weavers, cobblers, potters, basket-makers, story-tallers, oil-pressures, would cutters and cattle dealers.

It can be safely assumed that a large part of the workers that lost their traditional avenues of living had taken to agricultural labour partly or fully. These shifts are noted by the authors in their visits to some of the villages of Anantapur districts located in the mandals of Kadiri, Rayachoti, Rayadurgam, Prnugonda, Uravakonda and Dharmavaram, especially during the latest trips in 2001 to some of these areas. The proportion of agricultural labourers

Table 5. Variation of Agricultural Labours in the Districts of Andhra Pradesh, 1951-1991

District	*1951*	*1991*	*Variation*
Adilabad	99837	303877	204.37
Nizamabad	70404	307454	336.70
Karimnagar	144214	528187	266.25
Medak	76482	386929	405.91
Hyderabad	41574	2257	-94.57
Rangareddy		288925	
Mahbubnagar	135625	627454	362.64
Nalgonda	156361	555594	255.33
Warangal	157295	537236	241.55
Khammam		463976	
Srikakulam	204143	423258	107.33
Vizianagaram		32330	
Vishakhapatnam	103355	310353	200.28
East Godavari	302656	842372	178.33
West Godavari	219274	80226	-63.41
Krishna	15146	751812	4863.77
Guntur	210866	967327	358.74
Prakasam		648254	
Nellore	172561	488647	183.17
Cuddpah	51808	368470	611.84
Kurnool	19265	66434	244.84
Anantapur	78554	533512	579.17
Chittoor	79418	490360	517.44
Andhra Pradesh	2650154	11625159	338.66

Source: Census Reports, Government of India, India.

to the total agricultural workers in the state had increased from 28% in 1951 to 50% in 1991 (see Table 6). Each cultivator is surrounded by an increasing number of labourers in each successive decades leading to increased volume of unemployment and low wages.

Table 6. Proportion of the Agricultural Labourers to the Total Agricultural Workers in the Districts of Andhra Pradesh, 1951-1991

District	*1951*	*1961*	*1971*	*1981*	*1991*	*1951-91*
Adilabad	33	31	35	38	41	8
Nizamabad	22	25	30	33	41	19
Karimnagar	31	45	36	40	43	12
Medak	16	26	31	30	38	22
Hyderabad	28	31	32	33	49	21
Rangareddy					42	
Mahbubnagar	26	31	32	29	38	12
Nalgonda	26	32	37	36	43	17
Warangal	29	32	38	41	43	14
Khammam	29	35	42	43	51	22
Srikakulam	26	32	41	39	49	23
Vizianagaram					40	
Vishakhapatnam	18	24	32	27	35	17
East Godavari	43	70	59	58	72	29
West Godavari	40	49	58	54	69	29
Krishna	33	45	54	54	64	31
Guntur	32	39	51	51	60	28
Prakasam					55	
Nellore	31	36	53	50	58	27
Cuddpah	19	33	43	42	46	27
Kurnool	23	40	50	51	55	32
Anantapur	19	28	38	35	41	22
Chittoor	16	27	34	35	41	25
Andhra Pradesh						

Source: Census Reports, Government of India, India.

There are two implications that follow from this kind of trend. If the total number of hours of employment in agriculture had grown in the same rate as that of the agricultural workers in a given period, the per capita employment remains the same, if it varies in either direction, volume of employment per capita changes. And in the case the volume of employment declines, it is the labourer that has to accept a cut in the days of hired employment or low wages or both. Further and micro level village studies are required to ascertain the changing levels of poverty and deprivation in the rural areas.

The foregoing analysis shows that number of agricultural labourers in Andhra Pradesh had increased over the last one-half century both in absolute and the relative terms. But their wage levels did not increase by any significant extent. In the backward regions of Telangan and Rayalaseema their living conditions and to uplift them out of poverty in the next quinquinniums of the present 21st century. Increased agricultural productivity can provide an immediate and direct solution, but to a limited extent. Increased industrialization can provide a medium term solution; but it needs some structural changes, as the unskilled labourers cannot directly be absorbed into industries in any large numbers. The last but promising resort is the expanding service sector that can absorb workers with diversified skills and possibly on the sustained basis. It is likely to be less polluting than the industrial growth using the present technology. What is immediately required is that the people of any nation have to be imparted with the necessary skill.

References

1. *Census Reports* 1961 to 2001, Serie II India, Part III, B Series, Andhra Pradesh, Government of India, India
2. *Census of India* 1961 to 1991, Series III India, Part III, B Series, District Wise including all the District of Andhra Pradesh, Government of India, India.
3. *Census Atlas,* National Volume-1, 1991, Office of the Registrar General & Census Commissioner, India (Map Division), Ministry of Home Affairs, New Delhi.
4. *Economic Survey 2001-2002,* Ministry of Finance, Government of India.
5. *Seventh Five Year Plan 1985-90,* Vol. II, Government of India, Planning Commission.

34

Gender and Employment in India: An Agenda for the 21st Century

C. Muthuraja

Introduction

Women are part of labour force. They produce not merely goods and services, but are a part of labour force. They produce not merely goods and services, but are a prime source of accelerating human race. Thus, from the point of view of increasing labour force as well as of involving themselves in production and service activities, their active and positive participation can not be overlooked. But, throughout the world, the rural women have been under-represented in the development process. The male-dominated society, never recognizes their proper contribution.

At the end of the United Nations Decade for Women, a world conference was held in Nairobi in 1985. The Conference adopted the forward-looking strategies for the advancement of women from 1986 to 2000 AD Employment is the most recent approach (Women's Employment phase: 1986 to date), articulated by the "Third World" women. It seeks to meet women's strategic gender needs, due to their subordinate position to men, through bottom up mobilization around practical gender needs according to their accepted role in society. It aims at increasing women's power in terms of their self-reliance and internal strength to determine choice in life and to influence the direction of change.

Women's Employment in India

Women contribute greatly to the economy. Employment of women is an index of their economic status in society, especially with response to equality. According to the census data, the work participation rate (i.e. the proportion of employed or total workers to population) of women steadily rose from 14.22% in 1971 to 19.67 in 1981 and to 22.27 in 1991. The rise in work participation of rural women has been even steeper from 15.92 in 1971 to 26.79 in 1991.

The image of India as an agricultural economy is firmly etched in the minds of policy makers, planners and people, as 70 per cent of the population is still based in the rural areas. About 87 per cent of all economically active women derive their livelihood from the agricultural sector, and 48 per cent of self-employed farmers are women. This is the sector where women's role as unpaid labour in productive activities is most prominent, and is responsible work for conferring on women a non-working status, but their contribution is often made invisible by statistical biases, work on their own farms, wages etc.

According to 1991 census, 27 per cent of rural women are found to be workers of whom 19 per cent are main workers and 8 per cent are marginal workers. Of the main workers, 31.68 per cent are found to be cultivators and 48.83 per cent are agricultural labourers. Agriculture therefore, is a major field of women's employment. In India, almost all are working as wage labourers, unpaid workers in family farm enterprises or farm combination of the two. The rural India is witnessing a process, which could be described as Feminisation of Agriculture. Between 1977 and 1991, the ration of the female to male agricultural labour went up from 57 to 60 per cent. Similarly the rate of female to male cultivators has risen from 14 to 19 percent.

Women's employment in the organized sector has revealed significant increase from 1.9 million in 1971 to

4.0 million in 1993, constituting 14.4 per cent of the total employment of 27.18 million. Of these 2.47 million women i.e. about 62 per cent were employed in the public sector and 1.6 million i.e. 38 per cent in the private sector. As compared to women in the organized sector, the representation of men is almost six times more. About 56 per cent of women's employment in the organized sector is in community, social and personal services, 16 per cent each in transport, storage and communication and financing insurance, real estate and banking services. Of the total employment of women, the organized sector employment forms only 4 per cent whereas, for men, organized sector employment constitutes 10 per cent of total employment.

The total share of women's employment in the agricultural and allied activities sector has also been increasing steadily from 67% in 1901, 78% in 1951 to 87% in 1991. It becomes apparent that, so far, any assumption that with development there would be diversification to the tertiary sector/urban areas does not hold good for women. Further the ratio of number of women per hundred men in this sector is also increasing: in 1971 these were 14 cultivators and 50 agricultural labours, which increased to 26 cultivators and 64 agricultural labourers in 1991. These trends emphasize that the significant presence of women in the agricultural sector interventions needs to respond more to their need and interest.

The percentage of female non-agricultural workers in the rural work force at the all India level rose from 10.3 per cent in 1961 to 12.3 per cent in 1983. The proportion of female non-agricultural workers was much lower than that of male non-agricultural workers, and the increase in this proportion was also much smaller. While most states have shown an increase in the proportion of female non-agricultural workers, the exceptions were Himachal Pradesh, Kerala and Punjab. Kerala, however, retrained its top ranking in 1983. The percentage of non-agricultural workers in the total rural labour force ranged from 6.0 to 38.0 per cent for 14 NSS regions in 1977-78 and the coefficient of variation was 44.6 per cent. The coefficient of variation of the percentage of female non-agricultural workers was higher (84.6 per cent) than that of male non-agricultural workers (37.4 per cent). Obviously, there is a much greater variation of female non-agricultural workers ranging from 1.3 to 57.9 percent.

Ninety-four per cent of the total women workers are in the Informal sector in 1991. Women in the informal sector outside agriculture are often found in tasks, which are an extension of the role they play within the household. Women have little opportunity to upgrade the skills and move into better paying jobs. The double burden of work shouldered by women leaves them with very little time to unionise. The lack of unionization among women implies that women are often displaced from their jobs depending in the level of production. Very little legislation is made provocation of the rights of women in the informal sector.

A matter of great concern is the unemployment rates for workers in recent years. The rate of unemployment is more significant for urban females. The same trend is visible for current weekly status of unemployment, which stood at 2.1% for rural females and 5.3% for urban females in 1990-91. The unemployment rates for current status also present a similar trend, i.e, increasing for urban females even more than urban males and almost stagnant for rural females.

In India, there has been a gradual shift over the last decade or more towards policies for a more open economy, the 1991 policy declaration was more of a formalization of that phenomenon than a radical shift to a new outlook. However, available macro-statistics indicated that, in India, in a period of relative liberalization of the economy, the trends in women's employment pattern were, in the 1970's but the late 1980's it went down from 36 per cent in 1983 to 34.5 per cent and had remained there till 1993-94. There was a slight rise in women's share in the urban work force, which, according to Visaria, reflected mainly in growth in women's rate of urbanization. With that, the fall in their share in country's overall workforce from 1983-94 was small but nonetheless it was a fall.

Table 1. Profile of Women (Relative of men) in the Workforce of India*

Male	*Male*	*Female*	*Total*
Total population (mns)	435.00	403.00	838.00
Total workforce (mns)	224.00	90.00	314.00
Work participation rate	51.56%	22.73%	
Unemployment rate(1987-88)	5.50%	7.60%	
Employment in Urban areas (87-88)	24.70%	13.50%	
Employment in Rural areas (87-88)	75.30%	86.50%	
Self-employment (87-88)	53.80%	53.10%	
Regular salaried employment	18.00%	8.30%	
Casual wage employment (87-88)	28.20%	38.60%	
Annual rate of growth of employment (1977-78 to 87-88)	1.90%	1.95%	
Annual rate of growth of employment of the educated (1977-78 to 87-88)	6.07%	8.58%	

* Population and Workforce Figures are Based on 1991 Census Other Data are Based on the Figures of the NSSO.

Source: "Women Labour in India", V.V. Giri National Labour Institute, Noida, 1996.

Gender and Employment: Some Issues

Women's participation in employment is not only mediated by gender, but also by caste, ethnicity, age and marital status. Dalit and tribal women have significantly higher work force participation rates than the rest of Indian women. In the upper caste and Muslim households women are withdrawn from the labour force as soon as their economic status improves. In export processing zones, being promoted under the New Economic policy, women's entry into the labour market is also determined by age. Employers prefer to employ young single women. Marriage results in retrenchment because it is assumed that they cannot work for long hours, especially after childbirth.

In spite of such significant contribution in agricultural production process, women are yet to be perceived as participants rather than beneficiaries of development programme. Women are primarily treated as consumers of social services (like health care education and Nutrition) rather than producers. They are kept away from development programmes in agriculture and allied fields, lack of access to cash income is one of the reasons of the above situation. Moreover, women's work is considered ancillary even though the rural women are involved in numerous unpaid domestic as well as family agricultural enterprises. The subordinate status of woman has made her head of the household. Thus, farmwomen do not have any access to resources, credit, inputs and other agricultural interventions.

India is a big nation and it accommodates many variations in conventions regarding these rights of women. But the majority is deemed property rights at least on par with their male partners. This seriously erodes the material base on which they can operate as independent economic agents.

Several factors account for this situation. Among these are the absence of appropriate skills. Women also tend to get easily displaced by new technologies and are either pushed out or pushed down when job requirements call for skilled and trained persons. With the introduction of new macro economic policies skill and vocational training for women assume key importance.

Even in 1987-88, 87% of rural women workers as compared to 55% of rural male workers were literate. In urban India, too, 60% of women workers as compared to

Table 2. Employment in the Organised and Unorganised Sector During 1971 to 1991 (in 100,000s)

Year	*Male*			*Female*			*Total*		
	Organised Sector	*Unorganised Sector*	*Total*	*Organised Sector*	*Unorganised Sector*	*Total*	*Organised Sector*	*Unorganised Sector*	*Total*
1971	155.60 (10.43%)	133.16 (89.57%)	1491.76	19.30 (6.16%)	294.15 (93.84%)	313.45 (17.36%)	174.90 (9.69%)	1630.21 (90.31%)	1805.1
1981	200.86 (11.0%)	1625.75 (89.0%)	1826.61	27.93 (6.13%)	427.59 (93.87%)	455.52 (19.96%)	228.79 (10.03%)	2053.34 (89.97%)	2282.13
1991	229.53 (10.23%)	2014.11 (89.77%)	2243.64	37.81 (4.21%)	859.86 (95.79%)	897.67 (28.58%)	267.34 (8.51%)	2873.87 (91.49%)	3141.31

Note: Figures in Parenthes are % Ages with Respect to Totals.

23% of male workers were illiterate over 90% of male and 80% of urban women workers are married; they presumably carried a major load of reproductive work which drastically curtailed their mobility and choice of jobs. Even with widespread state financed arrangements for girl's education, their literacy, school enrolment and retention rates remain much below those of boys. And those girls who do get education are crowded into training for a few approved occupations and subjects.

Poverty is a structural problem that cannot be solved by just programmes, projects or plans with a 'top down' approach. Rather, the involvement and utilization of human resources of the poor, to achieve growth with equity, in an environment conducive to their participation is required. There is need for attitudinal change from seeing poor women as passive and defenseless to recognizing their creativity and entrepreneurship.

The urban labour market in India was slowly getting feminized through flexible labour over the eighties. Women were increasingly absorbed by the urban economy but mostly in low-paid and insecure employment. In most jobs where they replaced men. They were forced to accept wages discrimination. Yet their incomes though low were precious for their subsistence. It was their poverty that left in with limited options. They lacked education, skills or both and were forced to accept any work either at home or outside. A large majority of the new entrants in urban female workplace are absorbed in jobs in manufacturing and services.

S.R. Hashim observed that the youth being the later entrants to the job market bear the brunt of the unemployment problem. The youth unemployment is much higher than the general unemployment almost everywhere. Educational level among the young people is increasing, they are more informed than ever before. Education and information raise their aspirations and hence they are also likely to develop reservations about certain kinds of job which they perceive as mental or just manual. The level of education and information among youth females are higher than youth males. This trend is a continuous one in Indian context.

There is a higher incidence of unemployment in urban areas as compared to rural areas. A matter of great concern is the unemployment rates for female workers in recent years. The rate of unemployment is more significant for urban females at 4.7% compared to 0.3% for rural females. At the end of 1994, the number of women on the live register of the employment Exchanges in the country was 80.90 lakhs as against 78.50 lakhs at the end of 1993. Several factors account for this situation. Among these are absence of appropriate skills. Women also tend to get easily displaced by new technologies and are either pushed out or pushed down when job requirements call for skilled and trained persons. With the introduction of new macro economic policies skill and vocational training for women assume key importance.

A close observation of the present trend suggests that inspite of these positive signs there is really no reason to rejoice: the new millennium is unlikely to bring about a qualitative improvement in the position of women in the labour market. Rather, Indian women appear doomed to continue being crowded in a limited number of low paid, low productivity, uncertain jobs, which hold out little prospects for advancement and career-building:

An Agenda for the 21st Century

The government has made some special efforts to open up new venues of employment for women particularly in the administrative, banking and insurance sectors. Also, several occupations like teaching, Community and social services or telecommunications where women had got an early entry expanded particularly fast in this period, mainly as the result of the expansion of government sponsored activities.

Table 3. Unemployment Rates

All India

Year		*Rural*		*Urban*	
		Male	*Female*	*Male*	*Female*
1972-73	*(i)* Usual Status	1.2	0.5	4.8	6.0
	(ii) Current Weekly	3.0	5.5	6.0	9.2
	(iii) Current Daily	6.8	11.2	8.0	13.7
1977-78	*(i)* Usual Status	2.2	5.5	6.5	17.8
	(ii) Current Weekly	3.6	4.1	7.1	10.9
	(iii) Current Daily	7.1	9.2	9.4	14.5
1983	*(i)* Usual Status	2.1	1.4	5.9	6.9
	(ii) Current Weekly	3.7	4.3	6.7	7.5
	(iii) Current Daily	7.5	9.0	9.2	11.0
1987-88	*(i)* Usual Status	2.8	3.5	6.1	8.5
	(ii) Current Weekly	4.2	4.4	6.6	9.2
	(iii) Current Daily	4.6	6.7	8.8	12.0
1989-90	*(i)* Usual Status	1.6	0.8	4.4	3.9
	(ii) Current Weekly	2.6	2.1	4.5	4.0
1990-91	*(i)* Usual Status	1.3	0.4	4.5	5.4
	(ii) Current Weekly	2.2	2.1	5.1	5.3
1992	*(i)* Usual Status	1.6	1.2	4.6	6.7
	(ii) Current Weekly Status	2.2	1.2	4.6	6.2
1993-94	*(i)* Usual Status	2.0	1.4	4.5	8.2
	(ii) Current Weekly	3.0	3.0	5.2	8.4
	(iii) Current Daily	5.6	5.6	6.7	10.5

The figures represent size of unemployment as per cent of labour force. The results of 45th, 46th, and 48th Rounds are based on thin sample.

(i) Usual status approach with a reference period of 365 day preceding the date of survey.

(ii) Current weekly status approach with a reference period of 7 days preceding the of survey.

(iii) Current daily status approach with each day of the 7 days proceeding the date of survey as the reference period. (Strictly speaking this approach attempts classification of persons dates and not persons).

Source: National Sample Survey Organisation: 27th, 32nd, 38th, 43rd, 45th, 46th, 48th and 50th Rounds.

Unacceptable levels of poverty and the gradual feminisation of such poverty are the most daunting of all our challenges. The eradication of poverty and a special focus on women in all poverty alleviation programmes have been major strategies since the seventies. Special components for women have been built in almost all programmes in the social sector. The following are the specific agenda for action in the 21st century.

- Not only have additional employment opportunities to be generated by using the suitable structure of investment and production, but also distributive justice must be done.
- The minimum age limit to enter the public service should be higher in the case of women workers as against men workers. Because, they have to play a dual productive economic role as unpaid labourers at home and as paid workers in the fields, factories or offices.
- Better infrastructure facilities need to be provided for encouraging self-employment among the educated unemployed women. Efforts have to be made to bring about the development of different skills in line with social need and give opportunities for unemployed women.
- Special entrepreneurship courses should be run for unemployed women.
- Larger variety of Vocational Courses particularly for girls, who do not intend to continue their general education beyond elementary or secondary stage, should be introduced.
- Educated women should be encouraged to form co-operative societies to be controlled and run exclusively by women themselves.
- There is need for change of attitude on the part of male members of our society also. Women have

been given due participation in the developmental activities of the home and country.

- Lobby with the government to cut back its expenditure on defence and increase its expenditure in Public distribution system, health, education, housing and employment and recognize as rights of people which cannot be abrogated to the private sector.
- Evolve alternative development paradigm sensitive to gender cast, class, religious identities and environment.
- Organize and train poor, dalit and tribal women to take part in the economic activities.
- Evolve a gender desegregated date based on the above issue so as to lobby effectively with the government and plan development projects which are sensitive to survival needs and strategic gender interests.
- Over and above more and special educational facilities are to be provided for the women.

References

1. AIACHE, (1999) "Documentation on women, children and Human Rights"; New Delhi, Jan-March.
2. Banerjee. N (1991), "Indian women in a changing Industrial Scenario" Sage, New Delhi.
3. Banerjee. N, (1995) "Women's employment and All that", The Administrator, Vol. 40, No. 3.
4. Baud, I.S.A. (1992) "Forms of Production and Women's labour gender aspect of industrialization in India and Mexico", Sage Publication, New Delhi.
5. Binita Verma, (1993) "Exploitation of women labour in India-Employment pattern and wage discrimination", Deep, Government of India, (1995) 'Fourth world conference on women, Beijing 1995: Country Report; New Delhi.

6. Government of India, (1975) "Towards equality: Report of the Committee on the status of women in Indian-1947", New Delhi.
7. Hashim, S. R. (1999), "Employment and Unemployment in a Society in Transition" (Presidential Address) India Society of Labour Economics (41st Annual conference), Mumbai.
8. Jeemol Unni, (1991), "Regional Variations in Rural Non-Agricultural Employment- An Exploratory Analysis", Economic and Political Weekly.
9. Jeemol Unni, (1992) "Women's participation in India Agriculture" Oxford & IBH Publishing Co., Delhi.
10. Mahajan, V.S. (ed), (1989) "Women's contribution to India's economic and Social Development", Deep & Deep Publications, New Delhi.
11. Muthuraja, C, (1990) "Report women in Indian Agriculture" Khadi Gramodyog, Vol. 36. No. 8.
12. Muthuraja, C, (1997) "Womenfolk in Indian Agriculture: And Analysis of their participation and contribution' in Basant Mehta & Prakash Chandra Mehta (eds), "Perspectives of Tribal Economy" Intellectual publishing house, New Delhi.
13. Muthuraja, C, (2001) "Gender and Employment in India: An Agenda for the 21st Century" in S. Murthy (ed) "Women & Employment" RBSA Publishers, Jaipur (India).
14. Nitya Rao, (1996), "Employment through Organization of Women Workers in the Informal sector," Indian Journal of Gender Studies. Vol. 3, No. 2.
15. Patel, V (1992) "Women & Structural Adjustment in India " SNDT Women's University, Bombay.
16. Popola, T.S., (1992) "Employment of Women in South Asian Countries", The Indian Journal of Labour Economics, Vol. 36, No. 1, Jan-March.
17. Ranjini, K. Murthy, (1994) "Gender and Development in India: Experiences and Challenges Initiatives: Women in Development, Madras".
18. Sharada Gopalan, (1995) "Women and Employment in India", Har-Anand Publications, New Delhi.
19. Sarojini Ganju Thakur, (1995) "Making women visible: The Challenge for Indian Agriculture" The Administrator, Vol. XL.

20. Sheel C. Nuna, (1990) “Women & Development” NIEPA, New Delhi.

21. Sudha Deshpande, (1993) “Feminisation through flexible labour in India: Evidence and future prospects” (in the New economic policy and women) Indian Association for women’s studies (IAWS).

22. World Bank (1991) “Gender and poverty in India”: A World Bank country study’ Washington, D.C.

35

Problems and Perspectives of Labour in the Indian Leather Industry

C. Pulinda Rao, Girippa Kollannavar & D.R. Krishnama Naidu

Introduction

The perspectives of the Indian leather industry in the new millennium pose challenges on the economic development. There has been a perceptible change in the growth of the leather industry. The economic sustainability of the people depends upon many development factors such as population growth, working and living environment, social status, economic conditions, employment opportunities, wages, etc. The population of India was recorded at 102 crores and the total workforce over 38 crore persons. (2001). This shows that there has been an abundance of human resource base for the sustainable economic development of the country. At the global level, the human population is decreasing at a faster rate in developed nations, whereas in less developed nations it increases at a faster rate. In developing countries the annual rate of growth of labour force was 1.8% during 1960-70 and has increased to 2.8% during 1990-2000. On the other hand, in developed nations the rate of growth of labour force was 1.2% in 1970's and expected to fall down to 0.5% during the 1990-2000.

In developed countries, the dependence on agriculture has come down due to industrialization and technological innovations and in developing countries it is in progressing stage. The less developed nations are influenced by inefficient utilization of labour resource, resulting in unemployment, under employment and income inequalities. The economic progress depends upon the utilization of labour force, infrastructure facilities, investment, safety and security measures, protection from the regulations of Factory Acts and Labour laws. In India the main source of labour confines to Agriculture sector and Non-Agricultural sources contribute to some extent. India has two distinct regions viz. labour surplus and deficit regions. The labour surplus regions are Bihar, U.P, Tamil Nadu and Orissa, whereas the labour deficit regions are Mumbai, West-Bengal and Assam. Industrial sector attracts labour force from adjacent areas. The main industrial cities like Mumbai and Kolkata attract labour from neighbouring states of M.P., Bihar, and U.P. The major reasons for such mobility are economic necessity, increasing levels of incomes, expenditure, better employment opportunities, working and living conditions, social awareness, growing urbanization, education, medical, health awareness and improving standards of living.

Classification of Labour

The Word labour one of the factors of production is used in various senses. The word labour means workmen at a collective name. Labour in this sense is synonymous with human resources. In a narrow sense, labour includes only those civilian workers, who work for others and are not engaged in the work of supervision and management. In the other sense labour means workers engaged in the industry. In the leather industry the labour is classified as apprentice, casual, seasonal, temporary, unskilled, skilled, wageworkers, piece rate workers, monthly paid workers, probationary, permanent workers etc.

Characteristics of India Labour

The main characteristic of Indian labour is the presence of underemployment both in the agricultural and non-agricultural economy. The composition of the young generation shows high in the labour force due to social changes in terms of health care, education, training, standard of living and quality of life style. Hence, there exists a chronic surplus of labour in India.

Wages

Wages play a crucial role for the development of the nation's economy. According to payment of Wages Act 1936, wages mean all remunerations by way of salary or otherwise, expressed in terms of money, which would be payable to the person work done in such an employment. Wages include over time, leave period and production bonus. Wages do not include value of house accommodation, Provident Fund (PF), Travelling Allowance (TA), Gratuity, Bonus (Festival), Dearness Allowance (DA), and Over time Allowance (OT).

The wages paid to the workers seem to vary from one region to the need of the factories, the labour force is engaged and payment of wage is fixed suitably according to the nature of the work and skills of the workers. The wages and Over Time allowances are paid in the factory sector as per the provisions of the Factory Acts and Labour laws.

Labour Scenario in the Agricultural Sector

Being agrarian in nature, in India, the prospects and survival of the labour were mainly depending on the agriculture. After independence, economic reforms through plan periods were launched and wage policies and employment opportunities have shown drastic improvements.

Today the wages paid in the agricultural sector are rather at an upward movement. In agricultural sector, particularly in southern states like Tamil Nadu and A.P. a male worker gets Rs. 50 to Rs. 75 per day and female worker gets Rs. 30-45. In Non-agricultural sector a male worker earns Rs. 60-100 per day and female worker Rs. 30-50, depending upon the skills and nature of work. However, due to various benefits offered by the leather sector, in Tamil Nadu, most of the workers preferred to shift to leather sector for better advantage over agricultural sector.

Labour Force in the Indian Leather Industry

The land, Labour, capital and organization are the major factors of production. The labour as a human resource base towards economic development has a great impact in developing nations. In the leather industry, technological changes have brought higher levels of economic growth of the work force after entering into the factory work. The contributions of labour working in the factory sector of leather industry have become very significant. This paper aims to analyse the labour employed, pattern of wage payment in the factory sector of leather industry and their problems and perspectives for the sustainable development. The leather industry includes flaying, tanning, footwear, leather garment industries in India.

Leather industry is classified as Factory (organized) and Informal sectors. The Factory Sector is one resulting from planning where the pattern or structure is predetermined to carry out specific job or achieve goals. Whereas, Informal Sector or Decentralised Sector develops when people work together towards a specific object or goal. People with common interest generally get together and work.

Indian leather has witnessed remarkable structural changes in seventies. Technological innovations, mechanization in Production, favourable trade policies and export incentives are major factors for generating employment opportunities and enhancement of wages. The sectorial category of work force involved in various segments of leather industry include flaying, tanning, leather footwear, leather goods and leather garment manufacturing industries. The mobilization of labour force into the factory sector of leather industry took place after seventies. The labour employed in the tanning sector has made steady progress, whereas the leather products sector through introduction of assembly line of production has provided opportunity for creation of large scale employment. Since the women workers are best suited for swift handling of each specific job, they are employed in large scale in the factory sector of the products industry particularly in South India. The sectorial growth of labour force in the leather sector is as follows.

The census figures revealed that the total labour force employed in the leather and allied industries in India was registered at 5.73 lakhs in 1951, 8.06 lakhs in 1961, 5.50 lakhs in 1971 and 4.81 lakhs in 1981. Of the total employment of 4.81 lakhs, 74% of them were engaged in the leather footwear industry, leather tanning accounted for 14% of labour and the leather products manufacturing at 12%. It was noticed that in the subsequent years also the labour force employed in the footwear industry has shown an increasing trend. It is estimated that the leather industry provides employment to over 25 lakh persons (2000), of which the factory sector provides employment to over 2 lakh persons and the rest in decentralized sector (23 lakh persons). The details of employment of work force in the factory sector is presented in Table 1.

Table 1. Estimated Employment in the Factory Sector of Indian Leather Industry—200

(Fig. In 000's)

Category	*Men*	*Women*	*Total*
Tanning	0.71	0.02	0.73
Leather footwear & Components	0.38	0.32	0.70
Leather goods	0.16	0.15	0.31
Leather garments	0.18	0.17	0.35
Total	**1.43**	**0.66**	**2.09**

Source: CLRI.

With regard to the employment position, there is a difference between the census data and estimated employment position. The census data has confined to limited segments of the employment including flaying, tanning, footwear and leather goods in organized sector. Whereas, the data presented by the CLRI for the year 2000 is taken into account the over all employment position of the leather industry including raw hides and skins collection, flaying and carcass recovery, leather tanning, footwear components, Industrial leather manufacturing, leather goods and leather garment manufacturing. Hence. Variations persisted in the employment position in these two cases.

Mechanization and technological innovations, conveyor system of production in the factory sector of product industry have created large scale employment. Such changes have brought out a shift from traditional paradigm to the industrial culture. Large number of women workers have been attracted in the leather product industry. In factory sector of Tamil Nadu, about 60% of the labour force employed are drawn from rural areas and 40% from the urban agglomeration. Over 75% of the work force in the product sector including leather footwear components, leather goods, leather garments are women and 25% men.

Payment of Wages

With regard to the payment of wages, the factory sector of leather industry follows the procedures of the Factory Acts and Labour laws from time to time. The wages paid to the labour in this sector depends upon the educational qualification, experience, work discipline etc. The leather industry provides employment to the casual workers also. In such cases the unskilled worker gets daily Rs. 25 to Rs. 30, the skilled worker Rs. 40-75 and in some cases Rs. 100. These wages are paid as monthly salary.

Workers Benefits

The benefits of the labour force in the factor sector of leather industry are: Cleaner environment, in plant training for upscaling of wages/salaries, motivating efforts, fringe benefits such as productivity bonus, festival bonus, advances, free tea, uniform/dress twice in a year, free transport from home to place of duty, ESI facilities, annual increments, suggestion bonus, maternity benefits, health care, travelling allowances, workmen compensation for employment injury and Over Time allowance is paid at 1 1/2 times to that of normal pay of worker. The other benefits include safety and security, health and welfare, and employees service programmes including educational and recreation facilities, holidays, sick leave, housing facilities etc.

Workers prefer to enrole in the factories instead of working in the agriculture due to facilities mentioned. The rural young women workers are very much attracted to these benefits and accept for low wages. This sector has also been attracting labour force from the textile industry. The large infrastructure facilities, creation of conducive environment to produce export quality leather products by the entrepreneurs in the North Arcot district of Tamil Nadu have attracted women labour from both rural and urban segments.

Labour Problems

The problems of the labour force engaged in the leather industry are labour shift, lower wages, irregular employment, lack of technical skills through institutional training. The labourers who are entering into the factory without any educational back ground and previous experience get less wages and at times find it difficult to manage the family budget. Hence, in order to get better wages/salary, there is a need to provide proper education and training facilities to the workers engaged in the leather sector.

Perspectives

The perspectives of the labour engaged in the factory sector of leather industry in India depend upon many developmental plans. The five year plans have given due importance to resolve the labour problems. Besides these plans, efforts will have to be made seriously to minimize or to control labour problems that are facing the leather industry. The labour force without a minimum level of education are getting employment in the leather products sector. Education and experience coupled with skills and work-talents have direct impact on the salary composition of the labour force which is the main component to show their economic status. Inplant training will help to increase the socio-economic status of the work force. In most of the cases the workers satisfy the present job in the factories. There is an upward momentum of increasing the standard of living and socio-economic conditions of workers after joining product industry.

Keeping these developments in view, the factory sector of leather industry needs measures to enhance more employment opportunities and wage enhancement. Proper technical training and skill upgradation may boost up the skills and socio-economic conditions of the workers mainly the casual labourers or unskilled workers who are representing a sizable share in the total work force. In most of the cases, the implant training is being provided by the footwear factories to improve the quality of the products as well as enhancing the wages of workers but there are no exclusive technical training institutes to provide adequate attention to these deserving women workers. In the footwear factories even though more than 75% of the work force are women there is no exclusive technical training center for them.

The government may introduce leather footwear, leather goods and garment training centres exclusively for women in potential areas for all types of training skills required for them. Women candidates who are seeking for admission in these courses many be exempted from payment of fees. In addition to this, necessary stipend may be paid to trainees during the training period. Human Resource

Development through institutional intervention is an urgent need where commitment and dedication of women workers are remarkable in the leather products industry.

The industry, government and the developmental institutions such as Central Leather Research Institute (CLRI), Central Training Institute (CFTI), Prototype Development and Training Centre (PDTC), Footwear Design and Development Institute (FDDI), National Institute of Fashion Technology (NIFT), Indian Institute of Leather Products (IILP), National Leather Development Programme/ United Nations development Programme/United nations Industrial Development Organisation (NLDP/ UNDP/ UNIDO) may involve for evolving suitable and sustainable development action programmes for technical development of the work force. The other promotional measures include upgrading skills, better placement, career development, promotion, better salary, and strict compliance on labour welfare measures. These changes may bring in significant improvement in work performance, improvement in product quality, higher income resulting in better socio-economic conditions.

Wage composition is creating a greater concern for improving the standard of living of the work force. Majority of the work force are drawn from the low level income groups and due to the economic compulsions and lack of skills, workers are accepting low wages. In some cases skilled workers very often shift the jobs not only for job satisfaction, but also seeking higher salary in other factories. Owing to the shifting of jobs by these workers, the management face the problems in output delivery. In such cases, the factory loses potential workers who have already gained considerable experience in the factory and it becomes difficult task to train the fresh candidates.

In addition to the training being given by the factories, it may be suggested that new techniques of skill-oriented training programmes may be provided in the factory itself through Institutional interventions. Vocational training is another advantage for women workers to learn while earning in the factory.

Conclusion

The 20th century has witnessed technological revolution in various fields. India which has unique advantage of native skills and training through institutional interventions will certainly enhance employment opportunities and there by increase in wages. India has enough potential for the development of the leather sector. The improvement of skills and training of the workers in the leather sector and technological advancement became challenges in the new millennium. By utilizing the optimum level of its potential resources, India could resolve the wage as well as unemployment problems of work force to a large extent by implementing Action Programmes for the development of the Indian leather sector.

References

1. IBRD: "World Development Report" 1979, table 27.
2. Todaro Michael P: "Economic Development in the third world" 1981, p. 537.
3. & 4. Pant S.C.: "Indian Labour Problems"., 1973, p. 13.
4. CLRI: Nationwide survey on Leather Products Units, 1997, p. 65.

Note: The views expressed in this paper are those of the authors' only and need not necessarily reflect the institution to which they belong to.